DIGITAL LIBRARIES

Yan Quan Liu, Ph.D.

Connecticut, USA

2021

Published by Yan Quan Liu

Copyright @ 2016 by Yan Quan Liu
Revised @2019 by Yan Quan Liu
Revised @2021 by Yan Quan Liu

All rights reserved. No part of this publication may be reproduced, distributed, or transmitted in any form or by any means, including photocopying, recording, or other electronic or mechanical methods, without the prior written permission of the publisher, except for the use of brief quotations in a book review.

Liu, Yan Quan

Digital Libraries in Theory and Practices / Authored by Yan Quan Liu
Third Edition
    First edition or Course Pack edition was published in 2014
    Including bibliographical references and index.
    Size 6" x 9" (15.24 x 22.86 cm)
    1. Digital libraries. 2. Digital librarianship. 2. Information Technology.

ISBN-13: 978-1530170777
ISBN-10: 153017077X

This book is published through Kindle Direct Publishing (KDP), and is also available on Kindle.

Printed in the United States of America.

Table of Contents

Chapter One: Digital Libraries: Emerging Developments
1.1 What is a digital library?
1.2 History of digital libraries
1.3 The emergence of digital libraries
1.4 What are the characteristics of a digital library?
1.5 Are there different types of digital libraries?

Chapter Two: Digitization and Digital Objects
2.1 Why are we going digital?
2.2 What can digital libraries add to traditional libraries?
2.3 Impact of the digitization: will traditional libraries be replaced?
2.4 What are the digitization methods and technologies?
2.5 Digital objects, what are they? Origins and definitions
2.6 File Formats, migration and transformation
2.7 The process of digitizing material56
2.8 User access
2.9 Examples of digitization projects

Chapter Three: Collection Development
3.1 Collection development and selection policies
3.2 Harvesting
3.3 Document and e-publishing presentation mark-Up
3.4 Web (Push) publishing or pushing technology
3.5 Crawling

Chapter Four: Content Organization
4.1 How is a digital library collection organized?
4.2 Information architecture
4.3 What is metadata for digital libraries?
4.4 Resources description
4.5 Ontologies, classification, categorization
4.6 Subject description, vocabulary control, thesauri and terminologies

Chapter Five: Technologies and Architecture
5.1 What are the problems in merging systems?
5.2 What are some of the more exciting developments?
5.3 What are the workflows and processes of digital library software?
5.4 What are the key technologies used in construction of digital libraries?
5.5 Digital library models
5.6 Digital library architecture
5.7 Application software
5.8 Identifiers, handlers, DOI, PURL

5.9 Protocols
5.10 Interoperability
5.11 Security

Chapter Six: Design and Interface
6.1: Can the user be the weak link in a digital library?
6.2: How do the public view libraries?
6.3: What factors should drive the design process?
6.4: What are design philosophies for digital libraries?
6.5: How can digital libraries accessible with disabilities?

Chapter Seven: User Behavior and Interactions
7.1 Information needs and relevance
7.2 Online information-seeking behaviors and search strategy
7.3 Sharing, networking, and interchange (e.g., social)
7.4 Interaction design and usability Assessment
7.5 Information summarization and visualization

Chapter Eight: Services
8.1 What services may a digital library provide?
8.2 Digital reference services - trends and issues
8.3 Digital libraries and the change in reference services
8.4 Recommender systems
8.5 Personalization
8.6 Web crawling
8.7 Image retrieval
8.8 Location Based Services
8.9 Mobile apps developed for digital library services

Chapter Nine: Preservation
9.1 Preservation
9.2 Web archiving

Chapter Ten: Management and Evaluation
10.1 Project management
10.2 Evaluation and evaluation studies
10.3 Bibliometrics & webometrics
10.4 Cost/economic issues
10.5 Social issues
10.6 Evaluation resources

Chapter Eleven: Legal Issues
11.1 Intellectual property and intellectual property rights
11.2 Copyright and copyright laws

11.3 Legal issues and copyright in the U. S.
11.4 Using copyrighted materials
11.5 Privacy and security
11.6 Examples of legal disputes
11.7 International copyright protections

Chapter Twelve: Future Perspectives, Education and Research
12.1 Future of digital libraries
12.2 Education for digital librarians
12.3 Digital library science for digital librarianship

Bibliographical References

Appendixes
01 The List of the US Digital Libraries
02 Rubric Evaluation Criteria of the "Digital Library Review Assignment"
04 Rubric Evaluation Criteria for the "Digital Library Project"

Abstract

Intended as a textbook for a digital libraries course, this book is a presentation of various aspects regarding digital libraries for learners or interested parties who deserve a theoretical study of practices in designing, constructing and evaluating digital libraries. Topics include the following: digital library developments, digitization and digital objects, collection development, information & knowledge organization, architecture, user behavior and interactions, services, preservation, management and evaluation, and digital library education and research.

While the audience for this book is foremost students who are in information and library science classes at both undergraduate and graduate levels, its scope would be suitable, at an introductory level, for professionals, scholars and practitioners with a general interest in digital library science and technology. Moreover, this book will provide readers a thorough and comprehensive reference for teaching and learning of the growing area of digital librarianship.

Introduction

The definition of today's library changes depending upon who is asked. Many think of libraries as simple buildings holding collections of books and manuscripts, whereas some think it as a place for research and others bring in a technological aspect.

Over the past two decades there has been an evolutionary change in the world of libraries from mostly print based collections to today's current environment in which the phrase 'digital library' is no longer new, but rather, synonymous with the library itself. Witten and Bainbridge (2010) define a digital library as, "a focused collection of digital objects, including text, video, and audio, along with methods for access and retrieval, and for selection, organization, and maintenance of the collection." This is a broad definition that can be applied to various collections in public libraries, academic libraries, school libraries, special libraries, and organizations accessed through computers. The idea of a digital library that is different from a traditional brick and mortar library because of two: physical building boundaries are none and the information possibilities are endless. Digitization has made access to an abundance of information much easier.

Chapter One: Digital Libraries: Emerging Developments

What is a digital library?

From its inception, the term digital library has been applied to a wide variety of offerings, including collections of electronic journals, software agents that support inquiry-based education, collections of email to electronic versions of a public library, personal information collections, and even the entire Internet. The new emerging digital technologies are transforming the handling of information, and as a result are changing the nature of human activities and organizations.

Borgman (2000, 41-42) defines a digital library "as a system that provides a community of users with coherent access to a large, organized repository of information and knowledge."

Perhaps the most popular definition is that from Digital Library Federation: "Digital libraries are organizations that provide the resources, including the specialized staff, to select, structure, offer intellectual access to, interpret, distribute, preserve the integrity of, and ensure the persistence over time of collections of digital works so that they are readily and economically available for use by a defined community or set of communities." This definition covers all aspects of librarianship by considering the needs of users, providing information services, organizing and managing the information and making it available.

However, the definition proposed by Witten and Bainbridge (2003) is even more encompassing. According to Witten (2002, xxvi), "digital libraries are focused collections of digital objects, including text, video, and audio, along with methods for access and retrieval, and for selection, organization, and maintenance." This definition most accurately reflects role assigned to libraries as the providers and keepers of information. It deals with a diverse set of materials such as text, video, and audio; it mentions method of access and retrieval of the information (provider of information to users), and finally takes into consideration collection development and maintenance, including the selection and organization of materials.

Some authors on the subject do not individually define the digital library. They do, however, define a virtual university as "an institution, or a set of institutions, engaged in a delivery of degree granting programs in higher education, using technology and methodology outside a traditional classroom (Buchanan, Luck and Jones, 2002). The digital library becomes an integral piece of the virtual learning environment, especially when librarians collaborate with distance educators to provide students with remote access to information literacy instruction.

A digital library certainly works in a virtual environment by integrating services such as information literacy tutorials in order to satisfy the human need of understanding how to evaluate information. Most importantly, these services need to be provided any time and any place. The digital library serves as a bridge connecting the expertise of the librarians and the information they can provide with online users, for example, students, who have a requirement for information and a need to evaluate it.

The scope and definition of digital libraries have been the subject of intensive debate, which is well summarized in Borgman (1999). The integrative nature of the field could be simply described through three definitions that show such combinations:

- Library = library + archive + museums
- Distributed information system + organization + effective interfaces
- User community + collection (content) + services

Fox (2001) made his own favorite definition, drawing upon the 5S framework, with its five key constructs: societies, scenarios/services, spaces, structures, and streams: "Thus, digital libraries are complex systems that:

- help satisfy information needs of users (societies),
- provide information services (scenarios),
- locate and present information in usable ways (spaces),
- organize information in usable ways (structures), and
- communicate information with users and computers (streams)."

Chowdhury (2003) attempts to focus the crux of the definition by saying that there are two categories of definitions, one that "focuses on access and retrieval of digital content," a definition suited for computer scientists and engineers, and the other "focuses on the collection, organization and service aspects of a digital library," a definition suited for library and information professionals.

History of digital libraries

There were many valuable tools in the library and technological world that preceded the digital library and played roles in its continuing development.

Perhaps the most influential of all of these was the invention of the printing press in 1444 by Johann Gutenberg. The printing press used moveable type, which allowed books to decrease in rarity and cost (Wedgeworth, 1993, p. 709). This coupled with the ability to mass-produce paper in the 1800's, books were able to be mass-produced and were no longer considered treasures for only the elite few with higher station in life (Tedd, & Large, 2005). This meant that although it was once considered a waste of time to teach those of the lower class to read, now with books (and in particular, the Bible) more accessible education became more universally acceptable. In many ways, Guttenberg's invention was one of the major steps toward information dissemination and intellectual freedom. Now these ideas have developed even further as digital libraries, and the possibilities of a Global Information Infrastructure attempt to cross the digital divide caused by culture, social and economic class.

Other wonders followed between the time of Guttenberg and the most recent digital libraries. These included what Joseph NicéphoreNiépce produced and called a heliograph in 1826. His invention was later recognized as the first of what we now call photographs (Harry Ransom Center, n.d.). A little more than thirty years later, in 1859, the first patent for the microfilm was given to Rene Dagron. In 1935 Kodak's Recordak division began filming and recording the New York Times in microfilm, a project which still continues with films stored at the Center for Research Studies in Chicago (Heritage Microfilm, n.d.). This was the dawning of a new age for libraries, which quickly took to using the technology for archival purposes, to preserve their own periodicals. This would later be used to replace the originals as a more compact storage option as "information overload" became a more common term and libraries began to run out of space for new materials (Tedd, & Large, 2005).

In the 1940's photocharging and audiocharging were introduced to circulation procedures (Reynolds, 1985, p. 11). During this same period, in 1941, Kodak introduced color film (Bellis, n.d.). In the 1950's both the tape-producing auto typewriter and the copy machine were invented (Reynolds, 1985, p. 21; Rice, 1984, p. 30; Salmon, 1975, p. 45-49; Tedd, & Large, 2005). These were valuable predecessors to the image scanner, which was invented and manufactured under Russell Kirsch in 1957 (Nakate, 2010). Today many photographs, periodicals, books and other documents and images are scanned using this technology or technology based on it today. These scanned images in turn often make up a large percentage of some digital libraries.

The emergence of digital libraries

Vannevar Bush is probably the first to describe something similar to what is now known as a digital library in 1945 as he described his envisioned "Memex" machine: "Consider a future device for individual use, which is a sort of mechanized private file and library...device in which an individual stores all his books, records, and communications, and which is mechanized so that it may be consulted with exceeding speed and flexibility" (Bush, 1945, as cited in Office of Science and Technical Information [OSTI], 2007, February 8; Witten, Bainbridge, & Nichols, 2010, p. 16). Interestingly enough, Bush's vision came even before general-purpose computers had become introduced into the library world. This didn't happen until 1961 (Wedgeworth, 1993, p. 41).

Shortly after the introduction of the general-purpose computer the first online public access catalogs (OPACS) appeared. The first was installed in

1963 at the Ontario New Universities (Salmon, 1975, p. 4). Later in the 1960s, catalog systems became more uniform when Machine Readable Cataloging (MARC) was introduced to standardize the collection of metadata (Rice, 1984, p. 54; Salmon, 1975, p. 5, 73).

In 1964 the technological world was further revolutionized by Lawrence Roberts and Thomas Merrill of the Massachusetts Institute of Technology (MIT). They experimented with the idea of packet-switching, the first form of a network, and were successful in connecting a computer in Massachusetts to a computer in California via a low-speed dial-up telephone connection.

In 1965, JosephLicklinder predicted in his book *Libraries of the Future* that publishing would become primarily electronic at some point. He predicted the feasibility and actuality of digital libraries occurring around the year 2000 and described the incorporation of computer science into the library world and blending of many disciplines together, using the term "precognitive systems" (as cited in OSTI, 2007, February 8). It turned out digital libraries were closer than he thought. Right around the same time, in 1965, James T. Russell and his invention of the compact disc (CD) went unnoticed (Dudley, 2004; "James T. Russell," 1999, December).

Lawrence Roberts of MIT brought his research to the Defense Advanced Research Projects Agency (DARPA) and together they collaborated to create the Advanced Research Projects Agency Network (ARPANET), in 1969, which became the first version of the Internet (Cerf et al., 2003). Douglas Englebart and a team at Stamford Research Institute in California were later able to build off of this technology to develop hypertext (named later by Ted Nelson). Englebart was also behind the development of the cursor, windows software environment and online help systems (Tedd, & Large, 2005). When ARPANET became public in the 1970s, the Ohio State University System linked 21 libraries to one online public access catalog (OPAC) (Cerf et al., 2003; Reynolds, 1985, p. 47, 113).

As the 1970s progressed, James T. Russell further developed his invention of the CD. The fruit of this work was what we know today as the CD-ROM. By 1985 he owned 26 different patents for his new technology (Dudley, 2004; "James T. Russell," 1999, December). In 1971, the Online Computer Library Center (OCLC) became accessible to library systems online and by 1977 they were the nation-wide printer of the card catalog (Reynolds, 1985, p. 56-57; Rice, 1984, p. 55-56). Michael Hart invented e-books in 1971 and also founded Project Gutenburg, a digital library, which is the oldest and largest single collection of e-books still in existence today (Hart, 2008, November 3).

Fujio Masuoka invented and patented what he called electrically erasable, programmable read-only memory (EEPROM), in 1981. This later became nicknamed "Flash Memory" (Hall, 2006, April 3). Shortly after, Sony and Philips realized the potential of James Russell's invention. They introduced the CD to the main market in 1982 (Dudley, 2004). This is the same time period that John E. Creps describes digital libraries or remote library access through portable mobile devices before their dawning. In 1983 he is quoted as describing the ideal mobile device as "The package that lets me have my library with me, to read when I want and need to read, when I need to search, when I want and need to do my work without clock watching" and the next big "breakthrough" for the information world (Creps, 1983, as cited in OSTI, 2007, February 8). In 1984 Kodak demonstrated the first digital camera and in 1985 Pixar introduced the first digital imaging processor (Bellis, n.d.). From 1989-1992 the Mercury Electronic Library project at Carnegie Mellon University in Pittsburgh Pennsylvania became one of the first campus-based digital libraries of journal articles (Tedd, & Large, 2005).

In 1990 Kodak further developed James T. Russell's invention when they introduced the photo CD as a digital imaging storage medium (Bellis, n.d.). The Report of the American Psychological Society Task Force on Electronic Information Systems in 1991 called for the creation of the National Physics Database to integrate "all of the world's scientific literature information in an electronic information system." The original goal for the project was 2020, due to the suspected lag in the necessary technology to accomplish such a feat but the early stages of the database actually became a reality in the year 2000 (Task Force on Electronic Information Systems, 1991, as cited in OSTI, 2007, February 8).

From 1991-1995, another milestone occurred for digital libraries when Elsevier Science provided nine of the leading universities in the US with digitized content from 43 journals in The University Licensing Project (TULIP). This was a project designed to fine tune network delivery, the use of journals at user desktops while focusing on technical issues, user behavior and organizational and economical questions (Tedd & Large, 2005). While Elsevier was launching TULIP, the Association of American Universities began examining new approaches to the "collection and dissemination of scientific and technical information (STI)" in 1994. They called for the development of a national repositories system with non-profit access to STI to promote scientific research and exchange. They envisioned scientists having remote "desktop access to campus, national, and even global STI" from anywhere (OSTI, 2007, February 8).

That same year, the National Science Foundation (NSF), the National Aeronautical and Space Agency (NASA), and the Defense Advanced Research Projects Agency (DARPA) began in Digital library Initiative I (DLI-1) during 1994-1998, to be followed by Digital library Initiative II (DLI-2) (Tedd & Large, 2005). Under DLI-1 six digital library programs, among the first of their kind, were funded and developed: The University of Michigan Digital Library Project, the University of Illinois at Urbana-Champaign Digital Library Project, the University of California at Berkeley Digital Library Project, the Carnegie Mellon Digital Library Project, The Stamford University Digital Library Project and the

Alexandria Digital Library Project at the University of California at Santa Barbara (Li, 2010; Tedd & Large, 2005).

The University of Michigan Digital Library Project focused on earth and space sciences. The University of Illinois at Urbana-Champaign Digital Library Project was a database of full-text journal articles concerning physics, engineering and computer science. The University of California at Berkeley Digital Library Project consisted of a growing collection of photographs, satellite images, maps, and documents focused on environmental studies and information. The Carnegie Mellon Digital Library Project (Informedia Digital Video Library) was a study of multimedia digital libraries with digital video, audio, images, and text information. The Stamford University Digital Library Project focused on the development of interoperability and uniform access to an array of materials. The Alexandria Digital Library Project at the University of California at Santa Barbara focused on spatially referenced and geographic materials such as maps and satellite images (Li, 2010).

In 1999 the US President's Information Technology Advisory Committee issued a report "Information Technology Research: Investing in Our Future" which supported the idea of citizens having free access and use of information. The use of digital libraries and accessing technical journals online that would allow "readers to download equations and databases and manipulate variables to interactively explore the published research." This free access included making queries and printing "magazine[s], data item[s], or reference document[s]...by simply clicking a mouse" (OSTI, 2007, February 8). One of the recent endeavors since then began in the year 2000 when the National Science Foundation (NSF) began the National Science Digital Library (NSDL), a library which combines and allows access to the resources of over 100 science, technology, education and mathematic projects (Roth, 2003, January 3).

What are the characteristics of a digital library?

Assumptions about a digital library

There are certain assumptions in discussions of a digital library. Levy and Marshall (1995) summarize these as: digital libraries are collections containing fixed, permanent documents, which are based on digital technologies and are used by individuals working alone.

Cleveland (2003) gives a list of the characteristics of a digital library:
- Digital libraries are the digital face of traditional libraries that include both digital collections and traditional, fixed media collections. So, they encompass both electronic and paper materials.

- Digital libraries will also include digital materials that exist outside the physical and administrative bounds of any one digital library
- Digital libraries will include all the processes and services that are the backbone and nervous system of libraries. However, such traditional processes, though forming the basis of digital library work, will have to be revised and enhanced to accommodate the differences between new digital media and traditional fixed media.
- Digital libraries ideally provide a coherent view of all of the information contained within a library, no matter its form or format
- Digital libraries will serve particular communities or constituencies as traditional libraries do now, though those communities may be widely dispersed throughout the network.
- Digital libraries will require both the skills of librarians as well as those of computer scientists to be viable.

Fixity of content

The concept of a fixed and permanent document is based on the printed book: while a title may be reissued in a revised version, once a specific volume is printed and bound, it remains unchanged. Fixity creates a comfortable environment in which to perform certain library functions. Cataloging practices have evolved around the largely fixed and permanent document. Fluid or transient documents, such as pamphlets and news clippings have been largely uncatalogued and stored in unclassified areas, such as the vertical file [cabinet]. The perception of lack-of-fixity in fluid digital documents, especially the Internet-based documents, leads to the assumption that digital items are ill equipped for cataloging and other library functions.

This concept of the fixity and permanence of a volume is, in itself, flawed. For example, marginalia, notes entered by the reader, gives a book some degree of fluidity. Marginalia can contribute error-correction, critique, and even new content to the volume. Marginalia is viewed as an important addition to certain texts. In addition to marginalia, vandalism, such as removal of pictures or pages from a book, makes it difficult to predict that two books, identical at binding, still contain the same contents on any library shelf.

In classifying books as fixed and permanent, the ways of altering a book after issuance have been dismissed. What has, in fact, been cataloged is the pristine just-off-the-press edition. Certainly, many digital-based texts could be archived as a pristine edition, with many fluid copies existing at other sites, and perhaps even linked to and from the archived edition. While the range of variation from a digital pristine copy would certainly have the potential to facilitate and exceed the variation from a print pristine copy, the practice of cataloging and archiving documents at certain points of development can extend to digital media. Fluid copies on the Internet could be considered manuscripts in progress (just as some authors circulate paper-based working drafts of manuscripts to colleagues for reading, comment and use) and at some point, a revised version could be cataloged and archived, not unlike revised editions of print-based texts.

This is a simplistic discussion of fixity in print and digital media; it does illustrate the point that fixity is a relative concept and does not necessarily belong exclusively to the print medium.

Are there different types of digital libraries?

Metaphors for digital libraries

In early literature, there was little discussion or agreement about what constitutes a digital library. Harter (1997) juxtaposes two extreme views: the most inclusive view, which takes a digital library to be essentially what the Internet is today, and the metaphor of the traditional library, which involves a highly selective vetting process. The essential differences between these two metaphors deal with their (presumed) properties of location, content, selection criteria, organization, authority control, authorship, stability, access, user groups, services and fees. The Internet has no physical or logical location, no quality control and no entry barriers, no organization scheme, authority control, or surrogates; no concept of author; and is fluid and transient.

At the opposite end of the spectrum, the idea of a digital library as a version of the physical library means that much like a brick-and-mortar library caters to its community, the "traditional" digital library would have a very specific audience. Where the Internet has no controls or stability, the digital library may have a highly selective content selection process, a specific target audience, and a detailed authentication process for its users.

Types of digital libraries

What are synonyms for the term digital library? Several terms have been used, including electronic library, virtual library, library without walls, bionic library, hybrid library, and electronic resource sharing consortia. To distinguish its goals or missions, the titles may include research oriented DL, service oriented DL, preservation DL, and commercial DL.

Sloane (1995) looks at the ways networks and multimedia are organized and at the problems encountered by home-based (and library-based) users of digital libraries. Sloane presents three models of multimedia information provision: communications complex, media complex, and hybrid models. The typical example of the media-complex model is the CD-ROM: all the media is stored on one device and there is no need to communicate with other servers. For the home-based user, this would require physical distribution of the CD-ROM, including updates, to the user.

An example of a hybrid model is one in which a multimedia information system contains search clients or engines which would link to external databases to locate information not available on the contained system. An application of the hybrid model is a CD-ROM encyclopedia which could be used to gain introductory knowledge of a topic and then, after exhausting relevant knowledge available in the encyclopedia, request an online search using either pre-designated or user-created search strategies for current research articles on an aspect of the topic to gain more current or in-depth information. While pre-designated search strategies would be fixed and stored on the CD-ROM, the databases searched would be online rather than on disk, thereby permitting access to the newest updated information.

The communications complex and hybrid models would seem to be the models of choice except for the issue of useful access to the remotely stored information. In earlier age, the speed of data transfer (available bandwidth at user-end) was currently limited. The current generation of fast modems is somewhat adequate for the transfer text; however, large files and high-volume loads on networks combine to give the home user long waiting times for retrieving information. A recent Web-delivered government registration form of a series of about 200 check-off questions, one question per screen was reported by one institution to take about 5-6 minutes to load each screen. In order to complete the required form, the institution needed to hire someone for 40 hours for two weeks. Needless to say this system has since been improved.

When creating digital libraries intended for home users, capability of the users' equipment to receive the information in a reasonable amount of time must be carefully considered. A media complex (CD-ROM) model could cause the user to feel psychologically cut-off from the parent library. The hybrid model, in which a fairly fixed body of reference material could be issued on CD-ROM with links available to various levels of media format at the parent library, could be an acceptable alternative.

Most of the problems home users encounter with digital resources can be, according to Sloane (1995), categorized as navigation and document referral (classification, indexing and shelf location in the book environment). The current systems of referral provide reference at the book or document level. In a digital environment, the preference would be, as Sloane puts it, at the level of "information nuggets." This would be equivalent to a back-of-the book index compiled by an expert human indexer. Now of course, many libraries now provide online pathfinders, subject guides and webliographies that serve as finding tools.

Adam, Bhargava and Yesha (1995) confirm this needed level of granularity and point out that in order for digital libraries to be exceptionally useful, they must be highly organized with useful indexes and intra- and inter-document linkages (p. 3).

Conclusion

Comparing to traditional physical libraries, digital libraries are still fairly young, though there is a long history of inventions and innovations that have made their existence a reality. If one looks at the tools that are used in a digital library, we come to realize that there is a great deal of history that preceded them that is well worth looking at. The digital library should not be seen as merely a digitized collection of information objects plus related management tools, but as an environment bringing together collections, services, and people to support the full cycle of creation, dissemination, discussion, collaboration, use, new authoring, and preservation of data, information, and knowledge.

Gutenberg's invention of the printing press in 1444 may seem to have little to do with electronic collections but many of the materials included in those collections existed first and primarily in hardbound or printed format (Wedgeworth, 1993, p. 709). They were often scanned as early as 1957 by the early-invented scanner (Nakate, 2010). None of this could have been accomplished without the invention of the computer and its capabilities would have been greatly limited had not the Internet allowed people from any locations to access the same materials of one digital library (Cerf et al., 2003; Wedgeworth, 1993, p. 41). Project Gutenberg may have been one of the first digital libraries but its history began much earlier (Hart, 2008, November 3). As new technologies are discovered digital libraries will continue to find new ways to develop.

Study questions for Chapter one

- Digital Library Origin. Why suddenly all the digital libraries and digital projects - Do you think patrons are asking for digital libraries, or could it be technology the library community is "pushing" onto the patrons?
- What do researchers say about digital libraries? There may not be a single definition for what a digital library is. From your readings, such as Borgman, Lesk, Stielow, Hodge, Lynch Levy, and many others, what have these researchers said about digital libraries, and what are the similarities or differences in their definitions? Have you come across any definitions that are similar to or different than these researchers?
- Whitten and Bainbridge tell us "It is clearly essential for digital library developers to consider how their creations will affect other

people" (p. 35). They also distinguish between a digital library and a website (p. 8). Present an argument on the differences between a digital library and a portal, gateway, regular website or something else.

Chapter Two: Digitization and Digital Objects

Digitization is a starting and crucial element in building a digital library. The initial questions for digital library builders/designers/planners may include: what media should we include in the collection? Will the collection include items that were born digital? What are the best ways to convert our printed materials into electronic formats? How will we protect digital information from degradation? What is the plan for data migration? Although many issues may be involved when libraries digitize or build up their collections, many digitization projects have been accomplished since those pioneer digital libraries were born, putting their materials in digital form and distributing it through digital channels. Many endeavors that have been made to increase access to a range of materials crossing different types of databases, libraries, languages and cultures in an effort to further education, awareness and research have achieved great success.

This chapter outlines the technical considerations for creating, processing, storing, and retrieving digital images in detail, through explaining the underlying structure of digital objects and how that affects text, image, video and other multimedia formats.

2.1 Why are we going digital?

Digital coherence

Coherence means sticking together or having continuity.

The one property these various entities have in common for digital projects is their digitization or digital coherence (Atkins, 1996). Digital coherence means all the objects in a digital library, whether sounds, images, texts, or some other media, can be treated in essentially the same way. In a physical library, CDs must be treated differently from books simply because of size and other physical differences. Digitally, all media can be viewed in the same manner while searching and viewing their information. Therefore, digital coherence, as the word coherence implies, signifies the uniformity of various materials in the digital format.

Prior to digital coherence, libraries needed to treat various media, for example, books, journals, videos, and musical recordings, differently (Harter, 1997). One could say that digital coherence is the mechanism that permits a form of equality among various information resources. This equality is important for the delivery and integration of information.

In a digital library, traditionally separate media such as text, image, audio, video, citations, and algorithmic information can be included in the same compound document. With the development of the Internet, we are beginning to invent new genres -- new socially agreed upon ways to create, disseminate, preserve, and use data, information, and knowledge. We are already well into the world of hybrid information - the coexistence of both print and digital information resources that meet human needs.

For the home-based user, digital coherence affords increased access to a library's collection, from an online catalog that can be accessed remotely to full-text which can turn a home or office into a reading room.

How does digital coherence affect DLs?

A digital library is composed of digital objects --whether the object is a book or a video or a song, it still is stored, transmitted and integrated as digital entity.

Digital coherence is simply the fact that all media in a digital library are digital objects and the range of library functions performable on those objects is therefore essentially the same.

Although the items in a digital library might have very little else in common since they come in an endless variety of formats, such as prints, videos, web sites, photographs, etc. all of the items in this collection have digital coherence, because they are in a digital format.

Digital coherence, therefore, is a property that allows all digital library objects -- sounds, images, text and other media -- to be treated essentially the same way. "Treated" here refers to the storage, organization, search, and retrieval of digital information. The main principle that DLs rely on therefore is the concept of digital coherence.

What are benefits that digital coherence brings to DLs?

- **Storability**. Digital coherence offers contrast to the way libraries traditionally had to deal differently with the storage and retrieval of information sources depending on the media involved. A great advantage to digital coherence is that it is much easier to store and share resources.
- **Accessibility**. Digital coherence permits a broader range of information to be available to those who are disadvantaged in accessing to information by locality or disability. (Sloane, 1995)
- **Deliverability**. For libraries, this means that items that utilized different delivery systems and were treated differently for the purposes of cataloging/organizing can now be treated the same way.
- **Searchability**. Digital coherence would permit patrons to search for text, images, and multimedia materials through a common interface and uniform system of cataloguing. Search functionality in a DL is based on the concept of digital coherence.

- **Manipulation capability.** Materials can be downloaded to a computer or ebook for a limited period without the patrons needing to leave their own homes.
- **Advanced learning ability.** Because of digitization, users can experience a multimedia-learning environment. For example, it is not necessary to watch videos through a VCR, listen to music through a CD player, or to read from a book, because these digitized resources are all accessible via a computer.
- **Information integration.** Digital coherence allows equality among different information resources and promotes integration of information.

Are there any barriers for DLs because of digital coherence?

- **Requires high processing speed.** Digital coherence may not be easily attained due to the fact that audio, video, and image files tend to be larger and take longer to load than text does.
- **Requires advanced technology.** The more complex digital formats require the user to have an adequate system in order to be able to access them and may also require additional software or plug-ins for viewing them.
- **Requires computer literacy.** Users need to understand the functionalities of different application, and to be familiar with their optional features. Software is continuously evolving and improving the level of computer literacy.

2.2 What can digital libraries add to traditional libraries?

Some writers, such as Levy and Marshall (1995) recognize that the application of digital coherence to libraries is not simply moving text from a paper format to a digital format, though much of the text found on the web is precisely that. The print journal, especially the research journal, is not so rigidly held sacred. This may be largely due to the perceived reduced access to many journals in the collection that do not circulate.

Printing on Demand

Digitization offers new opportunities for libraries, such as replacing photocopying with publishing-on-demand. In a joint project between Yale University Libraries and Yale University Press, a publishing-on-demand service offered through Yale's library network to Yale students and faculty, where out-of-print books from Yale University Press can be available for viewing on the Yale Library network. After determining their need for a copy, the student or faculty member can order, as page images, the item online, selecting the desired paper quality and size and binding method. Ordered books will be printed and bound on campus and charged to the patron's account (Conway, 1997). This project no doubt has great significance in planning how libraries can deliver information to patrons using regulatory and economic models that will satisfy patrons, library services, and copyright holders.

Open Journal Project

The most innovative online journals are maturing rapidly with distinctive new features emerging. The foremost of these, the hypertext link, forms the basis and hope for a new, highly integrated scholarly literature which will exploit relationships at the level of journal content, both in categorization by topic and reference to other articles on the same or similar topics.

Previously many journals were appearing on the web as direct replications of their print form rather than breaking new grounds in evolution of the journal. There is a rich body of resources, including primary and secondary resources, and forward (works that cite the current document) and backward (works cited in the current document) citations and references, which can enhance the value of access for the user. It was expected that by 1998 the need for electronic journals would stabilize (Hitchcock, Harris, Hey & Hall, 1997). Once the market stabilized, the focus would concentrate on new services within existing markets.

Access to journal articles has become increasingly difficult for many library users. The cost of journals has continued to rise as library budgets have continued to fall. As a result, many individuals and libraries have limited their subscriptions to journals. More to the point, with rising costs, individuals are relying more and more on their academic libraries for the articles they need. While at the same time, the academic libraries are concentrating on reducing their journal collections, due to a combination of higher subscription costs and lowered overall budgets.

Current document delivery services are limited in the articles they can actually deliver to users and the costs of single articles do not compare well with, for example, a hardback book. Three randomly chosen articles of 17, 14, and 16 pages available from Open Access are available for a charge of $24.00, $20.75, and $27.00, respectively. There is no abstract or review of these articles so that the user may assess, prior to purchase, the fit between the article's content and his/her information need. One sampled article listed for $11 but there was no indication of the number of pages, which could be as low as one page. By contrast, one new 773 page hardback book from a noted author was listed for $27.50 at a notable large bookstore, but costs less than $20 with the 30% new hardback book discount. The book can be perused prior to the decision to purchase, even if this particular bookstore specially ordered the book for the customer.

Hitchcock, Carr, Harris, Hey and Hall (1997) suggest that the issue of access to journal articles will be a turning point in the migration of journals from print to digital format. For researchers, the issue of access is of great concern as academic research is based on the principle of progressiveness and one of its central tenets is that work should not be unnecessarily duplicated. This means that the user must have access to the full range of documents or risk loss of areas of knowledge.

Access alone, however, whether print or digital, is not sufficient to sustain users' needs. As early as Vannevar Bush's 1945 article and as recently as the Tulip Project's research the needs of academic journal users have been documented (see References under Bush and Tulip for URLs). These needs include access to all information from one (convenient) source, effective search capabilities, timely access to and publication of new information, sufficient coverage over time and publisher, and (convenient) linking of information. To meet these needs, publishers must focus on integrating their content with services, customer-driven product tailoring and the brokering of information (Hitchcock, Carr, Harris, Hey & Hall, 1997).

Some integration of the print literature is provided by services such as bibliographic cataloging, indexing, and abstracting. As print journals move to electronic formats, these services will be essential. New services will also become possible; for example, custom alerting services to bring new material promptly to the attention of users, and services that link citations and the cited articles.

One immediate obstacle to setting up these services is the lack of historical literature on the web. One exception to this is the literature in astronomy. The Astrophysics Data System (ADS), funded by NASA, under the system Urania, provides references to 20 years of texts of journal articles and all of it is linked both backward (references) and forward (citations to the article being read). That is, in reading one article, the reader can access, through selection of a link, an article referred to in the document being read. In addition, the reader can call up a list of articles which refer to the document currently being read and then, by selecting the link, move to any of these later articles. Unfortunately, many systems at this stage lack this electronic history that would form the backbone of these bibliographic services.

Even those systems that do include this electronic history and bibliographic references will notice that there are shortfalls within the system. For example, oftentimes reference in one article to another article does not necessarily indicate that the two documents are similar in coverage. In fact, after following a link, the reader may find that only one fact in an otherwise lengthy piece is relevant to the context in which it was referenced. This drawback can range from an annoyance to a loss of valuable and limited time. There is a need for an intermediate service between the reference and the referred-to document. The University of Southampton (UK)'s Open Journal Project has developed such levels of resource linking.

The Open Journal Project specifically addresses the issue of information coherence, such as between documents. The goal of the project is to develop a framework of information retrieval technologies that will make publications available as cooperating assets within an information delivery environment served by a progressive filtering or evaluation process. To illustrate, in the Open Journal project, the user accesses a certain article. In reading, the user is struck by a point or argument that carries a reference to another document, for example "Hitchcock et al. (1997)." By selecting the link "Hitchcock et al. (1997)," the reader is taken to the bibliographic reference (rather than to the full text). Here the reader can use the title and other publication information to assess continued interest in the reference. If still interested, the reader selects the bibliographic reference which links to an abstract of the document. If the abstract shows the document to be of continued interest, the reader may then link to the full text (if available) or to information on document location (such as the local journal collection or a document delivery service). Likewise, if the reader wishes to know, for example, how a presented theory has been applied in later work, the reader may link to a list of articles that cites the document being read. Again, a list of bibliographic information is retrieved and selection of a citation brings the reader to an abstract, etc.

Even when full text documents are not available online, this type of linking provides a great resource and service to the academic user and permits exploration of a body of knowledge and identification of resources with high probability of relevance to the information need. This process of linking between documents and/or various document representations is a knowledge-based activity that has been called a citation agent as it acts on behalf of the user to explore citations. Details of the search algorithm can be found in Hitchcock et al., (1997) and general information on the Open Journal Project can be found at http://journals.ecs.soton.ac.uk/. The associated issues of profitability and costing and of copyright and use will be dealt with later.

The book

The book as symbol of the library has evolved over many centuries to its current flexible, portable, and inexpensive paper-based form. Besides affording the qualities of flexibility, portability and economy, paper-based books offer the reader the ease of annotation--in the margins, on end sheets, between lines, within figures. While some software products permit the addition of some forms of marginalia to digital-based books, readers generally do not know how to take notes in a digital format (Ouhara & Sellen, 1997).

Marshal (1997) looked at the form, function, and importance of annotation for readers, particularly subsequent readers of a textbook. Marshall found annotation to be an unexpected valuable source of metadata. Through her observations, which included noting highlighting of user-added annotation as well as printed text by subsequent book owners, Marshall concluded that readers want to annotate and want annotation. Given this desire and the prohibition from annotating books in shared collections, such as in a library, the availability of a digital version of a text affords the ability of a collection to archive a pristine copy of a text while at the same time making it available (at least in RAM) for annotation.

Just as Marshall (1997) found some students valued an annotated (used) textbook over a new copy, we could well understand that a text annotated by certain readers could possess value far greater than the original work. In the case of a difficult text required in a college course, annotations of faculty and top students could be quite useful to others struggling to read and understand the material. Digitization makes possible the ability to display a portion of the text for reading with links to an annotation or layers of annotation (e.g., annotations of annotations) for passages that need further explanation, giving a type of online companion to a text. We should not overlook the fact that not all annotation is valuable to subsequent readers and that some annotation may be taken as valuable when in fact it is inaccurate or misleading to understanding. The matter of authority of annotation is not addressed by Marshall.

Various annotation tools are currently available. Some are based on a model of personal annotation (e.g., ForComment, Acrobat, LotusNotes); others on a model of public or work group commentary (e.g., CoNoter and NCSAUs HyperNews). Still others permit interpretive notes, ratings and paths (e.g., ComMentor), annotation by the text author (IntermediaUsInterNote), and side-by-side viewing by the text author of multiple text-anchored annotations (PREP editor). Annotations may also include drawings. One product, Electronic Cocktail Napkin, is a pen-based sketching mechanism that tries to facilitate informal, unconstrained notations (Marshall, 1997). (Note: Because of the authors' relocation, its website is moved to the 'design machine group' at http://depts.washington.edu/dmachine.)

Annotation has been observed to be a seamless activity with reading. However, annotation in an electronic environment has not achieved this flow, and it is suggested that digital annotation may be a distraction in reading, much as a color-coded highlighting system or highlighter combined with an underlining tool is a distraction in annotating paper-based text, as opposed to underlining and noting with a single tool--a pen or pencil (Marshall, 1997). Development of satisfactory annotation systems, combined with adequate mechanisms for preserving unmarked and annotated versions, could provide a strong incentive to publish certain books electronically. This could be universally attractive if the potential reader had the option to examine various versions and then order a paper-based copy of the text with selected versions of annotation applied.

Digital delivery of film, sound and images

Film is still favored over digital media for its exceptional resolution, its stability, and its low cost (Jim Reimer, Keynote Address, 2nd ACM International Conference on Digital Libraries, July 1997). Film is stable over a hundred-year period while the magnetic tape used to store electronic versions has suffered from problems with the glue used to adhere oxides to tape and has left oxides falling away from their tapes. Preservation initiatives have been undertaken by baking the tapes in order to remount oxides to their tapes. Each frame of film requires 20-30 megabytes of digital storage, making both film and tape media more efficient storage media than computer disk. In terms of universality, film is preferred, around the world, a 35 mm film projector can be found in almost any location and can be repaired for film viewing with only a screwdriver.

However, retrieval of images stored on film is so difficult that images are photographed over and over again; for example, advertising agencies, in the absence of a method for locating previously photographed images, re-photograph the image when it is needed. Vaults of film are more like garbage dumps: stories are told of rare and unreleased film (for example, a lost BBC recording of the Beatles) that have been found by accident when someone walking through a venue literally tripped over cartons whose contents spilled, revealing the location of lost material. Data management is a major problem and a new pioneering frontier in image retrieval. Digital libraries can offer search support to aid reuse of material and transfer of content without loss. Some problems still need to be solved: in order to retrieve the few best answers to a search query, heterogeneous and federated searching needs to be developed. Effective and efficient methods are also needed for indexing and abstracting images.

Digital libraries are a function of economics, that is, digital libraries are the economic engines that drive the reorganization of workflow and management. Digital libraries change the flow of cash and the reason people do work (for example, consider the ATM machine and banking). Digital libraries are still an emerging market: they are sufficiently difficult to create and are expensive. Issues and problems include scalability, security up and down stream, readability, openness (content independent storage-- interoperability among interfaces and vendor hardware and software), rights management (need for flexible alternatives), stream support (browse grade and a broadcast grade), complex search support, data modeling, and how we form metaphors to form searches. In terms of digital delivery of film, a rich data description is needed: frame by frame, who's in the frame, what's going on in the frame (Jim Reimer, Keynote Address, 2nd ACM International Conference on Digital Libraries, July 1997). This is certainly an area that will see exciting breakthroughs in research and development.

2.3 Impact of the digitization: will traditional libraries be replaced?

It has already been pointed out that current technologies' focus on the conversion of paper to digital formats and not on the conversion of the library in total to a digital format. In this way, digitization is comparable to the technology of microforms. It is probably more accurate to discuss the concept of digital libraries in terms of digital coherence and its application to library collections than to discuss the replacement of libraries in general with digital incarnations. Throughout this work, the term digital libraries will be used as a synonym for digital coherence.

Digital coherence can become a new tool with which the library can provide value-added information services to users--but first, those who apply digital coherence to libraries must understand the function and purpose of libraries. Many researchers seem to share the perception expressed in Wiederhold (1995) and believe "the functions of a library are to acquire works, store them, make the works available to the reader, and reimburse the author and the publisher for their efforts" (p. 95). The role of the librarian seems to be little understood as well. In a recent study, frequent users of libraries stated that professionally trained librarian could be replaced by volunteers, such as retirees in the community (Benton Foundation, 1996). With segments of the literature reducing the library to a second-hand shop and librarians to clerks, it is easy to understand how the current rush to raze the library arose. It is imperative that librarians take collaborative, if not leading, roles in the digital library movement and bring other fields and participants into the understanding of and appreciation for the knowledge and practices that have congealed over the past five or six millennia into what we know today as librarianship.

Historically, digitalization or automation in the library has emphasized the computerization of bibliographic tools such as catalogs, indexes, and other finding aids (Saffady, 1995). An area of current discussion is the computerized storage and retrieval of full textbooks and journals. However, some researchers see major distinctions between digital retrieval of information and digital use (reading) of that information. Further, it is suggested by other researchers that, as digital libraries develop, and particularly as issues surrounding intellectual property and fair use evolve, digital libraries will be location aids for documents stored off the Internet.

If we step far enough back in our survey of the history of digital libraries to view the methods people have used to store their thoughts, recollections, and impressions, we will see a lineage which begins with the single memory and moves on to include the human voice (such as bards and minstrels), clay, wood, papyrus leaves, reeds, animal skins, and eventually paper. The medium used depended on the local raw resources, available technology, and the cost of preparing the materials to store information. In this continuum, digital media can be viewed as another in a long list of materials upon which civilization has depended to carry the knowledge of one generation forward to further generations. Like the other materials, we can expect that it will be utilized in proportion to its local availability, supporting technology, its cost, and its reliability for storing and delivering knowledge to current and future generations.

2.4 What are the digitization methods and technologies?

When building a digital library, creators face two major questions, 1) what materials in the library collection should be digitized, and 2) what technologies and/or methods, including procedures and standards, should the library use in digitizing?

Materials to be digitized

The basic materials digitized include printed materials (books, journals, newspapers, manuscripts, archives), image works (paintings, illustrations, maps, photos/pictures, microfilms), and sound recordings (cassettes, records, films, videos) (Liu, 2004; Borgman, 42, 61). While digitization is possible, the process may not be effortless. Searching and retrieving material converted to electronic formats is a more difficult problem.

Textual material is probably the easiest to digitize, especially material with few graphic elements. The publishing industry, for example, has used computerized typesetting for many years. Scanners are commonly used to transfer printed matter from pages to electronic forms. Textbook publishers are now issuing CDs or offering online access to supplementary materials with little digital libraries of tests, readings, activities, graphic organizers, among other items to support material in schoolbooks.

Pictures and sounds also can be converted to electronic formats, for example, converting a song to a .wav file, or, adding background music to video by converting songs from ordinary music CDs to .wav files. The process just takes a little more effort than textual material.

Bibliographic amenities (such as indexes, searches, and retrieval) related to the storage of various media once it has been digitized pose a greater concern than the actual conversion of material to electronic formats (Borgman, 147).

Technologies in digitization

Digitization refers to the process of translating a piece of information such as a book, sound recording, picture or video, into bits. Bits are the fundamental units of information in a computer system. Turning information into these binary digits is called digitization. This digitization process can be accomplished through a variety of existing technologies. What technologies or methods libraries use in digitizing is a question usually associated with the types of materials to be digitized.

The binary coding technology

Binary coding technology is the basic technology for the creation of all digitized textual and image materials. Binary coding schemes take the data and convert it into one of three types of code, 7-bit, 8-bit or 16-bit code represented by ones and zeroes. The forms of these coding schemes are American Standard Code for Information Interchange (ASCII), Extended Binary Coded Decimal Interchange Code (EBCDIC), and Unicode. Unicode is of particular importance because it allows the representation of characteristics of other languages such as accents and special characters (Borgman, 42, 61). Computer languages are built using binary code schemes. Word processing, spreadsheets and database management programs (such as Microsoft Office and Acrobat products) are common tools used to create "new born" digital files, with file extensions such as doc, xls, and pdf files. Computer-based descriptive language systems are tools used to create the "newborn" digital files as well.

ASCII is a 7-bit code. There are many variants of this standard; typically these variations allow different code pages for language encoding, but they all basically follow the same format. Virtually every computer system in the world uses a variant of ASCII.

EBCDIC is a character encoding set initially used by IBM mainframes. EBCDIC uses the full 8 bits available to it, so parity checking cannot be used on an 8-bit system. EBCDIC has a wider range of control characters than ASCII.

Unicode provides a unique number for every character, no matter what the platform, no matter what the program, no matter what the language. Official representation covering the characteristics for all major languages uses a 16-bits-per-character representation.

Computer languages can be divided into three categories: operation systems include BIOS, DOS, Windows, UNIX, and Linux; utilities include statistical language and KWIC (Key Word In Context); and application programming software includes Basic, Pascal, Norton, C, C++, and Java.

The main standardized descriptive markup language systems include MARC, SGML, HTML, XML, Java script (Java, C C++ Perl), and SQL (Structured Query Language).

SGML-Standard Generalized Markup Language is tagged meaningful information that is contained within angle brackets. Example: <title>Asia Digital Library</title><author>University of Wisconsin-Madison</author>HTML-Hypertext Markup Language is syntactically a very similar language to SGML with the same kinds of formats. It supports hypertext links: <A HREF='HTTP://WWW.GOOGLE.COM'>GOOGLE</A>

XML-Extensible Markup Language is a markup language where you make up all the tags yourself. XML is the set of rules that this made-up markup language must follow and the ability to create your own tags is called "extensibility." It is used for documents containing structured information. Structured information contains both content (words, pictures, etc.) and some indication of what role that content plays. Almost all documents have some structure.

XML is a markup language derived from SGML (the parent language of XML and HTML). XML was developed because HTML could not handle certain types of data, such as financial data, software installation guidelines, or mathematical equations ('structured data'), and is limited to describing how data should be displayed by a browser, not describing what the data are.

XML describes content, not presentation. In XML, the user defines his or her own sets of markup elements to describe his or her specific content, and thus it is extremely flexible. In order to dictate presentation, XML can be used in conjunction with cascading style sheets (CSS) (as in HTML) or extensible stylesheet language (XSL). Use of these style sheets allows browsers to read the XML document as HTML, and thus the browser will know how to display the data. XML requires attention to detail that HTML does not: it is case-sensitive and requires closing tags, which HTML does not.

XML is fast becoming the new standard for markup language for the Web because HTML is too limiting and SGML is too complicated. XML is considered an extensible met language because users define their own elements (thus creating their own markup language). Because XML is nonproprietary, it is free, open to the public, and not constricted by computer platforms or software applications, thus offering interoperability. This platform neutrality suggests that XML offers the best chance at data longevity. XML also creates digital coherence, meaning that disparate data sources can be integrated if they share XML codes.

JAVA, designed by James Gosling at Sun Microsystems, is a language that can be interpreted. It is sufficiently limited in its capabilities (no file reading or writing) to be safe to execute. Java scripts are codes that run as an application inside a Web browser.

Popular standards for tags:
- AAP (American Association of Publishers) Electronic Manuscript Standard
- CALS (Department of Defense Continuous Acquisition and Life-Cycle Support) rules
- TEI (Text Encoding Initiative) standard

Optical Character Recognition (OCR) technology

Optical Character Recognition (OCR) technology is the technology used to digitize textual and image materials. It is a technology of machine identification of printed characters through use of light-sensitive devices that analyze electromagnetic spectrum frequencies. It is used for materials that are either not available as ASCII or not appropriate to store that way (e.g., a print book, a paper-based art work, an oversize print map, and so on), to convert them from their original formats into digitized formats. The purpose is that the creator of a .doc specifies what it should look like and the reader gets that appearance.

Software associated with this technology include:

PostScript - a general graphics language adapted to drawing letters from fonts. It defines fonts/logos by software that can generate any kind of graphic appearance.

Acrobat - Portable Document Format serves as a page-viewing interface.

Issues surrounding scanning focus on clarity, accuracy, cost and reformatting/manipulation.

Voice Recognition Technology

Voice recognition technology is the automated process of converting audio sound such as broadcast news into a text database using speech recognition technology.

Speech recognition is part of the technology that uses fixed length phoneme strings to search the phoneme space of the speech using an inverted index of phonemes. That is, the user enters a spoken search query, which the system converts, to a text representation of a fixed number of sequential phonemes from the spoken query. This is then submitted to an index of text representations of strings of sounds in the spoken news.

Voice-recognition tools such as the examples below are having an impact in three major areas: call centers, voice-enabled devices and desktop dictation-and-command software.

- IBM Via Voice
- Dragon NaturallySpeaking by Lernout & Hauspie Holdings USA Inc.
- The Voice C++/ActiveX, designed to build Interactive Voice Response (IVR) applications

Multimedia Recording Technology

Multimedia recording technologies include both conversion of analog video taping to digital video and digital video recording (DVR) technologies. The current recording technique on video tape requires a meticulous documentation of the identity of a given video sequence. Digital video recording (DVR) as well as other advantages has brought crisp video images and instantaneous playback of footage when compared with tape-based time-lapse video recording or VHS type video recording. With the advent of digital video recording technology, video images can now be stored in a digitized format with a unique identifier of every image on a given entity (such as tape or disc).

For documents that are not "born video digital" libraries now can use OCR scanning, voice recognition and speech recognition to convert text to a representation of digital format, or to convert pictures (GIF and JPEG), audio (MP3 and wave), and moving pictures (MPEG) to digital formats.

The Digitization Process

There are many processes in digitizing, such as microfilming, scanning images, recording or re-recording video or audio on to digital media, and retyping of actual texts. Objects that are often digitized include individual documents, pound volumes (prints, manuscripts, photographs, prints, and transparencies), microfilm and microfiche, video and audio, maps, drawings, art works, textiles, and physical three-dimensional (3-D) objects (Deegan, & Tanner, 2002). When these items are converted to the digital form, they need different treatment or handling. This may require using different methods and options (such as digitized photography), depending on the potential use of the digital collection as well as the resources available. This chapter contains more detailed information about some of the most popular Digital Objects including their different forms or formats, their history, and the potential outlook for these formats.

What technologies or methods libraries use in digitizing is a question usually associated with the types of materials to be digitized. One factor to think about is the purpose of the digitization. Is it just for preservation? Is it for putting on the website? Is it for printing? If the digitized document or picture is going on the web, then you have to consider the size of the document. If the size is too big it will be very slow to download. If the size is too small it might distort the original document.

However, sometimes digitization projects can easily consume vast quantities of time. Larger and more complex digitization work would certainly be very time consuming and potentially complex depending on the type of software and depth of utilization.

During a digitization project of images, librarians who work on this process have to carefully organize original and edited images by using appropriate names. The librarians should assign a concise and clear name to each image to manage all the images for their project

Print and images can be digitized using digital cameras, camcorders and scanners. Sounds can be digitized using recording software that turns sounds into digital files so they can be transmitted through phone lines and reinterpreted at the other end by a computer.

Most technological challenges to digitization are associated with paper-based materials. Microform digitization still poses a number of challenges. Digitization technologies for library-based applications, rather than business applications, are still relatively new and much of the hardware and software should be considered as first generation products. In all cases, the effective retrieval of digitized data remains a significant challenge.

The concepts and technologies connected with digitization are complex. There is a basic process that involves different sets of hardware and software technologies at each step. Determining the appropriate technology is directly linked to the anticipated use and purpose of the material being digitized.

Document -> Data Capture -> Data Processing -> Storage -> Retrieval and Display

Documents: examples include text, line art, photographs, color images

Data Capture: manual data entry (word processing), optical character recognition (OCR) or imaging

Data Processing: text may require conversion of diacritics or special characters; images may need enhancement, amplification or compression

Storage: examples include hard disk, magnetic tape or optical CD-ROM

Retrieval/Display: a myriad of technologies for viewing and displaying, concerns include network deliverability

The widespread use of word processors and desktop publishing software means that virtually all text creation is now digital. The challenges arise when the text is in a non-digital medium such as paper or microform and is converted into a digital format. The technologies and issues pertaining to the digitization of media such as sound or video are similar to those for the digitization of text or images.

2.5 Digital Objects, what are they? Origins and definitions

Digital objects either start as a digital file produced as a substitute for materials that already exist in analog format or, as Schreibman (2007) says, [are] "born digital," which means they have no analog counterpart. Most libraries hold a wide range of formats including manuscripts, print, and visual and audio materials from all periods, in many different sizes and conditions. All of these items may be candidates for the process of digitization. The process of converting any physical or analogue item into a digital representation or facsimile is called digitization and these converted items are Digital Objects.

Definition of digital objects

A digital object as defined by Kahn & Wilensky (1995) is "a data structure whose principal components are digital material, or data, plus a unique identifier for this material, called a handle." This digital object is then deposited in one or more repositories to provide access for others. The digital object will then receive a handle and will be registered with a system of handle servers. To deposit or access a digital object, one must use a repository access protocol (RAP). Once stored and registered, it is then considered a registered digital object, which may be used for widespread availability (Kahn &Wilensky, 1995). The digital collection as identified by the Online Dictionary for Library and Information Science (ODLIS, http://www.abc-clio.com/ODLIS/searchODLIS.aspx) (Reitz, 2010) is a collection of library or archival materials converted to machine-readable format for preservation or to provide electronic access.

Digital object architecture

An overview of the Digital Object Architecture can be found here: http://www.cnri.reston.va.us/papers/OverviewDigitalObjectArchitecture.pdf

Originally published in 1995, Kahn and Wilensky (2006), offer an early summary of the concept:

Conceptually, the System works as follows: An *originator*, i.e., a user with digital material to be made available in the System, makes the material into a *digital object*. A digital object is a data structure whose principal components are digital material, or *data*, plus a unique identifier for this material called a *handle* (and, perhaps, other material).

A digital object stored in a repository, and whose handle has been registered with the handle server system, is called a *registered digital object*. Registered digital objects are of primary concern to us here, as they are explicitly constructed to be known about by others, presumably for widespread availability. However, we do not constrain repositories to contain only registered digital objects. Nor are repositories constrained to operate only via the repository access protocol, although they must all support it.

Erickson (2001) refines this into four bullets:
- A *digital object* is a content-independent package that includes the content of a work, a unique identifier for the digital object (its handle), and other data about the object, which might include policy expressions dictating use of the object.
- *Repositories* logically store digital objects and are responsible for enforcing policies bound to aspects of their resident objects.
- A service request on a digital object produces a *dissemination*, which contains the results of the request (determined by the

parameters in the request) and additional data specifying the origin of the dissemination and the specific policies governing its use.
- Disseminations are not required to have the same data as the underlying, "source" digital object. Nor does a dissemination need to be some subset of the digital object's data (e.g., a dissemination that is the result of a service request for a single page of a book stored as a digital object). For example, a digital object may be an executable program and disseminations may be produced by running the program using the parameters in the service request as input.

Structure of digital objects

All digital data has the same underlying structure. This structure is composed of a "bit," or binary digit, which is an electronic impulse that can be represented by two states "on," or "off." These "on" or "off" states can also be written as "1" or "0." Almost any kind of information can be represented in these seemingly simple structures as patterns of the most intricate complexity can be built up, and anything can be digitized (Deegan & Tanner, 2002). The processes of digitization are numerous and include: Image scanning, microfilming and then scanning of the photographic surrogates, re-recording video and audio on to digital media, rekeying of textual content, OCR of scanned textual content, tagging text and other digital content to create a marked-up digital resource, and digital photography (especially for 3-D objects), or large-format items as art works (Deegan, & Tanner, 2002). The final digital objects of the digitization process can be text documents, images of pages, and multimedia, which may include sound, video, or software. These digital objects have changed their formats according to the differences in each digitization process. The following passages of this chapter will deal with many different types of digital object formats and their importance.

Text Resources

Perhaps the most widely used aspect of library digitization is the ability to digitize text. The most prominent success of computing has been in document preparation. Word processing is the most common computer application which enables users to create a document, edit it, store it electronically, and recall/display it on a screen. You can also highlight, underline, move sections of text, store it as an electronic copy or print it as a hard copy. Text can be stored in many formats using typesetting codes; each text document has a file type that indicates the type of code that data is written with. The HTML text is written in script Hyper Text Markup Language. This text file is indicated with (.html) or (.htm). There is also text typed using standard Generalized Markup Language, which is indicated with .sgml and the text document that is written using Extensible Markup Language, which is indicated with (.xml).

Text documents come in two types: plain text and rich text. Plain text supports standard ASCII characters, including numbers, symbols, and spaces, but does not support any type of text formatting. Therefore, we cannot apply bold, italic, or underlined styles, and cannot use different fonts or font sizes in a plain text document. Because plain text does not contain information about text sizes or styles, it is the most efficient way to store text (Reitz, 2007), ("Plain text," 2010). The rich text format (.rtf) includes formatting for style and page layout (boldface, underlining, italic, fonts, etc.). The document with rich text format could include multimedia (graphics, audio, and video) as well, unlike plain text (.txt), which can be read by most text editors and word processing software because it has not been encrypted but it does not include formatting for style and page layout or content definition (Reitz, 2007).

PDF (portable document format)

The best format for text can be the Portable Document Format (PDF) file. A PDF is usually created with software called Adobe Acrobat. Conceived of by John Warnock in 1993, PDFs are commonly created from other documents ("PDF file extension", 2010; DeFurio, 2005). A PDF is an image file that can be viewed on Microsoft, Apple, and Linux operating systems provided that system has the proper software installed. They are often used in digital libraries and online databases and are intended to let the creator specify what the document will look like (Lesk, 2005). [PDFs] may be composed of text, images, as well as other types of information and will carry the same formatting across different platforms ("PDF file extension," 2010).

Due to the fact that they can be created from both text and scanned images, many resources from magazines and journals are scanned and made into PDFs for digital use. Many search engines and online websites or databases allow users to view them using Adobe Reader. Leurs (2010) also notes that PDFs are smaller due to better compression algorithms when compared to PostCript. PDFs are also easier to modify and visualize, and are more independent and versatile (Leurs, 2010). They can be used to create new documents or store non-digitally created documents.

The drawback with PDF documents is the difficulty users have in making changes. Adobe offers software that enables users to make changes to PDFs, but it is not free. Users would have to copy the text and paste into a word processing application, and then save the changed document as a PDF. Copying text from a PDF and pasting into a word processing program is time-consuming and tedious.

Another problem is that errors can occur during the OCR process.

The National Library of Australia's Trove http://trove.nla.gov.au/ is a great digital library with a unified search interface. The result of the search Sydney Opera House yields journal articles, images, books, and other resources. In the screenshot below, the various views of digitized newspapers can be seen:

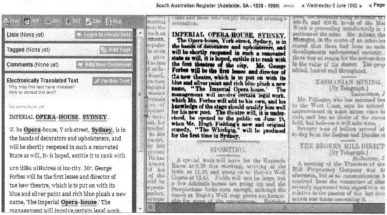

Figure 2.1

The left pane features "Electronically Translated Text", with the option of PDF, JPG, and TXT formats, while the image is in the right. The link, "Why may this text have mistakes?" explains the OCR errors and invites users to correct them. The errors are more apparent in the .txt format:

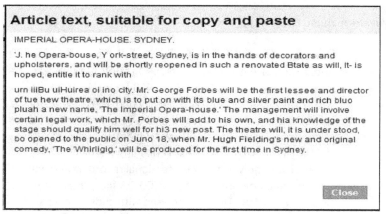

Figure 2.2

HTML and HTML with CSS are also suitable for viewing documents online, and are best for "born digital" documents. Documents may appear differently on different browsers.

Multimedia

Digital sound

Audio is perhaps among the simplest of non-text material to deal with. Digital audio as identified by PC Magazine Encyclopedia (2010) is "sound waves that have been sampled, digitized, and stored in the computer." The most common audio formatting includes a high-quality recording for music and a low-quality one for voice (Lesk, 2005). Widely used formats for digital audio include: music CDs, MP3s (or MP4 depending on the system), and WAV files. MP3s and WAV files are two of the most popular digital formats.

MP3 (MPEG-1 audio layer III)

MP3is derived from the audio sections of the MPEG-1 Audio Layer III. This audio compression technology revolutionized digital music. MP3 compresses CD-quality sound by a factor of 10, keeping intact most of the quality. Computer software such as iTunes or Windows Media Player can play MP3s, as can many handheld devices such as iPods. While most of the quality is preserved, it is still not as good as the original CD quality. Windows Media Player and iTunes both have "ripping" options, which allow a user to convert music from CDs into MP3 files on their computer. Stand-alone ripping software is also available. While 128 Kbps (kilobits per second) is considered the norm for MP3 files, MP3s can be ripped to bit rates from 8Kbps to 320 Kbps with the higher bit rate producing a better sound and larger file ("ZIP file," 2010).

Waveform Audio File (WAV)

WAVs are a type of uncompressed audio file which is short for Waveform Audio File Format ("WAV," 2009).[1] In WAV files, samples can be taken at 8-bits or 16-bits with 11,025 HZ, 22,050 Hz, or 44,100 Hz rates, the highest of which uses 88KB of storage per second ("File extension WAV," 2010). Size is also dependent upon whether the sound recording is mono or stereo ("File extension WAV," 2010). The WAV files use Microsoft Pulse Code Modulation (LPCM) as a form of bit stream encoding ("WAVE," 2009).

WAVs are commonly used for professional recording and editing, and take up about the same amount of space as CD-DA files, used for music CDs ("File extension WAV," 2010). They can be used with audio codecs such as the Microsoft Adaptive Differential Pulse Code Modulation (MS ADPCM) and uncompressed Pulse Code Modulation (PCM) to be played in Windows Media Player ("File extension WAV," 2010). However, WAVs take up much more room than the compressed MP3 files.

---

[1] Source not in original bibliography

Digital video

The term "digital video" refers to moving pictures that are stored on a computer hard disk for editing or playback. Digital video files vary in terms of their video resolution (measured in horizontal and vertical pixels) and their frame rate (measured in frames per second) (BMP, 2010). In order to edit video in the computer or to embed video clips into multimedia documents, a video source must originate from a digital camera or be converted to digital. Frames from analog video cameras and VCRs are converted into digital frames (bitmaps) using frame grabbers or similar devices attached to a computer. Uncompressed digital video signals require huge amounts of storage, and high-ratio real-time compression schemes, such as MPEG, are essential for handling digital video in today's computers. Other digital video formats include: AVI, FLV and QuickTime.

MPEG (Moving Picture Experts Group)

MPEG (pronounced "em-peg") is a standard for compressing full-motion video in digital format. More efficient than JPEG (the standard for compressing still images), MPEG is used to transmit a wide range of audio-video formats including DVD motion pictures. MPEG-2 requires bandwidth of 4-15 MB per second and an MPEG board for playback in most computers.

AVI (audio video interleave)

The AVI (Audio Video Interleave) is a common video format. This format was developed by Microsoft and uses less compression than MPEG files ("AVI," 2010). It allows users to capture, edit, and play video along with audio using multiple applications ("AVI RIFF," 2010). It is a type of Resource Interchange File Format (RIFF) and is the most common video format ("AVI," 2010). AVI files can be compressed with a number of codecs including DivX, XVID, Cinepak, and so on ("AVI," 2010).

FLV (flash video)

Flash video is commonly used on the Internet as a form of embedded videos and require Flash Player to view. It is used by popular video sites such as YouTube, Google, and Flickr ("Flash video," 2010). Originally owned by Macromedia, this company was bought out by Adobe in 2005 ("FLV File Extension," 2010). FLV files encode audio and video streams and make up for 80% of online videos today ("FLV/F4V," 2010).[2] It consists of a short header, interleaved audio, video, and metadata packets and is similar to the standard

---

2

Flash files (.SWF). Flash video is an open format that can be used by non-Adobe/Macromedia applications such as QuickTime ("FLV File Extension," 2010). With such support and mainstream usage, FLV files are likely to endure and remain a popular digital video format.

QuickTime

QuickTime (.MOV) is a video format that was developed by Macintosh in 1991 (QuickTime, 2010). It can be used by anyone for free and QuickTime Player can be downloaded for free on both Windows computers and Macs from the Apple website (QuickTime, 2007). It is used in conjunction with many Apple software or products including the QuickTime Player and iTunes (QuickTime, 2010). It is often used on the Apple website for high-quality movie trailers. Like the AVI file, QuickTime files also use codecs and third-party plug-ins (QuickTime, 2010). It also can handle a variety of formats including video, media clips, sound, text, animation, music, and interactive panoramic images (QuickTime, 2007).

QuickTime is also the basis for the MPEG-4 (MP4) format which is used frequently on iPhones and iPods (QuickTime, 2010). MP4s were introduced in 1998 and compress files without losing quality and can combine audio, video, subtitles, and still images ("What is," 2010). The MP4's quality is equal to the quality of a DVD and makes it easy to watch videos via the Internet ("What is," 2010). The high-quality and small video size makes these files easier to display on web pages or for digital preservation and storage.

Digital Images

There are many problems when storing digital images, especially those that aren't just pictures on printed pages. The complexity of adding color, texture, and shape in these pictures requires hundreds of different standards of image representation (Lesk, 2005). However, there are processes for converting any image into digital representation using the form of pixels, which can be read and manipulated by a computer, thus reforming as a visible image. There are many ways to convert an original document to an electronic format or to create digital documents using technology such as scanners, software programs (like Adobe Photoshop) and widely popular digital cameras (Digital Imaging, 2010). The digital images take different formats such as BMP, JPG, GIF, PNG, TIFF, WMF and EMF image. It could also be in a PDF file format. Image formats require the preservation of the resolution, color support, bit-depth and metadata of a very rich image file, the ability to store images in uncompressed or compressed formats using both lossless and lossy techniques and the ability to support the derivation of access copies (Schreibman, 2007).

Images in digital libraries are often used for viewing online, but are not to be re-used since there is usually a copyright. Images are usually stored as archival TIFF files, because they are the most faithful to the original, while displaying derivative JPEG files are more suitable for viewing on a screen. Often the TIFF file is not even offered for download since the JPEG is useful and TIFF files are large.

TIFF (tagged image file format)

The TIFF is a flexible format and saves 8 bits or 16 bits per color (red, green, or blue) for 24-bit and 48-bit totals, respectively, and usually uses either the .tif or .tif filename extension (Graphic Standards, 2009). The TIFF meets most of the general requirements for master images and is standard for textual images, graphic illustrations/artwork/originals, maps, plans, oversized photographs, aerial photographs, and objects/artifacts (Schreibman, 2007). TIFF images start to be scanned at the bottom and work their way up (Neuendorffer, n.d).

JPEG (Joint Photographic Experts Group)

JPEG is one of the most common types of image file (Lesk, 2005). It supports up to 24-bit color and is used much of the time for web graphics and digital photos ("JPEG file extension," 2010). It is a lossy compression algorithm and breaks an image into 8 x 8 pixel blocks (Lesk, 2005). This means that some of the original image's data is lost depending on how much loss can be tolerated ("JPEG," 2010). These files can be saved by the desired resolution, for high quality printing, low quality transmission, or anywhere in between ("JPEG," 2010). While JPEGs are great for images, text quality and information can be lost due to compression and low resolution ("JPEG," 2010). JPEG also is not as good for sharp computer-generated images (Lesk, 2005). However, while graphic interchange format (GIF) image files have been claimed to have a copyrighted algorithm by Unisys, JPEG is a "publicly defined and usable standard," (Lesk, 2005, p. 96). This gives the JPEG much more promise of flexibility for future usage, and the variety of compressions and resolutions, as well as having no copyright issues, allows its use for many purposes.

Digital libraries usually offer several image sizes. The Library of Congress offers two JPEGs and a TIFF in the screenshot below:

Digital Libraries in Theory and Practices

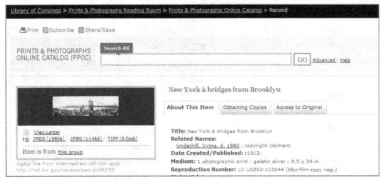

Figure 2.3

Bitmap (BMP)

Bitmap image files are uncompressed bit-mapped images and are stored in the device-independent bitmap (DIB) format ("File extension BMP," 2010). In this format, each pixel in the image is given a specific location and color ("File extension BMP," 2010). The color options for bitmaps include 1-bit, 4-bit, 8-bit, and 24-bit colors, which provide 2, 16, 256, and 16,000,000 colors ("BMP," 2010). In black and white BMPs, one bit will represent one pixel on the screen. With shades of grey and color BMPs, there are several bits to represent one or more pixels (bitmap, 2010). Unfortunately, since there is no compression, BMPs are often a lot larger than other image formats such as JPEGs, which use lossy compression.

Graphics Interchange Format (GIF)

The GIF file format is a common format in which the first pixel in the file goes in the upper left hand corner, and the second one goes just to its right. The image is scanned from left to right, top to bottom, until all the pixels have been specified (Neuendorffer, n.d). It is limited to an 8-bit palette, or 256 colors. This makes the GIF format suitable for storing graphics with relatively few colors such as simple diagrams, shapes, logos and cartoon style images. The GIF format supports animation and is still widely used to provide image animation effects. It also uses a lossless compression that is more effective when large areas have a single color, and ineffective for detailed images or dithered images (Graphic Standards, 2009).

Portable Network Graphics (PNG)

PNG is pronounced "ping" and its file extension is .png. The PNG file format was designed to replace GIF, because GIF compression is patented by CompuServe and software developers that use it (such as Adobe) have to pay a royalty. PNG, on the other hand, is free for everyone. There are two types

42

of PNG formats: PNG-8 and PNG-24. (The number refers to 8-bit or 24-bit color (Bloomsburg University Virtual, 2002).

2.6 File Formats, Migration and Transformation

File Formats

The National Digital Information Infrastructure and Preservation Program (NDIIPP) defines formats as "packages of information that can be stored as data files or sent via network as data streams" (Arms & Fleischhauer, 2007). A file is one type of these packages of information. There are many different kinds of file formats, and the vast number of different types can become a problem for those who need to decide which file format to use (File format, 2008). With so many file formats available, a digital librarian must consider carefully which formats to use so that the information contained in the digital library will be preserved in the best way possible. If the format chosen is proprietary, meaning that it is used, produced, or marketed under exclusive legal right of the inventor or maker,[3] then the digital library risks losing access should the owner abandon support for the proprietary file format. Choosing an open format instead of proprietary reduces that risk, but still the digital librarian must make sure that the file format chosen is easily accessible to users, which may sometimes require the use of a proprietary format due to its overwhelming popularity. NDIIPP suggests that there are seven factors that digital librarians should take into consideration when choosing a file format: disclosure, adoption, transparency, self-documentation, external dependencies, impact of patents, and technical protection mechanisms. Disclosure refers to the documentation available for the format – usually less available for proprietary formats and more available for open formats. The impact of patents can also affect the choice of format. If the owners of a format require a royalty to be paid for the use of the format, then that may affect the feasibility of its use for the digital library. Similarly, technical protection mechanisms often found in proprietary formats that keep a digital library from being able to preserve content must be considered. Adoption refers to the popularity of the format for users; designers take into consideration the wide use of some formats, but must keep in mind that "in some cases, the existence and exploitation of underlying patents may inhibit adoption, particularly if license terms include royalties based on content usage" (Arms & Fleischhauer, 2007).

Compression

---

[3] http://www.merriam-webster.com/dictionary/proprietary

Compression is the process of reducing the size of video, graphic, and audio files by eliminating redundant data (Bryn M. College, 2010). In the 1980s, Phil Katz developed algorithms for compressing files into smaller amounts of space, and his programs became PKZIP and PKUNZIP from PKWARE, Inc. The format became so popular that other companies such as Nico Mac and Netzip developed Zip and UnZip utilities, and the Zip/Unzip algorithms have been placed in the public domain ("ZIP file," 2010). There are two types of compression: lossy compression, and lossless compression. The lossy compression is a form of file compression that will compress data by a very great percentage (10:1 to 20:1). However, when the data is uncompressed later, there will be data lost. The lossless compression is form of file compression that allows compression and subsequent decompression without any loss of data. Compared to "lossy" compression, lossless does not compress the data to as great of a degree. The common compression file formats are ZIP file, and RARfile ("BMP," 2010).

ZIP file

A ZIP file contains one or more files that have been compressed into the ZIP format. Also called a "ZIP archive," "zipped file," or "zipped archive," the ZIP algorithm is the most popular compression method in use. ZIPs commonly have .zip extensions, however, there are other extensions as well. Files with the .gz extension are zipped files and can be opened using any UnZip program. JAR is a ZIP file in the Java world, using the .jar extension. Microsoft Word 2007 uses .docx files, which are ZIP compression, as well as Microsoft Office 2007's Office Open XML. These extensions are used to collect a number of files for a certain purpose, such as to provide simplified identification and transportation as a single object, and still contain the structure of a ZIP file ("ZIP file," 2010).

RAR (Roshal archive)

While ZIP files may be the most common and well-recognized type of compression file, RAR files are gaining popularity. RAR stands for Roshal Archive, named after its creator, Eugene Roshal (".Rar file," 2010). It is used with the program WinRAR and can be used to compress one or multiple files (RAR file format, 2010)[1]. In addition to compressing files as a ZIP file does, RARs also allow for multi-part archives, tight compression, multimedia and text modes, recovery records, Unicode support, and more (RAR file format, 2010). Multi-part archives allows a user to divide a rar into smaller parts with extensions such as .r00, r01, r02, ..., .001, .002, .003, ..., or .part1.rar, part2.rar, part3.rar, ... which makes large RAR files a lot easier to handle (File extension RAR, 2010). This is convenient for e-mails, burning onto disks, or uploading to a newsgroup (RAR files, 2010). While the RAR file is newer than the ZIP file, it is becoming quite popular and the additional features make it more effective and useful than a standard ZIP file.

Emulation, migration and transformation

Choosing a format is not only important for the immediate needs of the digital library, but also the future needs of preservation of the digital objects in the library. Because digital objects can be lost if the hardware or software that their format relies on becomes obsolete, digital librarians often must migrate the information to new formats. There is another option, however: emulation. With emulation, the original file can still be accessed through software that emulates the original software that has since become obsolete (Granger, 2000). In this way, the original look and feel is maintained. Also, when a format is very popular, there is an increased likelihood that tools for emulation will "emerge from industry without specific investment" by the digital library (Arms & Fleischhauer, 2007).

Emulation is not always an option due to feasibility and, sometimes, property rights issues (Granger, 2000). The most frequent approach to saving information from obsolescence of its format is through transformation and migration. Leidig (2010) defines transformation as "the process of altering the format of an object." Caplan (2007) summarizes format migration as "the process of creating a version of a file in a more current format, particularly if the format of the source file is in danger of becoming obsolete." The point of migration is to allow users to continue to access the same information even if the tools used to access the information and the format of the information change. The information contained in the file that is to be transformed for migration must remain as similar to the original as possible in order to "preserve the content and functionality" of the digital object (Leidig, 2010). Hedstrom (1997) argues that the process of migration will likely lead to some level of degradation of the original file contents, and that while some may be acceptable, others may "destroy the meaning of the document." She suggests several important strategies that can help the digital librarian when considering issues in file preservation (Hedstrom, 1997):

- transfer to paper or microfilm; store in "software-independent" format
- retain in the native software environment
- migrate to a system that is compliant with open standards
- store in more than one format
- create surrogates
- save the software needed for access and retrieval
- develop software and hardware emulators

A designer must consider the feasibility of these options. For example, keeping a hard copy of each file in a "software-independent" format may just not be feasible due to monetary or space limitations. Storing a file in more than one format may be a good option to hedge bets against obsolescence, and developing emulators and saving software can help if obsolescence becomes an issue. Creating surrogates is a form of redundancy that might also be used to combat unforeseen future problems.

The National Library of the Netherlands (KB) defines three specific types of migration: 1) periodic update, in which a file format is updated to a current format, 2) normalization, in which a file is permanently converted from one format to another, and 3) migration-on-request, in which a file format is transformed only when requested by the user. KB, for example, is currently normalizing all Microsoft Office formats into .PDF format "to ensure... long-term accessibility" (Kool & van Wijk, 2007).

Not all migration is done by the digital librarian. Sometimes, when content is user-created and submitted to a digital library, the link between the user and the library can filter the format by allowing only specific formats to be submitted. In this way, files are transformed to a standard file format. If this filter does not exist, then the digital librarian may find the need to migrate files to a standard format themselves, or to a newer format. Newer is not always better, as one can see with the difference between Microsoft Word's .doc and .docx file extension types. Users who had not adopted the newest version of Microsoft Word were unable to access the information in the .docx format until an update was available for their older software. In some cases, the problem may not lie in just the software, but in the hardware as well. For example, audio information stored on a cassette tape can be accessed through a cassette tape player, but not readily through a computer. One may migrate the information on the cassette to an audio file format (such as .mp3) that can be accessed through a computer, but one must take into consideration the degradation of the data that will occur during such a transformation. The designer must assess which is the more important goal: easier access or better preservation (Leidig, 2010). This process begins when the designer initially chooses a file format type while keeping in mind the future possibilities of transformation or emulation in order to preserve both the information data and access to the information.

Digital Libraries and Digitalization

Converting materials to a digital format has many benefits. Items are easier to duplicate, easier to store and easier to maintain. Often, physical documents and images fade and yellow after several years. Digitizing these documents prevents this from happening. As previously mentioned, digital libraries often have to make digitization recommendations or choices rather than purchasing recommendations. In this case, a selection policy is important for choosing which resources to digitize. "The utility of digital images is most likely ensured when the needs of users are clearly defined, the attributes of the documents are known, and the technical infrastructure to support conversion, management, and delivery of content is appropriate to the needs of the project" (Cornell University Library/ Research Department [CUL/RD], 2003). Thus, selection of materials to be digitized is based on value, use, condition, characteristics of original and appropriateness for use and access (Library of Congress, 2006a).

"Digitization is the process of taking traditional library materials, typically in the form of books and papers, and converting them to electronic form where they can be stored and manipulated by a computer" (Vrana, 2010). Digitization also allows users to access fragile materials they may not otherwise have the opportunity to view. Vrana explains mass digitization and non-mass digitization as the two types of digital efforts employed by libraries. Mass digitization involves an industrial level of digitizing everything within a repository. This effort is typically used by national libraries. Non-mass digitization involves the "careful and individual selection of materials to be digitized" and is aimed at building collections and preserving rare or fragile materials (Vrana, 2010). Depending on how content has been created and made available to users, DLs, or their content, can be broadly classified in three ways, each of which has its own advantages and disadvantages: born digital, turned digital and gained digital (Mahesh & Mittal, 2009).

Born digital, as its name suggests, is content that has been created and is meant for use and storage in digital formats. This gives libraries the opportunity to be involved in content creation, which can also be helpful when dealing with copyright issues. The problem with this method of library building is that it can be time consuming and requires significant resources.

Turned digital content is material, such as books or photographs, which the library has converted into a digital format, using scanning technology (Mahesh, G., Mittal, R., 2009). This type of content allows libraries to offer users access to material that formerly existed only in an analog format, and can make populating the DL a much quicker proposition. Some of the disadvantages to this type of library include copyright issues, equipment cost, and storage capacity, as scanned documents require more storage space than simple text.

Gained digital material may have been born digitally or been digitized by another individual or institution, but the DL had nothing to do with its creation as a digital object. An example of this is a subscription to an electronic database that gives users access to e-journals; users can view content, but the library had no input in its creation or digitization. While this may be the quickest way for libraries to populate their collection, costs are high and fixed, since subscriptions must be maintained in order to allow continued access to content.

There is a fourth option not mentioned by Mahesh and Mittal that can be valuable in avoiding duplication of content or for DLs with financial limitations or manpower issues, and that is linked digital content. Chowdhury and Chowdhury (2003) point out that material selection for digital libraries has its own challenges. Since there is no single source from which to choose materials for a digital library, libraries may have to resort to scouring the web to find appropriate digital materials. In this case, material is hosted somewhere other than the DL and the library points users to its location, meaning the library has no control over its content or responsibility for its maintenance (Berkeley). This can be very helpful for DLs when trying to avoid the cost of digitizing content that is already hosted by another institution; rather than creating an identical item digitally, users can view the exact same content at another site. Linking to material can also be a valuable tool for DLs with limited resources, although some would argue that if the majority of a DL content is linked, it might cease to be a digital library. However, since one of the primary goals of any library should be allowing as many people as possible access to as much information as possible, linked content is a very valuable resource.

While larger DLs might easily combine all four of these models in their collection development policy, the manpower and financial limitations faced by many, if not most, DLs will make it necessary for many digital libraries to focus on one strategy. There is no "right" choice for any particular DL, each one must weigh the advantages and disadvantages of each type, while considering its own unique circumstances. Regardless of the origins of the resources, several factors need to be considered.

Standards

Although no rules exist as far as digital libraries are concerned, many standards have been developed. The Getty Information Institute urges libraries to choose open standards (instead of proprietary standards), which are more likely to promote interoperability and longevity (www.getty.edu). The Digital Library Federation (DLF) has outlined a set of benchmarks involved in setting standards for digital reproductions. They state that "faithful reproductions" should be created in order to contain the same content as the print version. The DLF sets minimum standards for page image reproduction requirements, functions required when applicable and functions that are strongly preferred (diglib.org).

2.7 The process of digitizing material

Once a library has chosen the material to be digitized, the next step is deciding how to digitize it. One option is to use a commercial digitization company; another is to digitize works "in-house" (Tennant 1998). The Getty Information Institute notes, "The cost-effectiveness of each approach will depend on the volume, type, and fragility of materials being scanned, the required quality of the resulting digital objects, and the expertise and equipment available in-house."

Cornell University Library and Research Department break down the technical infrastructure of digitizing materials into the "digitization chain" (library.cornell.edu 2003). While the digitization chain is broken down into three seemingly simple components, hardware, software and networks, Cornell University Library (2003a) specifies:

A truly comprehensive view of technical infrastructure also includes protocols and standards, policies and procedures (for workflow, maintenance, security, upgrades, etc.), and the skill levels and job responsibilities of an organization's staff.

Selecting the hardware used for digitizing materials is dependent on the materials selected for digitizing, as well as the budget involved. Image creation from documents involves using a device that can capture an image, typically a scanner. The four most general types of scanners are flatbed, drum, film and digital cameras. When choosing any scanner it is necessary to ensure the bed of the scanner is compatible with the size of the items to be scanned and will not damage items during the scanning process.

Scanners

A flatbed scanner can range from $100-$3000. A flatbed scanner that costs around $500 is, according to Tennant, suitable to most digital library purposes (1998). It is important to consider the optical resolution; which refers to the pixels or dots per inch (dpi) the scanner can capture. [Cornell University Library (2003b) defines resolution as:] the "ability to distinguish fine spatial detail. Adjusting the resolution of an image prevents it from being blurry. The DLF sets the benchmark standard at 600 dpi for a black and white document reproduction and 300 for gray or color reproductions.

Bit depth is the number of bits used to make up a pixel. The number of tones used increases with the amount of bit depth. [Another way to say this is that bit depth or color depth refers] to the number of gray or other color shades a scanner can capture. The higher the bit depth capacity, the more accurate the reproduced image will be. The DLF standard is 1bit for black and white reproductions; 8 bits for gray; and 24 bits for color reproductions. The image below from Cornell University Library (2003) shows the number of bits used in a bitonal image, gray scale and color image:

Digital Libraries in Theory and Practices

Figure 2.4: Bitonal Image (Cornell University Library, 2003b).

Bit Depth: Left to right - 1-bit bitonal, 8-bit grayscale, and 24-bit color images.

Drum scanners are much more costly than flatbed scanners; however, drum scanners are capable of producing the highest resolutions, up to 12,000 bpi, useful for enlarging images. Drum scanners are very slow and require a high level of skill to use. Cornell University Library states that drum scanners are not conducive to scanning brittle or fragile materials (2003a).

Microfilm scanners are used to digitize existing film, fiche and aperture cards. "Although [microfilm] scanners are still essential for conversion of older library contents, new image come directly from digital cameras (Lesk 2005). The digital cameras used in the creation of digital libraries are more enhanced than the typical consumer models. Tennant explains "They are most often attached to a copy stand that allows the camera to be moved up or down above a table, upon which the item being photographed is placed (often under a sheet of glass to force the original flat" (1999). Digital cameras are useful to capture images of fragile objects, although the lighting involved may result in damage.

In addition to the four scanners discussed, the increase in mass digitization projects has resulted in very innovative technology to assist with scanning materials. The Stanford University Libraries and Academic Information Resources (SULAIR) have created a robot scanner, which uses air pressure to turn pages, resulting digitizing up to 1,600 pages per hour (library.stanford.edu 2004). SULAIR's robot scanner cost up-ward of $300,000 and is not a possibility for most digital library efforts (Stanford University Libraries, 2004).

Scanner software

The Digitization Chain states that once the scanning process has occurred it may be necessary to edit the scanned images. It may also be necessary to convert files to a user-friendly format, scale images by reducing resolution or bit depth and create optical character recognition (OCR), which converts scanned text to searchable machine-readable text. It is also necessary to create metadata for the digitized works (library.cornell.edu 2003). The Colorado Digitization Project (2008) states:

There are two types of software that are needed for most digital imaging projects. The first is the scanning software that comes with the scanner. The second type of software is the image editing software, normally applied to the image after it has been scanned, choose scanning software that is at least capable of saving image files into standard formats such as TIFF, JPG, GIF, etc. This functionality will help production and also ensure a wide range of image delivery options. Software that converts image files from one format to another may also be useful.

System software

Cervone (2006) states, "Selecting software for a digital library project is not an easy task. In addition to the standard issues that arise in any system software selection process, digital library software poses its own distinct problems" (2002). The two basic choices for digital library software are commercial and open-source. The Open Source Initiative (OSI) has become a certification body for open source software under a commonly agreed-upon definition for "open source". Highlights of the OSI's definition of open source include: free distribution and redistribution of software and source code; licenses that allow distribution of modifications and derived works and non-discrimination against persons, groups or fields of endeavor (Goh et al., 2006).

A variety of open source software exists for library use. The United Nations Educational, Scientific and Cultural Organization (UNESCO) (n.d.) has published the "Free and Open Source Software Portal" on their Webpage unesco-ci.org. Goh et al. (2006) have constructed a checklist for digital library software and conducted an experiment using the checklist to evaluate and score the four digital library software packages that met the checklist criteria. The four software packages and their scores are: Greenstone 82.17; CDSware 81.35. Fedora 75.01 and EPrints 66.49. Cervone (2006) states:

For digital library projects, if you pay particular attention to security and authentication issues, long-term cost and maintenance considerations, vendor viability, training and documentation as well as the functional requirements, you will be on the right track to a successful implementation."

Dynamic range, file size and compression

Other attributes must be considered to properly digitize an item. Dynamic range shows the variety in the lightest tone of an image and the darkest tone of an image. This is an important feature "for continuous-tone documents that exhibit smoothly varying tones, and for photographs it may be the single most important aspect of image quality," (Cornell University Library, 2003b). [See an example below:]

Figure 1.5: Dynamic Range (Cornell University Library, 2003b).

File size is determined by calculating the surface area of a document multiplied by the bit depth and dpi2. Compression is then used to reduce the image size so it is suitable for transfer or storage. Images are often very large and can overrun the network. File formats are used when saving a document or image. Such examples are jpeg, tiff, etc. A full table of common file formats is below (Cornell University Library, 2003b):

Name and Current Version	TIFF 6.0 (Tagged Image File Format)	GIF 89a (Graphics Interchange Format)	JPEG (Joint Photographic Expert Group)/JFIF (JPEG File Interchange Format)	JP2-JPX/ JPEG 2000	Flashpix 1.0.2	ImagePac, Photo CD	PNG 1.2 (Portable Network Graphics)	PDF 1.4 (Portable Document Format)
Extension(s)	.tif, .tiff	.gif	.jpeg, .jpg, .jif, .jfif	.jp2, .jpx, .j2k, .j2c	.fpx	.pcd	.png	.pdf
Bit-depth(s)	1-bit bitonal; 4- or 8-bit grayscale or palette color; up to 64-bit color[1]	1-8 bit bitonal, grayscale, or color	8-bit grayscale; 24-bit color	supports up to 2^{14} channels, each with 1-38 bits; gray or color	8-bit grayscale; 24 bit color	24-bit color	1-48-bit; 1/2/4/8-bit palette color or grayscale, 16-bit grayscale, 24/48-bit truecolor	4-bit grayscale; 8-bit color; up to 64-bit color support
Compression	Uncompressed Lossless: ITU-T.6, LZW, etc. Lossy: JPEG	Lossless: LZW[2]	Lossy: JPEG Lossless:[3]	Uncompressed Lossless/Lossy: Wavelet	Uncompressed Lossy: JPEG	Lossy: "Visually lossless" Kodak proprietary format[4]	Lossless: Deflate, an LZ77 derivative	Uncompressed Lossless: ITU-T.6, LZW. JBIG ossy: JPEG
Standard/ Proprietary	De facto standard	De facto standard	JPEG: ISO 10918-1/2 JFIF: de factostandard[5]	ISO/IEC 15444 parts 1-6, 8-11	Publicly available specification	Proprietary	ISO 15948 (anticipated)[6]	De facto standard[7]
Color Mgmt.	RGB, Palette, YC$_b$C$_r$,[8] CMYK, CIE L*a*b*	Palette	YC$_b$C$_r$	Palette, YC$_b$C$_r$, RGB, sRGB, some ICChttp://www.library.cornell.edu/preservation/tutorial/presentation/table7-1.html - ftn9# ftn9[9]	PhotoYCC and NIF RGB,[10] ICC (optional)	PhotoYCC	Palette, sRGB, ICC	RGB, YC$_b$C$_r$, CMYK

Web Support	Plug-in or external application	Native since Microsoft® Internet Explorer 3, Netscape Navigator® 2	Native since Microsoft® Internet Explorer 2, Netscape Navigator® 2	Plug-in	Plug-in	Java™ applet or external application	Native since Microsoft® Internet Explorer 4, Netscape Navigator 4.04, (but still incomplete)	Plug-in or external application
Metadata Support	Basic set of labeled tags	Free-text comment field	Free-text comment field	Basic set of labeled tags[11]	Extensive set of labeled tags	Through external databases; no inherent metadata	Basic set of labeled tags plus user-defined tags.	Basic set of labeled tags
Comments	Supports multiple images/file[12]	May be replaced by PNG; Interlacing and transparency support by most Web browsers	Progressive JPEG widely supported by Web browsers[13]	Multiple resolutions, progressive display, tiling, region of interest coding and many other advanced features	Provides multiple resolutions of each image; wide industry support, but limited current applications	Provides 5 or 6 different resolutions of each image; unclear future	May replace GIF, though market penetration has been spotty	Preferred for printing and viewing multipage documents; strong government use
Home Page	Unofficial TIFF home page	GIF specification	JPEG home page	JPEG 2000 home page	FlashPix home page	Photo CD home page	PNG home page	PDF home page specs

Table2.1: Table of Common File Formats

2.8 User access

Unless a digital library is created for in-house use only, it will be necessary to use a network to allow users access. A heavily trafficked digital library will require a faster network than a library that is providing just email and Web-searching. It is also important to consider the size of images being viewed; large files sent over users' slower networks will result in lengthy downloading times. Cornell University Library (2003a) suggests offering multiple versions of images to satisfy a variety of users.

Legal restrictions

Legal restrictions dictate that libraries consider whether materials are restricted, and if so, whether it is due to privacy, content, or donor concerns (CUL/RD, 2003). Another equally important concern is copyright, which is "protection...provided to authors of 'original works of authorship,' including literary, dramatic, musical, artistic a certain other intellectual works [which] is available to both published and unpublished works" (U.S. Copyright Office, Library of Congress, 2008). According to a former library law professor from San Jose State University, it is safe to assume that anything published before 1922 is public domain and can be digitized (Minow, 2004). However, if a material is in the last twenty years of its copyright period it is illegal to post a digital copy on the Internet and can only be used in-house. If the material is in fact copyright protected, the library needs to consider whether it has the right to create and disseminate digital reproductions (CUL/RD, 2003).

Other considerations

In addition to legal implications, there are issues relating to the resources themselves. For instance, document attributes need to be considered; it must be determined whether the material can be digitized and whether the content can adequately be converted to digital format (CUL/RD, 2003). Another consideration is whether the original resource would be damaged by the digitization process itself (CUL/RD, 2003). On the other hand, if the original resource were too fragile or damaged to be used in its original state, then digitization would reduce the use of the original thus preserving it longer (CUL/RD, 2003; Library of Congress, 2006a). [...] The expected frequency of use of the collection, the user's needs to access the digital resources, security of the collection, the ability to control unauthorized use and ability collaborate and share the collection [also need to be considered] (Wikiversity, 2010).

Another critical consideration is whether the library has the "requisite technical infrastructure to manage, deliver, and maintain digital materials" (CUL/RD, 2003). That is, if the library does not have the financial and technical abilities to provide and sustain the resources, then the expense and labor required to digitize material would be wasted.

2.9 Examples of digitization projects

The UCLA digital library describes two examples of adding materials to a digital collection: The first example involves the preservation of frequently needed items, that while not necessarily rare, were, due to the threat of deterioration unable to be circulated. Adding these to their digital collections would involve dismantling the book, scanning the pages and creating PDF files. The second example involves vinyl audio records, which are valuable to the study of ethnic culture. The records are not in fragile condition, but heavy use would cause them to deteriorate. Digitizing these materials is costly and will result in large audio files, which could not be stored on-line. Decisions will have to be made about what kind of audio file to offer to users, what kind of server software to use, and how to compress the original file so that it can be accessed easily through a database of metadata (http://digital.library.ucla.edu).

Another example of a digitization project is the Google Books Library Project. Google has partnered with 18 libraries, including Oxford University, University of Michigan and Stanford University among others to digitize out-of-copyright books and make them available through the Google Book Search (Wikiversity, 2010). This search is free of charge. According to the University of Michigan library website the partnership between Google and the other libraries is instrumental because only "through partnerships can digitization of this scale be achieved," (University of Michigan, 2010). The Google Books Library Project emphasizes how important the digitization process is and how it is quickly changing the way people view libraries.

Yale Law School's Avalon Project (https://law.yale.edu/yls-today/news/yls-avalon-project-provides-link-history/) includes digital copies of documents on law, history, and politics. The digital documents can include hyperlinks to related documents. (YLS 2001) The texts are presented as-is, without any editorial additions. The Project includes documents from 4000BC to 2003. Most documents are from the 17th, 18th, and 19th centuries, with none after 2003. The documents are focused on the United States and are mostly treaties. It seems that the Avalon Project was the project of one librarian in the late 1990s and early 2000s, and it does not look to be continually updated. The strength of the Avalon Project is that it collects a huge number of documents in an online format. The weaknesses of the Project are that these documents are not easily searchable and have not been updated.

The Columbia library digital collection (https://dlc.library.columbia.edu/) is comprised of reproductions, photographs, images, drawings, objects, and other digital objects that are a part of the specific library made up of the many branch libraries that makes the university libraries. The digital collection draws from items that are a part of the greater rare collections, or non-circulating libraries such as The Avery Architecture and Fine Arts Library, The Rare Book & Manuscript library, and from other collections such as the C.V. East Asian Library, and the Burke Theological library. The digital library collection highlights many of the library's collection and avails visibility to items parts of the collection that may not otherwise be viewed because they are in a special collection library. Items that are displayed in the digital library collections can also additionally be accessed on the library's page, for example under The Avery Architecture and Fine Arts Library, one can see there is a digital collection.

Conclusion

There are many factors involved in creating digital coherence, which is essential to effective digital library design. It requires a clear view of the big picture and an understanding of the details at work. Digital object formation is outlined and the considerations necessary to create, process, store, and retrieve them is described in this chapter.

Digital objects come in a variety of formats. There are a number of formats for text, images, audio, video, and compression. Each type also requires its own unique way of either converting it from the original source to a digital format, or to create it electronically in a digital format. Many of these have their own advantages and disadvantages, but the formats that will be the most successful will be the ones that can store the most amount of information and preserve the best quality while storing it in the smallest amount of space possible. In choosing the format for a digital object a librarian has many things to consider including the longevity of the format in regards to preservation and accessibility. Very often the processes of emulation, migration and transformation must be utilized in order to maintain accessibility to these objects in a quickly advancing technological world.

Making informed decisions about these issues will help to build well-designed digital libraries that adapt to changing technology.

Study questions for chapter Two

Information can now be accessed through computerized network systems. Acting locally and thinking globally is one of phenomena described by many researchers including Christine Borgman in her book (Borgman, Christine L., 2000, From Gutenbergto the global information infrastructure: access to information in the networked word. p.209). Such ideas can be also seen at this site http://dlis.gseis.ucla.edu/people/pagre/tno/august-1995.html. What do you think the possibility of a Global Information Infrastructure (GII)? Do you think that the application of this concept is "beyond our understanding of technology"?

Chapter Three: Collection Development

The most important aspect of a digital library is its collection; without it, a digital library would not exist. The selection of resources for the collection of a digital library takes careful consideration and extensive evaluation, from its scope to its content, to better accomplish its purpose to support the success of the library's mission.

Collection development in digital libraries is a subject that has gained significance in the present culture of information. The development of information technologies has changed collection development into a solution to assure that users can obtain information under current standards of quality. Prevalence of electronic formats can provide larger quantities of information to a larger number of users (Quesada & Vignau, 2006, para.1).

In this aspect, collection development and selection for a digital library does not differ greatly from traditional libraries, which often collect resources in varying formats, including print and electronic ones. In general, regardless of resource format, each library must create a collection development and selection policy that supports its overall goals and mission statement. As with any library, questions often are considered including: why an item should be added to a digital collection, what purpose it will serve, who the audience is, and so on must be answered. However, a digital librarian must also investigate to figure out if an item is born-digital, and if not, what is the process for converting it to a digital file? Other considerations must also be made, such as ways to search for and access information in various markup languages, and whether alternatives to print publishing may exist.

From a technological standpoint, "collection development involves the formulation of a systematic general plan for the creation of a library collection that will meet the need of the library's clients" (Clayton, Clayton, Clayton & Gorman, 2001 as cited in Chowdhury pg. 90). In a sense, developing digital collections is a logical consequence of inserting information technologies in organizations for specific users. "Collection development policies have largely been guided by the principle of 'the best book for the right user at the right time.' This role will be even more crucial in the digital world, since there the problem is not availability of information but 'information overload', and therefore digital libraries should use appropriate mechanisms for filtering out what is unwanted" (Chowdhury & Chowdhury, 2003, p.8). Therefore, the ultimate purpose of a digital library collection development policy is to provide guidelines that the library will follow in the selection, creation, and development of digital objects and collections.

Collection development takes into account selection and management policies, digitization, harvesting, document and e-publishing / presentation markup, web publishing and crawling.

3.1 Collection Development and Selection Policies

Collection development / collection management

The phrases "collection development" and "collection management" are sometimes used interchangeably. The latter term is more accurate, for it reflects the varied activities that are involved in building and managing a library collection (Chowdhury & Chowdhury, 2003). Traditional collection development may be viewed in part as a "process of evaluating what is published and making purchasing recommendations based on these evaluations." Chowdhury and Chowdhury (2003) clarify that *collection development* is the actual plan to build a library's collection that meets the users' needs, whereas *collection management* refers to the management of "planning, composition, funding, evaluation and use of a library's collection" (Chowdhury & Chowdhury, p. 90; Newsom, 2005). Collection management for digital libraries follows the same guidelines used in traditional libraries, but Chowdhury & Chowdhury (2003) note that "technical, economic, user and usability issues" must also be considered (p. 91).

The representation of the process of Digital Collection Development is shown in Figure 3. 1.

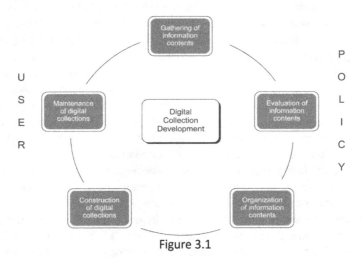

Figure 3.1

Figure 1. (from Quesada & Vignau, 2006).

Collection & material selection policies

"One of the most important services performed by archives, libraries, and museums is selection because it entails choosing from the many products of the living those few items which will best tell their stories. Digitization means that cultural caretakers will find themselves conducting yet another series of selections among their collections. Every institution knows its own audience best and thus will have its own set of selection criteria based upon its audience's needs" (North Carolina ECHO, 2007).

Selecting materials to be added to collections has been an integral part of building a successful library for as long as libraries have existed. According to the National Information Standards Organization (NISO, 2008), a successful digital library has "an explicit collection development policy that has been agreed upon and documented before building the collection begins." This is especially true as the number and types of materials available grows steadily over time, increasing the importance of having a comprehensive selection policy. In the year 1850, 600 periodicals were being published in the United States, and while this may seem like a relatively small number when compared to the thousands available today, it dwarfs the 26 in publication only 40 years earlier (Johnson, 2009, p. 4). While such a significant increase over a short period of time may seem unusual, it is actually quite similar to the challenges libraries currently face. Compared to fifty years ago, the brick-and-mortar library of today has a greatly expanded range when it comes to different formats (CDs, DVDs, e-Books), as well as more choices within those formats. The explosion of the Internet and the World Wide Web, combined with tremendous advances in computing power and storage, have made the choices available for DLs even greater, and make a solid collection development and selection policy even more crucial.

There are many good reasons for having a collection development policy. Although it takes much thought and time to develop a good policy, it is well worth it for the future of the organization. A collection and selection policy can help assure continuity and consistency despite inevitable changes in staff and funding. The use of a policy can also help defend a library's choice when potentially controversial material is selected. Good collection and selection policies often include gift policies. These gift policies can serve as "a very gentle way to say 'no thanks' to an inappropriate gift without hurting the donor's feelings" (Bond, 2007).

Evans and Soparano (2005, p. 50) distinguish between selection policies, acquisition policy, and collection development. Selection policies often omit evaluation, deselecting, and intellectual freedom, whereas acquisition policies tend to focus on the mechanics of acquiring materials. Collection development is inclusive, and a written collection development policy should be developed. The collection policy, among other things, identifies all the fields being covered and assures a balanced development; otherwise, one librarian and then another might just develop areas of personal interest.

A key question that must be asked when creating a digital library, before a single item has been selected for inclusion, is: what "kind" of DL is this going to be? It is important to know what other digital libraries exist, especially in the same subject area, in order to avoid redundancy. Physical libraries may have identical items in their collections to best serve the people living nearby, and make use of interlibrary loan to bring other items to them. Digital libraries, in contrast, can be accessed from almost anywhere an Internet connection is available and allow numerous people at various distances to simultaneously access a resource. In some ways, digital libraries can and do practice cooperative collection development. The digital library must have a clear mission statement and well-articulated goals.

There are many resources that can be consulted for assistance in writing a collection and selection policy. Chowdhury and Chowdhury (2003) cite Clayton and Gorman's criteria for material selection: author's authority, scope of coverage, treatment and level, content organization, format and special feature. For instance, Utah State University (2008) selects "materials based upon their uniqueness, research merit, potential for curriculum support, and appeal." In addition to determining whether prospective materials support the university's teaching or research, twenty questions are utilized to address such issues as revenue generation, funding support, added value to the original, and creation of collaboration opportunities (Utah State University, 2008). The University of California, Berkeley (2008) considers the suitability of a resource in regards to its scope, intended audience, timeliness, author's authority, documentation and objectivity. Sandler (2010) considers material selection from a financial perspective. He argues that libraries should consider the financial aspects of collections; libraries "should be mindful of [their] roles in the creation process and advocate for arrangements that support [their] long-term interests and those of [their] users" (p. 118).

Other criteria related directly to digital resources exist as well. For example, the "Library of Congress Collections Policy Statements Supplementary Guidelines" for their electronic resource at https://www.loc.gov/acq/devpol/electronicresources.pdf. Smith (1997) created a "Toolbox of Criteria" for librarians in which he suggests considering the currency, uniqueness and links to other resources. In addition, the graphic and multimedia design need to be considered as do workability, user friendliness, cost and required computing environment. Chowdhury and Chowdhury (2003) point out that not all resources are created equally. Variations may exist in the "quality and completeness of the data and images, coverage, accuracy and authority of the publisher" (p. 93). Other considerations of digital libraries are the user interface and information retrieval, both of which are integral in users' ability to search and locate information.

In 2008, The National Information Standards Organization (NISO) released *A Framework of Guidance for Building Good Digital Collections*, which "provides an overview of some of the major components and activities involved in the creation of good digital collections and provides a framework for identifying, organizing, and applying existing knowledge and resources to support the development of sound local practices for creating and managing good digital collections" (Abstract). The collections section of this document can prove especially helpful to those developing a digital library collection and writing a policy. NISO (2008) outlines nine principles for collections as follows:

- A good digital collection is created according to an explicit collection development policy.
- Collections should be described so that a user can discover characteristics of the collection, including scope, format, restrictions on access, ownership, and any information significant for determining the collection's authenticity, integrity, and interpretation.
- A good collection is curated, which is to say that its resources are actively managed during their entire lifecycle.
- A good collection is broadly available and avoids unnecessary impediments to use. Collections should be accessible to persons with disabilities, and usable effectively in conjunction with adaptive technologies.
- A good collection respects intellectual property right.
- A good collection has mechanisms to supply usage data and other data that allows standardized measures of usefulness to be recorded.
- A good collection is interoperable.
- A good collection integrates into the user's own workflow.
- A good collection is sustainable over time.

Each principle is described in more detail on the website (http://www.niso.org/sites/default/files/2017-08/framework3.pdf). In particular, Principle 1 states "There are a few cases where a selection policy may not be required: digitization on demand, when an organization is creating digital content based on end-user requests, and mass digitization programs, which are often indiscriminate" (NISO, 2008). Even in these cases, however, planning is necessary, and good habits for collection building should be followed as much as possible. Another common occurrence is for digital libraries to encourage users to deposit their own intellectual property. In this case, a published collection policy is still important, "but it may have to be fairly flexible in acknowledgement that the users may be the best judges of relevance" (NISO, 2008).

Along with these selection criteria, there are some additional challenges that must be considered when choosing items for inclusion in a DL. For example, "the speed at which digital material can disappear or become inaccessible means decisions to select and acquire must be taken earlier rather than later" (Library and Archives Canada). Thus, while it behooves a digital librarian to look more closely at the quality and value of an item, it must be done quickly, or they risk the chance of not being able to obtain it. Because of how quickly digital structure and content can change, DLs must also be equipped to react with their own hardware and software changes in order to ensure access to objects.

Chowdhury and Chowdhury (2003, p. 92) review the selection criteria recommended by Clapton and Gorman (2001). The selection policy should consider the following points:

- **The authority of creators** – authors, publishers, etc.
- **Scope** – the breadth and depth of coverage
- **Treatment and level** – suitability for the intended audience
- **Arrangement** – organization of content
- **Format** – accessibility and searchability, readability, portability, durability, etc.
- **Special features** – what makes an item different from similar products?

Additional criteria should also be considered for digital resources, such as hardware and software requirements, access and user interfaces, and licensing and preservation, although content should always be the first concern. For instance, the terms of use for a subscription database may include controlling access to authorized users only. Chowdhury and Chowdhury (2003, p. 93) again review Clapton and Gorman's criteria for digital resources, which include the following:

- Content, quality, currency, etc.
- Hardware, software and network requirements
- The version of the product – network or standalone version (for the CD-ROM product)
- The number of concurrent users allowed
- Access control – through password, proxy server authorization, etc.
- Price and licensing and copyright agreements
- Database features, the retrieval engine and the user interface(s)
- Ease of use and user training/efforts required
- Archiving procedures

One example of collection development policy can be seen at https://about.biodiversitylibrary.org/about/collection-management/collection-development-policy/. The Biodiversity Heritage Library's collection goal is to "build and maintain the BHL as the largest reliable, reputable, and responsive repository of biodiversity literature and archival materials." (BHL n.d.) All materials in the library are free to access and use. In-copyright materials are available for non-commercial use. Biodiversity is a broad term that encompasses differences between species and ecosystems. As such, the BHL includes materials concerning "all levels of organismic organization, from genes to ecosystems, as well as other disciplines affecting the study of the biodiversity of life on Earth." (BHL n.d.)

The International Children's Digital Library (ICDL) (http://www.childrenslibrary.org) mission states the following: "The ICDL Foundation's goal is to build a collection of books that represent outstanding historical and contemporary books from throughout the world. Ultimately, the Foundation aspires to have every culture and language represented so that every child can know and appreciate the riches of children's literature from the world community.

The following are governed under University of Maryland (UM) Library policy. The selection criteria must be in line with the University of Michigan Libraries' aims for creating an electronic information ecosystem.

1. Electronic resources considered for acquisition should fall within current collecting guidelines as described in the subject collection development policies and other appropriate guidelines.
2. All electronic materials should be relevant and appropriate to a significant segment of the libraries' user community and reflect current academic needs and the University's mission. Special attention should be given to electronic resources that provide coverage of underrepresented or high-priority subject areas.
3. In the selection of electronic materials, the availability of appropriate hardware and software should be considered. For CD-ROM products, consideration also needs to be given as to whether the product is networkable. If additional software needs to be acquired to run the product, this factor should be noted.
4. If the electronic resource duplicates another resource already available in the Libraries, the proposed electronic resource should offer some value-added enhancement; for example, wider access or greater flexibility in searching. If a product changes format, it should be reevaluated and a selection/retention decision made in the appropriate manner.
5. In addition to the cost of the product, if any, the following hidden costs need to be considered: licensing fees, hardware, software, staff training and continuing education, cataloging, duplicating support materials, updates, maintenance, and any other costs.
6. The product should be user-friendly, that is, provide ease of use and guidance for the user via appropriate menus, help screens, or tutorials.
7. The product should reflect the quality expected of similar materials in other formats.

8. Additional selection guidelines are available for free web-based resources and electronic publications." (University of Maryland, 2020)

By actively searching out and promoting barrier-free access to quality material, the University of North Texas (UNT) Libraries endeavor to accommodate the research needs of all users, including community users. The libraries acquire authoritative born-digital resources through a number of acquisition strategies, including the purchase, harvesting, and subsequent hosting of online items, as well as referrals to open access content not held by the UNT Libraries. For the purposes of this policy open access and born-digital materials include:
1. Resources clearly designated as open access, provided via the Internet with unrestricted access to peer-reviewed scholarly research;
2. Resources clearly designated as open content, provided via the Internet with unrestricted access to information for which the creators have formally asserted a statement that the information is licensed under open content standards, such as a variety of Creative Commons licenses; and
3. Resources that are freely available via the Internet, that meet standards of quality and value as described in the Selection Guidelines portion of the general collection development policy, and that are otherwise known or assumed to be under copyright.

3.2 Harvesting

Collection development in digital libraries includes the specific task of integrating the individual digital library collection with other relevant collections into one whole digital library collection. Arms, Dushay, Fulker and Lugoze (2003) noted that "the goal is to integrate tens of thousands of collections ranging from simple web sites to large and sophisticated digital libraries, into a coherent whole that is structured to support education and facilitate incorporation of innovative, value adding services."

The concept of collection development in digital libraries is changing due to the effect of vast and diverse digital resources easily accessible on the Internet. There are many and varied search engines on the Internet but it is still hard to locate and concentrate only on materials relevant to a specific task. In 1999, the Santa Fe Convention, comprised of computer scientists, librarians, and scholars, designed an approach to collect digital library resources called *harvesting*. Stern (2009) describes harvesting as a "clearinghouse" and a "relational database created by sophisticated harvesting of distributed data and metadata and the preprocessing of this material for end-user searching." Tennant (2005) puts it in simpler terms: "Collecting records into a central location for indexing and searching." (p. 32).

Harvesting involves providing summarized access to related material scattered over the network. The material held in the libraries is harvested (converted into summaries) according to the definition of an Information Specialist (IS). Sharon and Frank (2000) simply refer to it as "metadata with pointers to the holdings that are "one click away" in Cyberspace."

As more and more institutions file their digital collections online, technical services staff will continue to face the growing issue of distributed metadata harvesting. "Unlike their print cousins, today's institutional repositories and digital collections give rise to metadata of a distributed nature that require technical services departments to think creatively and produce workflows that encourage repurposing data" (Reese, 2009, para. 38). As new tools like the Open Archives Initiative Protocol for Metadata Harvesting (OAI-PMH Harvester) simplify the process by allowing nontechnical users to harvest metadata without having to deal with issues relating to XML validation or character encodings, more technical services departments will likely turn to metadata harvesting and capture as a viable method of generating metadata for digital collections (Reese, 2009).

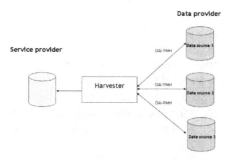

Figure 3.2. Metadata Harvesting by OAI-PMH from Pharo (2011).

What is metadata and metadata harvesting?

The process of harvesting metadata is an important resource in developing digital libraries. Metadata is commonly defined as data about data. To elaborate on this definition the National Information Standards Institute (NISO) describes metadata as structured information that describes, explains, locates, or otherwise makes it easier to retrieve, use or manage an information resource (NISO 2004). Libraries use metadata to describe their digital or non-digital objects. This assists in discovering and organizing resources, managing collections and preserving information. Library catalog cards, data used to describe the book it represents, are an example of metadata.

Metadata can contain enough description of a resource to allow a user to assess its potential without retrieving the actual item (Rhyno, 2004). Given the exponential amount of information available today, users are likely to use resources provided in digital formats. "Digitization combined with carefully crafted metadata can significantly enhance end user access" (Baca 2004). Metadata is necessary in digital libraries to ensure information has not been altered, track its origins and to ensure it will survive and be accessible in the future (NISO 2004).

Metadata harvesting according to Greenberg (2004) is "automatically gathering metadata that is already associated with a resource, and which has been produced via automatic or manual means." He also states that harvesting "occurs when metadata is automatically collected from META tags found in the "header" source code of an HTML resource or encoding from another resource format (e.g., Microsoft WORD documents), and the "harvesting process" relies on the metadata produced by humans or by full or semi-automatic processes supported by software. For example, Web editing software (e.g., Macromedia's Dreamweaver and Microsoft's FrontPage) and selected document software (e.g., Microsoft WORD and Adobe) automatically produce metadata at the time a resource is created or updated for "format," "date of creation," and "revision date," without human intervention. This is simply information resource gathering by web crawling.

Harvesting metadata is indispensable in digital libraries, enabling users to discover information from multiple libraries through a single provider. Woodley explains "it is a protocol that allows the gathering or collecting of metadata records from various repositories or databases; the harvested records are then 'physically' aggregated into a single database, with links from individual records back to their home environments" (Woodley 2008).

Open Archives Initiative

In 2001, the Open Archives Initiative (OAI), recognizing a need for low-cost interoperability in the digital library community, developed the Open Archives Initiative Protocol for Metadata Harvesting, or OAI-PMH, to distribute metadata for digital objects. Interoperability, a key factor in metadata harvesting, refers to the "ability of multiple systems with different hardware and software platforms, data structures and interfaces to exchange data with minimal loss of content and functionality" (NISO 2004). Interoperability allows for a more seamless search experience.

OAI focuses on creating a framework where metadata can be harvested from multiple repositories (digital library collections) and centralized in a single service (Breeding, 2002b). This means that OAI-PMH involves OAI service providers gathering metadata from various repositories, collecting this metadata in an "aggregated metadata index," and sharing it with users (Cole & Foulonneau, 2007, p. 7). Cole and Foulonneau (2007) write, "by the end of 2006, the aggregation of harvested metadata records indexed by OAIster had grown to more than 10 million items" (p. 21).

"Since both an OAI-PMH data provider and an OAI data harvester must conform to the same basic information exchange protocols, metadata records can be reliably retrieved from the provider(s) by the harvester" (Gill, 2004). Users can then search this easy service and choose whatever metadata they need, with the service providing links that allow them to reach specific materials from the original digital libraries (Breeding, 2002b). Lynch (2001) breaks down the technical aspect of the OAI-PMH protocol:

> OPI-PMH uses a very simple HTTP-based request-response transaction framework for communication between a harvester and a repository... The server returns a series of sets of metadata elements (in XML) plus identifiers (i.e., URLs) for the objects that the metadata describes.

Cole and Foulonneau (2007) have detailed some of the key technical concepts. First, a metadata *item* is distinct from a metadata *record* (2007). Item metadata is intrinsic to the repository and is shared in the form of records (2007). Second, the identifier must persist, not change or be used for a different object; be unique, one-of-a-kind for the particular repository; and follow the syntax specifications for Uniform Resource Identifiers by the World Wide Web Consortium (2007).

The technical process of OAI-PMH relies on verb arguments sent over HTTP from a service provider to a client (Cole & Foulonneau, 2007). The verbs enable the provider to identify the repository, get a record, or list metadata records, formats, or identifiers (2007). These verbs determine the metadata content in the record distributed by the client (2007). However, all records have an <OAI-PMH> root element, which is followed by the date when the client responded to the verb, and the identifier of the client repository, which received the argument of the verb (2007). OAI (2002) provides this example of the response to a GetRecord request:

> <OAI-PMHxmlns="http://www.openarchives.org/OAI/2.0/"
> xmlns:xsi=http://www.w3.org/2001/XMLSchema-instance
> xsi:schemaLocation="http://www.openarchives.org/OAI/2.0/
> http://www.openarchives.org/OAI/2.0/OAI-PMH.xsd">
> <responseDate>2002-05-01T19:20:30Z</responseDate>
> <request verb="GetRecord" identifier="oai:arXiv.org:hep-th/9901001"
> metadataPrefix="oai_dc">http://an.oa.org/OAI-script</request> (3.2 XML Response Format).

The anatomy of a record response provided to an OIA-PMH service consists of a header, metadata, and about information (OAI, 2002). The header contains a mandatory date stamp and identifier. Records are required to have date-stamps recorded in Coordinated Universal Time, and the granularity must be the same for every record. Allowable schemas include either year, month, day or year, month, day, hour, minute, second (Cole & Foulonneau, 2007). Also, it may include other optional information about whether the record is about a deletion of item metadata or whether it is part of set, which is like a sub-collection of records (2007).

Cole & Foulonneau (2007) state, "the data provider must disseminate all metadata items in a repository in at least simple DC" (p. 66). The metadata is disseminated using a prefix related to a namespace and schema, so additional metadata may be shared in the record (OAI, 2002). Moreover, optional information includes rights and provenance information, which is recorded within an about element conforming to a schema (2002). An annotated example using OAI (2002) content follows:

```
<?xmlversion="1.0"encoding="UTF-8" ?>
<OAI-PMH xmlns="http://www.openarchives.org/OAI/2.0/"
xmlns:xsi=http://www.w3.org/2001/XMLSchema-instance
xsi:schemaLocation="http://www.openarchives.org/OAI/2.0/
http://www.openarchives.org/OAI/2.0/OAI-PMH.xsd">
```

Above is the namespace and schema.

```
<responseDate>2002-05-01T19:20:30Z</responseDate>
<request verb="GetRecord" identifier="oai:arXiv.org:hep-th/9901001"
metadataPrefix="oai_dc">http://an.oa.org/OAI-script</request>
<header><!--This element is the header-->
<identifier>oai:arXiv:cs/0112017</identifier>
<datestamp>2002-02-28</datestamp>
<setSpec>cs</setSpec>
<setSpec>math</setSpec>
</header>
<metadata><!--Begin the descriptive metadata section-->
<oai_dc:dc
xmlns:oai_dc=http://www.openarchives.org/OAI/2.0/oai_dc/
xmlns:dc="http://purl.org/dc/elements/1.1/"
xmlns:xsi="http://www.w3.org/2001/XMLSchema-instance"
xsi:schemaLocation="http://www.openarchives.org/OAI/2.0/oai_dc
http://www.openarchives.org/OAI/2.0/oai_dc.xsd">
<!--The prefix is specified according to the schema, either OAI DC or simple DC-->
<dc:title>Using Structural Metadata to Localize Experience of Digital Content</dc:title>
<dc:creator>Dushay, Naomi</dc:creator>
```

More descriptive data is included:

```
</metadata>
<about><!--Here is the "about" information.-->
```

```
            <provenance
            xmlns="http://www.openarchives.org/OAI/2.0/provenance"
            xmlns:xsi="http://www.w3.org/2001/XMLSchema-instance"
            xsi:schemaLocation="http://www.openarchives.org/OAI/2.0/proven
ance
            http://www.openarchives.org/OAI/2.0/provenance.xsd">
            <originDescriptionharvestDate="2002-02-02T14:10:02Z"
altered="true">
            <!--More about information goes here-->
            </originDescription>
            </provenance>
            </about>
```
(OAI, 2002, 2.5 Record section).

Once the metadata is gathered, it may be augmented or normalized (Cole & Foulonneau, 2007). Normalization may consist of removing empty elements, "artificial value strings," symbols indicating missing information (i.e., N.A., unknown), and otherwise meaningless de-contextualized elements (2007, p. 142). Normalization may also involve transformation or semantic mapping of metadata to a service provider schema (2007). Spatial or date information may be displayed in a specified format (2007).

The OAI-PMH as acknowledged by Hao Ding and Solvberg (2004) has a low application barrier capability and as a result has been widely adopted in a few institutions for harvesting metadata records from other digital collections. Harvesting using the OAI-PMH has another major function, which is the primary mechanism for exporting metadata from the Metadata Repository, with the main aim of sharing metadata in a manner that is easy to implement and use. OAI-PMH is broad and intentionally "free of content, making it useful to a wide range of areas, not just scholarly information" (Witten, 2009, p. 345).

It is important to stress that OAI-PMH is not a search protocol; rather it gathers metadata into a single location conducive to harvesting. The harvested data is used by a service provider as a "basis for building value-added services such as central indexing and searching." This allows the service provider to offer its users a searchable index, assisting in locating the desired materials from individual repositories (Rajashekar, 2004). The diagram adapted from Gill's model (2004) gives a visual of the OAI-PMH process:

| OAI | OAI Serv | Custo | Use rs |

Figure 3.3: Metadata Harvesting Model (adapted from Gill 2004).

OAI-PMH is able to support any metadata schema that uses XML formatting. Dublin Core is the minimum the OAI-PMH has adopted as its standard.

OAI first requires "data providers" or primary owners/maintainers of information to run software that allows their information to be available in bulk to other participants. They must also maintain a repository, which is usually a digital library. The metadata must be formatted according to the Protocol for Metadata Harvesting. The protocol relies on an HTTP framework, in which requests are encoded into URLs. Results are returned as XML records (Witten, 2009). The digital objects themselves need not be available, only the metadata. Also, data providing is strictly voluntary in OAI, and the providers must load an OAI interface in order to allow harvesting using PMH (Breeder, 2002). The data provider is not responsible for deciding how the metadata records will be used, only to supply them. Should a request result in an incomplete set of records, data providers will use a tool called a "Resumption Token" to let the harvester know when the full set of records will be available. It is advantageous to data providers to be harvested, as their metadata records will likely receive more traffic than they would alone.

In their study, "A Framework for Harvesting Digital Libraries (HDL) on the Web," Uri Hanani and Ariel Frank (2008) described a logical harvesting model. They stated that an information scientist who is interested in constructing a DL on a specific domain of interest initiates an HDL harvesting:

> The initiating information scientist/librarian invokes the **Harvester** with a harvesting query. The **Harvester** generates the initial harvesting request and passes it to the **Locator**. The **Locator** uses various network search techniques to enrich the initial collection of URLs to be harvested. The next component to be invoked is the **Gatherer**. It uses each top-level URL, in a recursive descent manner, to gather all referenced resources from the Providers (see figure 3.3), and passes them to the **Filterer**. The **Filterer** is responsible for blocking the non-relevant documents from reaching the focused HDL. It uses various levels of filtering that all remaining documents have to pass to be considered relevant.

Service providers -- the other end of OAI-PMH-- are simply the harvesters, collecting metadata from various repositories to create portals on specific topics (Breeder, 2002). It is important to note that service providers can also be data providers within the same institution (Witten, 2009). Service providers use PMH to extract metadata records from each repository they are using. This act is the literal one of "harvesting." The harvested records are then loaded into the service provider's database. At this point, the final step is to make the metadata records available to end-users through a search-and-retrieval interface, not unlike a search engine on the Internet. Citations or full-text can be available, along with links to such sources directly.

PMH itself is highly flexible; the minimum requirement for metadata is to be formatted according to Dublin Core. Otherwise, data providers and service providers can decide the set up. This allows quite a bit of freedom that can benefit or obstruct the user and service provider alike. Data providers format their metadata records in "set" and as of 2004 there are no clear rules (excepting the very simple Dublin Core) as to what makes a set. A provider can arrange sets by digital format, subject, department, or individual collections. The Digital Library Foundation, along with several other institutions, is currently formulating a comprehensive protocol for sets. As of yet, it seems that while OAI-PMH is designed to require little human support, a trained staff is necessary. Witten (2009) cites an example demonstrating how low human effort interfered with a large-scale effort to harvest metadata. The United States National Science Digital Library attempted to create a digital library in 2003 by harvesting metadata using Dublin Core and OAI-PMH. Their results were unsatisfactory. Witten (2009) quotes "We discovered that the WorldCat paradigm, which works so well in the shared professional culture of the library, is less effective in a context of widely varied commitment and expertise. Few collections were willing or able to allocate sufficient human resources to provide quality metadata." (p. 351).

Some notable metadata formats that have been used in OAI have been MARC, TEI, EAD, and IMS. As Dublin Core has proven to be ineffective for the needs of many, some have created their own metadata format. Breeding (2002b) cites an example of Open Languages Archives Community, which developed the OLAC Metadata Set for the OAI Metadata Harvesting Protocol for OLAC-MS.

PMH, like Dublin Core, is designed to be simple to use. Data providers need very little programming to become providers, and can accomplish it in hours. Even service providers need little programming. One can implement OAI-PMH through Java, C++, Perl, and other basic programming languages. As it is designed for metadata records in bulk, it does not need to be as specific as an OPAC would. It relies on mere request and response between data providers and service providers. The requests commands are limited to six basic requests:

1. *GetRecord*, the request for a metadata record.
2. *Identify*, where the harvester can ask the data provider to provide more information about itself.
3. *ListIdentifiers*, a request for list of record headers.
4. *ListMetadataFormats*, a request to share what metadata formats the data provider uses.
5. *ListRecords*, the actual harvesting of the records.

6. *ListSets*, a request for the definition of the sets within the repository (Breeding, 2002b, p28).

Metadata harvesting and collection development

Exposing metadata in standardized formats, like OAI-PMH, makes content easier to discover and access. Collection development librarians use the exposed metadata to provide services to their target audience. By harvesting metadata, collection librarians can create searchable indexes of the information available from other repositories, to either provide direct access to their users or inform them of the resources available from other sources.

The Online Computer Library Center (OCLC) Website states that the OAI has over 23 million records from 1,100 data providers (oclc.org). These resources provide a substantial opportunity for collection development librarians to access them. The ability to harvest metadata from data providers throughout the world results in expansive services for the users of individual libraries.

3.3: Document and E-Publishing Presentation Mark-Up

Document and E-publishing is parallel to Web publishing because it is comprised of creating documents and publishing them. Document and E-publishing also involves tagging within the documents. One difference between them is that Web publishing entails various paradigms to publish content.

In creating a digital library, librarians must keep in mind that how the DL's resources are displayed to the user is a critical component in the DL's effectiveness. While a digital library may contain very valuable knowledge, a user's attempt to access this knowledge may be difficult or impossible if the document is not represented as originally intended by the resource's owner. Thus, it is imperative that a digital librarian ensure that the layout and presentation of documents be presented exactly how the librarian strategically envisioned that page as looking when a user accessed the page. The digital librarian of today is in essence a publisher, and as publisher, he or she is responsible for ensuring that the presented information reaches the user in such a way as to promote an optimal and rewarding learning experience. The digital librarian is responsible for presenting the library's collection in the most understandable, aesthetic manner possible, so that someone who is researching a document will not be hampered by structural errors with the document itself. As a publisher, today's digital librarian must effectively utilize markup techniques, so that a computer can be provided with all of the relevant information needed to produce a document to the exact structural specifications designed by the digital librarian.

According to Lie and Saarela (1999), "Structured document formats...encode the document's logical structure. Among the reasons for doing so is the preservation of device independence, document searchability, and information re-use in general" (p. 96). Since the first standard was developed in the 1970s and 1980s, many updated languages, each with their own positive attributes, have been introduced, along with various ways to control the presentation of documents.

Presentation markup (PresML) is a language with "specialized XML-based HTML-like markup specialized for efficient creation of "slide shows" to be displayed with a Web browser. The presentation is created by making one text file that describes the structure and content of the presentation" (Norderhaug, N.D.). PresML is a tool to efficiently create presentations, which can be displayed on a web browser, instead of uploading them as images. "PresML is an XML document type similar to HTML, supporting bulleted lists, enumerated lists, sub-headers, and other constructs used in a presentation, including specialized tags for slideshows with more advanced features scheduled in future versions." (Norderhaug, N.D)

PresML is also found at the Library of Congress' American Memory Digital Library. Initially, the MARC descriptive records and transcripts were linked to the presentations at Michigan State University as the works digitized are owned by the Special Collections Division of the Michigan State University Libraries and the Clarke Historical Library at Central Michigan University. Bibliographic displays for the books housed in American Memory provide links for the texts at both sites ("American Memory Project", 2012).

By employing presentation markup methods, a librarian will be better able to execute his/her vision of how the library's collection will be represented to the user. These markup techniques will invariably carry over to use throughout the World Wide Web. Markup methods will not only assist a digital librarian in presenting documents in the most optimal manner, but to virtually create the web pages that will present the library's collection to the public.

The presentation of the transcripts at the Library of Congress and at Michigan State Libraries is very different, yet are produced from the same markup. "This provides an excellent demonstration of the combination of markup that describes the structure of the document and the use of a stylesheet (or equivalent transformation) to control online display based on the structural markup" ("American Memory Project," 2012). Each book at Michigan State University is presented as a single file. While a single file download is convenient and makes for easy searchability, it does have the potential drawback of long download times. On the other hand, "the American Memory presentation uses the markup to divide the work into smaller chunks and construct a table of contents "navigator." This is useful for skimming a work and provides chunks that are individually faster to display.

Searches of the full text of the entire collection return a chunk from a work rather than the entire work." ("American Memory Project," 2012)

What is markup?

The term markup comes from the traditional publishing practice of "marking up" a manuscript, which involves adding handwritten annotations in the form of conventional symbolic printer's instructions in the margins and text of a manuscript or printed proof. For centuries, this task was done primarily by skilled typographers known as "markup men" who marked up text to indicate what typeface, style, and size should be applied to each part of the document, and then passed the manuscript to others for typesetting by hand (Woods, 1963).

During the late 1960's, the Electronic Age was dawning and innovations in computer technology had made electronic publishing a reality. Before this, a document might be dictated to someone who typed it. Then a copy would need to be proofed and revised, and edits and corrections would be made (markup), and then sent back to be retyped. One would have to make sure that the document was laid out in such a manner that did not interfere with the intended structure or meaning. For example, the typesetter would need to know "where a header belongs" or "what begins new paragraph." With the advent of the Electronic Age, the quest was how to use computers to help with this process. Computers couldn't "see" the document visually like we could, and they couldn't understand the meaning of the text. Computers only understood plain text characters (i.e., ASCII). They had to read a document one character at a time, starting from the beginning. So, the question was how to "mark up" a plain text document so that a computer could understand commands? How could one insert directives that are separate from the contents of the document itself? One solution was to use tags.

Tags are like commands, or annotations, that instruct the computer to perform a task and were very important in the development of electronic markup languages, which will be discussed in the subsequent section. In defining markups, it should be noted that there are three general categories of electronic markup: *Presentational, Procedural,* and *Descriptive* (Bray, 2002).

- *Presentational markup* is used by traditional word-processing systems; binary codes embedded in document text that produced the What You See is What You Get (WYSIWYG) effect. Such markup is designed to be hidden from human users, even those who are authors or editors.
- *Procedural markup* is embedded in text and provides instructions for programs that are to process the text. Well known examples include troff, LaTex and postscript; it is expected that the processor runs through the text from

beginning to end, following the instructions as encountered. Text with such markup is often edited with the markup visible and directly manipulated by the author. Popular procedural-markup systems usually include programming constructs, such that macros or subroutines can be defined and invoked by name. An example of descriptive markup would be troff's .bd, which instructs the processor to switch to a boldface font.

- *Descriptive markup* is used to label parts of the document rather than to provide specific instructions as to how they should be processed. The objective is to decouple the inherent structure of the document from any particular treatment or rendition of it. Such markup is often described as "semantic."

There is considerable blurring of the lines between the types of markup. In modern word-processing systems, presentational markup is often saved in descriptive-markup-oriented such as XML, and then processed procedurally by implementations.

Markup languages

In 1969, three IBM researchers created GML, a formatting language for document publishing. These three letters were the initials of its creators, Charles Goldfarb, Edward Mosher, and Raymond Lorie, though the term GML later came to be understood as General Markup Language. As Goldfarb has stated in his recollections, "later in 1971, when product development was imminent, I gave GML its present name so that our initials would always prove where it had originated (Goldfarb, 1996). GML allowed text editing and formatting, and it allowed information-retrieval systems to share documents. Instead of a simple tagging schema, GML introduced the concept of a formally defined document type containing an explicit hierarchy of structured elements. GML freed document creators from specific document formatting concerns such as font specification, line spacing, and page layout required by SCRIPT/VS. Using GML, a document is marked up with tags that define what the text is, in terms of paragraphs, headers, lists, tables, and so forth. The document can then be automatically formatted for various devices simply by specifying a profile for the device. For example, it is possible to format a document for a laser printer or a line printer or for a screen simply by specifying a profile for the device without changing the document itself.

The development of GML was a landmark development in terms of the advancement of electronic publishing, and in terms of building the technological world that many of us take for granted today. Goldfarb shed light on the communication innovations that were to result from his developments: The DCF GML User's Guide (IBM SH20-9160) includes the first published formal document type "descriptions" (DTDs), for this "General Document" and also for a "GML Markup Guide" document type. The General Document example, except for the delimiter strings, should look very familiar. It was not only the source for the homonymous DTD in ISO 8879, but also, thanks to Anders Berglund's championing of DCF at CERN, it was the source for the World Wide Web's HTML document type as well. The User's Guide itself became the first working paper of the ANSI SGML committee (X3J6/78/33-01) (Goldfarb, 1996).

Standard General Markup Language (SGML)

As the Electronic Age advanced into the late 1970s, major concepts of GML were implemented in mainframe publishing systems, and the language achieved substantial industry acceptance. IBM had adopted GML and by the early 1980's was producing over 90% of its documents with it. Goldfarb and IBM continued work, and ultimately developed, another document markup language known as Standardized General Markup Language, or SGML. SGML was designed to allow the sharing of machine readable large project documents in government, law and industry. SGML was also extensively applied by the military, the aerospace field, and industrial publishing businesses (Goldfarb 1996).

SGML specified a syntax for including the markup in documents, and for separately describing which and where tags were used (the Document Type Definition (DTD) or schema). This allowed authors to create and use any markup they wished, selecting tags that made the most sense to them and were named in their own natural languages. Thus, SGML is properly a meta-language, and many particular markup languages are derived from it. SGML found wide acceptance and use in fields with very large-scale documentation requirements.

The first system for structural mark-up was ratified as an International Organization for Standardization (ISO) international standard in 1986, and it was known as the Standard Generalized Markup Language (SGML) (Witten, Bainbridge, & Nichols, 2010, p. 152). According to Lie and Saarela (1999), "The philosophy of SGML is to define a general meta-language that can be used to build application-specific languages to encode structured documents" (p. 96). This mark-up language, and others that have been developed from it, is used to denote presentation of a document, including font size, italics, text justification, image inclusion, and much more. Since the late 1980s, most substantial new markup languages have been based on an SGML system (Kay, 2005).

SMGL ascertains that a document has four basic parts of speech:
1. *Elements* - containers that consist of a start tag (like <step>), some text or data contained within, and then an end or closing tag.

2. *Attributes* - special rules for an element Attributes each have a name and a value and can be placed inside tags.

- <step optional="yes"> Add tomatoes to the mix</step>. The optional ="yes" pair is an attribute of the step element to indicate the step is optional.
- The value of an attribute (here the value is "yes") is generally placed inside double quotes.
- Some attributes are implicit and don't always have to be typed out. For example, here it is implicit that a step is required. Unless you specify otherwise, an element could have more than one attribute.

3. *Entities* - a fragment of content or text or data
- These are the characters that make up the body of an element, which is the content of your document
- Special entities start with an ampersand (&) and end with a semicolon (;) some examples:
    - &copy = copyright symbol
    - < which becomes<
    - > which becomes a double quote
    -   this is an invisible, non-breaking space character that means don't wrap the text here.

4. *COMMENTS* - notes to the reader about the SGML document <!--a comment-->
- These are special tags that are hidden from view and ignored by the SGML.
- These tags start with an exclamation point followed by 2 dashes.....and end 2 dashes) (Holton, 2010).

HTML and the World Wide Web

As the 1990's began, it seemed to many that SGML would be limited to commercial and databased applications while What You See is What You Get (WYSIWYG) tools would suffice for other document processing applications. This changed when Tim Berners-Lee, working at CERN used SGML syntax to create HTML (Lee, 1997). HTML stands for Hyper Text Markup Language, and it resembles other SGML-based tag languages. The Hypertext

Markup Language (HTML) is a type of SGML that was created as a way to simplify the earlier standard's complex structure.

Created in 1989, and formally adopted as an SGML DTD in 1992, HTML included features that "played on people's desires to exert more control over how their documents appear" (Witten et al., 2010, p. 152). Allowing for images and objects to be embedded and able to create interactive forms, it became the predominant markup language for webpages; HTML documents contain both HTML tags and plain text. These documents describe web pages. The purpose of a web browser (like Internet Explorer or Firefox) is to read HTML documents and display them as web pages.

The browser does not display the HTML tags, but uses the tags to interpret the content of the page:

```
<html>
<body>
<h1>My First Heading</h1>
<p>My first paragraph</p>
</body>
</html>
```

Example Explained

- The text between <html> and </html> describes the web page
- The text between <body> and </body> is the visible page content
- The text between <h1> and </h1> is displayed as a heading
- The text between <p> and </p> is displayed as a paragraph

So in essence, Tim-Berners Lee invented the World Wide Web with HTML as its publishing language. Many argue that HTML's use of descriptive markup (and SGML in particular) was a major factor in the success of the Web, because of the flexibility and extensibility that it enabled (DeRose, 1997).

Because of HTML's wide use on the Web, most digital library interfaces use this language, presenting their source documents in HTML (Witten et al., 2010, p. 158). But despite the popularity and success of HTML through the years, with many different and updated standards being created since the early 1990s, the language is somewhat limited. Certain elements do not exist in HTML and additional mark-up is not easily built (Lie and Saarela, 1999, p. 97). "You might hesitate before tampering with source documents by inserting new metadata...When developing a digital library you need to consider whether it is wise...to add new information that cannot be disentangled from that present in the source document" (Witten et al., 2010, p. 158). In order to alleviate some of the problems of HTML, XML was created.

XML

XML (Extensible Markup Language) is a meta-markup language that is now widely used. It is a simplified version of SGML, providing "a flexible way of characterizing document structure and metadata, making it well suited to digital libraries. It has achieved widespread use in a very short stretch of time" (Witten et al., 2010, p. 152). XML was developed by the World Wide Web Consortium (W3C), in a committee created and chaired by Jon Bosack ("Jon Bosak", 2010). The initiative to create XML began in 1996 and it was available for use two years later.

According to Lie and Saarela (1999), "XML includes SGML's ability to define new elements. For content providers, this means XML can encode semantics more gracefully than HTML. In addition, XML removes the burden of having to validate documents against a document type definition (DTD); XML documents may refer to a DTD but are not required to do so" (p. 97). XML remains a meta-language like SGML, allowing users to create any tags needed and then describing those tags and their permitted uses.

XML adoption was helped because every XML document can be written in such a way that it is also an SGML document, and existing SGML users and software could switch to XML fairly easily. However, XML eliminated many of the more complex and human-oriented features of SGML to simplify implementation environments such as documents and publications. However, it appeared to achieve middle ground between simplicity and flexibility, and was rapidly adopted for many other uses. XML is now widely used for communicating data between applications.

XML has grown exponentially since its inception. For digital libraries, it means that file formats can be "rationalized and shared" (Witten et al., 2010, p. 162). Many organizations have created DTDs focused on different academic areas, including the Text Encoding Initiative (TEI), which created a DTD for representing academic works in the humanities and social sciences (Witten et al., 2010, p. 162). For this reason, many of the largest digital libraries use XML in a way personalized to their content, including the Perseus Digital Library Project at Tufts University, the Oxford Text Archive, and Der Junge Goethe (Witten et al., 2010, p. 162).

XHTML

Since January 2000 all W3C Recommendations for HTML have been based on XML rather than SGML, using the abbreviation XHTML. The language specification requires that XHTML Web documents must be well-formed XML documents; this allows for more rigorous and robust documents while using tags familiar from HTML. One of the most noticeable differences between HTML and XHTML is the rule that all tags must be closed: empty HTML tags such as <br> must either be closed with a regular end-tag, or replaced by a special form:
 (the space before the '/' on the end tag is optional, but frequently used because it enables some pre-XML Web browsers, and SGML parsers, to accept the tag). Another is that all attribute values in tags must be quoted. Finally, all tag and attribute names must be lowercase in order to be valid; HTML, on the other hand, was case-insensitive.

Presenting web documents

According to Lie and Saarela (1999), "The notion of style sheets is complementary to structured documents; documents contain content and structure, and style sheets describe how documents are to be presented. This separation is a requirement for device-independent documents and simplifies document management, since a style sheet can describe many documents" (p. 98). There are two main types of style sheets used: CSS and XSL.

CSS

Cascading style sheets (CSS) "produce presentable documents with minimal effort. They were developed principally in support of HTML, but also work with XML" (Witten et al., 2010, p.163). CSS consists of rules to assign a certain style to a different "class" within XML or HTML. Put more simply, in an XML or HTML document, the language might denote a name, a headline, or a paragraph. CSS states that anything denoted as a name will be 12-size font, blue, and in italics; anything denoted as a headline will be 16-size font, red, and bold; and anything denoted as a paragraph in 11-size font. This makes life much easier for web page developers, as now hardware and/or software will automatically format text properly (Lie and Saarela, 1999, p. 98-99).

XSL

The Extensible Stylesheet Language (XSL) takes CSS to another level by being able to transform document structure. "For example, an XSL sheet can automatically generate a table of contents by extracting all chapter titles from a document" (Lie, & Saarela, 1999, p. 99). XSL is made up of three parts: formatting objects, transformations, and XPath, which is a way of selecting parts of a document. Formatting documents is similar to CSS, while transformations and XPath select and alter portions of the document in order to create tables, lists, and other functions (Witten et al., 2010, p. 170). There are drawbacks to XSL, namely in the form of complexity. Because it is designed for XML, XSL cannot be used with all HTML forms -- only those that are XML compliant (Witten et al., 2010, p. 170).

3.4: Web (Push) Publishing or Pushing Technology

Web publishing defined

Web publishing refers to the collection and provision of digital resources served to users through the World Wide Web. Any digitized asset, not just electronic print resources, may become a resource in a Web-based service, including streaming media clips, digital photos, audio files, and Web pages. Web publishing also tends to feature a number of automated services that are designed to collect and distribute large amounts of information with minimal human intervention once the infrastructure is put in place (Karia, 2010). Essentially, web publishing can be defined as "the act of collecting web pages, images, videos and other digital assets and hosting them on a particular domain over the World Wide Web," and "as providing a web service that automates information services that are conducted over the Internet, using standardized technologies and protocols that simplify the exchange and integration of large amounts of data over the Internet" (Fox, 2009).

Librarians and other information professionals have embraced this technological advance for multiple reasons, including the ability to automate the provision of resources and to encourage patrons to play a collaborative role in creating, editing, tagging, and serving their own content (Karia, 2010). After taking the time to develop, write, and organize a digital library, sharing it with others becomes a priority. One way to do this is to publish your work on the Internet through web publishing. PC Magazine Encyclopedia defines web publishing this way:

> Creating a Web site and placing it on the Web server. A Web site is a collection of HTML pages with the home page typically named INDEX.HTML. Web sites are designed using Web authoring software that provides a graphical layout capability or by hand coding in HTML or both. Distributing the site requires copying the resulting HTML pages and graphic elements into the appropriate directories on the server (http://www.pcmag.com/encyclopedia_term/0,2542,t=Web+publishing&i=54333,00.asp).

Nearly 20 years into the Internet revolution, it is quite clear that our technology embraces widespread publishing. Traditional forms of publishing techniques are expensive and time-consuming procedures, the antithesis of communication techniques and procedures of our electronic age. Traditional publishing involves specific tasks executed by specific people, a process that runs up cost and the amount of time needed to publish a book. First, there is an author, the one who writes the material and owns its content. The author wishing to share his work contacts a publisher. Publishers take the work, mass produce it and distribute it to third party institutions. These institutions can be schools, universities, bookstores, etc., that store and make the work available to the consumer. The consumer (e.g. students, library patrons, learners, etc.) is an interested party wanting to read and learn from the work.

An author who publishes on the web can single-handedly perform the tasks of several people, dramatically cutting down the cost of labor and materials, and eliminating the need to wait an excessive amount of time for a publication to reach the masses. Technology affords a web publisher the ability to easily update a document, to modify and restore information in that document, and to collaborate with multiple users to maintain and manage correct information. Web publications also offer users remote access to resources, as well as access to resources of multiple users. Rather than a researcher/writer, publisher, and consumer agreeing to spend money on producing and purchasing a bound book or journal, the author instead presents his or her information on the World Wide Web, with or without a publisher, and the consumer can find it there free or for a nominal fee. Considering these benefits, it is easy to see why a digital librarian would opt to publish a collection over the World Wide Web rather than for the traditional process.

How does it work?

Web (Push) Publishing (also known as webcasting or netcasting) can be described as receiving information via the web. The information is "pushed" towards the user, instead of the user "pulling" the information from the web. As Jennifer Kyrnin states, "In order to get information from one source to the consumer, it must be transmitted. In general terms, there can be only two ways to transmit that information - "pull" or "push" (Kyrnin).

When Internet users visit a website, read a newspaper, book or magazine they are "pulling" information for their consumption. They choose which information is pertinent and which is not. Push publishing is exactly the opposite; information is broadcasted to users without them making an effort in obtaining it. A Web server "ostensibly 'pushes' information to the user rather than waiting until the user specifically requests it." (Whatis.com)

TV shows, radio stations, Internet advertisements, Tweet Deck, WeatherBug, Yahoo News, etc. are examples of push publishing. According to Kyrnin, "the most common use of push technology on the web is for stock price announcements and sports scores, but it can be used for all types of things to keep web consumers informed." (Kyrnin) Microsoft Internet Explorer also uses webcasting. (Whatis.com) Because these applications and methods are immediate, they differ greatly from e-mail and listservs (Umbach, 1997).

The Channel Definition Format (CDF) standard was created in order for a standardized data representation for Push technology to be possible. The CDF is "an XML application that allows web publishers to push content from their servers to their consumers as often or seldom as necessary. As a consumer, you can subscribe to channels that have information of interest to you and the data will be pushed from the web server to your browser. As a publisher, you can make sure that your readers have the most current information available on your product or service" (Kyrnin).

Web Publishing Paradigms

All web publishing paradigms share the common characteristic of being able to be updated constantly, without hassle, and quickly. There are three common paradigms used within web publishing: RSS, Wikis, and Blogs. RSS (Really Simple Syndication) enables the audience to keep up with dynamic Web content that can be channeled into special programs or filtered displays in an automated manner. Wikis allow users to collaborate to manage, organize, and create published content. Blogs act as personal diaries which provide personal commentary in a corporate or personal manner.

RSS

"Really Simple Syndication" is a web based format that allows websites who regularly publish Web content to syndicate their content. It uses XML to produce an RSS Feed which is "basically a specially coded web page that feeds the information to those who request it"(Hock, 2007). Some examples where RSS would be found includenews headlines, events updates, and/or podcasts. An RSS generated web feed is a full or portioned content of text updated by the website. This content can be surveyed using a "RSS Reader."Using a link provided by the website, the user can subscribe to the feed. The new feed is automatically updated and notifies the user when new content is available (http://technet.microsoft.com/en-us/security/bulletin/secrssinfo, 2012).

There are two types of RSS Readers. The first is web-based in which all feeds come to a web reader which is accessed online by the user after the user logs in to the web reader website. The second is program-based and in this type the user can directly run the program to download the feed onto their computer.

There are numerous web-based tools for RSS. Google Reader was one of the earliest examples. It was created in early 2005 by Google engineer Chris Wetherell and launched on October 7, 2005 through Google Labs but unfortunately discontinued on March 13, 2013. This web-based tool continually checked the user's favorite websites for new content and updates the status immediately. Google Reader abridged the reading experience for the user by presenting all favorite websites in one place. Along with making it easier to access new information, Google Reader also allowed collaboration by granting the user the ability to recommend feeds to friends and vice versa.

Figure 3.4. (from Google Reader, 2012).

RSS services are updated frequently to add new Web publishing tools and functionality. Google Reader, for example, a function whereby Google Reader users could display shared items as a "clip" on a blog (Figure 3.5).

Figure 3.2: Library-related resource pushed to RSS feed reader, Google Reader.

As one of the more popular RSS readers, Google Reader constantly checked favorite Web sites for new content and updates their status immediately. It simplified a user's reading experience by showing favorite websites in one convenient place.

Web-based readers, one of primarily types of RSS readers, where all the feeds come to a Web reader which the user access online by visiting the Web reader's home page and logging into it.

It is easy to see how a digital librarian can integrate RSS feeds into a digital library to supplement a user's experience. Someone accessing a digital library can find particular documents and information in text format related to their search, and then also enjoy additional information on the topic in video or audio format. And whenever there is an update or new information added to the RSS feed, the users will automatically be notified so they can further explore the information they are seeking. One can believe that RSS feeds transcend the traditional methods of accessing data in a library, and incorporating this technology into a digital library will make for a more interesting and rewarding learning experience for the user, who may remember the experience and deem this digital library as an important and relevant source of information.

A digital librarian can incorporate RSS feeds into a collection and enhance the digital library by providing video and audio RSS. An RSS document is called a "feed," and the content of these RSS feeds can be viewed by using an RSS Reader. The user subscribes to a feed by entering the feed's link into the reader. The user can also click on the RSS icon on the Web page and subscribe to the feed. Many program-based tools exist online which can be downloaded for free from News Gator (www.newsgator.com) (Fox, 2009).

An alternative to RSS is Atom. Atom works the same as RSS but has tried to clarify some of the problems associated with RSS. Atom was adopted by Google and has been added to Google related services such as Blogger, Google News, and Gmail (Wikipedia).

Wikis

Wikis are software that grant users access for collaborative editing, linking, and organization of content online. The term 'wiki' is Hawaiian and means "quick," which refers to the the instantaneous nature of the publishing. They are generally used for reference purposes and educational groups when collaboration is needed. They can be used in businesses to provide knowledge management. All users of a Wiki are able to edit the website or create new websites using normal browsers. Information is able to be built upon and modified by several users (http://computer.howstuffworks.com/internet/basics/wiki.htm, 2012). Wikis are web communities that allow users "to collaboratively create, edit, link and organize content online" (Karia, 2010).

Common tools used for web publishing with Wikis are: Wikiversity, MediaWiki and PBwiki. PBwiki later was changed to PBworks, and no longer

uses standard wiki markup - it's changed to using a WYSIWYG simple page editor instead. These tools offer features such as tagging for better content management. They also provide a navigation sidebar to allow users to browse through their collection of websites. The wiki's creators usually have the option to either make the wiki public or private, and give levels of editing and/or commenting privileges to specific collaborators or the public at large. PBwiki/PBworks allows comments to be made where the creators can see suggestions on how to enhance their websites.
(http://computer.howstuffworks.com/internet/basics/wiki.htm, 2012)

It is quite easy to see how wiki technology could influence the development of a digital library. By encouraging active collaboration, there could be a very dynamic influx of information made available to a digital library's collection, users could access a particular document regarding a particular topic of information, and the users themselves might have their own pertinent data or resources related to the library's holdings that they might want to contribute. The digital librarians and the user community would be able to instantly interact to discuss any number of topics regarding the library and its resources, in essence making the users digital librarians themselves, as they would have a stake in the creation and maintenance of the digital library. This collaborative approach would also serve well in checking information for errors or discrepancies, as a community of participants would more effectively be able to make sure that the information a digital library offers is accurate.

There are many examples of wiki sites. According to Warren (2009), Yale University Press has experimented with making e-books available on wikis and blogs: "The wiki site presents a new free collection of scholarly books published by the Press, to which anyone can contribute though comments, summaries, and links; the site also makes available a free, downloadable PDF version of each book" (p. 87). Warren goes on to note that the wiki is not meant to be a substitution for the printed book, and sales for printed books have not suffered.

Jose Lopez, a library science student from Southern Connecticut State University, describes his experience with a wiki used to facilitate class collaboration:

Among the courses I've taken at Southern Connecticut State University, an ILS 504
>
> Reference course taught by Steven Jones required the students to utilize a PBWiki account. From my experiences the collaborative nature of the process certainly assisted me in executing required assignments. The assistance of my peers greatly helped me when I was confused about a particular assignment, or when a peer would offer advice or enlighten me toward relevant resources. From these experiences I would believe that a digital library that employed the wiki platform would greatly enhance users experience in accessing

that library for their needs, as they would be active participants and be an integral component in the digital library itself.

The most famous wiki is Wikipedia, an online encyclopedia that is written and edited for free by its users. While there is some controversy about its legitimacy for research purposes, it provides information for non-academic purposes quickly, and as most Wikipedia entries have at least some citations of outside articles or books, the site can provide an entry point to the research process.

Once a wiki is established, users may create new content, edit, add hyperlinks, and organize content within the tool (Yang et. al, 2008). Made popular through Web sites such as Wikipedia and Wikiversity, these Web publishing tools provide a public environment for fruitful collaboration by authors and also offer a system for checks and balances on the quality of information. Wikis are also frequently used as knowledge management tools by organizations such as Substance Abuse Librarians and Information Specialists, a special library group who publish a password-restricted wiki space for committee and planning purposes (Figure 3.6).

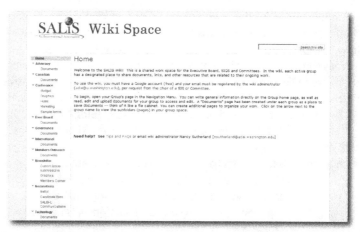

Figure3.3: Wiki – Substance Abuse Librarians and Information Specialists collaborative work space (SALIS Wiki Space, 2010).

Blogs

The term blog comes from the contraction of "web" and "log". Blogs are websites which sometimes act as personal diaries or soap boxes. They are spaces to express opinions and information which is constantly updated. Blogs "are either personal diaries or Websites providing news or commentary arranged in a reverse chronological order" (Karia, 2010). Blog readers or followers are allowed to leave comments. Blogs can be used by companies of any nature and can be linked to other blogs.

Blogs are displayed in reverse chronological order so the current posts will be the first ones read. They can contain text, music, images, and video clips. Blogs can have specialized content, such as photoblogs, or be classified by genre, such as an Anime blog (http://www.bloggingtips.com/2007/11/01/blogging-for-beginners-how-blogging-software-works/, 2012). According to Blood (2000), "the original weblogs were link-driven sites. Each was a mixture in unique proportions of links, commentary, and personal thoughts and essays"(para. 5).

Blogs provide commentary or news on a particular subject such as food, politics, or local news. Blogs can also function as more personal online diaries. A typical blog contains text, images, and links to other blogs, web pages, and other media related to its topic. The ability for readers to leave comments in an interactive format is an important part of many blogs (Swinburne University, 2009). Again, the collaborative nature of blogs is an attractive vehicle in providing the user of a digital library with an interactive experience that would involve the user on a more personal level. The user would possibly have access to video or audio feeds that could support the information presented on a topic, but the user would also be able to communicate with others who could share knowledge and insights regarding the given topic. Blogs, like wikis [which we discuss above], are examples of how collaborative methods of learning and sharing information continue to increase in popularity throughout the Internet. The website blogpulse.com sheds some light on the increase throughout 2009 of collaborative methods on the web: " Total blogs online - 126,861,574. New blogs in last 24 hours- 42,234. Blog posts indexed in last 24 hours- 769" (BlogPulse, 2010).

Most blogs are textual, but there are multimedia blogs with video clips, music or images,
such as YouTube. Five factors for a successful blog are:
1. Personality – blogs should reflect the personality of the author in a conversational tone. A dull blog will be an unpopular blog.
2. Opinion – providing a strong opinion will give visitors a platform to agree or disagree.
3. Participation – the strength of a blog comes from the community that surrounds it. A response should follow all comments. Making the community feel important will ensure a repeat visit.
4. Value – the blog should bring something interesting to the readers adding value to the community.
5. Availability – the author should be available to the community through email and responses. Successful blogs are updated frequently so that visitors start to rely on them for useful information.

How is web publishing useful for libraries?

Service-oriented architecture (SOA) is a conceptual model put forth by Fox (2009) that enables digital libraries to be more responsive to current and future patron needs. Traditional libraries have used "pull" technologies, such as traditional Web pages and blogs that visitors "pull" information from, in an effort to reach out to the off-site library user (Fox, 2009). "Push" technologies, on the other hand, sends information out *to* patrons who access and utilize it in their own places, on their own terms.

Today's library users are accustomed to minute-by-minute information. Today "students expect more choice now and more personalized [sic] services from universities, and we should not be surprised when this new behavior [sic] spills over into students' expectations of their library service" (Sykes, 2007). There are many ways in which librarians should consider using push technology to their advantage.

Using push technologies may mean that library updates arrive on a user's RSS Feed Reader, or that a pre-defined search generates a text message when a new resource matching the pre-set criteria is added to the digital collection. Lib-X, a browser plug-in for libraries, also features embedded cues visible to potential patrons as they browse books on Amazon, read a New York Times article online, or engage in other information-seeking behavior: a small library tag appears next to a title, author, or other metadata encouraging the user to search the library catalog for that or related resources (Lib-X, 2010) (Figure 3.7).

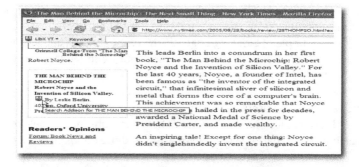

Figure 3.4: Embedded browser plug-in pushing library catalog data (Lib-X, 2010).

Many universities generally have their own information and communication systems. In order to combat this library illiteracy, Regis University designed a push notification system in 2000 called the Library Notification Module. This module works in conjunction with the university's "Student Information System to identify new students, and then generates an e-mail welcome message to them from the library. The message encourages students to apply for a RegisNET account, essential for remote access to library databases, and provides a hot link to the application form. Messages are tailored to declared programs of study, so students are also directed to Web lists of recommended licensed databases: MBA students, for example, will click on a link to business resources, and nursing students to a guide for health sciences resources" (Riedel, 2004).

Libraries should also consider using push technologies to notify students of information on their smart phones: "The growing popularity of the single multi-functional device means that it is now possible to reach a very significant majority of our students in one hit by pushing messages out to these mobile devices. Text messages, SMS and instant messaging, all have the potential to streamline the sending of information from libraries to students" (Sykes, 2007). Some examples of the importance of using these notifications in libraries that Sykes (2007) noted are:

- Global Messages (changes in hours, weather related closures)
- Group Messages (class readings, reserves, full text reading assignments)
- Individual Messages (due date reminders)

Librarians may also be able to use push technology to help patrons become "information specialists." David W. Powis-Dow (2006) wrote in his article about push-pull technologies in corporate libraries that "librarians' and information specialists' roles may be varied in the future: helping users to refine their search strategies and become 'information gathering independent,' on the one hand, and venturing out on the information frontiers to find information vital to the corporation's future endeavors, on the other.

An example of bleeding-edge "push" Web service is being conducted at the Community General Hospital Medical Library in Syracuse, New York (Fox, 2009). There, users utilize a tool called LibWorm to set up a custom search, which then runs against over 1500 library-related RSS feeds and returns results to the users (LibWorm, 2010).

These are just a few examples of how librarians may be able to utilize push technology to better serve their patrons and their audiences.

3.5 Crawling

For many people, the World Wide Web appears to be the biggest digital library in existence; unfortunately, as many students and scholars have discovered, that is not the case. "The World Wide Web is a very large and mostly unedited medium of publication. In contrast, a number of digital libraries index a more controlled set of quality documents that are of interest to an organization or a community of researchers" (Pant, Tsioutsiouliklis, Johnson, & Giles, 2004, p. 142). More and more media are being published on the web rather than in print, or rather, published online before it is printed as a hard copy (assuming it ever actually goes to print). The formats themselves have broadened beyond article and traditional formats. Documents such as government forms or even personal blogs have the potential to be part of collection development (Tennant, 2005).

Depending on its size, subject and collection method, the process of populating a digital library with data found on the Web can easily become one of the most time-consuming and labor-intensive operations involved in its start-up, maintenance and expansion. Considering the staggering amount of information available on the Web, literally billions of pages of information, searching by hand for items to add to a collection is simply not an option for many digital libraries. And even when searching for and analyzing data by hand is feasible, as could be the case for some smaller DLs or collections with a very narrow or focused topic, it is still a tremendous drain on human resources that could be spent elsewhere. One of the most useful and versatile ways to at least partially automate the process of adding items to digital library collections, thereby freeing up individuals for other tasks, is to employ a computer program known as a Web crawler.

Background

Web crawlers have been in existence for nearly as long as the web, with the first crawler, Matthew Gray's Wanderer, introduced in early 1993. Wanderer was designed to track the growth of the Web, and early versions had few controls and "ran rampant through the net and caused a noticeable netwide performance degradation" (Tang, 1999). Despite initial problems, the potential for crawlers was obvious, and search engines soon developed their own bots to find relevant subject pages. Crawling is now employed by a variety of different web services, both legitimate and nefarious, from shopping engines that employ crawlers to find product and price information, to spambots that search the web for email addresses.

What is web crawling?

Web crawling can be summed up as using specific software to "crawl" or look for information on the web. Search engines use spiders or bots to "crawl" for information on the web. Crawling is the strategy that Google uses to harvest hits for the end-user (Tennant, 2005). Below are various definitions about web crawling from scholarly sources:
- "... The activity of using software to recursively download web documents by following links. There are a variety of crawl methods, including: focused crawl, smart crawl, incremental crawl, targeted crawl, and customized crawl" (CDLib, 2010).
- "A web crawler is a relatively simple automated program, or script, that methodically scans or "crawls" through Internet

pages to create an index of the data it's looking for ... Search engines use web crawlers to collect information about what is available on public web pages. Their primary purpose is to collect data so that when Internet surfers enter a search term on their site, they can quickly provide the surfer with relevant web sites. When a search engine's web crawler visits a web page, it "reads" the visible text, the hyperlinks, and the content of the various tags used in the site, such as keyword rich meta tags. Using the information gathered from the crawler, a search engine will then determine what the site is about and index the information. The website is then included in the search engine's database and its page ranking process" (What Is a Web Crawler, 2010).

In their article *Crawling The Web,* Pant, Srinivasan, and Menczer (n.d.) stated that "the large size and the dynamic nature of the Web highlight the need for continuous support and updating of Web based information retrieval systems. Crawlers facilitate the process by following the hyperlinks in Web pages to automatically download a partial snapshot of the Web." The authors further concluded that "due to the dynamism of the Web, crawling forms the back-bone of applications that facilitate Web information retrieval. While the typical use of crawlers has been for creating and maintaining indexes for general purpose search engine, diverse usage of topical crawlers is emerging both for client and server based applications. Topical crawlers are becoming important tools to support applications such as specialized Web portals, online searching, and competitive intelligence" (Pant, Srinivasan, & Menczer, n.d.).

Examples of Web Crawlers:
- Google Analytics: https://www.google.com/accounts/ServiceLogin?service=analytics&userexp=signup&hl=en#utm_campaign=en_us
- Dice.com: http://www.dice.com/resumepost/
- Mozenda: http://www.mozenda.com/web-crawling

Crawling methods

A Web crawler, also known as a spider or bot, is "software that automatically traverses the web by downloading documents and following links from page to page." (California Digital Library, 2010) A typical web crawler starts with a seed set of pages, a list of relevant Uniform Resource Locators (URLs) chosen by its user. It downloads the seed pages, extracts any hyperlinks, and then crawls the pages found through the links, repeating the process until there are no pages left to crawl, or a set boundary, such as time or bandwidth, is reached. (Brandman, Cho, Garcia-Molina, & Shivakumar, 2000) All crawlers work by using this recursive or loop process, but there are two different methods available when beginning a crawl: depth-first and breadth-first.

Depth-first crawling "follows each possible path to its conclusion before another path is tried (Schildt & Holmes, p. 169, 2003). A depth-first crawler finds the first link on the first page, crawls that page, finds its first link and follows it, repeating the process until it reaches the end of that particular path. It continues that process until all paths from all links have been exhausted.

In contrast, breadth-first crawlers look at each link on a page and only then continue on to the next page. Initially, every link on the first page is crawled, followed by every link on the first page's first link, with the process repeating until all of the links have been checked (Schmidt & Holmes). Both strategies are often modified with a limit of how many links away from the original seed URL they will travel, since it is likely that the further away from the original page the crawler gets, the less relevant the information will be. Both strategies are effective at retrieving relevant documents, and often the nature of the crawl and its desired results will dictate whether breadth-first or depth-first is employed.

Crawling techniques

Whether a crawler is breadth-first or depth-first, there are several different crawling techniques that can be employed to modify the crawl and improve its accuracy.

Focused Crawl. A focused, or topic-driven, crawler searches the Web selectively for specified topics by using a, "page classifier to determine the relevance of crawled pages to the target topics and a link predictor to select the candidate URLs that have a high probability of being relevant" (Huang & Ye, p. 519, 2004). Rather than collecting every page indiscriminately, a focused crawl will analyze a page, comparing it to keywords and topics that are relevant to the search being conducted. The crawler will discard irrelevant pages, thus increasing its accuracy and saving time.

Smart Crawl. "A focused crawl based on dynamic criteria. For example, a crawler could be programmed to analyze and evaluate a website for volatility, the presence of metadata, or the structure and content of a site, etc. The more it crawls, the smarter it gets about what to crawl and what not to crawl" (Kresh, D.) Smart crawls take into account not only the topic being searched for, but also other variables that can affect the quality and reliability of data. If the content of a webpage is updated or changed frequently, a smart crawl can learn to discard that page because it is more likely to become obsolete or irrelevant to the subject being collected.

Incremental Crawl. Traditionally, a crawler searches and collects web pages until, according to whatever parameters have been set, the collection is "complete", and then it stops. When it is time to refresh the collection, the crawler follows the same procedure as before and creates an entirely new collection, replacing the original. Incremental crawlers follow a different set of guidelines. Once a collection is complete, an incremental crawler will continue to visit pages, both new and already added to the collection, in order to update and refresh existing pages while at the same time replacing less useful pages with new ones. This strategy can not only save time, since the entire crawl does not have to be repeated over and over, but can also keep a collection more current, since individual pages can be added as found, rather than waiting for the full search to be completed (Cho & Garcia-Molina, 2000).

Targeted Crawl. This is a means to collect data in a sharper way. Rather than using a massive search engine such as Google, an end-user can use specific website that will crawl to find the most relevant hits, without ulterior motives (such as corporations paying to be on top of the hit list) or irrelevant hits.

Targeted crawling, unlike Google or other search engines, makes use of librarians and trained human staff. Librarians must use their expertise to evaluate the applicability of particular web sites to patrons (Tennant, 2005). The ultimate purpose of targeted crawling is to harvest proper materials beyond basic searches, to better serve end-users and patrons.

Crawler characteristics

The following characteristics[4] built into web crawling programs can increase the speed of the search and the accuracy of the data it returns:

Parallel and Distributed. A parallel web crawler "runs multiple crawling processes simultaneously," while avoiding overlap, which helps maximize the download rate and speeds up the crawling process (Lee, J. & Lee, S.). The problem is that parallel crawlers are only as powerful as the machine they run on. This issue can be solved by using crawlers that can be distributed across multiple machines that share the workload, thus increasing speed.

Scalable. With the rapid, continuous growth of the Web, web crawlers must somehow increase their speed in order to simply maintain their current rate of coverage. This can be achieved both through distribution, as well as judicious use of main memory. Designing distributed web crawlers that use a bounded amount of main memory and store data on disk allows users to keep pace with Web growth (Abello, Pardalos & Resende, p. 26, 2002).

Extensible. Since no two crawling tasks are identical, it is important that users be able to adapt the functionality of the crawler without having to modify its core components.

Crawling in digital libraries

---

[4]Changed the word "attribute" to "characteristic" to go with heading.

Crawling is used in digital libraries "to build collections of documents related to pre-specified topics" (Bergmark, Lagoze, and Sbityakov, 2002). Crawlers are programs which are used by search engine services to "scan the Internet to identify new sites or sites that have changed, gather information from those sites, and feed that information to the search engine's indexing mechanism." (Hock, 2007) Crawler technology was developed in the late 1990's the benefit of search engines. It is considered an important tactic when building digital libraries. Some crawling technologies can be exploited when building collections. Bergmark, Lagoze, and Sbityakov (2002) explain:

> For example, to make such collection-building crawls more effective, focused crawling was developed, in which the goal was to make a "best-first" crawl of the Web. We are using powerful crawler software to implement a focused crawl but use tunneling to overcome some of the limitations of a pure best-first approach. (p. 45)

Tunneling encompasses prioritizing links from webpages consistent with the webpage's relevance score, and by approximating the value of the link and adding priority on that as well. "We add to this mix by devising a tunneling focused crawling strategy which evaluates the current crawl direction on the fly to determine when to terminate a tunneling activity" (Bergmark, Lagoze, and Sbityakov, 2002). There have been indications that a combination of crawling and tunneling can be an effective tool for building a digital library.

The California Digital Library (CDL) is working on creating tools for digital collection that development librarians could use to aggregate content. The purpose of these tools is to offer methods to digital librarians to select websites to be crawled,

> [...] with the intent that the resulting collections would be made available directly to end users or in association with other resources via metasearch software [...] Sure, Google crawls (or attempts to crawl) everything, but sometimes what isn't searched is as important as what is. As long as users have a need to narrow in on useful and appropriate information resources, there will be work for collection development librarians. It just won't be the work that most librarians do now (Tennant, 2005).

What models are used for developing national/international information resources sharing consortia?

As Lesk (2005) points out, many countries have digital library initiatives underway. Due to economies of scale and low entry costs, information technology is an appropriate national goal in many countries. Lesk contrasts the approaches used by these countries in supporting their digital library initiatives. Many nations decide to base digital library initiatives around either libraries or computer science research departments. At one extreme is the United States, where the digital library effort is run by the National Science Foundation (NSF). The focus is on computer science research, creating digital library tools, and new methods of access. The digital library collections are of less importance. It is felt that the tools developed in NSF supported projects can be applied by other institutions in building their collections. In contrast is in Japan, where the major digital library initiative run by the National Diet Library is focused on collections. European nations are said to be following a mixed policy because they are focusing neither on tools nor collections exclusively.

In the United States, the government and the NSF have always been involved in information delivery research. Starting in the 1950s, the NSF and other government agencies provided the funding for research in information retrieval. This has led to the development of the United States' world leadership in information services. As Lesk notes out, government funding has led to the development of many private information services such as DIALOG, which started as a venture between NASA and Lockheed. Other projects funded by the NSF have led to MOSAIC (an early browser capable of working with many different computing platforms), the Library of Congress' Thomas system, and Netscape, which grew out of the High Performance Computing and Communications program at the University of Illinois. The NSF's major initiative in digital libraries began in 1994. In cooperation with DARPA and NASA, six digital library projects were funded in the $30 million Phase 1 of the Digital Libraries Initiative. In 1999, the $55 million Phase 2 (DLI-2) included 36 projects supported by the NSF, DARPA, the National Library of Medicine, the Library of Congress, NASA, and the National Endowment for the Humanities, with the participation of the National Archives and the Smithsonian Institution. This funding was provided to develop innovative digital library technologies and applications. DLI-2 has also included a number of international digital library projects.

The six original projects funded in 1994, Digital Library Initiative I, each involved a consortium of cooperating institutions, but each was based at a single university. Each of the projects is involved in digitization and researches into the use of electronic materials. The programs are meant to explore different areas and are designed to advance technologies important to digital libraries rather than merely convert materials into digital collections. The focus is on performing research and creating tools that will advance the state of digital library technology. This technology can then be passed on to other institutions. The six original projects include:

University of California at Berkeley. Berkeley's collection focuses on environmental information. The research being done in this project includes attempts to develop new tools for automatically searching images for colors, shapes, features, etc. These search features can be used in conjunction with text searches in order to improve the users' abilities to efficiently access images in a digital online collection. Further research is being done to create the ability to make numerical and textual queries into documents that contain tables in order to extract information that can be placed in a spreadsheet or database. Research on multivalent documents allowing users to search and view multiple forms or different representations of the same document is also being done at Berkeley. Finally, natural language processing is being studied in order to create a process for reducing lexical disambiguates by determining the proper sense of a word based on statistical analysis of the document.

University of Michigan. This DL project deals with the earth and space sciences and includes journal articles, books, and video and audio recordings of scientists discussing research questions in the collection. Michigan's research deals with the intermediaries or gateways needed to perform operations on large-scale digital libraries. This project is trying to create interoperability between formats for different search services and to determine the appropriate sources to be searched for each query. When using this so-called 'conspectus search' method, agents are used to route arriving queries to the appropriate server. This method allows unlimited scalability since new collections can continually be added. Michigan has also included an educational element in its project by creating the Internet Public Library, which serves as a large-scale testbed to provide resources for public schools, college students, and others. Other digital library initiatives such as JSTOR, TULIP, and 'Making of America' are being integrated into the DLI-1 project.

University of Illinois. This digital library project focuses on creating a base collection of scientific journals. The items of this collection are either received from publishers in electronic form with SGML structure already embedded or in paper format, which are then transformed automatically with the articles being put into digital form. The Graduate School of Library and Information Science is performing a sociological evaluation of this testbed, technological development of semantic retrieval, and the design of scalable information systems, which they have dubbed the 'Interspace'.

Stanford University. Like the Michigan project, Stanford's project focuses on investigating the role of intermediaries and gateways in performing operations in large-scale digital libraries. The Stanford DL project is largely an infrastructure project focusing on interoperability. Stanford has a collection of computer science literature, but the main focus of the project is research on basic networking and database infrastructure to support digital libraries. The goal is to create a system that allows different projects to interact in searching, billing, etc. Stanford's research is aimed at creating a system in which systems are described in a formal model and are then linked by their database software. This is in contrast to documents on the WWW where all documents are in the same format.

University of California at Santa Barbara. This project is concerned with maps, aerial photographs, and other 'spatially indexed' information. The goal of this project is to create the ability to manipulate new media that were previously impossible to index and search. Research is being performed to allow for indexing of the geographic images in the collection in order to provide rapid and accurate responses to queries. Like the Berkeley project, research that will allow searching by color, texture, location, and other features is ongoing.

Carnegie Mellon University. Like the UCSB project the Carnegie Mellon project is seeking to develop tools that will allow for the manipulation of new media that were previously impossible to search and index. The CMU project consists of segmenting and indexing video by means of automatic speech recognition and knowledge about program structure. Among the tools applied to the video scenes and soundtrack in addition to speech recognition are image analysis, face recognition, and natural language understanding.

As stated previously, all of the NSF funded projects are intended to develop technological tools that will improve digital libraries' abilities to provide access to materials. The collections themselves are not the major focus of these projects.

As Lesk states (p. 252), other digital library projects have been more concerned with preservation and access to collections in digital format. In 1994, the same year as the NSF Digital Library Initiative, the Library of Congress created the National Digital Library. The National Digital Library Foundation is a joint effort with 15 large research libraries to provide a digital service that makes information on American heritage and history widely available. Different institutions are providing resources for the project. For example, Cornell and the University of Michigan are working together on the 'Making of America' project that will digitize important works and documents dealing with American history. The number of digital library projects has grown exponentially with the advent of the Internet. This growth makes it impossible to present even a cursory discussion of the varied projects and initiatives being undertaken.

Lesk mentions many of the initiatives being undertaken in the United States and internationally. The list is growing daily. Due to the relative ease of creating digital library projects and the trickle down of technologies developed by the larger DL projects, smaller local institutions and individuals are now undertaking their own projects. Since these projects are generally available on the WWW, they become part of a larger global information infrastructure. Items created locally and intended for a relatively small audience may be used by others and provide valuable information to information seekers elsewhere. Therefore, local digital library projects can serve a valuable function in supplementing the information provided by the larger institutions. The locally produced DL projects might provide expertise on subjects that may be overlooked by the larger institutions.

Due to the infrastructure provided by past research, especially that which is provided by government backed DLI initiatives, many institutions are now capable of making important collections available online. Digital libraries are not inexpensive propositions. An important challenge may be to come up with the appropriate funding to support digital libraries. Decisions to fund digital libraries must often come at the expense of traditional library services, which may be detrimental to the overall level of services provided by the institution. In order for digital libraries to meet their potential, proper funding mechanisms must be identified and developed.

We have seen that research into digital libraries has played an important role in their development. Although this process has been ongoing, it appears that 1994 was the watershed year when digital library research began in earnest with the NSF-funded creation of the 6 original DLI projects and the Library of Congress' NDL project.

Conclusion

As with a traditional library, collection development/management in a digital library is an essential task of a library's operation and sustainability. Underlying this work is the firm belief in the continued need for curating of content, e.g. selecting, organizing, and providing access to a world of resources that are appropriate to particular audiences and/or purposes.

The functions of selecting and maintaining resources and digitizing materials are the foundation of effective digital libraries. In addition to the large amounts of available material for inclusion in a digital library, there are also a variety of resources to be digitized. And there are also alternate ways to search for and access information. Accessing information also requires new methods as the vast number of materials available online continues to increase. This is where tools such as harvesting and crawling are invaluable. As the ubiquitous nature of the World Wide Web continues to grow and more software, hardware and applications are created, the task of collection management will continue to evolve with the digital libraries themselves.

An advanced stage of progress has been reached when the popularity of electronic formats allows for providing larger quantities of information to a greater number of users. The presence and change in the digital environment have forced us to rethink the term Collection Development, because despite the existence of large repositories of printed information, resources and collections of digital information increase daily in the information market. At present, Web norms and technologies support integration of diverse contents into digital collections. For the user, the implications of this process point to the possibility to consult simultaneously information in several formats; the digital form is one of the most popular for academic and scientific activities. Everything will depend then on how the user can access the information in an easier and more organized way with the implicit quality standards of the digital environment.

Study questions for Chapter Three:

- To develop a digital library, usually one needs guidelines and best practices for references. Each DL has its own unique mission and features made by libraries and affected cultural institutions around the world. The International Federation of Library Institutions and Associations (IFLA) in early 2007 established the IFLA-World Digital Library Working Group on Digital Library Guidelines. There are also a number of lit dealing with this. Share your views, news or information you find on the matter, and use them to conduct your DL Reviews assignment.
- What are the main themes around building digital? Early in Chapter 1 in Lesk the author states that, "it is particularly difficult to provide a survey of what is being done around the world in digital library projects." If you were to write a Fulbright to study digital libraries around the world, what qualities, issues or themes in digital libraries would you want to research?
- In looking at the history of digital libraries, many of the advantages of digital libraries seem obvious (easy access, accurate preservation, compact storage, search effectiveness, etc) but often discussions fail to consider the flip side of the coin - the disadvantages and worries that would be of concern with digital collections. It will be important to consider the possible short and long-term worries that go hand in hand with digital libraries. Along the same line is one of the quotes mentioned in this unit that refers to the belief that history is prone to repeat itself. There might be various mistakes/problems that have accompanied the growth of digital libraries that we should focus on so as to not repeat or magnify these earlier difficulties/challenges.

Chapter Four: Content Organization

In this chapter, we focus on the organization of library materials; specifically, how resources are best organized and retrieved to achieve a digital library's goals. Two important concepts we will use are resource organization and resource description.

For these matters, we need to discuss issues of information retrieval for users through questions like these: how is digital information organized? How should collected resources be described? How is anyone going to find anything of use? What are some of the problems of searching in a digital library, and how do digital libraries improve user environment? In answering these questions, we will consider the use of metadata schemas, retrieving text in images, retrieval in a pictorial digital library, retrieving information from spoken documents, indexing of the Internet, database models, and identifying relevant documents for linking and metadata for digital libraries.

4.1 How is a digital library collection organized?

Three questions are frequently asked when a digital library is built:
- What are the basic ways of organizing a digital library collection?
- Which is the most logical way to depict the library collection, and
- How can resource descriptions be made cost-effective yet efficient for retrieval?

The first and second questions are related to the resource organization, the second one is resource description.

Ways of collection organization

With digital libraries becoming a more popular method of storing and accessing information, there is a greater necessity for a good organization system. Because not all classification systems are appropriate for all DLs, determining which one is best for each DL is critical. A DL can use a variety of various types of organization methods. Library classification, subject headings, directories, and indexing thesauri are among them.

The methods used to organize and arrange knowledge in traditional libraries in order to make searching possible, simple, effective and powerful are also possible for resource organization of a digital library. These include:
- Library classification
- Subject headings
- Directories
- Indexing using thesauri

The difference between classification and subject heading is, as any cataloguer can tell you, in a classification system, all subject headings are arranged hierarchically, while in a subject heading system, subject headings are listed alphabetically.

Classification systems commonly used in United States libraries include:

- The Library of Congress Classification (LCC)
- Dewey Classification Decimal (DCC)
- Universal Decimal Classification (UDC)

Subject heading systems commonly used in the US libraries include:

- The Library of Congress Subject Headings (LCSH)
- Sears Subject Headings (SSH)

Directories are listings in which information sources are categorized by subject and are used to store information about the objects of interesting.

Thesauri are collections of controlled vocabularies or preferred terms or descriptors, in which equivalent terms, hierarchical and associative relationships are linked and identified by relationship indicators. The list of preferred terms is organized and structured in a way that equivalence, homographic, hierarchical and associative relationships among terms are displayed clearly and identified by standardized relationship indicators.

Common thesauri used in the United States are the following:

- Alexandria Digital Library Feature Type Thesaurus
- The Art and Architecture Thesaurus (ATT)
- The Astronomy Thesaurus
- The ERIC Thesaurus
- General Social Science Thesaurus
- Humanities and Social Science Electronic Thesaurus
- Merriam-Webster's Thesaurus
- Roget's Thesauri
- National Agriculture Library Agricultural Thesaurus (NALT)
- UNESCO Thesaurus

Digital libraries may use different organization systems to sort and retrieve different resources. In their study, Knowledge Organization Systems in Canadian Digital Library Collections, Shiri (2005) reviewed 33 digital libraries. 20 of them were academic and 13 were governmental. (Shiri p.3). Of these libraries, fifteen used the Library of Congress Subject Headings. Four used the Canadian Subject Headings. Three each used the Dewey Decimal Classification and the Art & Architecture Thesaurus. One used the Répertoire de Vedettes-Matière, and four used a source index. Eleven used a locally developed taxonomy. Shiri identified several problems with how these digital libraries organize their search functions. Some only offered a single search bar without the possibility of using limitations. Others had browsing capabilities that were hidden from the user entirely. (2005, p.4)

4.2: Information Architecture[5]

Librarians have been organizing information for usability and findability for millennia. Since the advent of the printing press, that task has become challenging, exacerbated over the past twenty years with the advent of the Internet and the World Wide Web, as shown in the diagram, below by Rosenfeld and Morville (2002):

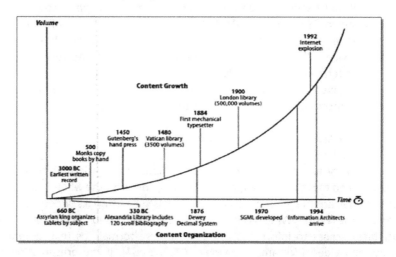

Figure 4.1: Information Growth (Rosenfeld, & Moreville, 2002, p.51).

The end products and structures underlying data on the Web—hypertext, hypermedia, metadata, classification schemas, controlled vocabularies, and thesauri, for instance—are what digital librarians use to organize resources so they are both findable and usable in this vast sea of information. Without these often-invisible structures, the information explosion of the 20th and 21st century would indeed be an unmanageable, useless morass.

While other components make up the hardware and software aspects of the World Wide Web and its supporting delivery structure, the Internet, in this chapter, we are primarily concerned with the structural underpinnings of information as it is delivered and organized on the World Wide Web. These building materials, unlike those comprising browsers and other interfaces, are behind-the-scenes, and include information architecture

---

[5]Please see Appendix B for an outline on Information Architecture and Organization that may contain more information.

constructs such as hypertext, hypermedia, metadata, classification schemas, and controlled vocabularies.

What is Information Architecture?

When we think of architecture, we generally think of buildings, both ancient and modern. The term architecture refers to the process or end-result of the act of building, and can be applied to physical as well as conceptual structures, including buildings, computer hardware and software, and even novels ("Architecture," n.d.).

Richard Saul Wurman first appended the term *architect* to the term *information* in 1975, and in 1994, the term began to be applied to the systematic, library science-like organization of information for the World Wide Web (Morville, 2004, p. xii). Today, the Information Architecture Institute defines the term *information architecture* as "the art and science of organizing and labeling websites, intranets, online communities and software to support usability" (Information Architecture Institute [IAI], 2007, p. 1).

Information Architecture on the World Wide Web

Every architectural structure is composed of basic materials that, when applied together in an organized fashion, comprise the whole. Buildings, for instance, are made up of physical materials such as bricks, wood, or steel girders. The World Wide Web is a "multi-media based technology" that facilitates access to information in such diverse formats as text, graphics, audio, and video (Williams & Sawyer, 2007, p. 64). If the presentation of information is the end product of architecture applied to the World Wide Web, its constructive components can be thought of as *hypertext* and *hypermedia*.

According to the World Wide Web Consortium, the term hypertext was coined by Ted Nelson around 1965 during "Project Xanadu, inspired by *As We May Think*, a Vannevar Bush essay" in which Bush describes a "microfilm-based machine (the Memex) in which one could link any two pages of information into a 'trail' of related information" (Bergman, 2010).

As a concept, "hypertext is text which is not constrained to be linear," and which "contains links to other texts" (World Wide Web Consortium [W3C], n.d.). Hypertext is a concept for information connectivity where data can be effectively linked to other data to create a chain of related, but not necessarily linear, information, concepts, and facts (Cailliau, 2006).

The following graphics illustrate how clicking on a link to the subject "artificial turf" in a Wikipedia hypertext document about "associationfootball" navigates to a distinct resource:

> **Association football**
>
> From Wikipedia, the free encyclopedia
> (Redirected from Soccer)
>
> "Soccer" redirects here. For other uses, see Soccer (disambiguation).
>
> **Association football**, commonly known as **football** or **soccer**, is a sport played between two teams of eleven players with a spherical ball. It is the world's most popular sport. [1][2][3]
>
> The game is played on a rectangular field of grass or green artificial turf, with a goal in the middle of each of the short ends. The object of the game is to score by driving the ball into the opposing goal. In general play, the goalkeepers are the only players allowed to touch the ball with their hands or arms, while the field players typically use their feet to kick the ball into position, occasionally using their torso or head to intercept a ball in midair. The team that scores the most goals by the end of the match wins. If the score is tied at the end of the game, either a draw is declared or the game goes into extra time and/or a penalty shootout, depending on the format of the competition.
>
> The Laws of the Game published in England by the Football Association in 1863 remain the basis for the way the sport is played today. Football is governed internationally by the *Fédération Internationale de Football Association* which organises the World Cup every four years.[4]

Figure 4.2: Wikipedia hypertext document "Association Football."

> **Artificial turf**
>
> From Wikipedia, the free encyclopedia
>
> **Artificial turf** is a surface manufactured from synthetic fibers made to look like natural grass. It is most often used in arenas for sports that were originally or are normally played on grass. However, it is now being used on residential lawns and commercial applications as well. The main reason is maintenance — artificial turf resists heavy use, such as in sports, better, and requires no irrigation or trimming. Domed, covered, and partially covered stadiums may require artificial turf because of the difficulty of getting grass enough sunlight to stay healthy.

Figure 4.3: Document Linking (Wikipedia.com).

Document linking is valuable as an information architectural concept because it mimics the way the human mind processes and organizes information, that is, via "hooks" or associations (Rosenfeld & Morville, 2002).

When designing information resources that use linking as an organizational concept, it is important to keep in mind the visibility of such links (Rosenfeld & Morville, 2002). Additionally, subject matter experts and information architects should be employed to vet linked terms in order to provide a logical yet intuitive information navigation pathway (Rosenfeld & Morville, 2002).

Linking, as a concept, can also be extended to objects beyond text, such as sound, graphics, and video files. *Hypermedia*, also a term coined by Ted Nelson, describes hypertext that is applied to digital objects other than text (W3C, n.d.). For instance, Ancestry.com allows users to click on a location link associated with a person record. This link brings up a map with virtual pins that link to database records associated with each discrete piece of information associated with both the person and the location on the map. See the example, below:

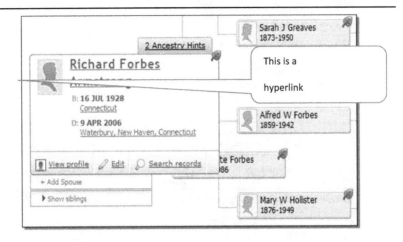

Figure 4.4: Hyperlink example (Ancestry.com).

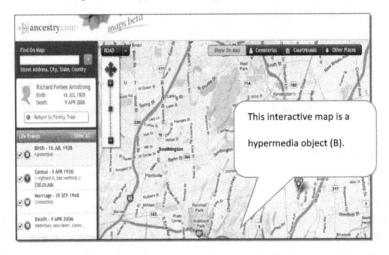

Figure 4.5: Hypermedia Object (Ancestry.com).

The hyperlink is the term, *Connecticut*, associated with the person record (A). The interactive map that results from clicking on the hyperlink is a hypermedia object (B).

The terms *hypertext* and *hypermedia* are often associated with databases; however, they should not be confused with the databases themselves (Lowe & Hall, 1998). Hypermedia, especially, is prone to this confusion in association. While hypermedia does not have to be as interactive as the Ancestry.com map provided in the example, it is one which utilizes more dynamically the information interrelationships inherent to the data being connected and presented (Lowe & Hall, 1998).

As a concept, hypertext, or hypermedia, can be applied to any application that allows information to be linked in a non-linear fashion; however, it is perhaps best known in relation to the World Wide Web and markup languages such as HTML (Borgman & Henstell, 1989). HTML, according to Williams and Sawyer (2007), "is the set of special instructions [called "tags" or "markups"] that are used to specify document structure, formatting and links to other multimedia documents on the web" (p. 68). When applied to information, a markup language controls the presentation and—when associated with specialized tagging schemas and controlled vocabularies— organization of information.

4.3: What is metadata for digital libraries?

One problem that plagues the online world is the propagation of many varied and sometimes drastically different forms and formats for search and retrieval. Baldonado, Chang, Gravano and Paepcke (1997) address this problem by designing metadata architecture for digital libraries.

Metadata is data that tells us about other data. For example, we may have data about a bill we just received: it is for $50, it is from the South's Garage, etc. Metadata about the class of object fields a bill might include the following attributes: a date, an amount due, an interest rate, a customer name, a customer address, etc. The metadata allows for translation modules between systems. For example, a user might want to copy the data from South's Garage into an automated budget and banking service program that manages the company's bills and payments. The metadata translator would know to write the value of the billing attribute "Total Due" into the budget attribute "Debt Amount" and the value from the billing attribute "Minimum Payment" to the budget attribute "Minimum Due." Metadata contains the knowledge required for the cognitive task of adapting one system's available data to the data requirements of another system. Translators facilitate this adoption by mapping the attributes of one system onto the attributes of another system. Currently, much of this mapping is performed through human effort.

Simply defined, metadata is information added to a document or object in order to help describe it. It can tell us what a data object is, where it came from, who made it, how it is formatted, and how it has transformed over time. If hypertext and hypermedia are the building blocks from which information on the Web are constructed, metadata is the blueprint that organizes information in a fashion that is useful. Constructing a collection of information without this blueprint can make data unmanageable, or even useless, much as constructing a building without a blueprint can result in a physical space that does not meet inhabitants' needs, or, worse yet, is structurally unsound.

The metadata architecture designed by Baldonado et al. (1997) provides a variety of services. These services include: finding resources that are likely to satisfy a given query, formulating queries that are appropriate for multiple sources, translating queries into those used by various sources, and making sense of query results. To provide these services, Baldonado et al. (1997) designed four basic component classes for their architecture: attribute model proxies, attribute model translators, metadata facilities for search proxies, and metadata repositories. For a full discussion of this design, refer to Baldonado et al. (1997). For now, the main thing to understand is that many systems purporting to be digital libraries or associated information services are not compatible with one another, disabling the desirable sharing of information. (The attribute of compatibility among systems has been termed interoperability.)

In essence, according to Rosenfeld and Morville (2004), "metadata is the primary key that links information architecture," allowing us to "reveal patterns and relationships within content...that can be used to better structure, organize, and provide access to that content" (p. 70, 223). Metadata may either be assigned by a person (human-created), or assigned by a computer program (computationally assigned) (Witten, 2010).

A familiar example of metadata is traditional library cataloging: the creation of bibliographic records to describe and organize a library's holdings. A metadata record includes a set of elements or attributes required to describe the object in question. A library catalog, for example, is composed of a set of metadata records with elements that describe books or other library items: title, author, date of creation or publication, subject coverage, and a call number that specifies the location of the item on the shelf.

Such elements may be contained in a record separate from the item (associated metadata), or it may reside in the resource itself (embedded metadata). Typical of associated metadata are bibliographic records residing in a library catalog, independent of the items (books, journals, recordings, etc.) that they describe. Examples of embedded metadata include the Cataloging in Publication (CIP) data printed on the verso of a book's title page, or TIFF tags embedded in a document digitized from an analog source using OCR.

The term metadata may refer either to a schema for describing data objects (such as MARC or Dublin Core), or to the data that describes a specific data object. In the latter case, the data object may be arbitrarily small (e.g., item-level description for a particular edition of *Beowulf*), or large (collection-level description of digital images in the British Museum).

Metadata is a critical component of digital libraries. Analyzing the metadata of digital libraries all over the world could be a crucial task. There are numerous challenges with metadata interoperability and transporting data between systems.

Collection-level description

Metadata records may describe collections of items as a whole, e.g., library collections or online depositories. A collection may be conceived of as any aggregation of individual items (objects, resources), without regard to the form or nature of the items. A description of such a collection may include information about the aggregate as a whole, or information about the individual items that constitute the collection, or information about groupings of the items that form a subset of the whole. For example, a collection-level description of copyright information may apply to all the individually described items in an archive of digital images. In this way, collection-level description complements item-level description.

All levels of metadata description entail a set of structured fields and the values that populate those fields. Standardized structure is implemented with metadata schemas, including metadata standards and metadata models. Further standardization is achieved through such tools as thesauri, taxonomies, controlled vocabularies, data dictionaries, and metadata registries.

The history of metadata

Metadata and digital libraries go hand-in-hand. In fact, the first known use of metadata in information science was with Machine Readable Cataloging or MARC encoding schema (Bergman, 2010). According to Bergman (2010), MARC was developed by Henriette Avram at the Library of Congress in the 1960s and is a set of standards for the representation and communication of bibliographic information in machine-readable form, and related documentation. MARC is the encoding schema by which the metadata (bibliographic data) is structured, much as HTML is the markup language by which text is structured for viewing in a Web browser (Taylor, 2003). The metadata standard, or schema, used with MARC is based on the Anglo American Cataloging Rules 2 (AACR2)[6]. An example of MARC encoding of AACR2 metadata, taken from the Library of Congress online catalog, is below:

---

[6]Just as librarians have a metadata standard, or schema, based on the Library of Congress Anglo American Cataloging Rules 2 (AACR2), other industries have developed their own standards.

```
100 1_ |a Mortimer, Ian.
245 14 |a The greatest traitor : |b the life of Sir Roger Mortimer, ruler of England, 1327-1330 / |c Ian Mortimer.
250 __ |a 1st ed.
260 __ |a New York : |b Thomas Dunne Books, |c 2006.
300 __ |a xiv, 377 p. : |b maps ; |c 22 cm.
500 __ |a Originally published: London : J. Cape, 2003.
504 __ |a Includes bibliographical references (p. 325-335) and index.
600 10 |a Mortimer, Roger de, |c Earl of March, |d 1287?-1330.
651 _0 |a Great Britain |x History |y Edward II, 1307-1327.
600 10 |a Isabella, |c Queen, consort of Edward II, King of England, |d 1292-1358.
600 10 |a Edward, |b II, |c King of England, |d 1284-1327 |x Death and burial.
650 _0 |a Nobility |x Great Britain |v Biography.
```

Figure 4.6: MARC encoding of AACR2.

In addition to bibliographic metadata standards for documents, metadata standards have also been developed for images (TIFF, or Tagged Image File Format, among others), audio (ID3 for MP3 files, for instance), video (AVI, MPEG-4, Flash, etc.), and multimedia and multimedia applications (MPEG-7, MPEG-21) (Witten, 2010, pp. 300-310). All of these metadata encoding standards are particularly useful for embedding metadata within the myriad digital objects that now constitute the Internet and that are being collected and disseminated via digital libraries.

The current state of rapid development combined with the diverse kinds of resources that must be cataloged for a digital library, along with the administrative metadata that must also be kept, has been cause for some concern over the sometimes fragmented direction all of the resources have taken (Gartner, 2008). It has, in a sense, been a "Wild West" for digital libraries and metadata standards.

Digital libraries, by the very nature of the diverse information formats they serve to a global audience, are complex to build, maintain, and catalog. Metadata standards are as potentially varied as the types of objects digital libraries collect. As such, a standard has to be set for metadata descriptions on the Internet. At this point that standard is XML or Extensible Markup Language and the MARC dataset combined into MARCXML (Guenther, 2007).

XML is "extensible," meaning that it can be extended or adapted to a great many different types of schemas. As such, it can be appended, adapted, or used with a variety of schemas for metadata preservation (PREMIS), metadata associated specifically with digital resources (MODS), hierarchical and location-descriptive metadata (METS), and metadata associated with images (MIX) (Guenther, 2007). When used along with controlled vocabularies, these four schemas have become the recommended best practice standards for metadata in digital libraries (Guenther, 2007; Gartner, 2008).

Metadata Schemes

With digital libraries becoming a more popular method of storing and accessing information, there is a greater necessity for a good organization system. Because not all classification systems are appropriate for all DLs, determining which one is best for each DL is critical. A DL can use a variety of various types of organization methods. Library classification, subject headings, directories, and indexing thesauri are among them.

4.4 Resources Description

The ways to describe library sources are mainly focused on the use of metadata. Metadata are a set of words, phrases or sentences that summarize and describe what is on a web site, or on individual pages or sub-sections of that web site, for the benefit of search agents. The methods commonly used now are the following:

Bibliographic citations. They are commonly in APA, MLA, Harvard, and etc. styles.
Machine Readable Catalog (MARC).
Dublin Core (DC).

Why do we use metadata?

Why do we need metadata? Metadata allows the sharing and exchange of resources consistently, it enables learners and instructors to search, evaluate, acquire and use learning resources effectively, and can be used to describe web sites precisely, so that search engines can accurately find them.

The term "metadata" currently refers to the bibliographical context used to answer the who, what, when, where, why, and how questions regarding a source of information:

- Who collected and who distributes the information?
- What is the subject?
- When was the information collected?
- Where was the information collected?
- What is the purpose of the information collected?
- How was the information collected and how should it be used?

Metadata can be structured or unstructured and can be stored in a number of places and in a number of different ways. At its simplest, it can take the form of a number of keywords that a web site manager feels sums up the content of the web page, or a short description in prose format that summarizes the site in a couple of sentences.

The use of metadata endeavors to place some controls on how information is described and retrieved over the Internet. Metadata organizes the search process into a clearer structure and so improves the retrieval of relevant information.

Metadata is a kind of information that is not visible to people browsing a site, but is visible to search engines or other programs that scan a site for relevant content. This information makes the job of classifying and searching the content of the Internet more efficient and a lot simpler.

Metadata standards provide the structure for the organization of digital collections, which allow the drawing in of content from a range of disparate sources through an improved retrieval process combined with high-quality descriptions of the resources.

The interchange of digital resources can be accomplished more effectively when resources are described in a uniform manner. Once a digital library has adopted a metadata standard it is possible to exchange data seamlessly within that group.

Metadata provides an environment for the development of interoperable systems. All data can be facilitated through a metadata standard such as Dublin Core metadata.

What are metadata standards and schemas?

A metadata standard defines the fields, or elements, to describe information. A metadata schema tends to be subject-specific and serve specified community group(s). Following are some of the key metadata standards among others.

IEEE LTSC LOM. The Institute of Electrical and Electronics Engineers Learning Technology Standards Committee (IEEE LTSC), formed in 1996, develops standards in a number of areas related to learning technology and applications. Their focus on metadata is taken forward through the Learning Object Metadata (LOM) group. The group has developed an elaborate metadata schema with a hierarchical structure. There is a strong emphasis on the educational category, which includes elements such as: 'interactivity type', 'typical age range', 'difficulty', and 'typical learning time'.

The IEEE LOM standard is at an advanced stage and has some notable implementations, such as the Instructional Management System (IMS) initiative.

VTC metadata schema. Virtual Teacher Centre (VTC) (http://vtc.ngfl.gov.uk/metadata) is based primarily on the IEEE Learning Object Metadata (LOM) standard and, to a lesser extent, on the Instructional Management Systems (IMS) specification. It is one of the key metadata schemas for the educational sector. The schema has been designed so that content on the VTC can be described quickly and accurately. It can map to other metadata standards, including mainstream Dublin Core and LOM sets, and more specific cases such as the National Curriculum standard as defined by QCA.

National Curriculum metadata standard. The National Curriculum metadata standard is a collection of keywords or phrases that describe distinct concepts in the National Curriculum. For instance, the following is a Key Stage 3 scientific enquiry requirement 1c: "Pupils should be taught about the ways in which scientists work today and how they worked in the past, including the roles of experimentation, evidence and creative thought in the development of scientific ideas."

It is tagged with the following metadata keywords or phrases:
- Ideas and evidence in science
- Creativity in science
- Science: historical & contemporary examples.

The metadata keywords label the ideas that are implicit within the information. This works in much the same way as a classification system does in libraries. Future developments to the National Curriculum standard will incorporate new keywords to address:
- Thinking skills
- Social, moral, spiritual and cultural development
- Financial capability
- Expertise and entrepreneurial skills
- Work-related learning
- Education for sustainable development
- Inclusion.

Metadata for Education Group (MEG). With a focus primarily in the United Kingdom, MEG seeks to reach a consensus on the description of learning materials across the full range of educational provision. It does this by gathering and disseminating best practice and guidance. MEG is an authority on the application of descriptive metadata and deals with policy issues surrounding this topic.

MEG also hosts the MEG Registry, which could become the most useful starting point for developers, as it is based on a shared practice in metadata development.

Wikipedia has a more comprehensive list of metadata stands at http://en.wikipedia.org/wiki/Metadata_standards. Also, "Putting Things in Order: a Directory of Metadata Schemas and Related Standards" at http://www.jiscdigitalmedia.ac.uk/guide/putting-things-in-order-links-to-metadata-schemas-and-related-standards.

What does metadata look like?

Metadata can be created manually or generated automatically with computerized and/or Internet-based tools. Below is a simple piece of metadata that describes a book:
<meta name = "DC.Title" content = "Small Boat to China">
<meta name = "DC.Title.Alternative" content = "One of the Oldest Counties">
<meta name = "DC.Creator" content = "Smith Miller">
<meta name = "DC.date" content = "1995">

The effectiveness of metadata in describing resources is greatly enhanced when element qualifiers are used, and the element refinement qualifiers' make the meaning of an element narrower or more specific.

What issues surround the use of metadata?

In the short term there is a shortage of skilled people to implement metadata solutions. As with any emerging technology, there are many areas that are still under-developed. Furthermore, most implementations have been research-based, with too few examples of commercial applications, and with the VTC being an exception. Tools for assigning metadata to resources are coming to market quite slowly.

Given these factors, any work to assign metadata retrospectively would incur expense in terms of human and time resources. However, as a general rule, any proposed future developments of learning resources or systems should take into consideration the increasing importance of metadata.

As metadata is a key issue in the development of all future public web sites, the issue cannot be ignored. One way forward at the moment would be to develop a 'controlled vocabulary' for the subject area in which you are interested.

Metadata schemas

Metadata schemes (also known as schema) are collections of metadata items created with a specific goal in mind. TEI (Text Encoding Initiative)-the Electronic Text Center Introduction to TEI and Guide to Document Preparation, EAD (Encoded Archival Description), VRACC (Visual Resources Association Core Categories), and GILS (Global Information Locator Service/Government Information Locator Service) are some of the metadata schemes used for resource description in digital libraries. Find a simple metadata scheme utilized in a digital library, illustrate it with your observations and comments, or analyze the value of the scheme to digital libraries.

Varieties of metadata schemas are used by repositories in order to organize their resources. Metadata schemas are established sets of elements designed to describe resources.

Metadata encoding and transmission standard (METS).

The Metadata Encoding and Transmission Standard (METS) is another metadata schema used in describing digital library objects. METS encodes descriptive, administrative and structural metadata in XML. According to the METS Website, this allows for metadata to remain connected to its digital files and can link multiple digital files (and their individual metadata) together. A METS document contains seven sections: METS Header, Descriptive Metadata, Administrative Metadata, File Section, Structural Map, Structural Links, and Behavior (Metadata Encoding and Transmission Standard, 2010).

Dublin Core.

Over the past fifteen years, another bibliographic metadata standard has emerged. This standard is called *Dublin Core*, named after a workshop on metadata standards held in Dublin Ohio in March of 1995. The impetus for the workshop was a conversation between Yuri Rubinsky, Stuar Weibel, and Eric Miller—the latter both of OCLC—regarding findability, semantics, and the Web (Dublin Core Metadata Initiative [DCMI], 2010). Dublin Core, as a metadata schema, was developed to address cataloging of Web and other electronic resources that do not traditionally fall under the purview of MARC or professional, trained catalogers (Witten, 2010, p. 294). The encoding schema most often utilized with Dublin Core for data transfer over the Web is called the Resource Description Framework, or RDF (Taylor, 2003; W3C, 2010).[7]

The metadata schema Dublin Core is a basic set of elements describing metadata for digital resources. Unqualified Dublin Core uses 15 core elements to describe metadata: Title, Creator, Subject, Description, Publisher, Contributor, Date, Type, Format, Identifier, Source, Language, Relation, Coverage and Rights. Qualified Dublin Core includes three additional elements, Audience, Provenance and Rights Holder, as well as a group of element refinements, or qualifiers that can narrow the scope of the elements (dublincore.org). An example of Dublin Core metadata is below (Taylor, 2003):

---

[7]It should be noted, as shown in the example, that RDF and HTML are not mutually exclusive, but rather combined, to form markup and metadata in one document.

```
<HTML> !4.0!
<HEAD>
<TITLE>Song of the Open Road</TITLE>
<META NAME="DC.Title" CONTENT="Song of the Open Road">
<META NAME="DC.Creator" CONTENT="Nash, Ogden">
<META NAME="DC.Type" CONTENT="text">
<META NAME="DC.Date" CONTENT="1939">
<META NAME="DC.Format" CONTENT="text/html">
<META NAME="DC.Identifier" CONTENT="http://www.poetry.com/nash/open.html">
</HEAD>
<BODY><PRE>
I think that I shall never see
A billboard lovely as a tree.
Indeed, unless the billboards fall
I'll never see a tree at all.
</PRE></BODY>
</HTML>
```

Figure 4.7: Dublin Core (Taylor, 2003).

Due to its economy and simplicity, Dublin Core has been described as a "small language for making a particular class of statements about resources" (Dublin Core Metadata Initiative, 2005). This language is composed of two classes of terms, elements (nouns) and qualifiers (adjectives), which can be combined into a simple pattern of statements. In this schema, any element can be qualified or refined. The *Date* element, for example, can be refined as *date created, date available, date issued, date valid, or date modified*. Within the Dublin Core basic element set, each element is also optional and may be repeated. Most elements are assigned a limited set of qualifiers or refinements, and these attributes may be used to further refine (but not extend) the meaning of an element. Two key principles underlie the relationship of DC metadata to the materials it describes:

1. *The Dumb-down Principle.* Element refinement in Dublin Core is guided by the so-called Dumb-down Principle: a qualifier can be safely removed and the element value interpreted as a simple element. In this way, a client may ignore any qualifier and use the value as if it were unqualified. Thus *date issued*, for example, may be safely interpreted as *Date*. While some specificity may be lost, the remaining element value (without the qualifier) will still be generally correct and useful for resource discovery. This principle enables Simple and Qualified Dublin Core to co-exist easily within digital libraries.

2. *The One-to-One Principle.* Dublin Core's One-to-One Principle states that each metadata record should relate to only one resource. When metadata is created to describe a resource, whether an analog object or a digital image, the description must take into account user requirements and provide the information

that users are looking for. For example, a description for a digital image of the Mona Lisa should be distinct from a description for the original painting itself. If the original *date created* of the painting were provided in the metadata description of the digital image instead of the digitization date, it would conflict with the One-to-One principle.

Dublin Core's reduction of complex descriptions to no more than 15 basic elements is so versatile that these metadata elements may easily be interpreted and applied in different ways by information providers. Accordingly, its combination of minimalism and versatility is both strength and a weakness. For example, among Dublin Core's 15 basic fields there is no placeholder for the name of a thesis-awarding institution. In its place some providers may use the dc:publisher element, while others may not. Creating further inconsistency, when the dc:publisher element is used, this institution may appear as [institution, school], [school, institution] or just [school] or [institution], with or without leading definite articles. Such variation among sources poses problems for third-party services that depend on consistency for resource discovery.

Thus, while Dublin Core's simplicity reduces the cost of metadata creation and promotes interoperability, its simplicity fails to accommodate the functional and semantic richness supported by complex metadata schemas. In effect it trades this richness for wide visibility, yet Dublin Core makes up for this loss by encouraging implementation of richer metadata schemas in combination with Dublin Core. Richer schemas may further be mapped to Dublin Core for export or cross-system searching. On the other hand, simple Dublin Core records may be used as starting points for the creation of more complex descriptions.

Gateway to educational materials (GEM) element set.
Dublin Core was developed with the underlying assumption that the set would be extensible in two basic ways: (1) additional elements could be added to meet the needs of particular domains, and (2) its elements could be enriched through the use of a broad range of qualifying schemas and types. In this way, extensions to Dublin Core could be developed for specific domains or user communities.

One such extension is the Gateway to Educational Materials (GEM) element set, a project designed to facilitate access to online learning objects. GEM originated as a consortium effort to provide educators with ready access to thousands of educational resources available on various federal, state, university, nonprofit, and commercial websites. While the general goals of GEM and Dublin Core were similar, the latter's simplicity was intended to serve coarse-grained networked information discovery and retrieval (NIDR) across a broad range of resources. By contrast, Dublin Core was less well suited to the more fine-grained NIDR of resources necessary to particular communities. For GEM's purposes, the basic DC metadata set was enhanced by the addition of a package containing five description elements (Audience, Duration, Essential Resources, Education Level, Pedagogy), as well as two evaluative elements and one meta-metadata element. Expanded in this way, the GEM element set provides educators with additional information in order to tailor a search for resources meeting specific learning objectives or pedagogical methods (Sutton, 1999).

Darwin core.

Similarly derived from Dublin Core is Darwin Core, a biodiversity informatics standard comprising a controlled vocabulary designed to facilitate NIDR of information about organisms, their spatiotemporal occurrence, and supporting evidence residing in biological collections. So-called *Simple Darwin Core* provides a predefined subset of terms in common use across a wide variety of biodiversity applications. A controlled vocabulary, the *Darwin Core Type Vocabulary* extends and refines terms from the Dublin Core Type Vocabulary [DCMI-TYPE] in order to describe and categorize resources more specifically for biodiversity applications. Terms include Occurrence, Event, Location, Taxon, PreservedSpecimen, FossilSpecimen, LivingSpecimen, HumanObservation, MachineObservation, and NomenclatureChecklist. Each term is provided with a definition and commentaries that are intended to promote the consistent use of the terms across applications and disciplines. In keeping with the goals and design of Dublin Core, Darwin Core may similarly be adapted to serve new purposes by adding new terms to share additional information (Darwin Core Task Group, 2009).

Metadata object description schema (MODS)

The Library of Congress' Network Development and MARC Standards Office developed the Metadata Object Description Schema (MODS) in 2002 for a bibliographic element set that may be used for a variety of purposes, and particularly for library applications. As an XML schema it is intended to be able to carry selected data from existing MARC 21 records as well as to enable the creation of original resource description records. It includes a subset of MARC fields and uses language-based tags rather than numeric ones, in some cases regrouping elements from the MARC 21 bibliographic format. As of June 2009 this schema is in its third version (version 3.3). MODS is expressed using the XML schema language of the World Wide Web Consortium. The standard is maintained by the MODS Editorial Committee with support from the Network Development and MARC Standards Office of the Library of Congress (Introduction and implementation, 2010).

EXAMPLE
<originInfo>
<place>

```
            <placeTerm                                        type="code"
authority="marccountry">nyu</placeTerm>
            <placeTerm type="text">Ithaca, NY</placeTerm>
        </place>
        <publisher>Cornell University Press</publisher>
        <copyrightDate>1999</copyrightDate>
    </originInfo>
```

ISBD-BASED DISPLAY AFTER XSLT TRANSFORMATION:
Ithaca, NY: Cornell University Press, c1999.

The relationship between MODS and MARC 21 elements.

Most MODS elements have equivalent ones in MARC 21, although there are a few additional elements or attributes in MODS that are particularly important for digital resources, a special target population for MODS. For <digitalOrigin> falls under <physicalDescription>. The MODS Editorial Committee keeps the MARC and MODS element sets in sync as much as possible (Metadata Object Description Schema (MODS) Official website [MODS], 2010).

MODS uses and advantages.

MODS could potentially be used:
- As an extension schema to METS (Metadata Encoding and Transmission Standard)
- To represent metadata for harvesting
- For original resource description in XML syntax
- For representing a simplified MARC record in XML

MODS is intended to complement other metadata formats. For some applications, particularly those that have used MARC records, there will be advantages over other metadata schemas.

Some advantages are:
- It is richer than Dublin Core
- It is more compatible with library data than ONIX (Online Information Exchange)
- The schema is more end user oriented than the full MARCXML schema
- The element set is simpler than the full MARC format
- Any set of cataloging rules may be used with MODS, as is the case with MARC 21 (MODS, 2010).

Limitations of MODS.

MODS include a subset of data from the MARC 21 Format for Bibliographic Data. As an element set that allows for the representation of data already in MARC-based systems, it is intended to allow for the conversion of core fields while some specific data may be dropped. As an element set for original resource description, it allows for a simple record to be created in some cases using more general tags than those available in the MARC record. An original MARC 21 record converted to MODS may not convert back to MARC 21 in its entirety without some loss of specificity in tagging or loss of data. In some cases, if reconverted into MARC 21, the data may not be placed in exactly the same field that it started in because a MARC field may have been mapped to a more general one in MODS. However, the data itself will not be lost, only the detailed identification of the type of element it represents. In other cases, the element in MARC may not have an equivalent element in MODS and then the specific data could be lost when converting to MODS (MODS, 2010).

Domain-specific metadata schema

Domain-specific metadata schema are those metadata developed by different communities to be used in specific situations for specialized resources. This metadata support description allows details needed by users searching for resources in a particular domain. Examples of domain-specific metadata are:

General International Standard Archival Description:
Designed to facilitate the creation of archival descriptions that "identify and explain the context and content of archival material in order to promote its accessibility. It contains 26 elements organized into seven areas of descriptive information (ISAD(G), 2000):

1. Identity statement area: information essential to identify the unit being described
2. Context area: origin and custody of the unit being described
3. Content and structured area: information about the subject matter
4. Condition of access and use area: includes information about the availability
5. Allied materials area: other information resources that have important relationship
6. Note Area: other information
7. Description control area: information about the preparation of the archival description (e.g., whom, when, how, etc.) (ISAD(G), 2000).

Visual Resources Association (VRA Core)
According to the website of this domain-specific metadata, the VRA Core "provides a categorical organization for the description of works of visual culture as well as images that document them." It includes 19 basic categories that include work, collection or image; agent; cultural context, date, description, location, measurements, rights, subject, technique, etc (Visual

Resources Association, 2010). Guidelines for description using the VRA Core are included in Cataloguing Cultural Objects: A Guide to Describe Cultural Works and Their Images (Baca, 2006).

Metadata "crosswalks"

The adaption of metadata standards for specific purposes may take place through metadata crosswalks. A metadata schema original to a specific library may be provided with a "crosswalk" or table displaying metadata elements in its own database and equivalent elements in another schema. For example, the crosswalk below maps MARC elements to Dublin Core:

MARC field		Dublin Core element
245 (Title Statement)	→	Title
300 (Physical Description)	→	Format.Extent
522 (Geographic Coverage Note)	→	Coverage.Spatial

(Library of Congress, 2008c).

Crosswalks indicate how to put data from one schema into a different schema, and in this way help databases using different metadata schemas to share information. Metadata mapping is frequently used by libraries, archives and other institutions to translate data to or from MARC, Dublin Core, MODS, and other metadata schemas.

Suppose, for example, a library has a MARC record in its catalog describing a recording, and it wishes to create a digital copy of the recording and make it available on the web along with the information from the catalog. The library will have to translate the data from the MARC catalog record into a format such as MODS, which makes materials with existing item-level MARC cataloging viewable in a webpage. Because MARC fields are different from those in MODS, decisions must be made about how MARC metadata should be translated into MODS.

Crosswalks may be applied to map elements with similar meanings from one community-specific schema to another, for example from archival to bibliographic records (Bountouri & Gergatsoulis, 2009). The EAD element "<unittitle>Ionian University Archive</unittitle>" maps to the MODS element "<title>Ionian University Archive</title>" (2009, p. 126, 128). Different standards may have different hierarchical relationships and/or relation models and mapping may also take place at the collection level (2009).

Namespaces and repositories

Each metadata standard may have multiple namespaces, one for each version of the standard (i.e. MODS 3.0 and 4.0). Namespaces are very often associated with XML. Liu (2007) defines a namespace as "a collection of terms identified by a uniform resource identifier (URI) reference" (p. 103). Each URI for a term must be unique.

Namespace URIs will be the authority space for the metadata standard. Namespaces allow XML documents to include multiple metadata standards by referencing multiple XML metadata schemas (2007). XML schemas define the structure of XML documents (2007). A partial XML document published by the Library of Congress (LOC) (2009) using the MODS schema and namespace follows. It is annotated with XML comments starting with "<!" based on the recommendations of Cole and Foulonneau (2007):

```
<?xml version="1.0" encoding="UTF-8"?>
<!--All content must be UTF-8 encoding-->
<mods xmlns="http://www.loc.gov/mods/v3"
xmlns:xsi="http://www.w3.org/2001/XMLSchema-instance"
xsi:schemaLocation="http://www.loc.gov/mods/v3
Schema namespace
http://www.loc.gov/standards/mods/v3/mods-3-3.xsd">
    <!--The latter element contains the "xmlns" namespace declaration, the "xmlns:xsi" schema instance, and the "xsi:schemaLocation" MODS schema and namespace-->
    <titleInfo>
    <!--"<titleInfo>" is an element, "titleInfo" is the value, all elements must have a value-->
    <title>Sound and fury :</title>
    <subTitle>the making of the punditocracy /</subTitle>
    </titleInfo><!--all elements must be closed with /-->
    <name type="personal">
    <!--The latter element has an attribute, which require a quoted value-->
    <namePart>Alterman, Eric</namePart>
    <!--Elements are case sensitive, no "<namepart>" is allowed-->
    <role>
    <roleTerm type="text">creator</roleTerm>
    </role>
    </name>
    <!--more descriptive content goes here-->
</mods>
```

Interoperable metadata

In May 2007, IFLA Working Group on Digital Library Guidelines commenced with the goal of writing the metadata chapter for the *IFLA Guidelines for Digital Libraries* (Zeng, Lee, & Hayes, 2009). In order to inform the content of this chapter, more than 400 "answers from individual professionals as well as collective answers from several national libraries and many institutions" were solicited from the IFLA listserv (2009, p. 176). It was concluded from comments that metadata sharing and interoperability were among the most significant concerns across the board including the issues of shareable "descriptive data, subject vocabularies," interoperable values, and "data elements and fields" (2009, p. 185).

Different techniques exist for interoperable metadata, each of which targets different metadata concerns. For descriptive data, federation is increasingly being accomplished through aggregation of records via harvesting (Beisler & Willis, 2009). OCLC is currently attempting to implement searching of harvested records of open access digital repositories within the WorldCat federated architecture (2009).

The variety of schemas used makes it difficult for repositories to share metadata. Metadata harvesting offers a solution to bridge this divide.

Harvesting of metadata is often employed using switching schemas (Bountouri & Gergatsoulis, 2009). For example, the Open Archives Initiative XML schema has been fine-tuned to import Dublin-core metadata for harvesting. When a switching schema is used, all rich metadata is put into a single homogenous standard for exchange, which may result in data loss. Deng and Reese (2009) relate an example where MARC21 XML is the switching schema for cataloging electronic theses and dissertations. In this case, diverse metadata records in MODS, TEI, or Dublin Core are converted to MARC via a software tool called MarcEdit, which employs extensible stylesheets (XSLT) and a processing engine (2009).

A number of researchers have studied the mapping of metadata from digital CONTENTdm (a digital collection management software) collections to the OAI simple Dublin core schema for harvesting. The inherent constraints of mapping metadata to a simplified schema are a challenge to metadata quality, which has been defined by Shreeeves, Riley and Milewicz (2006) as the six C's: "Content is optimized for sharing. Metadata within shared collections reflects consistent practices. Metadata is coherent. Context is provided." Beisler and Willis (2009) highlight issues with completeness and coherence in their case studies of mapped records from CONTENTdm. Many similar problems were confirmed in an analysis of 21 CONTENTdm repositories of digital special collections such as images and still images (Han, Cho, Cole, and Jackson, 2009). Incoherence resulted from erroneous mapping of elements including dimensions being mapped to description instead of extent, and:

URLs for related content (e.g., parent collection) that should not have been mapped to <identifier> in the item-level record, mappings of <record group>to <identifier> (instead of <source>), and mappings of <repository> and <place kept> to <identifier> rather than <publisher>, <relation>, or unmapped)" (2009, p. 231).

Another difficulty is when there is more than one date in a CONTENTdm collection because a one-to-one mapping will prevent confusion (2009). For example, in one record studied by Beisler and Willis (2009) the "date digitized" field was harvested. In another record, CONTENTdm displayed one date field as a decade range (1860-1870) and a date element for each year in the range (2009). Then the harvested record picked up all the individual years (2009). When this same record was mapped to a MARC record, it contained only the single year 1860 (2009).

These studies point to the need for careful consideration of whether or not metadata should be mapped (Beisler and Willis, 2009). In particular, Han, Cho, Cole, and Jackson (2009) emphasize not mapping fields that are only relevant to the local context as well as technical and administrative data. The authors stress that using qualified Dublin core for mapping and labeling on the user interface and mapping field names directly from other metadata standards is to be encouraged (2009).

Metadata schema registries

Another technique for ensuring interoperable metadata is the metadata schema registry, which is a "database of metadata schemas and application profiles" (Liu, 2007, p. 109). As Liu (2007) writes, "The metadata registry provides the tools for managing and disclosing metadata schema declarations, application profile declarations, and value space declarations" (p. 109). One of the more recent efforts to build such a repository is the CORES (2002) model (http://www.cores-eu.net/), which declares:

"The ambition of the CORES project is to build consensus on a shared data model for the declaration of element sets and application profiles. Such a shared data model would facilitate the re-use of existing schemas by other services, projects and initiatives" (2002).

CORES uses resource description framework (RDF) to encode element sets, element values, application profiles, and annotations (2002). For example, CORES contains application profiles for the British Library and simple and qualified Dublin Core (2002). Also one may browse indexes of all the elements used by standards in the repository (CORES Registry, 2002).

Administrative metadata

The Metadata Encoding Transmission Standard (METS) is widely used and can help one to understand the applications of administrative metadata to digital libraries. METS is "used for management of digital objects within a repository and the exchange of such objects between repositories" (Library of Congress, 2007a, p. 5). METS documents contain different sections such as file section, structural map, descriptive metadata section, and administrative metadata section. The structural map is the only required section of a METS document, and it contains elements that represent the structure of a document. Each item in the structural map can be associated with corresponding descriptive and administrative metadata using an ID (Library of Congress, 2007a, p. 5). IDs are what hold the document together for management purposes. An example of a physical structural map of a multi-page cartographic map of Alamosa dated 1890 from The Sanborn Fire Insurance Map Collection at Colorado University Digital Library (n.d.a) with example ID references follows:

```
<structMap TYPE="physical">
<div TYPE="map" DMDID="DMDala90" LABEL="Alamosa 1890">
<div TYPE="sheet" ORDER="1" LABEL="sheet 1 (index map)">
<fptr FILEID="ala90001"/>
</div>
<div TYPE="sheet" ORDER="2" LABEL="sheet 2">
<fptr FILEID="ala90002"/>
</div>
</div>
</structMap>
```

IDs are made meaningful through file-naming conventions. File naming conventions are exemplified by a project at the University of Colorado at Boulder, where historical maps were digitized and organized using METS records (Dulock & Cronin, 2009). The team developed file naming conventions, each record was named using the first three letters of the map's city and the last two numbers in the year published, thus the above map of Alamosa from 1890 became ala90.xml (2009). The descriptive metadata section ID is DMDala90, and the administrative rights metadata section ID would be AMDala90 (2009). Individual files and associated technical metadata are referenced similarly (2009). Each file in this two-file map received a File ID, which follow: FILEID="ala90001" FILEID="ala90002" (Colorado Digitization Project, n.d.a). These file pointer IDs are references to the files section of the METS document.

The file section is an "inventory of content files comprising the digital object" and subdivided into individual files specifying locations," usually by URL (McDonough, 2006, p. 149; 2007). That is, the <FLocat> element specifies the location of the individual file of the multipart object. The XML structure of the file section, file group, file with ID, and file location with URL follows:

```
<fileSec>
<fileGrp>
<file ID="MeaningfulID">
<FLocat                                    LOCTYPE="URL"
xlink:href="http://url.com/#MeaningfulID"/>
</file>
</fileGrp>
</fileSec> (2006).
```

The file section for an 1898 map from The Sanborn Fire Insurance Map Collection at Colorado University Digital Library (n.d.b) is a real world example. Multiple files are visible, the <file> element is repeatable:

```
<fileID="ala98001"                    MIMETYPE="image/tiff"
ADMID="TMDala98001">
    <FLocat LOCTYPE="URL"
    xlink:href="http://LibLuna.lib.ad.colorado.edu:8081/BrowserInsight
/BrowserInsight?cmd=start&cid=UCBOULDERCB1-21-
NA&iia=1&gwia=0&id=97622&ir=107746&iwas=2"/>
</file>
    <file       ID="ala98002"         MIMETYPE="image/tiff"
ADMID="TMDala98002">
    <FLocat LOCTYPE="URL"
    xlink:href="http://LibLuna.lib.ad.colorado.edu:8081/BrowserInsight
/BrowserInsight?c
    d=start&cid=UCBOULDERCB1-21
NA&iia=1&gwia=0&id=97641&ir=107747&iwas=2"/>
</file>
```

The administrative section of METS contains subsections for intellectual property of digital object, technical information, and information about the object being digitized and/or information about digitization of the object (2007). The technical metadata section of the administrative metadata may record information in various formats. There are officially METS approved metadata schemas for images and text such as "MIX XML Schema, NISO Technical Metadata for Still Images, and TextMD: Schema for Technical Metadata for Text" (2007, p. 23). Source metadata could include metadata in any form about the original object. Provenance metadata is often encoded in the PREMIS XML schema standard (2007).

METS has been applied to digital libraries for harvesting and preservation of websites such as New York University (McDonough, 2006). That is, METS can be used to "record life-cycle information regarding the curatorial processes to which a particular digital item is subjected" (2006, p. 153). Using either a single, or, preferably, multiple METS documents, information regarding biannual harvesting of the website is recorded in the structural map and/or in individual METS documents, which will contain associated technical and digital preservation administrative metadata (2006).

METS was designed with the goal of flexibility, so it has weak interoperability (McDonough, 2006). Two different METS files describing the same item may not be exactly similar in form and elements, like two different arrangement of a single composition (2006). Yet, this problem can be ameliorated by a METS profile document, which contains specifications for content standards (DACS, AACR2), thesaurus use, file formats, "structural requirements," and "local conventions and best practices" (2006, p. 153). A profile document will enable sharing between institutions that embrace the particular application (2006).

In review, Godby, Young and Childress (2004) write of a synthesis of METS and crosswalks in the form of a digital repository. In this repository, METS records reference metadata crosswalks in the form of extensible style sheets (XSLT) or similar scripts (2004).

Preservation metadata

Preservation information is used to ensure that digital objects are viable, tenderable, and understandable. These terms refer to the bit stream of a digital object, which has to be preserved in a way that it may be delivered in a usable way to computers and a clear way for human understanding. If a computer cannot use the bit stream, which composes a file, then a human has to be able to view the file in order to find errors or create a computer program that will emulate the program used originally. Emulation is necessary when old programs like Atari or Nintendo computer game systems are no longer available or functional for the use of a file. Also, considering that bit streams may decompose or be damaged and data is lost, it would be helpful to have some mechanism to maintain the bit stream. This is the place of preservation metadata. Dulock and Cronin (2009) define the purposes of preservation metadata: "(1) recording provenance information; (2) documenting ownership, rights, and licensing information; (3) providing technical metadata necessary for format migration and future access; and (4) providing technical metadata needed to verify the authenticity and validity of the digital object" (p. 302).

One widely used standard is preservation metadata: implementation strategies (PREMIS). Caplan (2009) stated that components of PREMIS data include inhibitors, provenance, and significant properties:

Inhibitors are defined as any features of an object intended to inhibit access, use, or migration. Inhibitors include password protection and encryption. Digital provenance is the record of the chain of custody and change history of a digital object. Significant properties are characteristics of an object that should be maintained through preservation actions. Any institution creating or acquiring digital materials for a user community should think hard about what features of those materials are important to that community and try to record this information for future use. (2009, p. 6)

The PREMIS data model includes information about digital objects, rights, events and agents of an intellectual entity (Caplan, 2009). The PREMIS data dictionary prescribes the content to be included in each of the component entities of the data model (2009). In the second version of the PREMIS XML schema, each of the data model entities is made to be a container element in XML (Library of Congress, 2008b). Also, PREMIS may be incorporated into METS documents, as is practiced by the British Library's eJournal system (Dappert and Enders, 2008).

The <object> element may contain the following information about a digital object: identifier, checksum, size, file format, name medium, digital signature, inhibitors, provenance, significant properties, and environment (Caplan, 2009). Environment is the context in which a file may be used (2009). Object information may be recorded each time the metadata for the object changes or each time the object changes. As Dappert and Enders (2008) report, this information may be recorded in the digital provenance section of the METS administrative section. The information recorded may be the unique identifier for the object divided into the type of identifier and the actual value of the identifier:

```
<object>
   <objectIdentifier>
      <objectIdentifierType></objectIdentifierType>
      <objectIdentifierValue></objectIdentifierValue>
   </objectIdentifier>
</object> (2008).
```

The <event> element may record a migration by using the same identifier/value process as described above, also included event IDs:

```
<event>
   <eventIdentifier>
      <eventIdentifierType>Type of identifier</eventIdentifierType>
      <eventIdentifierValue>Identifier value</eventIdentifierValue>
   </eventIdentifier>
   <eventType>Migration</eventType>
   <eventDateTime>Date</eventDateTime>
</event> (Caplan, 2009).
```

According to Caplan (2009), "The *Rights entity* aggregates information about rights and permissions that are directly relevant to preserving objects in the repository. Each PREMIS rights statement asserts two things: acts that the repository has a right to perform, and the basis for claiming that right" (3.5 Rights section). The agent section refers to "people, organizations, or software applications" involved in events or rights (2009, 3.4 Agents section).

Educational Metadata

Learning object metadata (LOM)

Learning objects are "any reusable standardized digital educational resource that can be readily adapted and reused to suit a single instructional objective in a variety of contexts" (Rogers, 2009, 2330). Learning object metadata (LOM) is one standard for learning objects. The IEEE Learning Technology Standards Committee (LTSC, 2004) proposed the following purposes involving the use of educational materials:

- To enable learners or instructors to search, evaluate, acquire, and utilize Learning Objects.
- To enable the sharing and exchange of Learning Objects across any technology supported learning systems.
- To enable the development of learning objects in units that can be combined and decomposed in meaningful ways.
- To enable computer agents to automatically and dynamically compose personalized lessons for an individual learner.
- To complement the direct work on standards that is focused on enabling multiple Learning Objects to work together within an open distributed learning environment.

Sharable content object reference model (SCORM)

SCORM was developed by the Advanced Distributed Learning (ADL) Initiative for the purposes of making learning object content interoperable with learning management systems (Zeng & Qin, 2008). There are five books pertaining to the SCORM standard (2008). Besides the overview, the *SCORM Content Aggregation Model* "describes the components used in a learning experience, how to package those components for exchange from system to system, how to describe those components to enable search and discovery and how to define sequencing rules for the components" (2008, p. 51). The *SCORM Run-Time Environment* book details how the content is run, exchanges messages with the LMS, and is displayed to the user (2008). The other two books are *SCORM Sequencing and Navigation* of content and *SCORM Conformance Requirements*.

Metadata for the semantic web

At the foundation of the semantic web are layers of data (Antoniou & Van Harmelen, 2008). These layers are hierarchical and increase in level of abstract logic as one moves up the hierarchy (2008). The stack of data layers consists of Unicode text and URIs, XML, resource description framework (RDF), resource description framework schema (RDFS), and ontologies, which results in the logic layer (2008).

RDF

RDF is most often constituted of XML and provides a *"data model.* Its basic building block is an object-attribute-value triple, called a *statement"* (Antoniou & Van Harmelen, 2008, p. 66). An example statement, Sam is taking ILS 565, has the subject "Sam," the predicate is "is taking," and the object is "ILS 565." Triples are comparable to 3-D, by abstracting the relationship between ILS 565 and student Sam an additional semantic layer is added.

With URIs and namespaces, this model can be expanded greatly. An example of the use of RDF/XML in digital libraries is describing the relationship between an item and an authority record for an author, each will have a URI namespace (Liu, 2007). For example, Yee (2009) has proposed a cataloging model in RDF that is intended to express the relational data model in the functional requirements for bibliographic records. Yee's (2009) model is intended to be digressive, which is "an old term used by bibliographers for bibliographies that provide great detail about first editions and less detail for additions other than the first" (p. 56). Yee developed her own name space, where the class entities and relationship predicate properties are defined (Yee, 2008b). Yee (2008a) offers an example by describing JASIST. First the namespaces and namespace prefixes are declared:

```
<rdf:RDF
xmlns:rdf=http://www.w2.org/TR/rdf-syntax-grammar#
xmlns:rdfs=http://www.w3.org/2000/01/rdf-schema#
xmlns:owl=http://www.w3.org/TR/owl-semantics#
xmlns:ycr=http://myee.bol.ucla.edu/ycrschema/elements/1.0/
xml:base="http://myee.bol.ucla.edu/ycrschema/">
```

One may notice that Yee uses the prefix "ycr" to define her namespace (Liu, 2007). Next, Yee (2008b) introduces the namespace for the resource. The namespace is in the form of a URL URI (2008b). In her example it is this URL: http://myee.bol.ucla.edu/Ex6JASISTwork.rdf (2008b) Yee uses the predicates in her model to state that this URI has the "Language-based Identifier for Work (Preferred Lexical Label) Identified by PrincipalCreator in Combination with Uniform Title" with the value "American Society for Information Science and Technology. Journal of the American Society for Information Science and Technology" (2008b; 2008c). Also, Yee (2008b; 2008c) uses RDF to state that the resource URI has a principal creator with the "Language-based Identifier (Preferred Lexical Label) for Work" with the value "American Society for Information Science and Technology." How this statement is written in RDF follows, one may notice that "ycr" is the prefix for Yee's model property types:

```
<ycr:Resource
rdf:about="http://myee.bol.ucla.edu/Ex6JASISTwork.rdf">
```

```
            <ycr:langidworkpcut>American Society for Information Science and
Technology. Journal of the American Society for Information Science and
Technology.</ycr:langidworkpcut>
            <ycr:keyidwork>W15</ycr:keyidwork>
            <ycr:principalcreator>
            <ycr:langidcorp>American Society for Information Science and
Technology.
            </ycr:langidcorp>
            <ycr:keyidcorp>n0043240</ycr:keyidcorp>
            </ycr:principalcreator>
```

4.5: Ontologies, Classification, Categorization

Ontologies

Another technique used for semantic interoperability is an "ontology," which enables shared conceptual frameworks "across applications for analyzing what entities their data describe" (Bountouri & Gergatsoulis, 2009, p. 102). Ontologies facilitate inter-community exchange and semantic integration of data (Bountouri & Gergatsoulis, 2009). In practice, the ontology employed is very similar to a switching schema, except that a semantic framework is used as opposed to a structural framework.

One example of the use of an ontology for mapping would be CIDOC Conceptual Reference Model (CRM) for collection-level description (Lourdi, Papatheodorou, & Doerr, 2009). This ontology involves entities such as E78 collection, E35 title, E55 type and E30 rights and properties such as P102 has title, P02 has type, and P104 is subject to (2009). Lourdi, Papatheodorou, and Doerr (2009) applied mapping from the Dublin Core Collections Application Profile to CRM and concluded that ontologies "provide rich semantics and therefore should be preferred as mediating schemas among other application profiles."

Application profiles (APs) are the detailed specifications that define a namespace encoded in an XML schema "based on an explicit documentation, endorsed by a specialized community, and registered in conformance to a general metadata standard" (Bountouri & Gergatsoulis, 2009, p. 101). Also, APs may be derived from synthesis or simplification of multiple schemas (2009). AP development "considerations should include the metadata element set, best practices guidelines and data content standards, data value standards, and authority files to be used to create metadata records," concluded the IFLA Working Group based on the survey (Zeng, Lee, & Hayes, 2009, p. 189). Also, they recommend, "specify localized refinements, required encoding syntax rules, and recommended controlled vocabularies. Create or use multiple crosswalks when multiple element sets are involved" (2009, p. 189-190).

RDFS "provides modeling primitives for organizing Web objects into hierarchies. Key primitives are classes and properties, subclass and subproperty relationships, and domain and range restrictions" (Antoniou & Van Harmelen, 2008, p. 18). These hierarchical relationships and concepts are further defined by ontologies.

According to Madalli and Suman (2007),

Ontologies are used to define fundamental concepts, relationships and rules to govern the digital domain... [and] make explicit the implicit relationships that exist among the defined formal description logic concepts while the set of rules or axioms define and constrain the semantics of concepts and relationships in the theory (p. 512).

Madalli and Suman (2007) propose the use of a unified modeling language to support query formulations in digital libraries. Basically, their ontology is based on the very broad concepts of Ranganathan's faceted classification schema: person, matter, energy, space, and time (p. 513). This should enable "decomposing and translating queries expressed in one or more high-level domain into a query plan for specific data sources" (Madalli, & Suman 2007, p. 514).

Lu et. al (2004) describe a digital library for preservation of endangered languages. This project would involve the construction of "a linguistic ontology which would serve as an interlingua for the various linguistic markups used so as to allow searching of diverse material" (2004). However, their project seems controversial because it involves mapping diverse endangered languages to a single integrating ontology (2004). So, it would be interesting to find out if essential meaning is lost in favor of retrieval capabilities (2004).

Metadata classification

As more collections go digital, it becomes increasingly difficult to find good-quality, interoperable metadata schemata, even among different departments of the same research institution. Although MARC remains very popular, particularly among research libraries, Dublin Core, Encoded Archival Description, and the Text Encoding Initiative are gaining ground as new, easier-to-use standards, particularly among non-research institutions. Proprietary metadata—including subject headings and thesauri—that are collection-specific are also gaining popularity among non-research institutions. Jung-ran and Tosaka recommend the Open Archive Initiative, an interoperable framework using Dublin Core standards that allows low-barrier metadata harvesting, to partially address this problem (Jung-ran & Tosaka, 2010).

Specialized metadata classification has both advantages and drawbacks. Authority librarians are working on standard terms that are more respectful of a given culture or social group, e.g., what classification to assign to lesbian/gay/bi/transgendered topics or incorporating Native American naming patterns to name authority files (Chambers & Myall, 2010). However, it's possible for a metadata schema to be so narrow that not only is it not designed to be interoperable with other metadata schemas, but it's not built to any sort of standard beyond the demands of its home domain content and the needs of its immediate users. Proprietary metadata schemas often remain proprietary because their designers lack the resources to make them "good enough" to share for more general use. And such systems lack documentation that would facilitate a retroactive adjustment to a broader standard (Jung-ran & Tosaka, 2010).

4.6: Subject Description, Vocabulary Control, Thesauri and Terminologies

Subject description/ analysis

Taylor and Joudrey define subject description/analysis as a process in the creation of metadata to identify and articulate the subject of the information resource being described. They enumerate three steps in this process:

1. Conceptual analysis to determine what the object is about
2. Written statement on the "aboutness" of the object
3. Assignation of controlled vocabulary/ classification
(Taylor and Juodrey, 2009).

Subject description refers to the assignment of specific subject headings or descriptors in order to fully describe an object's content and to serve in a metadata record as access points in a subject search of a catalog, index, abstracting service or bibliographic database. *Subject headings* are specific terms capturing the essence of a topic of a document (also known as an *index term*, *subject term*, or *descriptor*). Collectively, standardized subject headings constitute a controlled vocabulary for use in bibliographic records. Subject-based information retrieval in the context of digital libraries requires an adequate number of subject descriptors of sufficient quality.

Although some objects may have a single, easily determined subject, other may not be quite so clear, especially those with multi-faceted themes. Other factors that influence the conceptual analysis process are related to with the person performing the analysis (e.g., differences in cultural background, language, and education).

There are different methods in approaching the determination of content of the subject. Two of the most well-known approaches are those of Langridge and Wilson. Langridge's approach states that the cataloger or indexer should keep three basic questions in mind:

1. *What is it?* (Categories of knowledge—e.g., science, history, philosophy, technology, art, etc.)
2. *What is it for?* (Purpose of the object, how it might be used, specific audience, etc.)
3. *What is it about?* (Topic of the object—concepts, places, events, etc.) (Langridge, 1989).

Wilson's approaches are essentially four methods that can be used to understand what an object is about:

1. *Purposive method*: to determine the author's aim or purpose in creating the information resource
2. *Figure-ground method*: to determine a central figure that stands out of the background.
3. *Objective method*: counts references to various items to determine which ones outnumber the others.
4. *Cohesion method*: looks at the unity of the content, what has been included and what has been left out of the content (Wilson, 1968).

Vocabulary control

Natural language searching has serious problems that originate from the nature of language itself. Particularly problematic can be synonyms (different words that mean the same thing), and homographs (a single word that can have different meanings). The existence of synonyms and homographs may result in ambiguity, making it difficult to automatically map a given concept in the searcher's mind to a given string of text (Weinberg, 1998).

According to the American National Standard Institute/ National Information Standard Organization (ANSI/NISO) Guidelines for the Construction, Format, and Management of Monolingual Controlled Vocabularies, vocabulary control is used to improve the efficiency or efficacy of information storage and retrieval systems, Web navigation systems, or any other system that identify and locate content via some sort of description using language. Its main purpose is to achieve consistency in the description of content objects and to facilitate retrieval of that content (NISO, 2006). Vocabulary control has been defined as a list or database of subject terms in which all terms or phrases representing a concept are brought together. Usually one of these terms is designated as the preferred or authorized term (Taylor and Joudrey, 2009).

A *controlled vocabulary* is an authoritative list of terms used in subject indexing that provides a way to organize knowledge for subsequent retrieval. Such lists require the use of predefined, authorized terms that have been preselected by the designer of the controlled vocabulary. Controlled vocabularies are often based on systematic hierarchies of concepts and a variety of relationships defined between concepts. In this way they may be used to control polysemy, synonymy, and homonymy of natural language.

Controlled vocabularies are crucial for classification and subject description of networked information resources generally and digital library services specifically. When properly designed, they ensure consistent indexing across multiple documents, periodical articles, and websites. Types of controlled vocabularies include classification schemas, thesauri, subject heading systems (such as Library of Congress Subject Headings - LCSH), and ontologies. Periodical databases or indexes may use LCSH, but most have their own controlled vocabulary. Databases such as ERIC, PsycInfo, Social Services Abstracts, Sociological Abstracts, Linguistics and Language Behavior Abstracts and MEDLINE have developed very complex controlled vocabulary or thesauri. Vocabulary control can be achieved by three methods: "defining the scope, or meaning, of terms; using the equivalence relationship to link synonymous and nearly synonymous terms; and distinguishing among homographs [single word with different meanings]." (NISO, 2006).

By developing a word list and metadata to describe its equivalent (e.g., Theodore Geisel = Dr. Seuss), hierarchical (e.g., hand tool and screwdriver), and associative (e.g., Melvil Dewey and the Columbia College library school) relationships, this controlled vocabulary facilitates better and more detailed query matching by linking the query terms to the digital index of metadata (Papadakis, 2009). However, the typical OPAC search does not display these relationships in a way that helps the information retrieval process (Schwartz, p. 834). A controlled vocabulary is also essential for semantic interoperability, i.e., metadata for content meaning that follow different schemas (Franklin, 2003).

Subject heading lists

A working definition of subject headings comes from the National Institute of Health: "a system of terms involving definitions, hierarchical structure, and cross-references to index and retrieve a body of literature" (Maggio et al., p. 77). They are a form of vocabulary control, and the quality of their control is a measure of how good the library catalog using them is (Hearn, 2009). Subject heading lists have been created in library communities for years in an attempt to provide subject access to information resources by providing terminology that can be consistent and reliable. Terms in these lists follow structural hierarchies, meaning that they are presented in relation to broader, narrower, and related terms. Subject heading lists tend to be general in scope, covering a broad subject area or the entire scope of knowledge as is the case for the Library of Congress Subject Headings (LCSH) (Taylor and Joudrey, 2009A).

Library of Congress subject headings list (LCSH)

The United States' LCSH list is updated continuously, and a fully updated electronic version is available by subscription through Classification Web (LC Classweb, 2010). LCSH is perhaps the most popular subject-heading schema, with the basic format: *heading – subheading by topic – subheading by location – subheading by time – subheading by form/format.* Many traditional libraries use the LCSH controlled vocabulary of subject headings maintained by United States Library of Congress for use in bibliographic records. Recourse to LCSH offers several advantages for digital library contexts: LCSH is widely used, and thus promotes interoperability between library and/or digital library systems; it has rich vocabulary covering all subject areas and enjoys strong institutional support from LC; it imposes synonym and homograph control; and it has a long, well-documented history.

Use of LCSH persists for digital resources in the 21st century, even though the hierarchical component of the subject headings often doesn't combine well with Boolean query strings (Papadakis, 2009). Searchers typically cherry-pick words and phrases closer to their information needs, with searches successful only if searcher terminology matches terminology of underlying subject headings. A keyword match produced by such searching will still fail to exploit the ability of LCSH to shift from one subject heading to another. Search terms expressed as consecutive terms further suffer from possible polysemy and/or synonymy of words that constitute the search query.

Faceting and folksonomy

Several scholars endorse faceted subject classification to bypass the problems a strict adherence to hierarchical ranking brings to online searches. Faceting is a schema that assigns discipline terms, e.g., *place, time,* or *form*, to a topic and can also apply equally broad categories within each discipline, e.g., *thing, kind, agent,* or *process*. The process continues with arrays, or sub-facets (Broughton,53); the sequence of facet order ranges from the concrete to the abstract. This schema's abstract terms of compartmentalization can be an exercise in philosophical ontology as much as a classification schema, but the same terms may be applied to any field of study.

The Library of Congress has joined OCLC's Faceted Application of Subject Terminology (FAST) project to classify LCSH into facets; OCLC hopes to offer a subject-heading schema that makes LCSH more logical for non-librarian users, but compatible with legacy subject headings (Schwartz, p. 835; Broughton, p. 58). Another way to make LCSH more accessible is to make possible subject heading matches an intermediate step in the query process, instead of obtaining a hit list from a Boolean keyword search. Since we no longer have a subject card from the catalog drawer that contains a "see also" line, Papadakis recommends an analogous brief index of possible subject matches for the user to choose; this intermediate step in the query process offers more options and a potentially larger results list for a given query.

Faceted subject headings may also facilitate both the deep and broad extensibility needed in a subject classification system that will meet the search needs of contemporary users (Franklin, p. 96) as they engage with search queries that cross platforms, databases, and media types that do not have a consistent metadata standard.

Despite its participation in the FAST project, *On the Record* moves the Library of Congress's efforts away from being the keepers of authority records such as LCSH in favor of decentralized, collaborative standards. Professionals such as Thomas Mann are horrified that a central schema of authority control such as LCSH would be left to collect dust in favor of LoC librarians digitizing unique special collections, and adopting a subject classification philosophy closer to folksonomy tagging. However, where will the authority files that support subject headings for those specialized collections come from?

Dragon discusses the problem of proper subject analysis for a special collection of North Carolina postcards. She points out that many proper names from the collection contents are too specialized to have a listing in the LoC Name Authority file, and that the rules to determine a proper name in the absence of an authority file are not easy to use. Under such a circumstance, consistency is possible only from having the same person construct custom subject headings and name standards; collections that are large enough to have more than one authority librarian will have difficulties (Dragon, 2009).

While folksonomy tagging can augment the accessibility of a given tagging collection, it cannot replace traditional subject headings because it has a similar difficulty with consistency. Maggio et al. describe the use of folksonomy tags to teach Generation Y medical students the theory behind the Medical Subject Headings to help them frame efficient MEDLINE queries—and to illustrate folksonomy's limits (Maggio et al., 2009).

The faceted schema discussed in the context of subject headings also applies to the broader question of vocabulary control. A faceted classification schema is an excellent way to build a thesaurus because the facets provide the very interrelationships that are necessary for the effectiveness of a thesaurus. Such a schema also makes it easier for a machine to manipulate and index controlled vocabulary (Broughton, p. 50, 59-60). Faceted vocabulary control can also help a user who does not use good search strategies in his or her queries. Schwartz explains this "guided navigation" in the context of commercial websites that allow you to filter a product search for, e.g., a laptop case by manufacturer, price range, size, etc. with match totals for each filter to help the user in his/her selection (Schwartz, p. 838).

Natural language processing

Natural Language Processing (NLP) is an information retrieval system that can interpret users' information needs as expressed in free text. It also represents the complete range of meaning expressed in documents, and it is able to understand when there is a match between the user's information need and the document(s) that meet it (Rich and Knight, 1991). Natural Language Processing includes keywords, tagging and folksonomies.

Many of the existing social tagging applications have not been designed with information discovery and retrieval in mind. In this context people tend to use tags mainly to organize their documents (Tonkin, 2008). However, end-user natural language tags could cover aspects that are not available in a controlled vocabulary, especially when it comes to new concepts. The combination of tagging and controlled vocabulary seems to increase the quality of information retrieval and user satisfaction. A recent study by Enhancing Tagging for Discovery group (EnTag, http://www.ukoln.ac.uk/projects/enhanced-tagging/) shows the importance of controlled vocabulary suggestions for both indexing and retrieval: to help produce ideas of tags to use, to make it easier to find focus for the tagging, as well as to ensure consistency and increase the number of access points in retrieval (Golub, 2009).

"By understanding a scientist's interests, skills, projects, and activities, intelligent systems can give enhanced outcomes," Sateli et al. found in ScholarLens: Extracting Competencies From Research Publications for the Automatic Generation of Semantic User Profiles (2017, Page 2). It is still impossible to create automatic user profiles. To assess research articles and extract an author's competencies, the authors utilized a natural language processing method. They put it to the test in two user trials with groups of ten and twenty-five scientists. The authors concluded from these research that "the created profiles accurately represent the competencies of scientists." (2017, p.34)

The capacity to construct accurate user profiles automatically by NLP will aid in the creation of increasingly useful recommender systems.

Thesauri, authority control and the Text Encoding Initiative

Thesauri

According to the Encyclopedia Britannica, "the assembling of words into groups related by some principle, as by their meanings, can be done, and such a work is often called a thesaurus or synonymy" (thesaurus, 2010). Thesauri and bounded vocabularies are a form of authority control; they direct a user to a restricted list of terms to help sift through a collection to yield relevant results efficiently and consistently.

In information technology, the term *thesaurus* refers a controlled vocabulary following a standard structure, where all terms have relationships to each other and existing relationships between concepts are made explicit. The thesaurus is powerful in terms of organizing and searching large bodies of online information such as databases. It can be used to generate a standard set of headings and cross-references and may be available in printed form, online, or both. Such a tool enables users to locate Broader Terms (BT) and Related Terms (RT) if they wish to expand retrieval, or Narrower Terms (NT) to make a search statement more specific. In digital library contexts, thesauri may be useful in bridging the gap between metadata provided by the indexer and concepts presented by the searcher.

The High Level Thesaurus Project (HLIT)

HLTP (http://hilt.cdlr.strath.ac.uk/Sources/index.html) is a clearinghouse of information about controlled vocabularies, including related resources, projects, and an alphabetical list of thesauri. Some organizations maintain suites of thesauri for use within specific domains. Here are some examples:

The Getty Vocabulary Program
GVP
(http://www.getty.edu/research/conducting_research/vocabularies/aat/) is a thesauri for the visual arts, architecture, and material culture. It is known as The Art & Architecture Thesaurus (AAT) and is also available in Spanish (http://www.aatespanol.cl/) and Dutch (http://www.aat-ned.nl/).

MDA, terminology bank
MDA (http://www.mda.org.uk/spectrum-terminology/termbank.htm) is formerly known as the Museum Documentation Association, this thesaurus was conceived for museum objects, and includes vocabularies for describing archaeological objects, waterways, railways, costumes, and aircraft types.

Library of Congress authorities
LC authorities (http://authorities.loc.gov/) are authority files for bibliographic description, including a controlled list of subject headings, authorized forms of personal and corporate names, titles, and name/title headings. Authority files are used for authority control, which will be discussed below.

ICONCLASS
ICONCLASS (http://www.iconclass.nl/) is a classification system for describing the narrative and iconographic content of works of art and other visual materials. The master version is in English with translations into German, Italian, French, etc.

Simple knowledge organization system (SKOS)

One such thesauri-related system with potential application to LCSH used in digital library contexts is ONKI-SKOS. This system offers a uniform approach to accessing thesauri represented as Simple Knowledge Organization System (SKOS) vocabularies. Its user interface provides an auto-suggest function acting as an entry point for the entire thesauri-based information retrieval process. The hyperlink-based interface allows users to traverse the thesaurus as well as browse, search, and visualize vocabulary conforming to SKOS specifications (Papadakis et al., 2009).

Further improvements of vocabulary control in the current digital environment include better thesauri tools that can navigate between a user's customary query terms and multiple collections using different controlled vocabulary lists. However, Franklin points out the challenge of obtaining maximum interoperability between controlled vocabulary lists without sacrificing too much accuracy or precision in semantic mapping. It can be challenging to combine diverging thesauri (Franklin, 2003). Another improvement to thesauri involves using the semantic web to enhance resource descriptions to be searchable by concept rather than keyword; special thesauri would sort through Uniform Resources Identifiers and make inferences (Morales-del-Castillo et al., 2009). It may be eventually possible to generate useful thesauri semi-automatically.

Authority control

Authority control is a way to set labeling parameters to names and subjects to enable a user to find a larger number of matches to a given inquiry. When studying *Huckleberry Finn*, does a scholar need to look up both Samuel Clemens and Mark Twain? What is the correct spelling of the name of Libya's most famous contemporary leader: Quaddafi? Khadafy? Gaddafi? Authority control links authority records to bibliographic records to facilitate automatic file maintenance. Authority control is also a way to document cataloguing decisions that can be referred to at a later date (Dragon, 2009).

The single current topic of authority control that continues to make waves among the profession is the Library of Congress Working Group on the Future of Bibliographic Control's 2008 report that recommends the LoC no longer maintain serial authority files (LOC, 2008c). The report argues that bibliographic control is becoming decentralized, collaborative, and dynamic. While few would claim that library OPACS are the starting point of choice for online queries in this age of Google, it is disconcerting to read about the Vatican of American libraries planning to put more resources to digitizing special collections instead of maintaining authority control. Even the LoC's work on Resource Description and Access (RDA) and Functional Requirements for Bibliographic Records (FRBR. Chambers and Myall complain that RDA is moving too far towards Dublin Core and other web metadata "boogie-woogie Google boys." However, Roeder points out that traditionalists who are too set in their ways to discuss topics of interest to the Web 2.0 gurus will not be given an opportunity to offer the benefit of their experience as new standards get hashed out (Roeder, 2010).

The Text Encoding Initiative (TEI)

The text encoding initiative (TEI) "is an encoding standard for describing the physical and logical structure of textual material for the purposes of research analysis and data interchange" (Liu, 2007, p. 89). TEI is used in small institutions, such as for the authentic "historical texts" at Case Western Reserve University (CWRU) (Wisneski & Dressler, 2009, p. 266), in world-class projects at large universities such as Virginia Tech's "Paper's of George Washington: Digital edition" (Stertzer, J., 2010), and even in "an immense and searchable full-text literary corpus" such as Metadata Offer New Knowledge (Zillig, 2009, p. 187). TEI used in digital projects may be the basis of authority work, and TEI is grounded in standards for encoding and digitization.

The foundation of all text encoding is the actual encoding of the text. Fox (2008) writes,

"Unicode is the bedrock of all metadata in modern digital library applications.... Three of the primary design goals of the Unicode standard were to ensure that the encoding was universal, meaning that it is large enough to encompass all characters that will likely every [sic] be used; efficient meaning that it is easy for computer programs to parse; and unambiguous, meaning that a given Unicode point always and everywhere represents exactly the same character" (p. 140, 142).

Texts in XML TEI format have UTF-8 encoding as a default. There are two sections of a TEI document: the header and the text section, which includes "the bulk of the text itself... divided into front matter, body, and back matter" (Liu, 2007, p. 90). The TEI header resembles a MARC record and is based on the International Standards for Bibliographic Description (ISBD) (Liu, 2007; Wisneski & Dressler, 2009). Also, it contains administrative, structural, technical, and preservation metadata (Wisneski & Dressler, 2009).

TEI texts may be encoded at different levels from the fully automatic encoding of Level 1 through scholarly encoding of level 5 (TEI, 2010). "Texts encoding in P5, levels 4 and 5, involve structural mark up and attention to a text's specific textual nuances; texts are meant to stand independent of page images and allow for sophisticated search and retrieval" (Wisneski & Dressler, 2009 p. 270).

TEI may also be used for display by XSLT conversion to HTML for web publishing. This transformation may be applied to create tables of contents and indexes. Also, the analytical capabilities of TEI level 5 vocabulary may be put into a database (Tuohy, 2007). For example, the MONK project is intended "to create a new literary text corpus for the purpose of undertaking text analysis work" (Pytlik Zillig, 2009). In this case, TEI "markup for data structures useful in common analytical tasks (e.g. part-of-speech tags, lemmatizations, word tokens, and sentence markers)" is put into a relational database for the purposes of "data mining, principle component analysis, word frequency study, and n-gram analysis" (2009, p. 189). Similarly, Ulmin (2010) is attempting to extract geographic metadata from TEI encoded "nineteenth-century American manuscript travel journals, letters, and other... papers" to explore "a wealth of contextual information (references to countries, cities, regions, ships, landmarks, works of art, notable people, and so on)" (Ulman, 2010).

Tuohy (2007) describes the use of TEI in databases to create topic map ontologies based on XML Topic Maps (XTM). Their topic map consisted of TEI structural elements of the text, names of creators and those people in the text, and other bibliographic elements in the header (2007). Each topic is mapped by association; the main nodes used were "books, pictures, people, and places." The resulting topic map had some 50,000 nodes (Tuohy, 2007).

Terminologies in DL contexts

Terminology (also known as *nomenclature*) refers to the system of terms belonging to any science or subject. Controlled vocabularies such as LCSH are broadly adopted for conventional resources, but specific subjects or domains of activity may require comparatively small vocabularies tailored to their resources or users. Smaller than LCSH (though still quite sizeable), for example, is Medical Subject Headings (MeSH), a comprehensive controlled vocabulary used for indexing books and journal articles in the life sciences; also serves as a thesaurus that facilitates searching. A practical feature of the Dublin Core metadata set for such domains is its inherent extensibility, which allows for terminological enhancements by specific user communities, such as those using *Darwin Core* (q.v.).

Conclusion

Knowledge organization lacks a clear direction, much as the profession lacks effective, broadly applied metadata standards for the 21st century. Tensions between traditional catalogers and "Boogie Woogie Google Boys" makes it harder to achieve consensus in schemas that take advantage of, and effectively organize digital content to meet modern research needs. Organizational frameworks such as OAI and faceting offer some promise, but many digital collections are proprietary metadata islands that cannot interact with any others. We need metadata standards that benefit from the profession's bibliographic and cataloguing experience, but are flexible and extensible enough to be of use for the casual query of Google keywords.

As is evident from the many different types of metadata that can be utilized to define data, determining what your digital library collection is going to be made up of, who the end users will be, and what would be the most appropriate type of metadata to utilize to describe the resources, will make an enormous difference in the usability of your digital library. All of this information will lead into the next topic – searching the digital library in which all of the metadata choices will be critical in how easily a user is able to search this library.

Visually, organization of the digital library is typically enhanced by the use of subject headings that allow users the ability to see all the different topics that the digital library has to offer as well as understand the underlying organization of the digital library. Sidebars, main topics and subtopics all increase the usability of the digital library and will help keep the information better organized. Any way that the information can be organized and the layout of the digital library can be organized to make the user experience better will be paramount to a good digital library. Digital libraries are quickly becoming a more common occurrence and learning how to organize them in such a way that information is easily found will differentiate one digital library from another.

Study questions for Chapter Four:

1. How can we make an intellectual organization of a digital library? What are the basic methods that people have used to organize and arrange knowledge, with the idea of making searching possible, simple, effective and powerful?
2. There are a number of metadata schemas used for description of digital resources, such as TEI (Text Encoding Initiative)-the Electronic Text Center Introduction to TEI and Guide to Document Preparation, EAD (Encoded Archival Description), VRACC (Visual Resources Association Core Categories), and GILS (Global Information Locator Service/Government Information Locator Service). What are the basic metadata schemas used in digital libraries? Can you find their official websites? What are their significances to DLs? Are there any other schemas that you have come across that are important to DLs?
3. Find latest review on metadata strategies specifically for multimedia collections?
4. In her article Systems of Knowledge Organization for Digital Libraries, Gail Hodge describes the evolution of abstracting and indexing (A&I) services, saying that for many years they were "applied only by catalogers and indexers trained in using the KOS indexing for a particular product or products. The primary users of KOSs [knowledge information systems] were librarians and other professional searchers (p. 14). She notes that the "proliferation of electronic data, the explosion of

electronic publishing, and increasing concerns about the difficulty of locating information" has led to a renewed interest in these by professionals and also end users. With so many types of KOS--authority files, relationship lists, ontologies, etc.--how do we determine what is right for our digital library? Is the patron part of the process or just a recipient of the result?

Chapter Five: Technologies and Architecture

One of the primary differences between a digital library and a traditional library is the use of cyberspace and cybertechnology. Whereas a traditional library is a physical building, a digital library is founded on the Internet. Therefore, we must learn Internet technology in order to understand the new generation of libraries.

Technologies related to the construction of digital libraries include but are not limited to the following: architecture, system integration, interconnectivity and interoperability, cooperative and collaborative efforts, federated search and/or cross-sites or multiple database searching capabilities.

Before discussing architecture, one may ask several questions, including: what are the problems in merging systems? What are some of the more exciting developments? What are the basic technologies that are used for the construction of digital libraries and what are their functionalities? In answering these questions we consider non-uniform query languages, Web-based collaborative library research, complex information environments, and system interoperability.

5.1: What are the problems in merging systems?

Merging results

Voorhees and Tong (1997) explore the need for a single cohesive search across multiple databases, which can accommodate a wide range of topics, diverse vocabularies, and differences in depth of coverage. Ideally, this search system will combine the results of these multiple independent searches into a single, cohesive response. The most effective means of doing this is termed *database merging* or *metasearching* (Voorhees &Tong, 1997). The need for metasearching is exemplified by the following problem: If five databases are searched, each database might rank the order by the probable relevance of each retrieved item to the search query. However, the most relevant document in one database could be of low relevance compared to all five databases together; therefore, the items of all five databases need to be rank-ordered against each other for probable relevance to the search query. The use of a metasearch engine would alleviate that problem by ranking each search engine's results relative to the other engines' results.

One approach is to use published metadata, the information and statistics on each database (such as range of topics, depth of coverage, or probability of relevance). The problem with this approach is the user does not entirely control the search and the work is completed at the server end. One solution is to use agents that collect the history of user behavior (historical metadata of the long-term, stable information needs of the user and relevance patterns of prior retrieved documents). The benefit of an agent-assisted approach is that the system does not impose a cost to the user; rather, the agent is supported at the user end. Certainly, this is an area of high interest in research and development.

Non-uniform query languages

Chang and Garcia-Molina (1997) are concerned with non-uniform query languages, which make searching over heterogeneous information sources difficult. Their solution is to allow the user to compose Boolean queries in one rich front-end language, which then transforms the user query into a subsuming query that is submitted to the information source. As this method may retrieve more documents than are relevant to the original query, the results are then processed by a filter query before being displayed to the user. The problem with this two-process solution is that the costs of post-filtering may be significant. Another problem is that what the filter thinks the user is looking for could be completely wrong. Then the user, not being proficient enough to come up with an 'acceptable' term for the query, probably isn't proficient enough to A) realize that their query was filtered and B) how to resolve the problem.

This research evaluates the acceptability of the cost of this methodology.

There are meta-searchers on the Internet that share the goals of Chang and Garcia-Molina. Some of these are *SavvySearch*, accessible at http://www.savvysearch.com, and *Meta-Crawler*, now known as CNET Search.com, accessible at http://www.search.com. However, these meta-searchers are only slightly more powerful than the least common denominator supported by the sources they search (Chang & Garcia-Molina, 1997).

5.2: The more exciting developments

DLITE

One of the earliest developments in search is Digital Library Integrated Task Environment (DLITE) by Cousins, Paepcke, Winograd, Bier, and Pier (1997) of Stanford and Xerox PARC. DLITE is a digital library interface that provides a fully customizable work environment for users. DLITE offers something called workcenters; loosely comparable to work areas such as a kitchen or a hobby room, workcenters contain tools needed to accomplish a given task. The tools are represented as icons and are utilized through a drag-and-drop manipulation. For example, the user selects the icon for the bibliography-creation workcenter. In the create-query dialogue box, the user enters a topic. This causes a query icon to appear on the screen. The query icon can now be dragged to and dropped into the icon for the databases to be searched. The results are returned in separate documents for each search service. By dragging the various documents to a common folder, the results are merged. By dragging this result to another icon, the retrieved results will be formatted into a bibliography that can be appended to a paper or saved as a personal collection through which future written work can be passed to locate the complete bibliographic reference for citations within the work.

All workcenters contain five components: documents, collections, queries, services, and representations of people. *Documents* can be anything from a simple citation to a complex entity with hundreds of information fields and text and graphics documents uploaded from the user's local disks. *Collections* are containers for other components, such as documents, which seem to retain a memory of the activity that retrieved the contents. In the case of a database search, this would allow the user to reactivate the search to add additional references to those already found. *Queries* are expressions of the user's information need. Queries can range from simple lists of keywords to complex Boolean search strategies. One of the services available through the workcenter is a query translator that interprets a query into the form needed for various databases. Queries can be stored for reuse and sharing with other users. *Services*, available through the component termed the *InfoBus,* include summarization facilities, optical character recognition, query expansion, format translation, and bibliography processing. *Representations of people* (icons) are components that manage access control, communications, payments, and authorizations and which contain the information necessary to execute management tasks. For example, when a user logs on, an icon appears. Contained in the icon is information about that user, which will be passed on to the vendor as charges are incurred during an online search.

Documents in the DLITE environment do not necessarily represent digital materials. DLITE documents may also represent, through an abstract, bibliographic record, materials that exist on paper, film, etc. We would expect, in these cases, for as much information to be presented to the user as is available on gaining access to the materials.

As DLITE is being designed to work across the Internet, its developers have leveraged web browsers, such as Chrome, as a space to process and display retrieved documents. From there, documents can be transferred to a disk and word processing application.

While DLITE appears to be a technology that will please users, insofar as its mechanisms go, the graphic component may leave something to be desired. The picto-cabulary used in DLITE does not seem to be intuitive and seems to lack the camaraderie of the component-mechanisms. While impressive, this piece of work is in need of an equally impressive interface designer.

Web-based collaborative library research

Robertson, Jitan and Reese (1997) report on a design for web-based collaborative library research. A corporate research library has moved many of its resources and services to the organization's intranet. This library conducts information searches and research analyses for employees of the organization. The described web-based system makes library research activities highly visible and collects usage statistics as a background activity for purposes of billing and research visibility. As a research request is submitted, it generates its own interactive web page through which researchers and clients chat, share files, manage their activities, provide feedback, and learn about each other. Automatic listing and indexing of research requests (generated from collected statistics) are viewable, permitting possible future formation of interest communities who share common research interests.

Robertson et al. (1997) point out that while the major perceived advantage of digitization is to find information, observations of work that occurs in libraries show that interaction and collaboration are central to information-gathering. Research shows that library users intermingle their various activities (social, technical, data-gathering, analytic) while working in the library. From these observations emerge a new vision of technology bringing together otherwise dispersed knowledge workers for the sharing of knowledge and special expertise in an asynchronous collaborative workspace.

In this system, each client has a homepage that is generated when a new client enters the system. The client's homepage contains links to initiate a research request, view pending and archived research requests, view statistics about their own usage of research services, as well as a link to the group page of the client's business unit within the organization. There is also a "mailto" link that permits email to be sent to the client without having to know the particulars of the email address.

When the client selects the initiate-a-research-request link, a new request form--a webpage customized to the client--appears, and the client types in a description of his or her information need. The information-request webpage serves as a recording tool for all interactions between the client and the researchers regarding this information research request. The research request records a request number, date received, date needed, status of request, billing time, client's name and group, and assigned researcher's name. The page is divided into sections: *Comments* by the client, the researcher, or other employees who know of relevant sources; *Actions* of the researcher and billing time spent; and *Files*, consisting of hotlinks to digital copies with notations on source, topic covered, copyright and permissions.

Each researcher also has a personal page, allowing each to have a "sense of 'place'" on the web. Personal information on the researcher and on the client is carried automatically from the personal page to each action page created from the personal page. The system has many automated management and clerical functions and is an outstanding example of how technology can, at a relatively low-tech-user entry, greatly benefit and enhance the research function in an organization.

5.3: What are the workflows and processes of digital library software?

There are a number of questions that need to be considered when developing a digital library:
- What basic digital libraries' workflows and processes need to be considered during development?
- What are the basic software needs of digital libraries?
- How to determine the DL architecture and use of the software features?
- What open source software options are available?
- What are current development issues and trends for DL software?

There are various application areas that contribute to the construction of digital libraries:
- Knowledge management/content management, including managing and accessing internal/external information assets
- Archiving and preservation, including cultural, heritage, historical, special collections, local records, archives, and objects that need to be preserved in digital format
- System operation and management
- Copyright and legal issues, including intellectual properties and security issues

The following work flows and processes should be considered while constructing a digital library:
- Content selection
- Content acquisition
- Metadata description
- Content publishing
- Content uploading
- Content indexing & storage
- Content access & delivery
- Preservation
- Content management
- Usage monitoring and evaluation
- Networking and interoperation
- Maintenance

Although questions associated with these workflows of DL construction are based on the needs of individuals, there are some common questions that challenge software designers:
Content Selections:

- What are the different document types?
- What varieties of content will constitute the DL, such as internal/external, free/commercial, owned/licensed, print/electronic formats?
- Why? - Utility for today and tomorrow
- Who is going to use it? Internal vs. external, or both? How many?
- How will they use it? How frequently? Free vs. paid. Technology they need.
- Content volumes today and tomorrow
- Document types, for example: publications (books, journal articles, conference papers, technology reports, or progress reports), e-mail archives, news, policies and plan documents, drawings, software, press releases, presentations, courseware, lectures, best practices, etc.
- Document formats: HTML, Text, PDF, audio, video, PPT, multimedia presentations
- Multilingual content

Content Acquisition:
- How is the content of the DL acquired and loaded?
- Central vs. distributed?
- Already in digital form vs. to be converted to digital??
- To be converted?
- Conversion and conversion processes?
- Online & offline content acquisition?

Metadata Description:
- What metadata schema should be used?

Content Publishing:
- Content description (metadata) including
  - Objective description (author, title)
  - Administrative (date/time created, content life)
  - Subject categorization, indexing (manual or automatic?)
- Content tagging/ markup (full-text, XML, SGML)
- Uploading of metadata and e-documents to the DL such as central vs. distributed
- Content quality control

Content Uploading:
- Different document storage formats

Content Indexing and Storage:
- Index element extraction and updates of indexes (metadata and full-text)
- Metadata and e-document storage
- Physical organization of content in the DL Server

- o Databases, indexes, folders for efficient storage, search and retrieval
- o Compressed storage
- Automatic metadata extraction
- Indexing and data compression
- Efficient storage and search for metadata and document objects

Content Access and Delivery:
- Structured search (metadata-driven)
- Object search (full-text, multi-media object search)
- Global search and resource type search (e.g., bib database, e-journals, reports, experts)
- Multilingual support
- Structured presentation (display)
- Hierarchical browsing (subject schemes/ topic directory)
- Relevance ranking, hit/link based ranking
- Search refinement, search history, search set combination
- Personalization, customization
- Browse, hierarchical browsing
- CD-ROM distribution

Content Management:
- Access control for owned/licensed content
  - o User identification and password management
  - o Proxy/IP authentication management
  - o Unauthorized access
  - o License metering
  - o Management of access by mobile staff, branch staff, home-based users (off-campus)
- Content security
  - o Object identification
  - o Ownership establishment

Usage Monitoring and Evaluation:
- How do we know what digital sources are being used (and not used)? How much they are being used? And by whom?
- How is our system performing?
- How do we evaluate digital library and information services? Variables and measures

Networking and Interoperation:
- How do we network with other similar services?
- Standards compliance (XML, Dublin Core, Unicode)
- How do different digital information services inter-operate, exchange information and help users to find information
- Options: search/retrieval protocol standardization (e.g., Z39.50)
- Metadata harvesting (e.g., OAI)

- How do we federate access to different collections across the enterprise?
- Information portals (e.g., SciGate, SABIO)

Preservation:
- How to make an object unique, object identification
- How do we ensure perpetuity and long-term access through time and changing technologies?
- What do we want to preserve? Links internal and external
- Bits storage obsolescence (e.g. pits on CD-ROM) such as document formats and software for display and print
- Strategies such as
    o Bits replication (copying to new storage) CD-ROM
    o Link validators or link checkers, standards for persistent and unique object identification, digital object identifier (DOI), OpenURL
    o Document formats such as migration moving to new version of the software/ format (loss of data?), or use of TIFF format for archiving, or use of standard formats SGML, or XML
    o Software: Emulators.
- Content refreshment/migration plan such as monitoring of content due for refreshment and maintenance of support tools for refreshing and reading software
- Proven (additional) preservation media: such as acid-free paper, microfilm and photographic reproduction

5.4: What are the key technologies used in the construction of digital libraries?

One of the major tasks of developing a digital library is integrating and interoperating digital information.

Technologies used in building a digital library center on these areas: digitizing, storing or archiving, capturing, describing, organizing, designing, displaying, accessing, navigating, servicing, translating, managing, integrating, customizing, securing, preserving, and maintaining digital files/electronic sources. Classifying these technologies is a challenge, not only do some technologies overlap, but also the constant development of the software market and the concept of digital library organization and services. Below are some examples of the technologies.

Digitization and Archive Technologies

Digitization Technology

It includes text and image digitizing, sound and multimedia digital recording.

OCR (optical character recognition) technology

Utilizing the Adobe Acrobat Distiller program or PDF 95 or others to create a pdf, or creates an Adobe PDF Online document from a doc or htm file Adobe Acrobat Distiller program.

Utilizing a digital camera or camcorder to create a jpg, tiff, gif, or bmp file, with Adobe Photoshop, MGI PhotoSuite, ArcSoft PhotoStudio, Print Master or others.

Utilizing a scanner including printer/scanner/fax all-in-one to create a text and/or image file with the hardware genetic software or Publisher XP, PrecisionScan, and photo and imaging software.

Sound recognition technology

Utilizing a microphone with sound recording software to create a wav file, and then plays it with a speaker.

Video/Multimedia recording technology

Utilizing a video camera to create an mpeg, mov, or mp4 file, and then plays it with QuickTime, Window Media Player, iTunes or iMovie.

S-Picview: a software program allows users to preview, edit, and view images. http://www.yukudr.com/.

ABBYY FineReader 6.0, an optical character reader software package:http://www.abbyy.com/ocr_products.asp?param=1615

WinOcris a fast and highly accurate Optical Character Recognition (OCR) system:http://www.expervision.com/webtr6.htm

Converting technology

Music converters. Convert from optical to digital; or convert from analog to digital. DBpowerAMP Music Converter is a freeware software package that converts files from .wav to .mp3.

Storing or Archiving Tools

EPrints Archive Software (EAS) evolved from the practice of authors e-mailing pre-prints of their papers to peers for informal feedback. It was popularized through arXiv.org, started at Los Alamos in 1991 – the granddaddy of Eprint servers. EPrints is a free GNU General Purpose License (GPL) archive software developed at the E&CS Department of the University of Southampton. The primary goal of EPrints is to set up and maintain institutional eprint archives and facilitate free Internet access to research publications, as well as improve the visibility and impact of research results. It can be used for setting up an online repository of institutional publications.

EPrints provides a web interface for managing, submitting, discovering, and downloading documents. It supports several document types (books, conference papers, technical reports, etc.) and document formats (PS, HTML, etc.). It allows for quality control of submissions, and has strong OAI compliance, facilitating access to the content of worldwide eprint archives. Its current version is 3.0. Available from: www.eprints.org. One example is at http://eprints.iisc.ac.in. Its setup uses eprints.org Eprints Archive Software, and integrates Greenstone Digital Library Software (GSDL) for full text searching.

Pears Database Software PEARS (OCLC) – (www.oclc.org/research/software/pears/) The Pears Open Source software (OSS) project offers software that implements a Pears database layer. Pears databases have features that make them ideal for storing hierarchically structured data, such as bibliographic records, authority records and text documents. The software includes a stand-alone program to build a Pears database.

Resources description or organization technology

The entire total of man-made devices or established procedures that alter, refine, or create new commodities and services offered by companies is referred to as organizational technology. Electronics, software, papers, new methodologies, or any combination of these are all employed in service delivery. (Neuby, 2016)

Knowledge points are used to organize knowledge resources, making it easier to acquire, share, distribute, and visit information. Traditional tree structures, on the other hand, lack the ability to describe overall relationships and are inconvenient for searching for knowledge resources and positioning in distant situations. The Semantic Web is a tool that can explain complicated relationships between ontologies in great detail, as well as natural properties of distributed systems. The generic semantic Web, on the other hand, is not built around knowledge points. In this study, the semantic Web is developed so that it may be used to define knowledge points-based knowledge resources. (Sorge, 1991)

In recent years, the issue of information sharing in e-learning has gotten a lot of attention. It covers a wide range of topics, such as information integration and ontologies. One of the research projects proposes a semantic integration strategy to solving the problem of information sharing. The semantic annotated knowledge resource is created after an ontology-based knowledge organization model is constructed to improve the traditional information resource model. In addition, the semantic mapping findings are used to mediate the ontology defined resources. (Li & Wu (2009)

Encoded Archival Descriptions EAD

EAD Official Web Site: http://lcweb.loc.gov/ead/ has provided the archive community with a metadata standard appropriate for describing their collections (Bekaert, 2002). Implementation of harvesting protocols like the Open Archives Initiative – Protocol for Metadata Harvesting (OAI-PMH) would allow EAD finding aids to be searched using one interface, providing users with increased access to information.

EAD at Virginia: http://www.lib.virginia.edu/vhp/
EAD Official Web Site: http://lcweb.loc.gov/ead/

METS

Metadata Encoding and Transmission Standards (METS) is the brainchild of the Digital Library Federation (Cover Pages Technology Reports, 2005) and is maintained by the Network Development and MARC Standards Office of the Library of Congress. Its official webpage is located at http://www.loc.gov/standards/mets/. It designed to encode metadata for electronic texts, still images, digitized video, sound files and other digital materials within electronic library collections. It attempts to address the lack of standardization in digital library metadata practices that currently inhibits the growth of coherent digital collections (Gartner, 2002).

Markup languages

SGML. Virginia: http://etext.lib.virginia.edu/sgml.html. The SGML/XML Web Page, by Robin Cover: http://www.oasis-open.org/cover/sgml-xml.html

HTML. World Wide Web Consortium: http://www.w3.org/. HTML Introduction: http://www.w3schools.com/html/html_intro.asp

XML. Extensible Markup Language (XML) (https://www.w3.org/XML/) is a standard becoming widely spread throughout the library system, first published in 1998

XML.COM is a rich source of articles and other features about XML. http://www.arbortext.com/Think_Tank/XML_Resources/xml_resources.html

The SGML/XML Web Page, by Robin Cover: http://www.oasis-open.org/cover/sgml-xml.html

Xmetal (XML tool): http://www.sq.com/
NoteTab is a text and HTML editor: http://www.notetab.com/
XML SPY http://www.xmlspy.com/

XSL was made available by the World Wide Web Consortium (WC3) a governing body for the web that recommends methods for those producing content and tools for the web to code material.

Digital Libraries in Theory and Practices

Translating tools

Online language translation tools.
Xanadu – language translation tool http://www.foreignword.com
AltaVista Babel Fish-an online translation tool, http://babelfish.altavista.com

Internet Technologies

Interface designing technology tools, e.g. Common Gateway Interface

OntoNO is a Natural Language Interface Generator to Knowledge Repositories. Stavros (2006) describes the goal of this tool: to offer principles, approaches, and software to help automate the building of natural language interfaces to depositories of knowledge. Included in these interfaces are the abilities for pronouncement and management of new knowledge, in addition to querying, filtering, and ontology-spurred interaction formulation (Stavros, 2006). One great advantage of this is that a single architecture can handle syntactic and semantic ambiguities, can control ambiguity at both a domain specific and a general level, and can check the profiles of the various users in order to personalize the disambiguation. OntoNo can do a syntactic analysis of different types of sentences and word ontologies (Stavros, 2006). It would seem as though this technology would alleviate much of the concern associated with the syntactic and semantic ambiguity of queries.

Displaying tools

Accessing including searching, browsing, retrieving software, such as federated search tools, local search tools, intelligent search engines.
Intelligent Search Engine: Intelligent search engines provide search service of all the web information within IBM's Center for Advanced Studies (CAS), covering all the websites of CAS institutes, searching and indexing them periodically, to help users access information in websites of CAS institutional websites (including libraries). At the same time, it will trace authoritative websites of particular academic institutes, to help users discover the latest developments and hot spots.

Navigating

Including linking systems, such as openURL, Uniform Resource Name (URN), Digital Object Identifier (DOI), and Information Portals (e.g., SciGate, SABIO).
OpenURL linking system: Based on the OpenURL standard, to integrate all the full-text databases, abstracts databases, citation databases,

union catalog databases, ILL and document delivery, and virtual reference service, to support integrated access to multiple sources of information.

Integrating and operating software/systems and platforms

DSpace is a digital library system for converting resources into digital formats, electronically publishing academic journals, monographs and other forms of academic communication and data creation and providing for preservation of digital content over time. DSpace's operating systems: Cygwin (MS Windows), all POSIX (Linux/BSD/UNIX-like OSes). It is available under the BSD open source license for research institutions to run as-is, or to modify and extend as needed. It uses postgreSQL relational database. The latest version is available for download at http://sourceforge.net/projects/dspace/

Greenstone Digital Library Software is a comprehensive open-source software for constructing and distributing digital library collections. It supports Internet, intranets and optical media based collections, and was developed by the New Zealand Digital Library Project at http://www.nzdl.org/. It is distributed in co-operation with UNESCO and Humanities Library Project, version: 2.38, and is available from: www.greenstone.org. Key features include:

- Ease of installation and use
    - Web and command mode
- Collection building and configuration
    - Variety of document formats (PS, PPT, Word, PDF, etc.)
    - Internet, local content
- Indexing and storage
    - Automatic metadata extraction, format conversion to XML/HTML
    - Compressed storage
- Collection browse and search
    - Full text, Boolean, metadata
- Access and delivery
    - Internet, CD-ROM
- Collection administration
    - Usage monitoring, security
- Support for Unicode and Dublin Core
- Z39.50 and OAI compliance

Omeka **is** a free, flexible, and open source web-publishing platform for the display of library, museum, archives, and scholarly collections and exhibitions. It uses an unqualified Dublin Coremetadata standard. Completely web-based, it allows users to publish cultural heritage objects, extend its functionality with themes and plugins, and curate online exhibits with digital objects. It is a light-weight solution in comparison to a traditional institutional repository software like DSpace. Omeka is a project of the Roy Rosenzweig Center for History and New Media, George Mason University. Available from: http://omeka.org/

DLXS (The University of Michigan Digital Library eXtension Service) http://www.dlxs.org/

Dienst is a system for configuring a set of individual services running on distributed servers to cooperate in providing the services of a digital library. http://www.cs.cornell.edu/cdlrg/dienst/DienstOverview.htm

CONTENTdm is a software suite used to help create a digital library project, http://contentdm.com

IBM Digital Library is an earlier software for libraries. http://www-3.ibm.com/software/is/dig-lib/

DigiTool (The Digital Library Tool Kit) includes all the tools required for building and managing digital collections and as such constitutes a major component of an overall digital strategy. http://www.aleph.co.il/dtl/

DELOS is developed for a Prototype Peer-to-Peer (P2P) DL Network. A P2P Digital library is able to balance the autonomy and decentralized data organization that P2P architecture will grant (Christophides, 2006). It would seem as though this type of service would be quite useful today, when P2P presents different issues in terms of accessibility.

LionShare P2P is a technology to facilitate legitimacy among institutions around the world through the use of authenticated Peer-to-Peer networking. Designed for the exchange of academic, personal and work-related materials on an officially sanctioned and secure P2P network among participating groups and institutions globally, LionShare employs an authentication/trust model between institutions that allows an authenticated P2P network user at one institution to search and access resources at other participating institutions.

Fedora, or Flexible Extensible Digital Object Repository Architecture, is a repository system and an open source, a digital object repository system using public application programming interfaces (APIs)exposed as web services. The Fedora repository system consists of three layers: the Web Services Exposure Layer, the Core Subsystem Layer, and the Storage Layer. The Web Services Exposure Layer is comprised of three related web services described using Web Services Definition Language (WSDL).

CORBA (Common Object Request Broker Architecture) is the basis for Fedora and is used because of the easy way that CORBA integrates machines from so many vendors. This allows for reliability and scalability on sites with large client bases and high hit rates.

Customizing tools

MyLibrary: A customized gateway for individual users to build a personalized information service, by user customization, system recommendation and push, based on the user's subject and preferences. The system became available in September 2003, using the open source code of MyLibrary@NCState.

MyLibrary Software – by North Carolina State University [under development] http://library.open.ac.uk/aboutus/myolib/monthly_report-myolib-2002.10.doc

MySQL http://www.mysql.com/

Searching Tools

Federated search products allow a user to search across multiple, independent data sources with one search query using one search interface. Federated search products have been marketed for the past decade (Stuivenga, 2005). Leaders in the market include MetaLib and WebFeat. Feedback from some public libraries using WebFeat was not encouraging.

The implementation of federated search products in academic and, especially, public libraries has been heralded as a saving feature to attract a new generation of library users (Sommers, 2005). California Digital Libraries manager and Library Journal columnist, Roy Tennant, noted in his comments at the 2004 American Library Association conference that "only librarians like to search; everyone else likes to find. Users want a 'black box' to which they can pose their questions and get answers" (Miller, 2004).

Reference Tools

Real time chatting software.

MassAsks at http://www.247ref.org. NOBLE offers reference service by 24/7 Reference.

Refdesk at http://www.refdesk.com, a free site which bills itself as "The Single Best Source for Facts." Like many other websites related to digital and virtual libraries, Refdeskh as everything a "real" library might offer, including entertainment, news, world facts, photos, genealogy, sports, to name just a very few items. Although there aren't reference librarians behind Refdesk to answer your questions, there are links to several "Ask the Experts" sites where you could ask questions.

Ipl2 at http://www.ipl2.org/ has more than 40,000 "librarian approved resources" including ready reference resources, books, magazines, newspapers and other special collections. Ipl2 offers a free "ask a question" reference service and a free regular email newsletter.

Google Answer can be seen at http://en.wikipedia.org/wiki/Google_Answers.

Yahoo Answer has been around more than decades at http://answers.yahoo.com/.

Recommender systems can be one of the tools used by reference librarians providing subject oriented bibliographies. Some information on the topic can be found on these sites: http://en.wikipedia.org/wiki/Recommendation_system, http://www.cis.upenn.edu/~ungar/CF/, or any other sites with a Google search.

Security technology
Distribute movable user authentication. Support CAS users to access web resources legally and safely without the limitations of IP address, to provide a single interface for multiple web resources while effectively maintaining intellectual property.

Maintenance tool
OpenDLib is a management system for digital libraries, developed by DELOS partners.

Standards
Z39.50i is one of National Information Standards Organization (NISO) standards at http://www.niso.org/z39.50/z3950.html.

5.5: Digital Library Models

For the new generation of digital libraries, the fundamental requirements and capabilities are collaboration and interoperation. These capabilities are more likely to occur as a digital library community than as individual libraries. There are three main possible models of digital libraries. What we have seen so far are mostly either the centralized model or the distributed (or federated) model. Current researchers predict that the future will most likely favor the combination of these two models. This is called the hybrid model.

a) Centralized Model
A centralized model is based on the execution of the applications at one site. The concept is that one party controls the other's streams or that the center controls the flows. Many current information technologies are currently designed for the centralized model of digital library infrastructure. The centralized organization coordination is usually set at national levels such as the national digital libraries.

b) Distributed Model
In the distributed model, a digital library is open for participants. The services are governed by agreements, standards, policies, and mutual beneficiaries. The collaborations for distributed services can be considered at three levels: the client service level, the service engine level, and the asset

repository level. Service integration in three levels can be portal, service federation, and content sharing.

Client service in the distributed model is typically through a portal service. Users can go to each individual digital library from the portal service site. The advantage for this model is ease of implementation, in which each individual service system is able to use maximum automation. However, this kind of service is through individual service entrance points led by portals for each system, which can be inconvenient for users. Users have to go to each individual service site to search separately for what they want. Moreover, the service interface and search mechanisms can be different from one service provider to another.

Service federation at the service engine level is a typical distributed computing model, as introduced by CORBA. The digital libraries interact with each other through their service components. The service components for a typical digital library will be described in the following section.

The advantages for this model are the efficiency, service consistency, user experience, etc. It enables common service entrance points for all users. The disadvantage is the challenge of implementation under current technology. J2EE and .Net are making implementation possible.

Content sharing at the repository level is based on the contract or less-formalized agreements between collaborators. For this model, each digital library can have its own independent service engine and components, but the intellectual content they provide to users can be from the same resources. In this case, the individual digital library will compete for service quality while their resources will be the same.

c) Hybrid model

A hybrid model is locally centralized and globally federated or collaborated. This is likely the most preferable model for future acceptance, because of its flexibility and ability to enable multiple levels of collaboration.

Because of funding and resource limitations, there must be more collaborative projects undertaken on a national level as well as on a regional level. The goal is to cover a broader range of information needs; that is, coalitions of local libraries creating region-wide, shared union catalogs. When we talk about digital libraries complementing - and in some instances, replacing - traditional physical library services, this implies that the efforts should divert to make information available electronically.

Collaborators in such a model can be the following:
- National library to national libraries
- National library to the libraries in the country
- National library to Web publishers
- National library to content owners
- National library to global libraries

There are a number of issues associated with these three models. The digital library developers face challenges from system organization such as cooperation and collaboration among libraries, collection and connection, service aggregation or integration and implementation of standards, challenges from system interoperation such as interoperable repositories, internal and external search engines, interoperation and integration, multilingual capabilities, interface design, preservation, feasibilities, maintenance plan, and challenges from legal and political sources such as copyrights, licensing, ownership and legislation. These issues and challenges posed with respect to the individual digital library models (centralized, distributed and hybrid) are similar and must be assessed prior to implementation of such digital libraries.

Proposed Digital Library Model and Associated Services

A typical model for individual digital library architecture in the new generation digital library community is illustrated in Figure 5.1 below:

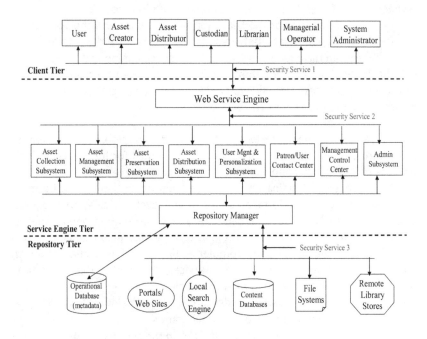

Figure 5.1: Typical Individual Digital Library Architecture

To build such an individual digital library six categories of issues need to be solved.

1. Asset collection includes Web content selection (including issues involving dynamic content), preservation, and distribution (including copyright issues), asset discovery, asset loading and transformation (one service component for different media handling: create collectable format for content), asset registration, and asset abstracting and indexing, which are based on content management scheme.
2. Asset management includes metadata standards, content catalogue and categorization, content navigation, search, and retrieval, content and service monitoring, digital object management, multi-media asset storage and retrieval.
3. Asset preservation includes life-cycle management, identification of service levels, e.g. on-line archiving, renovation of preserved assets (technical migration as a continuous effort) collaborative preservation, Web content preservation, dynamic content preservation, and storage management.
4. Asset distribution includes access control and secure distribution of digital rights and license management and presentation customization.
5. Intelligent service includes customization or personalization engines, workflow engines, rules engines, automatic agents and analytic engines.
6. Lastly, infrastructure service includes robust open platform, decentralized access to digital objects, distributed services application server and middleware, security and scalability, availability and maintainability after implementation.

The components of a digital library could differ greatly depending on the library's technological architecture as well as its mission and goals. Components that make up a DL could include collations or knowledge organization systems, services, managerial and operational tools. There are many architectures and frameworks for design, evaluation and interaction described in the literature. To simplify what a digital library should include, one model could be Figure 5.2 below:

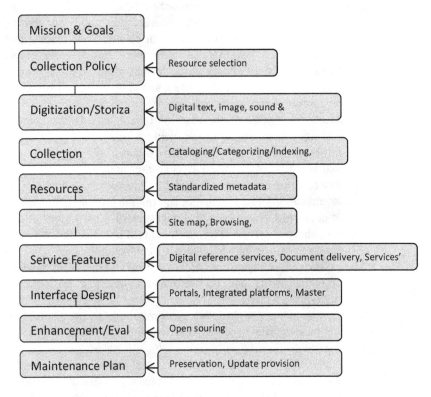

Figure 5.2: Digital Library Components

    Ultimately, digital library project construction and development require cooperation and collaboration not only with respect to information technology but also with respect to information policy. Some crucial policy issues concerning DLs include cooperation and collaboration between information service providers, collection development, intellectual property protection, the management and administration of the digital library project and public information services.

    Cooperation and collaboration no doubt play important roles in the successful formation and operation of such a DL. An example of such cooperation and collaboration that would allow ease of data flow and control within the organization sponsoring the DL is illustrated in Figure 5. 3 below:

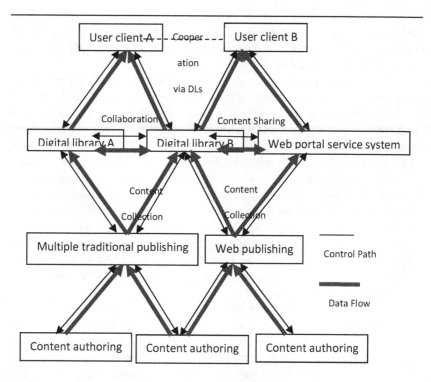

Figure 5.3: Cooperation & Collaboration of Hybrid Digital Library System

5.6: Digital Library Architecture

When creating a digital library, a great deal of consideration is needed regarding the collections, the digitization process, and the architecture. Architecture may be something that some librarians only consider in physical libraries, in terms of the layout of the bricks, tables or shelves. Nevertheless, planning the elements that go into a digital library is just as important. When we speak of digital library architecture, it is helpful to understand it as analogous to the architecture of an actual library building. This is not necessarily true for other kinds of software architecture, and only works very generally for digital libraries (Bass et al., 2003). However, a comparison is worth making, because digital libraries and physical libraries together form the library user's experience. In addition, the user may compare real services and structures to their virtual counterparts.

In the architectural plan of a library building we would include every detail that would affect the storage and usability of the materials, as well as our patrons' ease of finding and using the materials. We tend to take these architectural needs for granted in our local library, and assume that shelves, desks, chairs, and classification schemes are all we need in order to create a helpful and useful library atmosphere. However, when we move to the digital library, we need to reevaluate these needs, and make adjustments based on our new needs. We must ask ourselves what we need to understand in order to create a usable digital library architecture.

We are organizing and presenting digital objects, objects that differ from the usual monographic library mediums. According to Kahn and Wilensky, "the term digital object is used here in a technical sense of a particular sort of data structure, and not in the general sense of any object that may have digital form"(1995). That is, the digital objects that will be stored and accessed in our digital library will be highly specialized structures, including extensive information for storage and retrieval. Hence, we need a specialized architecture to deal with these objects and their data structures. This is not unlike requiring a special library room to deal with a collection of antique objects such as maps, including the need to tag and prepare the objects for both proper storage and retrieval. What we are looking for in the digital arena is "an infrastructure that is open in its architecture and which supports a large and extensible class of distributed digital information services" (Kahn & Wilensky, 1995).

Elements that fit under the category of architecture are application software, identifiers, handlers, DOI, persistent uniform resource locators (PURL), protocols, interoperability, and security. These elements are more in-depth than simply purchasing software for a set of computers in a library. The software that is selected must run on more than one operating system so that users are able to view the materials no matter the brand or type of computer they use. Furthermore, many digital libraries offer collections that have more than one type of digitized information, such as e-books, e-journals, music files, video files, as well as many others. Thus, the architecture must be able to support these systems and have a set of rules for handling all of the data, securing access to intended users, and preventing copyright violations. Therefore, the architecture of digital libraries is a very important issue.

Architectural structure

Digital libraries have multiple layers, which are revealed by architectural description. Bogen, Borowski, Heisterkamp, and Strecher from the German National Research Center for Information Technology describe a generic digital library system with four layers. The user sees the first layer, the interface, which allows him to request digital objects stored in the system. This is not done directly, however. Behind the interface is the digital library's middleware, which "includes toolkits for the development of interfaces and clients, directory and security services, and management facilities" (Bogen, et al., 2001).

This second layer is software such as the "out-of-the-box" version of Greenstone and other open source software, that allows for easy manipulation by librarians. Greenstone, for example, allows users to build indexes, import, export, and manage objects and metadata, and specify security (Witten, Bainbridge & Nichols, 2010).

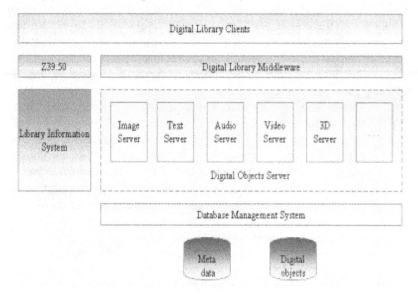

Figure 5.4: Generic representation of a digital library (Bogen et al., 2001).

Beneath this layer is the third layer, the digital objects server, which handles requests for digital objects. There are different servers for each type of material; text, video, audio, and other kinds of files all appear to the viewer in the same interface. The metadata and the actual digital objects are stored in the fourth layer, in a database management system, or DMS (Bogen et al., 2001).

The concepts behind these general architectural structures can be analyzed and discussed as well. There are eight general principles Kahn and Wilensky created, which were further discussed and explained by Arms in 1995; criteria like these should be considered when designing a digital library. The first three refer to broad scale issues of software architecture:

1. The technical framework exists within a legal and social framework.
2. Understanding of digital library concepts needs standard terminology.
3. The underlying architecture should be separate from the content stored in the library (Arms, 1995).

The first principle urges that laws and general mores of society must be obeyed, so structures must be put in place within the system to obey these rules. Often, legal issues relate directly to issues of intellectual copyright; the right to view and use information contained in a digital library may need to be restricted. Therefore, security and access must take a substantial role in the software's architecture.

The second principle describes the importance of terminology. Software architecture, as we have discussed, largely exists to explain how important parts of the system relate and react to other parts. The conversation can be derailed and misinterpreted because of inconsistent terminology.

The third principle relates directly to digital library architecture. The following statement sums up the importance of this principle:

> This underlying architecture is a base for extensions that can be tailored for various types of information. The extensions typically include specific formats, protocols, and rights management that are appropriate for the type of material. For example, the extensions for digitized movies will be very different from those for video games; texts are usually described by bibliographic terms, such as author and title, which are of little relevance to a computer program; a protocol designed for interaction with a database is unlikely to be useful in manipulating graphic designs. (Arms, 1995)

The other principles discuss various ways the digital object is actually kept separate from the software's architecture. The idea of designing a digital structure is that it remains flexible and able to store many types of materials, even ones that were not considered when the digital library itself was originally designed. Storage, transmission, and delivery of digital objects must remain separate from the underlying architecture (Arms, 1995).

Handles, which identify digital objects but remain independent from them, help to maintain this distinction between the underlying architecture and the objects themselves. Handles can also be referred to as "unique identifiers" (Arms, 1995), or object identifiers (OIDs). In Greenstone, for example, the librarian has a choice of assigning a random number to the digital object (this is called hashing), or by specifying a metadata element unique to the object (Witten et al., 2010). Whatever the user chooses to call an identifier, and however it is assigned, its purpose is to string the object to the system. The software performs a program on the digital object, the results of which are viewed by the user. This process of commands, which allows access to digital objects and metadata, is called "protocol" (Arms, 1995).

It is possible to discuss system architecture from the point of view of any of these aspects, which react to other aspects within the system. For example, describing the process from the view of the handler would be very different from describing it from the point of view of the digital object itself. The point of a broad understanding of digital library architecture is to have the ability to verbalize the process and come up with solutions to problems, as well as changing and restructuring the architecture when necessary. From a non-technical librarian's point of view, knowledge of the architecture (and a way to consider it and visualize it in his or her mind) can help him or her ask the right questions and communicate efficiently with IT. Ultimately, more understanding of the process leads to greater utilization of the digital library and its potential.

Principles of digital library architecture

The issues in creating a digital library architecture bring about the need for underlying principles to help in the planning stages. We will follow the eight principles laid out by Arms in his *Key Concepts in the Architecture of the Digital Library* (1995).

1). "The technical framework exists within a legal and social framework."

As with traditional library materials, digital objects also exist within a "legal and social framework," and copyright laws similarly apply. A digital library must be constructed in such a way as to honor any copyright or performance rights, such as in regard to audio or video digital objects. Just as traditional libraries are constricted as to the rights of the photocopying of copyrighted texts, digital libraries are constricted as to the rights of online distribution of copyrighted digital objects. The architecture of the digital library must reflect current legal and social laws in regard to its digital objects.

2). "Understanding of digital library concepts is hampered by terminology."

If any kind of worldwide consensus is to be reached about proper digital library architecture, the exact meaning of the terminology must be made fully explicit. Arms notes the confusion surrounding terms such as "copy, publish, document, and work."
If our digital library is to be a repository for documents or works or e-books or speeches, how do we define each one of these as a *digital object*?

3). "The underlying architecture should be separate from the content stored in the library."

Digital library architecture should not be content specific. Again, following Kahn and Wilensky, "the term digital object is used here in a technical sense of a particular sort of data structure, and not in the general sense of any object that may have digital form" (1995). Every digital object has its specific digital form, but digital library architecture should not be based on a specific digital object's form. The architecture should instead be based on general principles of data structure, parts of which include the object and its metadata. An architecture that is based on storing and retrieving any objects based on universal metadata can hopefully store and retrieve any kind of digital object, from an e-book to a music video.

4). "Names and identifiers are the basic building block for the digital library."

Just as in a traditional library, an identifying system based on permanent names is needed to retrieve objects. With the constant changing of digital collections on the Internet, Arms, and Kahn and Wilensky, proposes a system of *handles*, in which every digital object will be assigned a unique *handle* that will persist on remote servers even after that object's collection is gone.

5). "Digital library objects are more than collections of bits."

As we saw in Kahn and Wilensky, digital objects are data structures. For example, we could say that an e-book is merely a collection of bits that represent variations of letters, but when prepared for storage in a digital library the object becomes e-book + metadata + handle + other properties relevant to storage and retrieval. Digital library architecture must reflect this complexity.

6). "The digital library object that is used is different from the stored object."

Because digital objects are stored and presented to the user through a medium (computer processing and display), the object in storage is different than the object on the screen, or through the speakers. For example, Arms writes of a digital image, which is "stored in a library as a set of wavelets. To use it, the stored wavelets are used to generate an image with the characteristics requested. This is transmitted over the network to a user's computer, where it can be further processed or displayed." Furthermore, users may choose to have aspects of objects filtered or altered upon retrieving them (for example, viewing a small screen-sized photo instead of the original high resolution photo).

7). "Repositories must look after the information they hold."

Just as traditional libraries contain valuable material behind locked cases, so do digital libraries contain valuable material in need of security. Digital library architecture should take this into account.

8). "Users want intellectual works, not digital objects."

Arms writes that "digital objects are the basic building blocks of the digital library, but users of the library usually want to refer to items at a higher level of abstraction." These needs to be some way to group like kinds of objects, and place them under another umbrella of metadata (which he likens to a catalog record). Digital library architecture must provide the means to group digital objects based on each repository's needs.

D-space architecture

Among digital library software, the D-Space, Greenstone and Fedora are the general type of digital library architecture is the kind that you will most generally find when exploring digital library collections. Just as a physical library may hold a physical special collection and make this collection accessible through a reference desk, a library running the D-Space (or Greenstone or Fedora) software may make a digitized and stored collection available through a computer interface.

The architecture begins with an easily used interface through which librarians can add many kinds of digital materials to the system. Digital materials are assigned metadata and made into digital objects with a specific *handle*, not unlike assigning them a catalog card. The object's metadata is indexed, and the object is filed on the server with like objects, facilitating retrieval. Large clusters of digital objects are held and presented together, similar to disparate university collections. Digital material is preserved and "kept accessible as technology formats...evolve over time." At the end of the line, the user can browse or search for digital objects, and display these objects on a web browser, or the objects can be "downloaded and opened with a suitable application program" (DSpace diagram, n.d.).

The main idea of this general type of digital library is that digital objects are well-described, well-stored, and easily retrieved. We will see in the cases of Federated and Service-Oriented digital libraries that the architecture changes slightly, but the principles of digital library architecture are maintained.

Federated architecture

When one thinks of the architecture of a digital library, one usually imagines a combination of a main server holding all the digital objects with a computer program that retrieves and displays these objects on a website. However, this might only be a small part of the picture. There might be a need for "networked or federated digital libraries," which "are composed of autonomous, possibly heterogeneous information services, distributed across the Internet" (Goncalves et al., 2001). This need arose with:

> "Networked Digital Library of Theses and Dissertations (NDLTD), an international consortium of universities, libraries, and other supporting institutions focused on electronic theses and dissertations...Federation requires dealing flexibly with differences among systems, ontologies, and data formats while respecting information sources' autonomy." (Goncalves et al., 2001)

Imagine a computer program retrieving digital objects from one library. These digital objects have been cataloged by that library's metadata technicians, and the retrieval computer program has been tuned to the specific metadata conditions. Now imagine the same computer program retrieving objects from 200 libraries. Among these libraries, the metadata, language, protocols, etc. are all different. Because of this, searching a federated digital library can result in poor retrieval if there are discrepancies in metadata and content among libraries.

Goncalves et al. (2001) summarizes the problems with federated architecture:

1) **Autonomy:** Members manage most services for their scholars.
2) **Decentralization:** Members are not (yet) asked to report either collection updates or changes in their metadata to central coordinators.

3) **Minimal interoperability:** Each source must provide unique URNs and metadata records for all stored works, but need not (yet) support the same standards or protocols.
4) **Heterogeneity:** Members differ in language, metadata, protocols, repository technologies, character coding, nature of data (structured, semi -structured and unstructured, multimedia), user characteristics, preferences, and capabilities.
5) **Massive amount of data and dynamism:** NDLTD already has over 100 members and eventually aims to support all those that will produce electronic theses and dissertations (ETDs). New members are constantly added and there is a continuing flow of new data as theses and dissertations are submitted. (Goncalves et. al, 2001)

In any federated system there will always be problems, and using such a system may never be perfect, but steps can be taken to get the federation members to agree on common metadata formats and Internet protocols.

The problems in federated digital libraries arise mostly from users performing remote searches rather than local union searches. When the user performs a remote search, the search computer program connects to all the federated repositories and searches with the user's query (e.g., Mark Twain AND Connecticut). Because different repositories catalog and organize works differently from each other, and do not all use the same search protocols, this type of search can result in less than ideal returns. On the other hand, when each federated repository submits its holdings to a local "centralized data source," and these holdings are processed and made into one huge list of holdings, searches tend to be of a much higher quality—except that local searches may be dated, depending on when the repositories sent their holdings to the centralized source.

Service-oriented architecture (SOA)

This type of architecture is exemplified by the organization CiteSeer (http://citeseerx.ist.psu.edu). Unlike either DSpace or a federated digital library (which are programs that index and search repositories), CiteSeer, like similar service-oriented architectures, actively searches for materials on the Internet. It performs a *service* for scholars:

Rather than creating just another digital library, CiteSeer^x attempts to provide resources such as algorithms, data, metadata, services, techniques, and software that can be used to promote other digital libraries. CiteSeer^x has developed new methods and algorithms to index PostScript and PDF research articles on the Web (About CiteSeerx, 2010).

Along with promoting other digital libraries, Petinot et al. (2004) explains the system as an indexing site:

> CiteSeer is an automated service that discovers new academic publications on the Web, downloading, converting and processing them to allow end-users to browse the document collection following cross-document citations and to identify related publications using citation-based features such as co-citation and active bibliography.

CiteSeer performs this automated service through Autonomous Citation Indexing (ACI), in which a web crawler finds and indexes materials:

> An ACI system can automatically create a citation index from literature in electronic format. Such a system can autonomously locate articles, extract citations, identify citations to the same article that occur in different formats, and identify the context of citations in the body of articles. (Lawrence et al., 2004)

As we can see, a service-oriented ACI system can be quite helpful when it has access to a large community of metadata-rich materials, such as the scientific literature materials that have been discovered and presented by CiteSeer. Furthermore, proponents of the service-oriented architecture approach note that "CiteSeer has thus far been successful in facilitating access to a large amount of meta-data on the World Wide Web" and hope for further advances in gaining organized access to a greater portion of the semantic web (Petinot et al., 2004).

5.7: Application Software

The selection of repository software is a crucial, and often daunting, decision that must be made by the developer of a digital library. While it is possible for an institution to develop its own software—and indeed, popular digital library software often has its origins as an in-house solution developed by a university—most institutions seeking to create a self-contained digital repository are now better off using a third-party software solution than spending time and money reinventing the wheel (Tedd, 2005). There are dozens of open-source and commercial software solutions available for digital libraries (Tedd, 2005; Repositories Support Project, 2009). Among these, no single software package is obviously superior to the rest, although some are broadly popular for a given application, such as DSpace as a platform for institutional repositories (Markey, Rieh, St. Jean, Kim, & Yakel, 2007). The task of selecting software, therefore, is not a matter of choosing the "best" software, but of defining the requirements of the project at hand and deciding which software package will best meet those needs. Being able to prioritize needs is important, since, as Frank Cervone (2006) puts it in his article "Some Considerations When Selecting Digital Library Software," "the reality is that no software package will be able to perform all [potential requirements] in the exact manner the organization would like."

Digital library software provides a structured, browse-able, and searchable gateway to a moderated and metadata-annotated collection of electronic documents. In general, the digital library software packages that have received the most press in library and information science writing are open-source software packages. This may be in part because open-source software can be downloaded and evaluated free of charge. Open source and commercial software both have strengths and weaknesses that will be discussed later.

It is impossible and unnecessary to provide an exhaustive list of the digital library software currently available; technology trends are in constant flux and today's most popular solutions may be less prominent tomorrow. This section will offer introductions to some of the best-known software packages in order to provide an overview of the current state of the art.

Open source digital library software

Open source software, as defined by the Open Source Initiative website (2010), is software that can be freely distributed and redistributed, has freely available source code, and can be modified or reused in derivative form. Commercial software, conversely, is supplied by a for-profit vendor, has an upfront cost, and is limited in its ability to be modified, because the source code is usually not available to the purchaser.

Important open-source digital library software includes DSpace, Fedora Commons, Greenstone, and Eprints. DSpace and Fedora are now both overseen by the DuraSpace non-profit organization (DuraSpace, n.d.b). DSpace was developed as a collaboration between MIT Libraries and the Hewlett Packard Company and released in 2002 (Tedd, p. 123; DuraSpace, n.d.a).

DSpace is very popular as an institutional repository; the 2007 MIRACLE census of institutional repositories reported that 46.4% of the surveyed universities that had institutional repositories used DSpace software. Over 700 organizations are currently using DSpace. Written in Java, DSpace can run on any operating system and can be used to store a wide range of files including documents, images, audio, video, and other file formats such as computer programs, websites, and learning objects. Its support for different metadata schemas is somewhat limited, by default only supporting a customizable version of Dublin Core (DSpace, n.d.). DSpace conforms to the OAI-PMH protocol for standardized metadata harvesting (OAI-PMH and other protocols will be discussed later on) (Repositories Support Project, 2009). Its popularity as an institutional repository platform means that it excels in offering security and user profile-related features (security will be discussed later in the chapter). DSpace has its own authorization system or can be integrated into an external system. In addition, control over user permissions is extremely granular, so that a given user's ability to access files can be controlled on a per-file basis. The DSpace project recognizes the importance of preservation and provides bit-level preservation—keeping files intact in their original state—as well as providing functional preservation for supported formats through format migration or emulation. The software is available in more than twenty languages, making it accessible to an international audience (DuraSpace, n.d.a). DSpace's primary training offering is a free online course hosted on their website (DSpace, n.d.).

Fedora Commons, also maintained by DuraSpace, was developed at Cornell University and released in 2003 (Fedora Commons, n.d.a). There are currently more than 170 known Fedora projects in existence (Fedora Commons, 2010). Fedora is also Java-based and has been tested on Windows, Solaris, Linux, and Mac OS X. Fedora is somewhat more multipurpose in its aims than DSpace; it can store any type of digital content, supports all metadata schemas, and conforms to OAI-PMH (Fedora Commons, n.d.a; Repositories Support Project, 2009). Fedora has its own authentication system and can be integrated into an external authentication system (DuraSpace, n.d.c; Fedora Commons, 2009). Fedora's default distribution is English only, but support for other languages can be manually added (Repositories Support Project, 2009). The Fedora Commons project provides online documentation and a wiki as training materials (Fedora Commons, n.d.).

Greenstone is another popular software package that, like Fedora, is multipurpose in its aims, although its main use appears to be as a repository for cultural and historical items. Greenstone began in 1995 as the New Zealand Digital Library Project and has worked in partnership with UNESCO to create software accessible to an international audience (Witten & Bainbridge, n.d.). Greenstone runs on Windows, Unix/Linux, and Mac OS-X. Greenstone can manage documents, images, audio, video, and other file types such as source code. Within Greenstone itself, the Dublin Core and RFC 1807 metadata schemas are available, plug-ins allow for the import and export of a variety of file and metadata types including specialized import/export to and from DSpace. Greenstone complies both with OAI-PMH and with the Z39.50 protocol for standardization of search and retrieval from remote databases, and can import and export its metadata according to the XML-based METS standard (Witten, 2009). Greenstone offers granular authentication settings, but it is limited insofar as it cannot be integrated into an external authentication system (Greenstone Wiki, 2009; MIDESS, 2006). Due to its involvement with UNESCO, Greenstone is highly multilingual, with full documentation in five languages, the librarian's interface available in ten languages, and the general reader's interface available in fifty languages. In addition to extensive online documentation, Greenstone runs training workshops in developing countries (Witten, 2009).

The last open-source software that will be described is EPrints, which was first developed at the University of Southampton in 2000. Like DSpace, EPrints is primarily used as an institutional repository. It runs on Windows, Linux, Unix, and Mac OS X, and in 2010 was being used by over 200 organizations (EPrints, 2010d). EPrints primarily manages documents and images, but the software is easily extensible and with third-party add-ons allow it to support video, audio, and other formats (Repositories Support Project, 2009). EPrints has a customizable plug-in architecture that allows it to import and export a wide range of metadata (EPrints, n.d.b). Natively it supports Dublin Core and MARC, as well as the METS and OAI-PMH standards (Repositories Support Project, 2009). EPrints has its own authentication system and can be integrated into an external authentication system (EPrints, 2010a). EPrints, like DSpace, specifically addresses preservation issues through its work with the KeepIt project, funded by the Joint Information Systems Committee (JISC), to provide preservation tools as part of EPrints (EPrints, n.d.a). EPrints has been translated into almost twenty languages (Eprints, 2010b). In addition to its free online documentation and training materials, the EPrints project provides fee-based hosting, training, and/or consultancy support (EPrints, 2010c).

Commercial digital library software

Commercial digital library software packages are also an important presence in the digital library software world, but the dizzying variety of commercial software available makes it hard to summarize the field with a few examples. Nevertheless, CONTENTdm and DigiTool are two popular examples of commercial digital library software. CONTENTdm was developed at the University of Washington and was acquired by OCLC in 2006 (OCLC, 2006). CONTENTdm runs on Windows, Unix, and Solaris and is used by almost 2000 organizations (Repositories Support Project, 2009; OCLC, 2010a). CONTENTdm supports all file types and uses Dublin Core and VRA metadata schemas, while allowing for the customization of these schemas. It complies with Z39.50 and OAI-PMH standards. CONTENTdm can be integrated with a variety of authentication systems and offers granular control over user permissions. OCLC provides a separate Digital Archives preservation service with which CONTENTdm can be used (OCLC, 2010a). CONTENTdm's web interface is available in five languages (OCLC, 2010b). Support includes an online documentation support center, live Web tutorial sessions for new users, and OCLC-sponsored regional training, workshops, and user meetings (OCLC, 2010c).

DigiTool is another commercial digital library software package that has been produced by Ex Libris, a library automation company, since 2002 (Shigo, 2002). DigiTool advertises itself for use in institutional repositories, e-learning systems, and general digital collections (Ex Libris, 2010c). DigiTool runs solely on Linux/Unix and Solaris. It can support documents, images, video, and audio (Repositories Support Project, 2009). DigiTool supports MARC and Dublin Core schemas and supports OAI-PMH, METS, and MODS standards. It is compatible with a variety of external authentication systems (Ex Libris, 2010c;

Repositories Support Project, 2009), like OCLC. Ex Libris also offers a separate digital preservation solution, Ex Libris Rosetta (Ex Libris, 2010b). Ex Libris provides subscribers with extensive online documentation, including a learning center with training materials, a customer-run wiki, and live web training sessions (Ex Libris, 2010c).

Selecting a software package

Digital library software may be easily reduced to a laundry list of features, but product specs alone cannot provide complete guidance in choosing the optimal software for a given project. Goh et al. observe in "A Checklist for Evaluating Open Source Digital Library Software" (2006) that "much effort has been put into DL research and practice but not so much on evaluation." Since then, a great deal of useful writing has been produced on the selection and evaluation of digital library software. Cervone reminds project managers that software-related decisions must be made with the question, "What problem are we trying to solve?" in the forefront of their minds. For a digital library project to be successful, a project mission statement must be formulated. The mission statement must be specific—it must state what formats of materials will be included in the library, who the user community will be, and whether the library intends to be a long-term storage solution (Cervone, 2006). With these questions answered, the project manager can select software designed to store the kinds of materials in question and to provide the ease of use and functionality necessary for the end user, and that appears to have the longevity that the project requires. Longevity can be hard to predict, but Cervone recommends that if a commercial solution is being considered, the license should have a clause that protects the product from going into limbo if the vendor goes out of business. Documentation and training should also be excellent, or the product will be extremely difficult and time-consuming to use (Cervone, 2006).

Budgetary concerns, of course, also need to be considered when a product is being selected. Open-source software has no upfront cost, but generally requires more in-house time and expertise to configure and maintain. Commercial software has predictable costs, but they can be high when maintenance is included, and local support may still be required (Cervone, 2006). As a result, it can often be difficult to predict whether a commercial or open-source solution will be cheaper, so the decision maker must do the math and make a careful decision.

Selection of digital library software can and usually should be a formalized process in which different software options are evaluated against a checklist of required features. Such checklists have been formulated by researchers at the Nanyang Technological University of Singapore and at the United States National Library of Medicine. The Nanyang checklist is designed to be extensible based on the needs of the organization performing the evaluation, but the areas that it suggests should be evaluated are content management, content acquisition, metadata schemas supported, search and browse support, authentication/user management, usage statistics and reports, preservation, interoperability, user interface, standards compliance, and support and maintenance (Goh, 2006).

Similarly, the National Library of Medicine created a set of "Master Evaluation Criteria" that evaluates potential software packages in the following areas:

- functionality (could the software fulfill the needs of the project?)
- scalability (the ability of the repository to manage large collections)
- extensibility (the ability to integrate external tools through an API or manipulation of the source code)
- interoperability with other repositories
- ease of deployment (installation and integration with other software)
- system security meeting the requirements of the organization
- system performance (response time and availability)
- physical environment (ability to be deployed elsewhere for disaster recovery or to have components in different physical locations)
- demonstrated successful deployments (a history of happy customers)
- system support (quality of documentation, training, and/or user community)
- strength of development community/organization
- strength of technology roadmap for the future (Marill & Luczak, 2009).

5.8: Identifiers, Handlers, DOI, PURL

Librarians have discovered that the Internet is a medium antithetical to cataloging. Pages come and go and URLs break, so that hyperlinks collected one day may be useless the next as the item they point to has moved to a different location. As digital content becomes vital to the information landscape, there has been an effort to create persistent labels for digital information, the Internet equivalent of a library call number. These identifiers allow a given resource to be located over time, even if its actual location on the Web changes. Such identifiers are extremely important in making digital libraries useful and sustainable, since they provide an external cataloging system that makes digital objects continuously available despite location changes.

There are several persistent identification systems currently being used. One, the Uniform Resource Name (URN), is a standard that simply provides a unique name for an Internet resource. The Internet Assigned Numbers Authority (IANA) oversees URNs and makes it possible to redirect the URN to its current URL, but there's no guarantee that the resource still exists or will be findable. One special use of URNs is the NBN, or National Bibliography Number, which is used by national libraries to identify publications without an ISBN (Tonkin, 2008). Much more widely used in a digital library context, however, are the DOI and PURL systems.

The Digital Object Identifier system (DOI)

The Digital Object Identifier System, operated and governed by the International DOI Foundation, is probably the most important identification system in current use. The Foundation was launched in 1998 and its applications first came into use in 2000. The Foundation oversees the creation and management of Digital Object Identifiers (DOIs). A DOI is a name that can be assigned to any item of intellectual property that exists in digital form. The DOI system is currently used by 4000 naming authorities, and 43 million DOI names have been assigned to date (IDF, 2009).

DOIs are alphanumeric strings following a standard syntax. The string can incorporate an in-house identification system such as ISBN, allowing the DOI to be meaningful within the organization that controls the information. DOIs can also have metadata associated with them, and DOIs that share a metadata schema and rules for name assignment can be associated in groups known as Application Profiles. This allows DOIs to be treated differently depending on whether they point to, say, a journal article or a sound file (DOI, 2010).

The IDF uses a name resolution service, the Handle System, that allows a user to input a DOI and receive the location where the item is found. DOIs can be resolved using a web browser by using the proxy server at http://dx.doi.org. DOI resolution can also be configured to represent more complex relationships; for instance, one DOI can resolve to multiple other DOIs, representing a hierarchical relationship among items (IDF, 2008). This means that DOIs can be assigned to parts of a work, such as individual songs or articles, as well as to the work as a whole (Wang, 2007).

The DOI system is implemented by individual Registration Agencies, operating either commercially or as member communities that follow the policies of the IDF (IDF, 2008). To assign DOIs to digital items, an organization must subscribe to one of these Registration Agencies, an example of which is the popular Crossref, which provides DOIs for scholarly publications (IDF, 2009). Once an object has been assigned a DOI, there are several ways to use and promulgate the DOI. A simple one is to visually include the DOI on the object itself or on a citation page associated with the object. You can also use the aforementioned DOI proxy server or a related service to create a hyperlink. An object with a DOI need not be publicly available, so gray literature and other non-public material can be assigned a DOI (IDF, 2010).

DOIs are usually assigned to all online copies of an item, but can be manipulated to resolve to a specific copy of an item that the user has access to, rather than a publisher-held generic copy; this is possible by using the OpenURL protocol to manage the transaction (IDF, 2010). The OpenURL protocol allows a user to be forwarded to the most appropriate copy of the item they are trying to access; for instance, a university student who wants to read an article will be forwarded to the copy of that article included in the university library's subscription databases (Ex Libris, 2010d).

Persistent uniform resource locators (PURL)

The PURL system is another system that provides persistent identification to shifting web resources. A PURL, or Persistent Uniform Resource Locator, is a Web URL, not a name like a DOI. The PURL system was developed by OCLC and provides a large-scale resolution service—the PURL points to the service, which in turn redirects the user to the current URL of the resource in question. An individual server can also run its own resolution service. The PURL software and the creation of PURLs are free; however, it is the DOI that has received widespread adoption by the publishing industry, and PURL does not have the same support for modeling complex relationships and including metadata that DOI has (Tonkin, 2008). Nevertheless, PURL can be an excellent solution for an individual library wishing to create proxy links to items in a potentially shifting digital collection.

5.9: Protocols

What are digital library protocols?

There are two widely used protocols, one for harvesting metadata and one for searching for metadata. We are interested in the ways information can move across computer systems. Through a look at these two protocols, we should get a general idea of the role of protocols in digital library communication, and be able to understand the role of other protocols within digital libraries.

In the "Introduction to Digital Library Architecture" section we mentioned federated digital libraries, such as the Networked Digital Library of Theses and Dissertations (NDLTD) (http://www.ndltd.org/), which lets users search for content on hundreds of small digital library collections. One way the NDLTD does this is to collect digital object metadata from all the digital library collections and put it together in one big index. We might ask what the protocol is for this system. For example, the protocol could be for librarians at their respective libraries to type up lists of their metadata and mail them to NDLTD. This would be a cumbersome and time-consuming project and would not allow NDLTD to be instantly updated.

In order for metadata to be transferred instantly and effortlessly to NDLTD, a better protocol is used, called the Open Archives Initiative Protocol for Metadata Harvesting, or OAI-PMH (NDLTD Union Catalog Project, 2008). This protocol does the work for the librarians, harvesting the metadata. In effect, "the OAI provided a mechanism to separate data providers from service providers" (Suleman et al., 2003). In this view of things, we have on the one hand all the loose data, and on the other hand a service provider that harvests this data and presents the searchable index to the user. We can see the similarities to CiteSeer, which crawls the web and harvests data to create an index. CiteSeer previously used an HTML protocol and merely scoured plain text, but as of 2004 also incorporates OAI-PMH (OAI News, 2006).

OAI-PMH is a *harvesting* protocol, and will not do any searching for the user. On the other hand, Z39.50 is a *searching* protocol, and will not harvest information, but will search and find information across libraries. "Z39.50 is a national and international (ISO 23950) standard defining a protocol for computer-to-computer information retrieval" (Z39.50 Gateway, n.d.). Again, this is a protocol for communication, similar to the OAI protocol. By using this protocol, a computer running OCLC Connexion and retrieving MARC records from another library can find the needed information (Nylink, 2009) "without knowing the search syntax that is used by those other systems" (Z39.50 Gateway, n.d.). Similarly, a digital library program can retrieve metadata from other digital libraries without running into problems of different syntax. That is, using this protocol the two digital libraries end up speaking the same language, and transferring information in that language.

Z39.50 gateway

The workings of Z39.50 are not as easy to explicate as those of OAI, primarily because Z39.50 is a complex set of rules for facilitating searches across libraries, or in our case digital libraries, and not just a harvesting technique

Z39.50 must be present in both the sending and the receiving computers in order for the computers to be able to communicate with one another. There must be total agreement between the two computers. "The basic function of Z39.50 is to negotiate a connection between the client and server on two systems, execute a search, and return the formatted results to the user's screen" (Niso Press, 2002). Without agreement on the protocol the search cannot be completed, not even in part. The protocol works along the following steps (refer to *Z39.50 — A Primer on the Protocol*: http://www.niso.org/publications/press/Z3950_primer.pdf):

    1) Z39.50 software begins a search request by designating the requesting computer as the *origin*, and the receiving computer as the *target*.
    2) Then "the Origin (client) and Target (server)...negotiate and establish a Z39.50 search session, known as a Z-Association."

The Z-Association establishes the rules that keep the computers communicating with each other.
3) A search facility is then used to search the target's collection by means of the client's request—all with regard to the rules established in the Z-Association.

The Z39.50 protocol is not as simple as merely requesting and receiving XML data, but it can do much more than OAI-PMH by also searching data with advanced search capabilities (Niso Press, 2002).

5.10: Interoperability

As we saw in the **Protocols** section, it is important for digital libraries to be able to communicate with each other in this world of different digital library programs and data needs. In fact, the whole time while we were talking about protocols we were more generally talking about interoperability. This section, then, is kind of an introduction to the protocols section, and deals with interoperability in a general sense.

Let's take a look at an example of the European Digital Library http://search.theeuropeanlibrary.org/portal/en/index.html. In an attempt to create the European Digital Library as a federated library system, the creators "envisage[d] a network of many digital libraries – in different institutions, across Europe" (Gradmann, 2010). A few things were realized at the beginning of the project that gave the project its form:
- Europeana is federating objects from distributed sources,
- Europeana is federating objects from heterogeneous sources with different community backgrounds,
- Europeana is part of a bigger framework of interacting global information networks including e.g., other 'Digital libraries', scientific repositories and commercial providers, [and]
- Europeana relies as much as possible on standards and existing building blocks as well as be based on web standards. (Gradmann, 2010)

These precepts of the need for over-arching interoperability inform the principles by which federated digital libraries' function.

Principles of interoperability – From the European Digital Library Agenda

Included here are four of the principles:
1). Interoperating entities can be assumed to be the traditional cultural heritage institutions (libraries, museums, archives) offering digital services, or again the digital repositories (institutional or not), eScience and/or eLearning platforms or simply web services.

2). Objects of interaction, the entities that actually need to be processed in interoperability scenarios. Choices range from the full content of digital information objects (analogue/digitized or born digital) to mere representations of such objects – and these in turn are often conceived as librarian metadata attribute sets, but sometimes also are conceived as 'surrogates'.

3). Functional perspective of interoperation. This may simply be the exchange and/or propagation of digital content. Other functional goals are aggregating digital objects into a common content layer. Another approach is to enable users and/or software application to interact with multiple Digital Libraries via unified interfaces (dynamic portals) or to facilitate operations across federated autonomous Digital Libraries. Others again seek to establish a common service architecture and/or common service definitions.

4). Linguistic interoperability (multilingualism) can be thought of in two different ways: as multilingual user interfaces to Digital Libraries (relatively well known) or as dynamic multilingual techniques for exploring the Digital Library object space. Three types of approaches can be distinguished in the second respect: dynamic query translation for addressing Digital Libraries in different languages, dynamic translation of metadata responding to queries in different languages or dynamic localization of digital content (Gradmann, 2010).

Interoperability and standardization of metadata is still a major issue today as it was ten to fifteen years ago. This lack of interoperability and standardization plays a major role in the digitization of materials as it creates problems between different library systems. Simic & Wick discuss a very similar situation of converting their metadata to become compatible and compliant to the best practices of digital collection platforms when Oregon Digital joined the Mountain West Digital Library and the Digital Public Library of America (2019). This case study also took place in 2019. There are many issues related to the digitization of library materials. Physical digitization quality and metadata interoperability and standardization are just wo examples of the challenges faced when digitizing library materials.

5.11: Security

When information is published online, many users may think that copyright laws are not in place. Nevertheless, copyright laws protect works, even when they are online, so the architecture of digital libraries must account for this. In addition, the architecture of digital libraries must protect users. Lastly, security measures should prevent unwanted access.

In a digital library system, documents are available in digital form and therefore are more easily copied and their copyrights are more easily violated. As Brin et al. point out, "the danger of illegal copies is not new, of course; however, it is much more time consuming to reproduce and distribute paper,

CDs or videotape copies than on-line documents" (p. 398). This is a very serious problem, as it discourages owners of valuable information from sharing it with authorized users. There are two main methods for addressing this problem: prevention and detection (p. 398).

Brin et al. (1995) offer one solution for this problem: "The key idea is quite simple: provide a *copy detection service* where original documents can be registered, and copies can be detected. The service will detect not just exact copies, but also documents that overlap [in] significant ways" (p. 398). This idea is similar to educators detecting plagiarism in students' papers. The copy detection service allows the digital library staff to see if a new item is added to the collection that consists of information taken from one of its other sources. Then, the digital library staff will be able to take steps to contact the person who digitized and published the new item and remove the item that violates copyright laws. One possible problem with this idea is "whether authors can be convinced to register their documents: Without a substantial body of documents, the service will not be very useful" (Brin, et al., 1995, p. 409). Nevertheless, if the architects and librarians of the digital library present the idea to authors and owners of information in the correct way, the authors and owners will see that this idea will actually protect the original works. In addition to the copy detection, Brin et al. (1995) offer other security measures for digital libraries: "There are a number of other important 'tools' that will also assist in safeguarding intellectual property. For example, good encryption and authorization mechanisms are needed in some cases. It is also important to have mechanisms for *charging for access* to information" (pp. 398-399). Hence, if users can gain access either through a fee, or another means, such as entering a valid library card number, there may be a decrease in copyright violations because information is tracked when a person logs in, though the information regarding what users' view is in many cases protected by law. If the federal government becomes involved, as it might if a copyright law is violated, the librarian may give the government information about the user. Thus, if users know that they have to login to the system in some way, they may be deterred from breaking copyright laws.

However, as stated in ALA Code of Ethics #3: "We protect each library user's right to privacy and confidentiality with respect to information sought or received and resources consulted, borrowed, acquired or transmitted."

Along with the idea that copyright laws will be protected, users want to ensure that they will be secure as well. According to H.M. Gladney and J.B. Lotspiech's (1997) article, "Safeguarding Digital Library Content and Users: Assuring Convenient Security and Data Quality" in *D-Lib Magazine*, "Readers must be confident of their privacy and of information authenticity, i.e., that information comes from purported sources and is not fraudulently altered" (n.p.). This relates to the earlier point that users' identities must remain anonymous unless there is a major problem and the government asks for information; this is part of the United States' Patriot Act (ALA, 2010).

Lastly, Joel S. Birnbaum (2004), senior technical advisor for Hewlett-Packard Company, discusses the idea of "cybersecurity" in his article, "Cybersecurity Considerations for Digital Libraries in an Era of Pervasive Computing." Birnbaum (2004) discusses the great influence that digital libraries have had on today's technology, and says that this role will continue to grow throughout time. He also mentions that, "since [digital libraries] will also inevitably become the target of malicious attack by people seeking unauthorized information, and by terrorists seeking to disrupt the global information infrastructure and the physical infrastructures built upon it, it is both timely and essential to study the cybersecurity characteristics future digital libraries will have to support" (Birnbaum, 2004, p. 169). In other words, Birnbaum stresses the idea that digital libraries have to protect resources from unwanted hands. This is difficult since the American Library Association (ALA) has rules against censorship. Nevertheless, each physical library requires users to have a library card to borrow materials; so digital libraries should also have some protection so that information is not widely spread without permission. If the digital library receives a request for the material from another library for an interlibrary loan program, then the digital library will share the information correctly by following copyright laws and without having someone hacking into the system. Lastly, Birnbaum predicts that as digital libraries become more popular, security measures will have to support the new trends in digital libraries. Thus, one important aspect to remember in regard to the architecture of security online is that the security measures should be able to be expanded when the need arises, especially to protect copyright laws and users.

Like any website, a digital library can be vandalized or its contents redistributed without consent, to the detriment of the library's ability to provide continuous service to its users and protect its intellectual property. Many digital libraries also have an interest in controlling the contents users can access based on the user's identity—in an institutional repository, for instance, the institution might wish to grant more access to a university member than to a member of the public. An access management system allows a digital library to set different levels of access depending on the identity of the user, as determined by electronic means. There are two steps to identifying the user of a digital library, or of any electronic resource—authentication, "the process of verifying who is requesting access to a resource," and authorization, "determining whether access should be granted to that individual based on information about that individual" (JISC, 2010).

In their article "Technologies Employed to Control Access to or Use of Digital Cultural Collections" (2010), Eschenfelder and Agnew point out that "few published studies of [technological protection measure] use at academic or cultural institutions exist." Their study of 154 museums, libraries, and archives using technology to protect their digital archives provides a good overview of various security solutions found in digital libraries. Examples used by institutions in the survey include providing low quality resolution images, streaming/limited length video or audio clips, placing visible watermarks on materials, or making materials available through a software decoder or viewer. However, institutions also used authorization-based methods such as identifying the user's computer by its network ID or IP address, implementing a user account system, or integrating the library into a cross institutional authentication system (Eschenfelder and Agnew, 2010).

Simple solutions like IP address verification are better for in-library use of digital resources, since users won't want their access to a digital library to depend on what computer they're using. A digital library with a user account system, or better, one that integrates into an institutional system, allows users to access resources wherever they are. An institutional system is superior because the user only has to remember one set of credentials. Using a single access management system for an entire library is called federated access management (JISC, 2010). Federated access management services include LDAP (Lightweight Directory Access Protocol), Athens, and Shibboleth (Repositories Support Project, 2009). Many digital library software packages are designed to be easily integrated into these systems and give the developer granular control over what resources a given type of user is allowed to see.

If a digital library does use an authentication system, following good password practices is an important way for the system security to remain intact. Poor password practices include using common dictionary words only followed by numbers or using birthdates, sharing passwords, or using a default password (Tassabehji, 2005).

Conclusion

Following the principles of digital library architecture, a successful digital library can be constructed that will aid both librarians and information-seeking patrons. Single-repository digital libraries such as D-Space are just the building blocks of Federated digital libraries such as NDLTD (http://www.ndltd.org/). Service-Oriented digital libraries such as CiteSeer take this to a whole new level by treating the Internet as a tremendous library, and creating a citation list of a part of it. Overall, digital library architecture is dependent on the end-user: Are your patrons finding what they need?

As we have seen, digital library protocols allow libraries to be universally accessed beyond the normal user experience. Instead of having to search through each and every digital library, the user can access an umbrella connected to thousands of digital libraries by means of digital library protocols such as OAI-PMH or Z39.50. Each and every digital library must make sure that its metadata conform to the protocol or protocols that will make the metadata accessible beyond the digital walls.

Although security is one aspect of architecture, it will be well worth librarians' and architects' time and effort to plan out security measures before implementing other areas of the architecture. The reasoning is that the software must be able to handle the security implements, the protocols have to include how often the security measures should be updated or enhanced, and the security systems have to be able to work on more than one system (interoperability). Thus, although all aspects of digital libraries are important, the planning that goes into the architecture is very in-depth and often requires considerations that will impact the rest of the library.

Digital items are naturally more vulnerable to theft and corruption. Hackers may be interested in stealing digital files of library items, user information, or corrupting the database. Program hacking was more common in the past. Today, security vulnerabilities are more likely to originate from the user's side than from the developer's side, because it's usually easier to get information from a user's mistake than it is to try to hack programs. Developers typically fix coding errors rapidly. The investigated digital library has security problems, as proven by Xie et al., such as insufficient password control, poor backup mechanisms, and delayed system updates (2020). Instead of bad programming, these are all user-side security mechanisms. Moving forward, digital libraries must be mindful of potential security concerns posed by developers. To keep their digital library as safe as possible, they must be especially cognizant of their own security policies.

Study Questions for Chapter Five:

1. What possible problems do we face as more DLs are developed? In looking at the history of digital libraries, many of the advantages of digital libraries seem obvious (easy access, accurate preservation, compact storage, search effectiveness, etc.) but often discussions fail to consider the flip side of the coin - the disadvantages and worries that would be of concern with digital collections. It will be important to consider the possible short and long-term worries that go hand in hand with digital libraries. There might be various mistakes/problems that have accompanied the growth of digital libraries that we should focus on so as to not repeat or magnify these earlier difficulties/challenges.

2. This chapter discusses a number of technologies relating to the interoperation and integration of information in digital libraries. The DLITE system discussed in the lecture provides a vision of a workcenter environment where-by the user can search and collect data from multiple sources including full-text digital information and bibliographic information for paper and film based resources. Additional technologies discussed included personalized, user-based, portals that provide access to resources while recording the users search history. This system provides a place for the users to store digital resources and provide access to other users with whom they are collaborating. While the DLITE project at Stanford University formally ended in 2004 ("Stanford digital library,") other projects with similar aims have come into

existence (Dorner, & Curtis, 2004). The Metalib service by Exlibirs is one such project ("Exlibris metalib," 2010).   As the Unit 4 Lecture 2 discusses exciting developments, what current products and projects extend and make available the ideas discussed above? Do you have any experience with digital environments that provide for collaborative research or utilize the workcenter approach as discussed with the DLITE environment?

3. Digital libraries are becoming part of the mainstream. What issues are these mature libraries facing in regards to their designs of structure? How do these issues differ from those faced by early digital libraries? In your answer, you could consider issues such as collection development, audience, funding, strategic planning, standards, etc.

4. Lesk discusses (p150) the debate concerning whether computer programs should be designed for expert users or novice users. As he explains, often a system that has enough explanations and menu choices to help novices is annoying or slow for experts. He goes further to explain the two basic arguments: 1). Since most people who buy a program use it many times, they spend most of their time as expert users, and so the program should be designed for experts, perhaps with some aids for novices. 2). Since many buying decisions are made by people who look at a program in a store or a trade show for only a few minutes programs should be designed for novices to increase sales. What do you think? What has your own experience been with software ñ either in building your digital library, or in general?

Chapter Six: Design and Interface

Interface design is not only one of the most important components for developing and constructing a digital library, but also an important skill for professional digital librarians.

Despite numerous small differences and origin stories, connection is the main goal of any digital library. The ability to connect various scattered users to a wide variety of information stored in countless locations is a crucial skill. However, there is more to connection than just the most up to date server or Wi-Fi router. Connection must also be achieved through those designing the databases and the patrons who will benefit from them. After all, is a digital library any good and are its goals really ever obtained if the public does not understand how to interact with the database?

Two of the most crucial features of a well-connected digital library are the design and interface. For our purposes, *design* refers to the way the information is organized and presented for patrons and users. The *interface* serves as the tools and methods patrons use to search, locate, and interact with the requested information. While both design and interface are separate entities, they are heavily linked and the successful (or not so successful) implementation of one will greatly impact the other.

6.1: Can the user be the weak link in a digital library?

It is essential that a digital library meet the needs of its users. What users are looking for and whether your digital library can satisfy those needs must be addressed. Usability is a hot study topic not only for information professionals, but also for system programmers, computer technology experts, and decision-makers across the board. Many studies have been conducted on digital library or website usability and its influence on system design and program evolution. Among many issues that connect to the usability studies, one question we ask in this unit is: Can the user be the weak link in a Digital Library?

Human attention: a limited resource

Levy (1997) considers the issues of reading and attention with applications to the digital environment. As Levy points out, there is a growing awareness that human attention is a highly limited resource; in the context of our information-enriched society, this presumably immutable limitation needs to be well understood. Levy recalls from the early psychologist William James (1890) that attention is "the taking possession of the mind, in clear and vivid form...Focalization, and concentration of consciousness are of its essence. It implies withdrawal from some things in order to deal effectively with others..." (p. 203). In the words of noted cognitive psychologist Herb Simon, "in a world where attention is a major scarce resource, information may be an expensive luxury, for it may turn our attention from what is important to what is unimportant. We cannot afford to attend to information simply because it is there." (p. 203)

Observation of attention has led to what W. Thorngate calls the *economics of attention*. Three of Thorngate's principles of attention economics are: "attention is a finite and non-renewable resource" (*principle of fixed attentional assets*); "attention can, in general, be invested in only one activity at a time" (*principle of singular attentional investments*); and "whenever we search for and choose attentional investments, the acts of searching and choosing themselves require attentional investments" (*principle of exploratory attentional expenses*) (p. 203 in Levy). To summarize, we have a fixed amount of attention, and it can be directed toward one activity at a time; the act of choosing among activities, itself, uses up attention. The overall effect in an information busy environment is that we may expend our attention on the single activity of trying to choose which other activity needs our attention (the *Catch 22* of the information society).

The relationship between reading material and our attention is of interest. During the Middle Ages, reading shifted to a primarily silent activity. Following the invention of the printing press, and the resultant explosion in the availability of books, there was an anxiety created by the sudden increased awareness of the amount of knowledge and the lack of organization of its various fragments. Between the end of the Middle Ages and the eighteenth century, an immense effort was put into creating vast organizational schemes and institutions to oversee these schemes. The expanded availability of books and the shift to silent reading, saw the development of *intensive* reading, that is, a rehearsed and varied knowledge obtained from rereading familiar material. The second half of the eighteenth century, with expanded book production, lending libraries, and newspapers, saw a shift to *extensive* reading habits, that is, the critical and avid reading of great breadths of material. The design of books, including typefaces, spacing, margins, and binding, aided the extensive reading process. More specifically, the design of books guided and focused our attention during extensive reading.

We have inherited the tradition of extensive reading. However, current trends in production of reading materials--from limited resolution screens to beeping and humming computers--work against the attention that is necessary to sustain extensive reading. Visually busy displays further compete for our attention. If digital libraries are to contribute to enhancing how we deal with information, designs for digital libraries must take into consideration what we know about how we read and to what we can attend.

Talking in libraries

Crabtree, Twidale, O'Brien and Nichols (1997) are concerned with the methodologies used in systems analysis and design, specifically in designing digital libraries. Crabtree et al. describe and justify their use of ethnomethodologically-informed ethnography to study query negotiation at the help desk of a university library. Crabtree et al. posit that the success of systems design depends on the social context into which the system will be placed. That is, to achieve success, the system must fit and complement the social character of the work setting. Ethnomethodologically-informed ethnography involves gathering descriptions of what is being done and the ways in which it is being done. This information must be gathered in the real world setting and activity.

In ethnomethodologically-informed ethnography, descriptions are gathered using a documentary method, that is, through recording the action on audio-tape (or video-tape, if appropriate) and analyzing the transcribed actions and interactions. This methodology permits the researcher to ask task-based questions of actors during the taping. Appropriate questions include *What are you doing?* And, *Why did you do that?*

This methodology helps uncover cooperative and sometimes subtle aspects of work that often go undiscovered using other methodologies. While the points made in this article are well taken, they are not well stated. The following work, notwithstanding Crabtree et al's criticism, is recommended for additional insight into the issue raised by these researchers:

- Taylor, R. S. (1968). Question-negotiation and information seeking in libraries. *College & Research Libraries 29*(3), 178-194.
- Works by Peter Ingwersen on interpersonal communication and library science are also worth reading, especially:
- Ingwersen, P. (1982). Search procedures in the library--analyzed from the cognitive point of view. *Journal of Documentation 38*(3), 165-191.
- Ingwersen, P & Kaae, S. User-librarian negotiations and information search procedures in public libraries: Analysis of verbal protocols. ED211051.

6.2: How do the public view libraries?

The Benton Report

The Benton Foundation, commissioned by the W. K. Kellogg Foundation, surveyed the public to determine the extent of their support of libraries, as libraries and their communities confront the digital world.

As a backdrop to this support, the Benton Foundation asked participants about their access to computers. 42% of those surveyed had access to a computer at home, 35% had access to a computer for personal use at work, and 40% had no access to a computer. Despite the perception that computers are ubiquitous, nearly half the population surveyed lacks access to computers and presumably needs a central (and we may infer free) location where they can learn about and have access to computers and newer information technologies.

30% of those surveyed mentioned (10% first mention; 20% second mention) the library as one of the first two places they would go to learn more about using a computer to find information through the internet and to learn about online services. 64% of respondents (41% first mention; 23% second mention) would ask somebody they know. 23% (7% first mention; 16% second mention) would buy a book or manual. 34% (17% first mention; 17% second mention) would take a class. Clearly, a well-planned and promoted information technology facility within a library could serve as an educational and information-gathering center for a community, particularly for the large numbers in the community without other access to computers.

In terms of future importance, 40% of those surveyed felt that libraries would become more important (as opposed to 19% who felt they would become less important) in the future due to the availability of information via computers. 37% felt it would be most important for public libraries to be a place where people can use computers to find information and to use online computer services (versus 35% who felt it is most important for public libraries to be a place where people can read and borrow books). Certainly, it is not unreasonable to look to libraries to fulfill both of these functions.

While some libraries seem to be hard-pressed for patrons who browse their shelves and use their reading rooms, some bookstores are doing a thriving business in this area. In comparing visits to a bookstore and to a public library for the purposes of browsing or purchasing of books, the bookstore was more frequented, notwithstanding a significant number who never visited either (22% did not visit a bookstore in the past year; 32% did not visit a library in the past year). One study (Brown, 1997) sheds some light on reasons why a bookstore may be more inviting than a library. Brown found non-library users preferred to read or purchase books in a bookstore because the clerks were more helpful in finding the needed material and the reading areas were more comfortable. This enhanced customer focus by bookstores is understandable, given the direct relationship between a bookstore's survival and the movement of customers and books through the store. Perhaps libraries need to consider their services in terms of a cost-benefit relationship. That is, placing a dollar value on each circulation and on each reference answer and measuring the volume of circulation and information given against the cost of operation of the circulating collection and reference desk.

Notwithstanding the found preference for bookstores, libraries are valued as potential hubs for community activity. 56% of those surveyed felt it was very important, and 26% felt it was moderately important for the library to serve as a neighborhood or community activity center, as a place for organizational or club meetings, and as a place to present concerts or lectures. Yet, the local school and community recreation center were named as the places that most often served these functions (combined first and second mentions: school, 56%; community recreation center, 50%; public library, 37%). Recall, the library took on more of a broader social function in ancient times, in some of the Carnegie Libraries in the United States, and in design of the Pompidou Center in Paris. Additional functions in these facilities have included a bath, a fitness center, game rooms, a reading garden, and a theater. Perhaps today's libraries need to view--and plan for servicing--information and information gathering in a broader social context as well as re-consider the social function of the public library in the community.

Funding computers and computer-based services for a library, however, can be somewhat problematic. When queried about sources of funding for libraries, 43% favored increasing taxes to cover the necessary costs, 39% favored charging user fees, and only 9% favored reducing services offered to the public. When asked how much a year in user fees the survey participant was willing to pay for library services, 35% responded 'nothing,' 27% responded $10, and another 27% responded $25.

One question has an interesting application to the funding problem. When asked "Now, imagine that you have a personal computer at home, which would you prefer: * Spending $20 a year to buy disks or information to install on your computer OR * Spending $20 a year in taxes that enable your public library to have an information service that you could access from your home computer." Among the respondents, 52% preferred to use the library, against 33% who preferred to buy disks. (In areas where it is difficult to find public sympathy for funding computer access, perhaps a shift in focus to funding information access via digital media would be more successful in raising bond and other monies for a public library-based technology center.)

In rating the importance of various library services for making difficult budget decisions, the following services were ranked as most important (to the individual respondent, for the community): reading hours and programming for children (83%, 84%); purchasing new books and printed materials (72%, 68%); maintaining, repairing, building libraries (65%, 62%); providing computers and online services to children and adults who don't have their own computers (60%, 60%); providing a place where librarians help people find information through computers and online services (58%, 59%); making access to library information possible from home computers (46%, 47%); purchasing computers and providing access to information and online services through computers (42%, 47%).

The Benton Report also looked at how library leaders viewed the library in the digital age. Though some voices in the field of library and information science envision a future of libraries without paper or walls, the Benton Report found library leaders, in general, want a hybrid institution that contains both digital and book collections (Benton Foundation, 1996). Library leaders and the public generally agree on the role of the library in at least the near future.

The Benton Group also conducted a focused group study with frequent library users. While focus group participants expressed many of the same ideas as survey participants, there were some discrepancies. The frequent library user did not see the library as a leader, especially in technology. In looking into the future, the focus group saw the library in thirty years as a museum of historical archives. Further, this group of frequent library users felt the trained library professional could be replaced with community volunteers. This group of frequent library users was also unwilling to increase taxes to support public libraries.

This study suggests that in the future the support for public libraries will come not from the current regular patron, but from those to whom the library is still a frontier. Most certainly, the library cannot afford to look past the needs of any group. Further, catering to the faithful could prove fatal in the end.

6.3: What factors should drive the design process?

There are at least five factors that affect the digital work:
- Foundations of human computer interaction (HCI)
- Understanding interaction design
- Understanding and conceptualizing interaction
- Understanding users
- Understanding how interfaces affect users

System interface design principles in general:
- Feasibility
- Integration
- Usability
- Consistency
- Reliability
- Security
- Recoverability

Feasibility principle. A system should be applicable to a broad scope of target situations including finance, time and benefits, and be compliant with technical standards, where appropriate.

Integration principle. Systems require users to interact with them to carry out their tasks. They should be configurable, predictable, and maintainable over all layers/subsystems, and should allow an organized approach to the derivation and revision of the different parameters. Interaction design is concerned with developing interactive products to support people in their working lives, and is multidisciplinary, involving many inputs from wide-reaching disciplines and fields. The barriers for knowledge integration include discipline-oriented mindset, different languages, naïve user-models and users as domain experts.

Usability principle. The idea here is to make a system easy to learn, easy to use and efficient to use. The system should be appropriate for different types of users, should not hinder user performance, and should use terms and concepts that are drawn from experience.

The goals of usability are that a system should: be effective to use, be efficient to use, have good utility, be easy to learn, and be easy to remember how to use.

- Effectiveness is a very general goal and refers to how good a system is at doing what it is supposed to do.
- Efficiency refers to the way a system supports users in carrying out their tasks. The system is efficient if it allows the user to carry out common tasks through a minimal number of steps.
- Learnability refers to how easy a system is to learn to use. A key concern is determining how much time users are prepared to spend learning a system. For more complex systems that provide a wider range of functionality, resources such as online help tutorials and web authoring tools may be appropriate.
- Utility refers to the extent to which the system provides the right kind of functionality so that users can do what they need or want to do.
- Memorability refers to how easy a system is to remember how to use, once learned. For example, users can be helped to remember the sequence of operations at different stages of a task through meaningful icons, command names, and menu options.

Consistency principle. Each subsystem/component should ensure its conformity to the system as a whole and ensure system sequence. The parts of the system should be visible or easily retrievable, accessible, or approachable.

Interaction design is increasingly concerning itself with creating systems that are: satisfying, motivating, fun, aesthetically pleasing, enjoyable, supportive of creativity, entertaining, helpful and more.

Traditional Design

The basic traditional design for a digital library has two access modes to obtain information. The first is a custom built interface that allows patrons to select a specific resource format such as books, articles, or mp3s. The patron selects one of these types and is directed to a search interface specifically for those resources.

Alternatively, the second most common design is a search engine that allows patrons to browse several different resource formats within a single search. This is often done through check boxes or drop down menus that enable the proper results. However, this can be much more taxing and time consuming from a technological and financial standpoint, so it is not as common as the first.

The following image shows a traditional digital collection design. Specifically, it is a screen capture from the Middlesex Community College articles and journals resource. This website is a collection of smaller and separately run databases that are available for use. However, there is no interaction or pooling of information between the various resources. Each database must be selected and searched independently from the others and the Middlesex page serves only as a central corralling point for the various search options.

Figure 6.1:

Obviously, there are some setbacks when running a traditional design, especially for the patrons. Each resource must be individually searched one at a time until the specified item is located; this can be quite time consuming even if the patron only has one search term to investigate. Also, some traditional designs are more tailored for the creators than the users. A longtime reference librarian might find this system simple enough. However, a first time patron with only Google search experience could be quickly overwhelmed by the wealth of search options provided. Sometimes less can be more.

Digital Work Environment (DWE)

Digital work environments are a sub-type of user based digital libraries. Digital work environments seek to eliminate the common traditional design problem of having all the various resources or databases isolated and not pooling information. The diagram below shows how various users and technologies within a digital work environment interacting and co-exist.

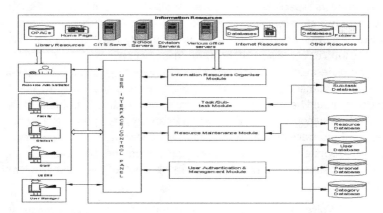

Diagram 6.1: A digital work environment interacting and co-exist

Digital work environments can go beyond the simple task of sharing resources. They allow a whole new degree of organization, planning, and interacting through the varying users of the resource.

Meyyappan (2002) explains how various users of an academic digital work environment could collaborate. The Information Resource Administrator is responsible for collecting information about sub-tasks, the information resources required to accomplish the task, and the creation and maintenance of the resource database. The User Manager, as the name implies, manages the overall collection of user-related information, creation of user accounts, maintenance of the user database and users' personal space data in the personal database. The General Academic Users are the end users of the DWE. They include faculty, students and staff who use the system to access the information resources to meet their information needs while accomplishing some tasks at hand.

Interface Principles

What exactly constitutes good interface design?
Traditionally, interface design has encompassed everything that appears on users' computer monitors, the method in which they view it, and the methods in which they are able to interact or edit the material. Sheneiderman, an expert in human computer actions, offered a number of general guidelines and suggestions for digital interface design.

Sheneiderman felt that interfaces should strive for consistency and closure. Everything should generally remain the same from page to page and day to day. Maintaining similar features such as layout, colors, fonts, buttons, and database specific language would help foster an environment of familiarity. Users would feel comfortable with the interface and believe they fully understood its capacities. The closure was also key to familiarity and good user interaction. Patrons need to be able to know when they've utilized a resource to its fullest capacity. Interfaces should plainly state when a user has run out of resources or viewed all the items in a category.

Sheneiderman's type of interface is also very forgiving. It is designed fully aware that humans constantly make small mistakes and is able to adapt to that. Users should be able to easily correct errors in a timely fashion. Tools needed to be designed to allow them to undo and reverse previous actions. Well-designed interfaces under these principles allow their users to quickly retrace their footsteps. Also, error messages cannot be ambiguous or in technical terms. Simple messages must inform the user of the exact problem and how to fix it.

There is also a heavy emphasis placed on customization and personal preferences. Alternative interfaces are offered to match the varying skill level of the user. Additional features or shortcuts should also be included for potential use by expert patrons. Feedback is also provided in a transparent way so users don't end up going around in circles.

Finally, a well-designed interface is convenient for the user. Interfaces should reduce the required short-term memory load by keeping a history of previous actions and allowing the user to quickly go back to former searches or tasks.

What are design challenges?

As with all early technology, there are some constant and serious challenges that digital library design faces. Often these problems arise from separate groups and institutions all working within their own preferred methods. Incompatibility becomes a frequent challenge as different computer types, file formats, operating systems, structuring, information organization and retrieval procedures are all forced to interact. Witten (2008) ponders if conformity is needed:

> An ideal approach would be to develop only one set of standards and ask that all digital libraries and other stake holders, such as information creators and service provides, follow them strictly. However, this approach is not only difficult to implement due to practical and political reasons, but it may not be desired, either. Forcing everyone to follow one set of standards may close the door to innovation. (p.70).

Even if conformity is not the answer, a better sense of communication and basic standards must be present in the future.

System Design Process

Conceptual design
- The set of activities required to answer the question: what does the DL look like for the process?
- Explicit construction of idea.
- Concepts that everyone needs to learn about such as what the goal is, what it can do, and how it is intended to be used.

Object-oriented design
- Object-oriented design is the method that leads to system structure/architectures based on the objects that every system or subsystem manipulates. (by Meyer)

User-centered design
- All systems need not be designed to suit everyone but should be designed around the needs and capabilities of those people who will use them.

The Design process for user-centered design includes these items:
- The design is the creation of user scenarios and analysis of their profile.
- Designers are device experts. Users are task expert.
- Designers must please their clients.

The right designer's perspective is to think how the DL and interface should support what the user wants to do, rather than what the system is capable of doing. The designers should know users and their goals.

There are four questions to ask early in the design process:
- Who are my users and how will they perceive the DL?
- What are the users' primary and secondary goals?
- What areas are used frequently, sequentially, concurrently, or are critical?
- What are their needs, interests, skills, and knowledge?

Visual based Interface Tools

Human beings are overwhelmingly visual learners, so it is no surprise that many interface functions are structured around visible flexibility and customization. Additionally, well-designed digital libraries will have an overall clean visual presentation that is easy on the viewers' eyes. For the purpose of ease and a kinder learning curve, many of the tools and functions are based upon or borrowed from common word publishers and web browsers.

One of the most prevalent visual tools is a magnifying glass that allows users to adjust the size. The standard array of movement is provided through the panning and rotating features. A similar, but less common option is known as focus plus context. The user gets to select a section of the article or book to focus on and the other pages will shrink or become blurred out to provide maximum attention.

From there the visual options offered get only more complex. A cone tree can provide a fish eye like view where the selected segments appear more towards the center of the screen and much brighter. The parts not focused on become smaller and duller. This view is most useful when overlooking a structural document such as a flow chart or family tree.

Perhaps the most unconventional tool is the perspective wall. Essentially, the screen is broken into three grey sectors to provide a three-dimension look. The middle third of the screen provides the most detailed view. The side sections are used mainly for context. The perspective wall is most commonly used and helpful for linear based documents such as maps and illustrated stories.

These are just some of the visual-based aids that are currently widespread and successful. New interface tools and visual-based technologies are constantly being proposed and experimented with. As the variety of items offered in a digital library expands, so will the need for new ways to examine and view them. Chowdhury discusses how these visually-based innovations are among the most popular and growing areas of study for librarians and designers alike:

> The digital library user interface is an exciting area of research and researchers from various fields are now working in this area. The first International Workshop on Visual Interfaces to digital libraries was held Roanoke Virginia, on June 28th, 2001. The one-day workshop drew an international audience of 47 researchers' practitioners, and graduate students in the area of information visualization, digital libraries, human- computer interactions, library and information science, computer science and geography. The primary aim of the conference was to raise awareness of several interrelated fields related to the design and use of visual interfaces for digital libraries. (p.166)

Eden (2005) also goes into much greater depth about types of information visualization and their potential uses.

By their very nature, digital libraries are very visual, which has an impact on the blind and visually impaired community's ability to use them. "Our analysis reveals that BVI users are vulnerable in DL environments because present DL designs do not sufficiently support these users' diverse skills in their interactions with the DL material and features," Han et al. write (2016). Simple features like the option to convert embedded content to descriptive text and the usage of easily visible labels can enhance the BVI community's digital library experience (Han et al., 2016). The lack of accessibility features in digital libraries makes it difficult for everyone to gain access. Moving forward, digital libraries must add accessibility elements into their digital platforms.

6.4: What are design philosophies for digital libraries?

When you visit a digital library, the first questions you may encounter as a digital librarian usually are these: what do you think about the design of the library, and what should we do better in terms of the designing?

There are two main questions we should ask in order to improve the design and increase the usability of a digital library: what are the basic principles for interface design, and what are the basic processes in interface design?

A digital library is a system, and the design should be based on system analysis, the process by which the analysis model is transformed into a model that is capable of being implemented, and describes the solution to the problems the system faces.

There are many different types of systems. An *open* system is a system interacting freely with its environment, and must evolve. A *closed* system does not interact with the environment. A *decomposition* system breaks large systems into smaller, more manageable components. A *modularity* system divides a system in modules of relatively equal size. A *coupling* system represents the degree of dependence among subsystems that should be relatively independent of one another. A *cohesion* system is the extent to which a subsystem performs a single function.

To view a system in its entirety, the designer should understand the system's scope and boundaries, identify the major functions to be performed by the system, decompose the functions into well-defined parts, understand the component inter-relationships, understand the workflow among components, and lastly, account for constraints imposed from within and from outside the system.

Digital Libraries Interfaces

Digital library interfaces can vary wildly from one collection to the next. The reasons for such discrepancies come from numerous factors such as intended users, institutional goals, content, item format, and designers. Similarly, the complexity of these interfaces runs the entire spectrum from simplistic to nearly impossible to navigate unless you are trained in the intended field.

To the untrained eye this may all just seem like frivolous customization and a stubborn allegiance to one's own system, but many experts feel the impact and importance of various interfaces goes well beyond personal preference. Chowdhury provides a few of these opinions:

Bates (2002) stresses that interface design is pivotal to the effective use of an information system, and that the application environment of information retrieval systems has its own distinct needs and characteristics that need to be understood and addressed in design. Hearst (1999) comments that an interface designer must make decisions about how to arrange various kinds of information on the screen and how to structure the possible sequence of user – system interactions. (p.163)

Digital Library Design Principles

Although digital libraries come in a wide variety of formats and are open to various designers' interpretation, there are some guiding design principles that are generally agreed upon. These aren't laws, but the most successful digital libraries often abide by them in their designing process.

Starting with the basics, a digital library must be created within a legal context. Additionally, a standard terminology should be used consistently throughout the system, and every item within the system must be assigned a name and identifier. This helps combat miscommunication with the various individuals or organizations working on the process and keeps files easy to locate. The same holds true for the terminology the patrons will interact with in the finished project.

It is also important that the digital library and the items within it remain monitored. Objects cannot just be uploaded and forgotten about for all eternity. Employees need to make sure the materials are still up to date, classified, obtainable, and not being used for any malicious purposes.

Arguably the most important principle is that the loyalties of digital libraries and their builders align with collections of knowledge rather than with current technology. It is dangerous for designers to get too attached or fond of one particular technology or file format. It may not be accessible to the majority of your patrons or it could unexpectedly become obsolete. It is more important to provide as many ways to utilize a resource as possible. Additionally, the users are more interested in the works than the digital formats. The ability to easily export the works in a variety of common formats is crucial to a digital library's usefulness.

User Centered Digital Libraries

User centered design principles:
- Important to know what design guidance is available and use what is already known
- Make it possible to determine what actions are possible at any time.
- Make things visible and understandable.

- Follow natural mappings between the intention and required actions, and between the actions and resulting effects.

Currently, most patrons interact directly with the interface to access outside databases or resources. The extra step in the process allows librarians to work as a intermediary to create and tweak a filtering system that takes patron searches and improves upon them in order to produce more useful results. Unlike the traditional model, more complexly designed libraries can also search across several resources and formats at a time.

One cornerstone of user-centered design is customization and personal preferences. Well-designed user centered databases allow patrons to add or strip away options to their display. These choices can serve more than just a cosmetic purpose; digital libraries can be tailored to match the education and research skills of different users. Thus, expert users can have the advance features and work-related quick links they desire, but newcomers won't be overwhelmed with options as sometimes is the case with traditional model digital libraries.

Some academic user-centered digital libraries take into account the studies and interests of the searcher when finding relevant results. Chowdhury (2003) elaborates about the Headline project:

> The Personal Information Environment (PIE) presents users with pages of resources that are relevant to their courses and / or departments. PIE users are also presented with an "All resources" page that contains all the resources accessible through the library. Users can create their own list of resources on their personal page. The headline model also stores information such as subject and course. This is used to generate information resources that are more relevant. (p. 70).

Even social networking trends and techniques have influenced the user-oriented digital libraries. Beyond creating their own custom pages and resource lists, some digital libraries now allow patrons to share their creations with other users. The most progressive (or some would say foolhardy) institutions are experimenting with user created content, allowing patrons to add, edit, and comment on information. The widespread acceptance of this is still far off, but even the first steps marks a radical shift in philosophy. Witten (2010) expands on this:

> Of course, librarians traditionally discourage patrons from adding value to paper materials (or defacing them, as librarians tend to see it). Neither did librarians permit users to add their own cards to the card catalog. However, with digital content, users can choose if they want to access the original versions or the user enhanced ones, because user content is stored separately from the original copies and can be combined or viewed separately as the occasion demands (p.67).

Multimedia Digital Libraries

As technology continues to advance and more of the global population gains Internet access, some digital libraries may evolve into systems that have very little resemblance to the ones utilized by today's patrons. The emphasis placed on text-based items might also be radically changed to suit an increasingly visual world. New visual based technology could help them gain access to valuable information in other languages and preserve their oral histories or myths.

The goal of multimedia libraries is to help less utilized information formats, such as audio recording or videos, gain a sort of first class citizenship within physical and digital library collections.

Often times, the collection development for such items has been neglected or the systems being utilized cannot handle their formats. However, crucial information does not necessarily need to be expressed in the written tradition, and these resources can prove crucial. Witten suggests how much medical knowledge and research can be supplemented with visual or audio resources. A specific example provided is a digital copy of *First Aid In Pictures* by M.B. Delong. This item with no words could be a big help to patrons of any language or culture.

Initially, this may idea may be too niche or a poor use of resources, but Witten describes the value it could serve everyone:

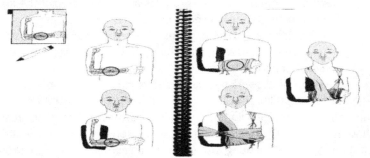

Figure 6.2

Imagine having access to collections that spring out of rich histories such as China or Arabia, created by people who had grown up in these cultures, without having to learn a new language. More practically (since you dear reader are culturally privileged and can probably access this information in translation) imagine giving someone in the highlands of Peru, fluent and literate in only her native language, access to first hand information in humanitarian collections from the Humanitarian Development Library. (p.427).

Such lofty goals will become increasingly more realistic as the price of audiovisual technologies continues to fall and their use becomes more widespread. Even children can now create a virtual photo gallery or edit a simple movie on a laptop; the things trained professionals will be capable of is simply staggering.

Still, there will always be those opposed to change. Many might even view the amount of focus on digital libraries currently offered as enough or too much. Witten argues that libraries must remain current and relevant to those they serve or risk becoming obsolete:

We book lovers may deplore the decline of the printed word, laud the sustained argument carefully built up over pages, and praise the power of the written word to conjure up some far more imaginative and powerful imagery than any TV can. We can lament the decrease in attention span, the reduction of arguments to sound bites. We may wish our children spent more time reading books and less time playing video games. But we must live in the world too, and the world is changing. (p.429).

6.5: How can digital libraries be accessible with disabilities?

When creating a digital library, one of the factors that should be considered is described by Are the websites of urban public libraries accessible to people with disabilities? (Liu et al., 2019) According to Liu et al., websites should comply with the Americans with Disabilities Act's standards (ADA). "...gave disabled Americans redress and an outlet to pursue the same rights as persons who do not suffer from a disability, as well as ensuring that private and public enterprises provide reasonable accommodations for those with impairments," according to the American Disabilities Act (Liu et al., 2019). Within the ADA, Section 508 is a set of minimal acceptable standards (Liu et al., 2019). Designing a digital library to fulfill the ADA's minimum standards can enable people with impairments gain access.

In their investigation, Liu et al. discovered that only seven out of 122 libraries had no Section 508 problems on their websites. Missing alternative tests, linked images with missing alternative text, missing labels, broken skip links, and contrast issues were among the errors. Because of the lack of these standards, visually impaired people will have a difficult time reading or using a screen reader on these homepages. Over half of the libraries' homepages would have been inaccessible to a screen reader, according to reports (2019).

Another difficulty with accessibility is device-dependent event handler circumstances, which make it necessary to navigate homepages using a mouse and keyboard (Liu et al., 2019). This makes navigation of webpages difficult for persons who are unable to use a keyboard.

The interaction of visually impaired and blind (BVI) users with digital libraries was investigated by Xie et al. BVI users want accessibility features like a clear menu bar at the top of the page where the screen reader starts, clear and meaningful menu item labels, transcripts for images and embedded text, clear and descriptive text describing the results of their search query, and step-by-step instructions with embedded descriptive text and hypertext on how to locate and access digital library items, according to the experimenters (2020).

Digital libraries should consider following the WCAG 2.0 guidelines. WCAG 2.0 is a set of standards developed by the World Wide Web Consortium (W3C). The W3C is an international organization that works to define web standards with members, full-time staff, and the general public (W3C, 2019a). Section 508 of the Americans with Disabilities Act (ADA) states simply that "websites, email, or web documents must be completely accessible to persons with disabilities" (Edelberg, 2019).

Section 508 has been using the WCAG 2.0 as guidelines since the Refresh of 2018. WCAG is a global standard, whereas Section 508 is specific to the United States. WCAG is a more rigorous and particular standard that is widely accepted around the world. W3C updated its accessibility requirements in June 2018. The list of suggestions is long and divided into four categories: perceivable, operable, understandable, and robust.

These guidelines are very helpful in giving detail on criteria and how to make a website accessible. W3C suggests that a website's information and operation be presented in a clear and intelligible manner when making it ADA accessible (W3C, 2018). Making text legible and understandable in human language is part of this. Human language refers to communication between humans that is spoken, written, or signed (through American Sign Language, visual or tactile, Braille). If jargon or idioms are utilized, the website should also include a means for defining these unique or odd phrases and pronunciations. Making web pages "look and work in predictable ways," according to the W3C, as well as providing input assistance to help users rectify and avoid mistakes in data entry, and "labels or instructions are presented when content requires user input," according to the W3C. (2018).

Conclusion:

While the new technologies and design philosophies behind digital libraries can often get quite complex, their main goal is quite clear: digital libraries must connect their users to their desired resources as quickly and easily as possible. Although the hard work behind design and interface can often go unnoticed, they are absolutely crucial elements to obtaining this goal. Without them a digital library is just a high tech storage room. The contents inside will go to waste unless given the key.

Study Questions for Chapter Six:

1. In designing user interfaces there is usually a conflict between novice and expert users. An interface can be well designed for a novice and irritate an expert. An interface may be well designed for an expert but too difficult for a novice. How would you design an interface that could be utilized

effectively by both novices and experts? What elements would such a system include?

  2. Lesk talks about the willingness/unwillingness of people to read from screens instead of paper. What do you think are the implications for interface design?

  3. What are the benefits of the CONSULS access interface/s as compared to a web search engine like Google? What factors might the library have taken into consideration in evaluating the interface/s of CONSULS?

  4. Is the time necessary to create a single user interface and thus the interoperability with other systems worthwhile? Are there any examples you would share where you think this has been successfully presented?

Chapter Seven: User Behavior and Interactions

The term "information behavior" has been used in a number of different contexts; indeed, it can refer to the entire constellation of responses that occur when people interact (or refuse to interact) with information from a variety of sources in their daily lives (Savolainen, 2007; Case, 2007). Information behavior also encompasses the related field of information use, which, together with information seeking and evaluation, comes under the discipline of information literacy.

Information seeking is a ubiquitous human behavior. Humans search for information actively and passively, for serious reasons and as a mere diversion. Some have even argued that ignoring and avoiding information are relevant areas of inquiry in the field of studying information-seeking behavior. Over the past twenty to thirty years, studies of information-seeking behavior have increased exponentially, with an estimated 10,000 documents crossing many disciplines (Case, 2007, p. 14).

The creation and proliferation of computers and the World Wide Web, the subsequent gathering of incredible amounts of information in one metaphorical place ("online"), and the limited ways to access this place (usually web browsers of one sort or another) are why so many studies on information-seeking behavior have occurred recently.

Understanding how users seek information is vital to designing digital resources that can be used effectively, and to providing instruction that can help users improve their searching skills. In order to discuss the field of information seeking, we shall first set it in context by providing some background, and then present some of the basic concepts used in the field.

7.1 Information Needs and Relevance

The success of a digital library can be judged by its sustainability. Sustainability for digital libraries can be accomplished when their methods of accessing, storing, and selecting digital content are based on their users' information-seeking behavior and needs. The methodologies used in contextual information and retrieval are important, but so are usability, social connectivity, and the interoperability of a digital library. Research studies indicate that the information needs of users have directly impacted technology in libraries; the changes in digital access to information and web users' experiences are shaping our libraries of the 21st century.

The organization of the digital library determines how the user will interact with the design. It has been found that users' cognitive styles impact their reactions to the organization of subject categories: "Whereas one group of users preferred alphabetical display, the other group of users seemed to favor the ordered display. The results indicated that users usually had their own preferences to different browsing interface designs" (Zhang, 2008).

Flexible interfaces are being used to accommodate the preferences of users with different cognitive styles, and the ability to offer flexible interfaces and user-customization should be a major advantage of digital libraries and digital information objects over traditional library collections.

Browsing is another important component in terms of interaction design for digital libraries. Browsing not only relies on the users' awareness of where the destination is, but also how to get there. This idea of "how to get there" is closely aligned with how the browsing interface design is constructed. Different designs may affect how users reach the wanted information and may end in different user performance (Zhang, 2008).

Tennant (1999) offers suggestions as to how to combat some of these issues. He believes system designers cannot ignore the responsibility to create a usable system. One of the principles he suggests is to talk to the users: "The best way to discover how users like your system is to ask them. That 'asking' can include focus groups, surveys, polls, and informal conversations. Methods that are always available (such as links from web pages) will encourage ongoing user feedback" (Tennant, 1999). Koohang (2005) agrees, arguing that a close relationship among design developers and users of digital libraries will result in a library that fits the users' needs in all ways. King (2009) discusses ways to understand library users and their needs and wants.

Developing measurable goals when redesigning an interface to improve sites is incredibly important, yet not always followed: "Redesign goals were often soft and, in some cases, even unidentifiable. Most site owners described design goals vaguely by saying they were 'updating their look and feel' or 'making their site simpler'" (Head, 2003) Creating a measurable goal, then creating a design that will meet that goal is important when thinking about interaction and interface design. This is when the use of personas may help the design team.

Wilson's model of information behaviors

There has been much research performed to help understand a user's behavior and need for seeking information. In this segment we will look at some of that research. One of the most prominent researchers in this field is T.D. Wilson, who developed two models of information behavior, many years apart, indicating growth in thought in the field. In this section, we look at the second model. In his second model he examines research performed in other fields, such as psychology, and consumer research, to complete his model. This model stresses the context of the individual who is doing the information seeking rather than the context of the system of retrieval.

Wilson and other researchers understood that individuals with information needs may differ in how they go about verbalizing their needs, then locating and retrieving that information. With the development of Wilson's model, researchers were able to discover stages where information seeking behavior would need further study, finding that this model was not complete. (For a view of Wilson's model see http://informationr.net/tdw/publ/2005SIGUSE.html)

The context of a seeker's need may be the person himself, "or the role demands of the person's work or life, or the environments (political, economic, technological, etc.) within that life or work takes place" (Wilson, 2000). Brenda Dervin worked on the sense-making aspect of information-seeking. This work coincides with Wilson's model. Her theory on sense-making states that a person's demographics, (e.g., ethnicity, race, gender, culture and class) influence how the seeker makes sense of information (Dervin, 1999). This is exemplified by Wilson's model under the middle sections of psychological, demographics, role-related or interpersonal, environmental and source characteristics.

Consumer information needs

Part of Wilson's research led him to study patient and doctor information-seeking and dissemination. Wilson notes in Weigt's article on *Patients' information seeking actions and physicians' responses in gynecological consultations* that information needs for patients followed these categories;
- Need for new information
- Need to clarify information already held
- Need to confirm information already held
- Need to clarify beliefs/values held
- Need to confirm beliefs/values held

The need for new information included the need to clarify information and to verify it as well. The patients wanted to realign themselves with information that they know is true and correct, that they understand it, and that it is accepted, or not.

Consumers need information that is readily available and trustworthy. It would be detrimental not to be able to access needed information or to have the information come at a high cost. A consumer health study revealed that patients were most likely to seek out health care providers for answers to their questions; utilizing the library was the second most popular option. Credibility is extremely important with consumers. Generally it is noted that information taken from publicity is thought to be more reliable than a paid advertisement while information from an objective source is considered the most trustworthy (Wilson, 1996).

Stress and coping

As a way of dealing with information or lack of information, Wilson borrowed the "Stress and Coping Theory" from the field of psychology. If a person does not have enough information they may tend to be stressed about the situation. However, one may also become stressed with too much information, or information overload. Therefore, the outcome of their situation is unpredictable. If the person has sufficient information stress is likely reduced. Two ways of understanding coping are problem-focused and emotion-focused. With problem-focused coping, one tries to change the circumstances of the situation and with emotion-focused coping one alters the way in which the situation is perceived. (Wilson, 1996)

Wilson notes that there is a range of stresses due to intolerance of uncertainty and anxiety that leads to becoming more sensitive to the information need and acting on that need, becoming vigilant in finding that information. The opposite end of this spectrum is that one is intolerant of arousal of interest in finding information and represses the need with constant avoidance.

Wilson found several variables to be barriers or instigators of action to seek information. They are psychological (cognitive dissonance), demographic (education level, economic status), role related (attitude of the information provider) environmental (lack of time, interruptions), information source characteristics (accessibility, credibility).

Psychological

Cognitive dissonance refers to recognition of conflicts that give people discomfort and their desire to get rid of this discomfort by resolving the situation. One way to resolve this is to find information that supports current knowledge, values, beliefs, or some information that can change these elements. Because some people don't have a desire to seek more information, it is believed that people have differing levels of cognitive need.

Demographic

Wilson found in studies that people with higher degrees of education often felt more knowledgeable on subjects and therefore didn't necessarily seek more information. However, there were also cases of information seeking when the subject matter was deemed to be of more importance.

Role related

A study noted that there were physiological characteristics (hearing, lack of medical knowledge, nervousness) that caused barriers for the patient while seeking information during medical consultations. Three factors were identified in the information-seeking behavior of patients:
1. Characteristics and perceptions of the patient
2. Characteristics in the patient's companion and the specialist
3. Characteristics of the organization and situation (Wilson, 1996).

Environmental

Outside variables can also factor in as barriers to information seeking. These can include:
1. Time- interruptions such as phone calls, stress of the situation and lack of familiarity with medical terminology.

2. Geographic location, gender, and age- Information knowledge decreased as age increased in urban areas, women in rural areas increased knowledge at a younger age, decreased slightly in middle age and then rose again as they got older. Older men in rural areas received much less information than younger men. (Wilson, 1996)

Risk and reward

A mechanism that was identified as activating information-seeking behavior is the "Risk/Reward Theory. "According to this theory, consumers will engage in more information-seeking when the risks are higher, with the idea that if there is high risk, there will be high reward.

There are various components to risk, in consumer research:
1. Performance risk: will the product act according to standard?
2. Financial risk: is the product affordable or could another product suffice?
3. Physical risk: is the product safe?
4. Social risk: will the product impress people?
5. Ego risk: will the product make the owner happy? (Wilson, 1996)

These components could be adapted for student information behavior:
1. Performance risk: Will the information found be sufficient for the information needed and help complete the project at hand?
2. Can it be obtained without much expense?
3. Will it get the student a good grade?
4. Will the student learn what is needed, or will more information need to be acquired?

Self-efficacy

Self-efficacy involves beliefs and is another mechanism of activation. If a user doesn't believe that having more knowledge about an issue will increase his understanding of that issue, he probably won't look for more information on the topic. However, if more information is perceived to help solve a problem, we are more likely to seek out information (Case, 2007).

Social learning theory

The "Social Learning Theory" explains another activation mechanism. This theory is the belief that it is possible to act on the behavior required to produce an outcome. Individuals can believe that a course of action will produce an outcome, but if there are doubts about being able to perform the necessary activities to produce the desired outcome, that still doesn't affect their behavior (Wilson, 1996).

Information-seeking behavior involves passive attention, passive search, active search and ongoing search. An example of passive attention is listening to the radio or watching TV; information may come to the seeker without the seeker actively looking for it. With passive search, one search may lead to the information seeker finding information pertinent to something else they want to know about. An active search for information is when a person is actively looking for information. Ongoing search for information occurs when the search has been established, but more research may add to the framework of what is already being worked on (Wilson, 1996).

After the information is gathered, it must be analyzed and used in some manner. Although there has been some research done on information processing, there is no guarantee that information found and processed will be used in decision-making (Wilson, 1996).

Anomalous state of knowledge (ASK) - Belkin (1980)

Nicholas Belkin states that information searching begins with a problem and a need to solve it. The information seeker hopes and assumes that the Information Retrieval (IR) system will help to satisfy that user's need. The IR system is a communication system. This system starts with an author who wants to express their knowledge of the world.

The role of the user determines the success/failure of an information system. Representing users' needs is as important to a system's success as representing the content of a system. Evaluation of an IR system is completed by the user, so it is important to have their needs considered when the retrieval abilities of the system are being mapped out (Belkin, 1980).

Belkin is known for his Anomalous State of Knowledge Theory. He states that IR is concerned with the transfer of information from a human generator (one state of knowledge) to human user (another state of knowledge) when a user is cognizant of a need for information, "the perceived inadequacy is interpreted as an aspect of the user's anomalous state of knowledge." (Belkin, 1980)

Anomalous state of knowledge (ASK) is defined as the following: "anomalous" refers to the unusual, "state" refers to a condition, and "knowledge" refers to understanding. If there are gaps in the mind of the information seeker, the seeker may not be clear on how to achieve information retrieval.

Belkin proposes that a search begins with a problem and a need to solve it; the gap between these is defined as the information need. The user gradually builds a bridge of levels of information, which may change the question or the desired solution as the process continues. (Belkin, n.d.)

Steps of the ASK model

1. User's UNSTRUCTURED Problem Statement (ASK)
2. ASK is converted to STRUCTURED category
3. Retrieval system selected
4. Information is presented to the user
5. User reviews information and then decides
    a. System's method of choice was
        i. suitable
        ii. not suitable
    b. Did the information relate to the problem?
        i. yes
        ii. no
    c. Have the information requirements changed?
        i. yes
        ii. no
6. Based on responses
    Finish or Return to step 3
7. System changes retrieval mechanism
    Finish or Return to step 2
8. System modifies problem structure
    Finish or Return to step 1 (Belkin, n.d.).

The user realizes his information need and so finds himself in an anomalous state of knowledge, which is then transformed into a request, motivating information-seeking behavior. However, this information seeking can be difficult because the user may not be able to specify what it is he/she is searching for.

Information needs (Taylor, 1968)

Many of the theories of these researchers are based upon insights gained by other researchers. Belkin's ASK model, for example, was built upon Taylor's model. Taylor "suggests that questions put to IR systems go through four stages, the first two being the visceral need or the internal, actual but unexpressed and perhaps inexpressible need for information, and the conscious need or the realized, within-brain, ambiguous and ill defined description of need" (Belkin, 1980).

Visceral need

The visceral need starts out as a need for information not existing in the remembered experience of the inquirer. The need can be vague. It will change form as more information is added to make it clearer as either analogy or as the importance of the need grows (Taylor, 1968).

Conscious need.

Conscious need is when the inquirer becomes aware of the need, but has a mental description that is ill-defined and there is indecision. It is possible that they will talk to someone to become clear about the need, still trying to define it. At this point, one of two things will hopefully occur: they will find that the person they're talking to understands the issue, or the ambiguity will continue (Taylor, 1968).

Formalized need

The inquirer can express the formalized need verbally. They can describe what the question is about, but not necessarily within the confines of the information system where they are seeking the answer. Also, at this point the inquirer may view the librarian as part of the information system itself, but not so the colleague that was questioned in the conscious need step. (Taylor, 1968)

Compromised need

With the compromised need we find that the inquirer discovers that the question may have to be reformulated to be able to retrieve information properly from the information system. This is due to the way the information system is indexed and cataloged. (Taylor, 1968)

Taylor's theory assumed that libraries should be communication centers, rather than passive warehouses. Effectively, librarians need to be skilled in taking the inquirer back to the formalized need, possibly even to the conscious need and then to translate these into an effective search strategy (Taylor, 1968). In digital libraries, users are often working alone without the support of a librarian. So, the designer must question: how can the system itself help the user work through their conscious and/or formalized need to formulate this effective search strategy?

Relevance judgments and their relation to information needs

User perception throughout the process of information seeking will result in the user's assessment of the relevance of retrieved information. These judgments are also made according to the user's satisfaction or dissatisfaction with the information retrieved. In the most fundamental sense, relevance has to do with effectiveness of communication. Relevance is considered as a measure of the effectiveness of a contract between a source and a destination in a communication process. (Saracevic, 1975)

There are two main classes of relevance in IR research. The first is system driven. This approach treats relevance as fixed and as an objective concept. The second class is the cognitive user-oriented approach, which describes relevance as a subjective mental experience that involves reforming thoughts in the individual's mind (Borlund, 2003). The system or algorithmic relevance describes the relation between the question asked and the collection of the retrieved information. Algorithmic relevance is calculated by giving ranked values to the retrieved information. (Saracevic, 1975)

Topical relevance

The topical or subject relevance is associated with the *aboutness* of a retrieved piece. *Aboutness* is also referred to as usefulness, usability, or utility of information objects (information retrieved) in relation to the fulfillment of goals, interests, and tasks associated with the user. (Saracevic, 1975)

Cognitive relevance

Cognitive relevance or pertinence is related to the information need as perceived by the information seeker. Pertinence is the relationship between the ingrained information need of the user and the retrieved information objects as interpreted by the user. (Saracevic, 1975)

Situational relevance

Situational relevance depends on the task interpretation. It is the usefulness of the perceived information object that is retrieved and how it pertains to the actual information need.

Motivational relevance

Motivational and affective relevance is goal oriented. This is the relevance between the intent of the user and information objects. (Saracevic, 1975) Most relevance judgments are subjective, relating to the user's situation. Because of their subjective nature, it is hard to incorporate them into IR experiments.

Topicality

Topicality (is the subject of the information my topic?) is usually the main consideration people use to make relevance judgments. There are also other factors that can be taken into consideration, including;

1. Novelty: uniqueness of the source; the user's familiarity with the source.
2. Currency: is the source is up to date?
3. Quality of the information the source provides: is it well-written, credible, and understandable?
4. Presentation and comprehensiveness of the information.
5. Is the source well-known in the field?
6. Information aspects of the source: does it describe techniques or provide examples?
7. Appeal: is the source interesting or enjoyable?

The relevance criteria most used was found to be topicality, the second most used was information aspects, and the least used was currency.

Salience

Salience is less often discussed in information seeking, and describes the degree to which information catches our attention. It is closely related to relevance, though an item that appears salient during a search may not be relevant to the problem at hand, while one that does not catch our attention may indeed be highly relevant. (Case, 2007)

Selective exposure

Selective exposure and *avoidance* are ideas that involve many factors, such as a seeker's tendency to accept or dismiss ideas that do not support previous beliefs, or the need to filter information for other reasons, such as taste, an overwhelming volume of data, or limited time. Case suggests that the available research indicates that most users do not actually avoid information, but rather simply choose not to use it (Case, 2007).

Yuan, Belkin and Kim concluded that the relevance criteria were core criteria and they applied to a wide variety of information use and information problem types. This study is thought to be the "first time that a direct representation of a person's information 'need' or problem has been shown to be related to the relevance criteria which that person would bring to bear when evaluating documents." (Yuan, 2002)

7.2 Online Information-Seeking Behavior and Search Strategy

Information seeking and search strategy are the process of iterative interaction between an information system and an information seeker. Typical online information systems are OPACs, online databases, search engines, and digital libraries. Information seeking can be intermediated or direct. Here we are concerned with direct, or end-user, searching. As the term implies, direct searching is when the end-user searches for information herself, as is the case with most online searching. Web search engines have come to dominate online searching to the point where the creators of OPACs, online databases, and digital libraries find it imperative to emulate search engine-like discoverability in order to attract and retain end users. Information seeking usually refers to interaction between a person and an information system (e.g., an OPAC), and information searching refers to the specific behavior exhibited when users engage an information system (e.g., entering search terms or browsing an OPAC) (Xie, 2009).

Basic concepts

Information need

In his book *Looking for Information: A Survey of Research on Information Seeking, Needs, and Behavior*, Donald Case (2007) emphasizes the difficulty in defining exactly what comprises information, from various theoretician's points of view. Information need is defined by Case as a state in an information seeker's mind that causes thoughts and actions through which they obtain something they desire. It is also described as the state in which a person recognizes that his or her knowledge is inadequate to satisfy an information-seeking goal (Case, 2002). He finally settles on the broad definition inspired by anthropologist Gregory Bateson, which he paraphrases as "whatever appears significant to a human being" (as cited in Case, 2007, p. 40). For the purposes of this overview, the definition of information can be reduced even further, limiting it to the narrow requirements set by the model Shannon proposed (as cited in Case, 2007): information must be useful, intentionally transmitted, recordable, and verifiable. Information within a digital library meets these requirements. Clearly, it is considered useful by the person who is seeking it. It is capable of being stored electronically, it has been intentionally placed for use by patrons, and it can be examined or verified. The information may be aural, visual, textual, perhaps even emotional, but luckily, the limitations placed on the nature of information that can be held within a digital library obviates the need to enter into heady existential questions of whether it truly *is* information.

Information seeking and information seeking behaviors

Information searching and retrieval has been studied within such areas as information studies, education, communication, psychology, management, business, medicine, and public health. (Case, 2007) Case describes information seeking as the conscious effort to acquire information in response to a need or gap in the seeker's knowledge. Information behavior encompasses information seeking and unintentional or passive behaviors, such as glimpsing or encountering information. It also encompasses purposeful behaviors unrelated to seeking, such as actively avoiding information. (Case, 2002, p.5) Information seeking is what seekers do in response to information needs, tasks, and problems.

Wilson defines information seeking behavior as the purposeful seeking of information as a means to satisfy some goal, in which the seeker may come in contact with manual or computer-based systems (Wilson, 2000).

Marchionini defines information-seeking behavior as the process in which humans purposefully engage in order to change their state of knowledge. (Marchionini,1999, Ch1)

Information browsing, searching & seeking

When considering information browsing, searching, and seeking, it is important to note that these terms are often used interchangeably in literature regarding information seeking. It is also essential that readers understand the appropriate meaning of these terms in the context of the literature. For example, older literature used the term information seeking, but what was really being discussed were the venues and sources for information seeking, not the actual act of information seeking (Case, 2002). Furthermore, contemporary literature often refers to searching as the actions taken by computers to match and display information objects, but for the purpose of this chapter, searching is used in the context of human behavior.

Browsing.

Browsing may involve viewing a series of items with no particular goal in mind, or it may be highly directed, as described by Chang and Rice (as cited in Case, 2007). The definition of browsing may change, depending on the context or environment in which it is used (Case, 2002). It is typically characterized in terms of a purposeful action with some source or channel of information (Case, 2002).

Serendipity is the happenstance location of relevant information as a result of browsing. Thomas Mann, in his book *The Oxford Guide to Research* (2005), praises the potential that serendipity holds in shelf browsing for finding unexpected treasures. Though research by scholars such as Toms (as cited in Case, 2007) suggests that browsing is not highly related to seeking specific information, who of us has not used this strategy as an alternative or adjunct method to a carefully-phrased search query? Terms related to browsing that are used throughout the literature include such words as "environmental scanning," "information discovery," "foraging," "and "shopping" (Case, 2007). Chase adapts the scheme developed by Chang and Rice to classify browsing goals for digital resources, ranging from the most to least well-defined, such as "find(ing) specific pages or records using controlled terms or attributes" or "follow(ing) links to pages that pique interest" (as cited in Case, 2007, p. 92).

Searching.

Searching is referred to by Marchionini as the behavioral manifestations of humans engaged in information seeking (Marchionini Ch1, 1999). The scope of meaning can be narrowed as being tied to specific searching techniques (e.g. keyword searching).

Seeking.

Seeking encompasses the broad nature of cognitive, perceptual, behavioral, and environmental perspectives of information seekers, as opposed to just dealing with the behaviors or actions of information seekers with browsing and searching (Case, 2002).

Online information seeking behavior models

Models are a "proposed set of relationships" used to develop theories which can be used to test assumptions (Bates, 2005, p. 3). Models are more specific than theories, applying to more limited cases and rooted in real-world experiences, though theories can lead to models that cover broader situations. They are streamlined versions of reality, and typically describe causal processes and conceptual relationships (Case, 2007, p. 120). Although Johnson insists that "models should answer the 'why' question" (cited in Case, 2007, p. 119), it is generally understood that models provide a framework on which a theory can be built. Instead of describing all the models in detail, it will be more useful to look at them globally, noting the major points of diversion and intersection.

The models presented by Case (2007) present an evolutionary overview of the understanding of information seeking from the perspective of several different disciplines. He describes the work of models developed by such researchers as Wilson, Krikelas, Leckie, Pettigrew, and Sylan, Johnson, and Wilson. Most of these models are represented by sequenced flowcharts, and all include a need or motivator and an information seeking activity. Some explicitly mention the use of sources, and some allow for feedback and looping, such as when a user evaluates information to reassess his needs. Some take into account both affective and emotional aspects on user behavior. Some, like Leckie, Pettigrew, and Sylvain, are specific to work roles, while others, like Savolainen, are applicable to personal or professional situations. Wilson's model is much more generally applicable to different situations, and his 1996 version takes into account different kinds of information seeking, perhaps making it the reason his is one of the most cited by today's scholars (Case, 2007). The Savolainen, Johnson, and Wilson models acknowledge the importance of sociological factors influencing an individual, such as education and age, as well as psychological factors, such as beliefs and attitudes (Case, 2007). Johnson notes the changing nature of an evolving search, as a user's knowledge changes as it progresses (as cited in Case, 2007), in much the same way as does Bates, in her *Berrypicking* model (2005).

Metatheories or paradigms, theories, and models

Marcia Bates (2005) helps us to make sense of the realm of information behavior study by defining the major descriptors used to talk about ideas within the field and throughout scholarly disciplines: metatheory, theories, and models. Metatheory is explained as "the philosophy behind the theory, the fundamental set of ideas" that describes how to approach a field (p. 2). Shifts in metatheories in a given field over time may depend on current trends in cognitive styles, such as favoring qualitative over quantitative work, or a humanistic over a scientific approach (Bates, 2005, pp. 8-14). These metatheories are analogous to what Case (2007) understands as "paradigms." Both Bates and Case are careful to clarify that there is no single metatheory or paradigm at work in today's study of information science. Some current approaches include those termed constructivist, bibliometric, cognitive, ethnographic, and user-centered design (Case, 2007; Bates, 2005). There are many ways to tackle a problem, and often, prevailing "fashions" in academia determine those that will be used.

Case (2007) places the concept of a paradigm at the top of the theory-model- observation hierarchy. Simplified, a paradigm is the point of view or approach from which information seeking behavior is understood. Case has identified 5 general approaches to information seeking, relying on psychological and sociological ideas, which he has categorized as follows: *Principle of Least Effort*, *Uses and Gratifications*, *Sense-making*, *Constructionism*, and *Play Theory and Entertainment Theory* (p. 151). At this point, in spite of the risk of oversimplification, a simple summary of each will be offered, because it clarifies the interrelationships between these ideas and their connection to information seeking.

The first, the *Principle of Least Effort*, based on the work of Zipf (as cited in Case, 2007) and investigated in various realms of human behavior, proposes that when given a choice between information that is easy to obtain but possibly not the most accurate, and information that is potentially highly accurate but requires more effort, people will most often make do with the information that requires the least effort. Bates (2005) terms this result the "most solid" in the entire realm of information-seeking research (p. 4). Perhaps this should be the guiding light for all designers of digital libraries; if it isn't easy to find, you may be wasting your time in including it in your collection, because users may simply accept the result that comes most easily.

The *uses and gratifications* approach views the user as an active seeker of information, and provides the "simplistic" rationale that people choose certain sources and actions because they expect to be gratified by them (Case, 2007).

Sense-making, the principal researcher of which is Brenda Devlin, owes a debt to the educational theory of John Dewey, insofar as its description of the processes that people pass through as their understanding evolves in tandem with the progress they make in solving problems (as cited in Case, 2007).

Constructivism, as it is understood in information seeking, appears to share some common roots with sense-making, though it focuses on language communication between individuals (Case, 2007).

Play Theory and Entertainment Theory essentially hold that because people "tend to mix work with play, "there is an important element of pleasure-seeking in searching for information (Case, 2007, p. 161). Though it has been applied in relation to users' interaction with communication media, it may be of value in the context of digital libraries, which are likely to contain holdings that have a high entertainment value because of their non-traditional or multimedia formats.

These paradigms or metatheories, and other, often overlapping theories, form the basis for much of the work being done in information seeking. Though there is no single all-inclusive theory of information behavior that is commonly accepted, the recent trend, notes Case (2007), is away from psychology and the social sciences, and toward the humanities.

The next step down the hierarchy from a paradigm, a theory is understood as "a system of assumptions, principles, and relationships posited to explain a specified set of phenomena" (Bates, 2005, p. 2). The theory will generally explain the "why" behind the model, which is subordinate in the hierarchy, and describes a set of observations that can be generalized.

A number of theories have been developed to describe information behavior in general, and information seeking in particular. In their collection *Theories of information behavior* (2005), editors Karen Fischer et al include no fewer than 72 theories, briefly presented by the scholars who delivered them at the ASIST 2003 SIG USE Symposium. Some of the more well-known theories include *Affective Load, Bandura's Social Cognition, Berrypicking, and Khulthau's Information Search Process*. Among those with the most provocative titles are *Chatman's Life in the Round, Face Threat, The Imposed Query, PAIN Hypothesis, Serious Leisure,* and *Women's Ways of Knowing* (Fisher et al, 2005, p. v-xi).

Most of these theories share some basic elements. Generally, they begin by acknowledging an information need, or gap in knowledge that needs to be filled. They are usually goal-directed, mostly toward some kind of information that is good enough to meet the user's immediate needs. Nearly all of them are illustrated by processes with linear steps or stages, though many of them allow for iteration of these actions, making them essentially non-linear, since the actions may occur in repeated cycles, depending on what the user experiences at a given moment. They almost all take into account both the user's effective needs, and his reactions to what is or is not found, as well as the cognitive component needed to form queries and determine relevancy.

Some are extremely abstract, while others treat the subject at the level of discrete activities and cognitive strategies, such as browsing and subject searching. Among the many theories that have been proposed, the following three are examples of work that has influenced other scholars, or is recently at the forefront of the field.

T.D. Wilson's theory, the *Wilson Model*, is actually presented as a broad behavioral model, or series of models. Case (2007) also acknowledges Wilson's important contributions in providing the basis for many other scholars' investigations. Wilson's own explanation for the value of his information-seeking models is that they form a broad base on which multiple factors from related disciplines, such as psychology or sociology, come to bear, and can be compatible with the theories of other scholars (Wilson, 2005).

Marcia Bates' (2005) theory, called *Berrypicking*, arose as a result of the need to change assumptions about information seeking due to shifts in the resources themselves. The very nature of search and retrieval systems has changed to encompass different databases and interfaces, with a range of material formats encountered in a single search session. Searches evolve and change during the process, not just with respect to adjusting the search terms to retrieve better results, but also in terms of the actual goal of the query, as more information leads to a refining of needs. Thus, information retrieved is not only judged by a final set of results, but also by the information picked up along the way. Bates identified some strategies used in digital resources, involving actions like searching for subjects, following footnotes to prior resources, searching citation indexes for authors building on prior works, scanning content pages in relevant journals and works, browsing through materials near relevant materials, and searching other works by a relevant author (Bates, 2005).

Carol Kulthau's (2005) *Information Search Process*, is expressed as a "conceptual framework" in which initial uncertainty and anxiety may become resolved as information is found, or may actually increase because of contradictions or lack of understanding, until the user begins to make sense of the information, at which point confidence increases. The applications for this theory have been important for information literacy education, as previously mentioned, since those moments of anxiety or low confidence during the process are susceptible to interventions, either by people or systems, which can help the seeker through the difficult moment, making it more likely for the task to be completed successfully (Kulthau, 2005).

While all theories attempt to make sense of observed behavior, some are particularly susceptible to real-life applications in digital resources, in ways that will help users find information. Bates (2005) has seen the implementation of her work in information system design, and Kuhlthau (2005) notes that designers can use the opportunities provided by the "zone of intervention" that uncertainties create during a search as optimal moments in which to offer help (p. 234).

As in research for disciplines that investigate sociological, psychological, and humanistic traits, the methods used in information behavior work include a wide range of formats, including case studies, surveys, interviews, discourse analysis, content analysis, and meta-analysis, with each type of study having its advantages and disadvantages (Case, 2007). Most of these methods assume that information-seeking behaviors are highly related to demographic characteristics, and do not rely so much on the context in which they take place.

The new paradigm in information seeking, exemplified by the work of Kuhlthau and Mick and Buhl, stresses the importance of context to the process, and uses qualitative methods in longitudinal studies (as cited in Case, 2007). What is clear is that in a body of literature that now includes over 10,000 works, the amount of effort being given to this discipline is increasing each year (Case, 2007). Information seeking has become more focused on the user, and less on the "channel" or source of information, while most studies are being designed to investigate a particular type of user, defined by characteristics such as demographics, social role, or occupation (Case, 2007).

Allen's information tasks (1996)

Allen's information tasks deal with what is accomplished by users of information systems as they interact with those systems (Allen, 1996). The need for information leads to the display of some response from the system, and Allen examines how information seekers deal with this response (Allen, 1996). Scanning the response is the first task, followed by evaluation, in which users will categorize results as useful, useless, or in between (Allen, 1996). The user then learns from the response, either determining that the information need has been met, or revision of the original query. Finally, the user enters the planning stage, where additional action to meet the information need is determined (Allen, 1996).

Scanning.

Allen refers to scanning as the preparatory task performed before the evaluation and use of resources (Allen, 1996). Scanning does not use resources in the same capacity as the more in-depth task of searching (Allen, 1996). Furthermore, the scanning process varies depending on the information system being reviewed. For example, users engaged in the act of scanning text will utilize the table of contents or index, and spend the most time on category selection (Allen, 1996). Depending on memory capacity, users will either scan inflexibly, sticking to set information seeking goals (low memory capacity), or shift attention to other interesting materials during the scanning process (high memory capacity) (Allen, 1996).

Because documents often contain figural elements in addition to text (pictures, graphs, tables, etc.), users often use additional resources not required in the textual scanning process (Allen, 1996). For example, in order for an information seeker to properly decipher a table, they must possess knowledge of symbol systems and conventions (Allen, 1996). Scanning figural information is similar to textual scanning on a base level. The user's goals and scanning abilities, as well as the topic and presentation medium all affect the scanning process. However, with figural scanning, there is also an element of "global processing," which requires "summarizing information into gist representations," understanding trends, and developing generalizations and abstractions from the information system (Allen, 1996).

Scanning electronic documents presents an additional layer of complexity. Studies showed that although students were able to find the same amount of information when scanning print and electronic versions of the same document, the process was more time consuming when dealing with the electronic version (Allen, 1996). Many of the cues present in printed sources to aid in scanning and comprehension were missing or different when dealing with electronic documents (Allen, 1996). A positive aspect of scanning electronic documents is that they contain hypertext. This allows users to browse from one point to another, quickly and efficiently (Allen, 1996). However, this requires users to possess an additional knowledge resource, not required for other texts.

Reviewing and Evaluating.

After information systems have been scanned, users must assess resources for their relevance to the original information need (Allen, 1996). During the review and evaluation process, seekers decide whether information is useful, useless, or somewhere in between. Criteria such as depth, accuracy, clarity, and relevancy are taken into account during this process (Allen, 1996). When evaluating text, users often consider information important if it begins or ends the text they are reading, begins a paragraph, or proceeds or surrounds examples of the main points being discussed in the text (Allen, 1996). Information seekers also tend to focus primarily on titles and abstracts during the review and evaluation process (Allen, 1996).

When evaluating documents containing figural information, a two-step assessment occurs: 1) the user evaluates the validity of the form of presentation, and 2) the user ensures that the information itself is useful and relevant (Allen, 1996). There are no additional evaluation techniques required for the evaluation of electronic documents, other than the use of additional critical judgment (Allen, 1996). Resources on the Internet are often difficult to evaluate for validity, quality, completeness, and accuracy (Allen, 1996).

Learning

Learning is the information seeking task that must be completed in order to meet information needs, and is comprised of three steps: 1) comprehension, in which new stimuli must be understood, 2) elaboration, where connections between existing knowledge are made to the new stimuli, and 3) the creation of new knowledge structures, during which memory structures of information seekers are enriched by new memories that can be recalled (Allen, 1996). When learning from text, both prior topic knowledge and the organization of text influence the process (Allen, 1996). Also, as is the case with scanning, the match between the organization of text in relation to the user's information goal plays a large role in the learning process (Allen, 1996).

When information seekers apply the learning process to documents containing figural information, a "dual-coding" approach is often used, in which users remember information as propositions and images (Allen, 1996). For example, documents containing textual and figural information about a place will result in information seekers remembering the words that describe the place as well as the picture or map (Allen, 1996). When users learn from tables, graphs, and illustrations, they "summarize information into gist representations, but also focus on "complex abstraction" (Allen, 1996). Learning from electronic documents incorporates all of the previously stated approaches in addition to users gaining the ability to explore the many ways in which the topic can be elaborated through the use of hypertext and hyperlinks (Allen, 1996).

Planning.

The planning process requires that users employ their knowledge of the task they are accomplishing, their state in accomplishing their plan, and their environment in developing plans (Allen, 1996). When planning for information retrieval, information seekers combine a particular goal, purpose, or objective with their state of knowledge and the nature of the information to generate a plan of action (Allen, 1996). The knowledge resources involved in this process include knowledge of heuristics and scripts in addition to topical and contextual knowledge of the information need (Allen, 1996).

Marchionini's browsing strategies (1999)

Marchionini defines browsing as "an approach to information seeking that is informal and opportunistic and depends heavily on the information environment" (Marchionini, 1999). Browsing occurs when an individual employs one of four informal browsing strategies as part of the information seeking process: *scanning, observing, navigating,* and *monitoring.* Information seekers exhibit different types of actions based upon "interactions among the information-seeking factors" (Marchionini 1999). Browsing strategies are determined by the individual's cognitive perspective and internal representations of the desired results (Marchionini, 1999). Observing, navigating, and monitoring are used in an opportunistic browsing environment when learning goals are ill-defined, or systems are unfamiliar or unstructured, while scanning is used in a systematic browsing environment where learning objectives are well defined in the seeker's mind and in the environment (Marchionini, 1999).

Scanning

"Scanning is a perceptual recognition activity that compares sets of well-defined objects to an object that is clearly represented in the information seeker's mind" (Marchionini, 1999). In other words, scanning may be performed to identify key landmarks or characteristics to form initial ideas and opinions about a scene or document. Users also scan to form relationships between scenes or concepts already known (Marchionini, 1999). The most effective environments for scanning are those that provide "clear and concise representations" (Marchionini, 1999). Marchionini states that scanning can occur in a sequential fashion, known as *linear scanning*, or take a sampling approach, known as *selective scanning*.

Linear scanning

Linear scanning "applies perceptual attention in continual and sequential fashion" (Marchionini, 1999). Individuals engage in this type of scanning when content or objects are cognitively arranged in simple patterns (Marchionini, 1999). The eye has the ability to recognize these simple patterns in less than 50 milliseconds, although this time is reduced when people know where the result will appear (Marchionini, 1999). Examples of linear scanning include scanning a results page to locate relevant material, or methodically flipping through television channels to locate an interesting program. One negative aspect to linear scanning is that it is fatiguing and taxing on the brain.

Selective scanning

Selective scanning "applies perceptual attention according to either an inherent or imposed stratification of the search space" (Marchionini, 1999). This type of scanning is used to break complex objects up into smaller, more manageable groups, or to gain an overview of content. Examples of this would be skimming a reference list in a journal article or section headings found in a chapter of a textbook. Selective scanning is sometimes used as a precursor to linear scanning. Samples of the "search space" are first identified and scanned for relevance before linear scanning takes place (Marchionini, 1999). Marchionini gives an example in which different screens of text are scanned for relevance before settling on a single screen to further analyze.

Observing

Observational strategies, the most general of all browsing strategies, have "minimal thresholds" for all browsing factors, except cognitive effort (Marchionini, 1999). When individuals apply these strategies, it is because they assume that they have found relevant information and react to stimuli from this information. The observation method also depends mainly on parallel input. For example, rather than scanning a busy street scene, a browser will utilize sights, sounds, and motion. Observational strategies are often subconsciously applied, because they are part of our "physiological and psychological survival instincts" (Marchionini, 1999).

Interpretation and reflection are required to process information in relation to the original information-seeking objective. Observation is the primary strategy used in casual browsing, because it admits the widest range of objects and unorganized environments (Marchionini, 1999). Marchionini recommends that interfaces aiming to support observational strategies should provide alternate views of information. Information should be clearly represented and labeled, because observational strategies yield significant control to the searching environment. He also recommends that alternative representations of information should be available for users to transform for pattern recognition, association, and reflection purposes (Marchionini, 1999).

Navigation

The navigation strategy strikes a balance between the influences of the user and the browsing environment. The user selects the information-seeking path, and the environment constrains browsing by supplying these paths. In order for information seeking behavior to fall under the navigation model, objects must be specifiable and seekers must have an initial idea of what they are seeking. They must also take a proactive role in interacting with the environment. Navigation may occur in unstructured environments, but high levels of organization on the part of the information seeker will aid the efficiency of the search (Marchionini, 1999).

The destination for information seeking is almost never predetermined; "intellectual space is highly amorphous" and most "navigation" deals with problem identification and clarification (Marchionini, 1999). With navigation, information is drawn to the seeker rather than transporting the seeker to the information, especially in an electronic environment. Marchionini suggests that navigation is an "attractive compromise between user and system responsibility" because the system provides links for the user to follow. Successful systems provide a level of navigational freedom somewhere in the mid-range, providing some choice to seekers while "suggesting directions and providing informative cues about progress" (Marchionini, 1999).

Monitoring

The monitoring strategy is often used in tandem with systematic browsing or other primary activities. It is similar to scanning, but tolerates unstructured searching environments, while scanning does not. An example would involve an information seeker passively looking for concepts related to another topic of interest while reading text about a specific topic. Monitoring is partly subconscious, but it requires the user to make connections between concepts in the mind and representations in the information space. This browsing strategy is "enabled by perspectives of the database," which include different cues (words, phrases, movements, etc.) found in the information environment (Marchionini, 1999).

Choo, Detlor & Turnbull's information seeking on the Web (2000)

Choo, Detlor, and Turnbull refer to Ellis' information seeking model as a helpful method for analyzing patterns of Web-based information seeking. The model identifies six information-seeking activities: *starting, chaining, browsing, differentiating, monitoring,* and *extracting*. In the context of a web-based environment, the model is used by information seekers to systematically work through specific websites or pages, through the use of search engines, to retrieve material of interest (Choo, 2000).

Starting
Starting refers to any activity performed by the seeker to initiate the search for information. This could include identifying sources of interest that will serve as jumping off points for information-seeking behavior. These "identified sources" are comprised of previously used sources, that are known to provide authoritative information, and unfamiliar sources that promise credibility. The likely and desired outcome of starting activities is the identification of initial sources that will lead to additional sources or references (Choo, 2000).

Chaining
The activity of chaining relies on the initial sources established during the starting phase. Chaining can be backwards or forwards, depending on the initial source. Backwards chaining occurs when pointers or references from initial sources are followed, and forward chaining happens when seekers identify or follow up on sources that refer to one of the initial sources (Choo, 2000). Both are effective in the information seeking process, but forward chaining tends to be used less than backwards chaining.

Browsing
Browsing is referred to as the activity of "semi-directed search in areas of potential search" that occurs after sources and documents have been located and established. Browsing often takes place in situations in which related information has been grouped together, such as title lists, subject headings, abstracts, and summaries. Information seekers utilize browsing activities to look for information at the "micro-event level" (Choo, 2000).

Differentiating
During differentiating activities, information seekers evaluate the nature and quality of sources through filtering, scanning, and applying criteria. In a study, social scientists assigned three main criteria to sources: substantive topic, approach or perspective, and level, quality or type of treatment. Differentiation varies among information seekers, depending on prior or initial experiences with sources, recommendations from colleagues, or published reviews about sources.

Monitoring

Monitoring activities are performed to monitor progress in a topic area by following updates to particular sources. Information seeking individuals identify and concentrate on a small number of "core sources". These core sources are usually made up of key personal contacts and related publications (Choo, 2000).

Extracting

Extracting is the activity of sifting through a specified source or group of sources to identify material of interest. This is achieved by directly consulting the source, or by reviewing abstracts, indexes, or online databases. This is a labor-intensive activity used in situations when there is a need for comprehensive or historical information (Choo, 2000).

David Ellis' "information-seeking patterns of behavior"

Developed from studies of academic social scientists in the 1980s and 1990s, Ellis's groundbreaking study focused on behavior and actions instead of cognitive activities. Ellis breaks the information seeking patterns down into six characteristics: starting, chaining, browsing, differentiating, monitoring, and extracting. These characteristics constitute the principal features of individual patterns, and together they provide a flexible behavioral model for information retrieval system design (Ellis, 1989).

Search tactics and search moves

Tactics are specific, incremental moves made by searchers such as query formulation and query reformulation (Fidel, 1985). A combination of tactical moves is called a search strategy; in other words, a search strategy is multifaceted and can involve many different approaches and resources (Bates, 1979). Taking a step back from the individual user, usage patterns describe aggregate search trends and search patterns revealed by examination and analysis of information system records and logs. Google analytics, for example, describe usage patterns (Arendt & Wagner, 2010). Search tactics are actions taken by a person while searching.

Researchers have identified many types of search tactics, but here we are mainly interested in search formulation and term tactics, as these are most relevant for online searching since they apply to initial and subsequent, refined searching (Bates, 1979). Also relevant are idea tactics, such as brainstorming, that lead searchers into new, previously unexplored areas. Finally there are what Shute and Smith (1993) call topic-based tactics that lead to the broadening, narrowing, and shifting of "knowledge areas."

Where search tactics occur within the searcher's thinking process, search moves are the result of human – information system interaction, specifically queries. In turn, search moves can be broken down into operational moves (where the query stays the same), conceptual moves (where the query changes, usually to refine results), cognitive moves (query changes brought on by analysis of returns), and physical moves (query changes assisted by information system functions) (Shiri & Revie, 2003).

Search strategies generally vary depending on the information system being searched and are incredibly wide-ranging in approach and nuance. Keyword searching and browsing, for example, are examples of very popular and straightforward search strategies. When it comes to structured information systems like online catalogues and databases, two of the most popular search strategies are "concept" and "trial and error." A very popular type of conceptual searching is called "building block," where the desired information is broken down into its major components, or building blocks, and searched for (Boolean searching works very well here: "Information seeking" + "World Wide Web"). Trial and error, as you would expect, is unstructured, almost free-form searching (Markey & Cochrane, 1981).

Search engine search strategies tend to differ from OPAC-related search strategies and are influenced by the way the World Wide Web itself functions and structures information. For example, Web searchers tend to repeat queries; multi-task; use metasearch engines; make extensive use of the back and forward navigation buttons; jump from page to page using hyperlinks; and use multiple search engines (Rieh & Xie, 2006).

Since user search strategies change with the type of information system being used (e.g., digital library, search engine), so do the patterns of usage, though there is overlap. Because patterns of usage are a measure of aggregated searches, we can get a better view of how most people actually go about looking for information; that is, how they formulate and then reformulate their queries (Spink, et. al, 2001).

For search engine Web searching, four general patterns emerge. Users tend to make brief queries; these brief queries are altered very little during equally brief iterative searching; search modifiers and operators are rarely employed by users, and they are often mishandled when employed; finally, users tend to look at only a small number of search returns (Moukdad & Large, 2001).

Findings for more structured online information systems such as digital libraries and OPACs show similar patterns of minimal effort on the part of information seekers. In this environment, however, search topics logically parallel subject content contained in the OPAC or digital library. Complex searching strategies, such as using Boolean operators, are more prevalent, too (Wolfram & Xie, 2002).

Search strategy development in online environments

Chowdhury's four-phase framework for information search in DLs (2003)

Chowdhury has taken the four major phases of searching, established by Schneiderman, Byrd, and Croft in 1997, and applied it to online information retrieval. Specifically, Chowdhury has identified the features found in successful search interfaces and applied them to this information seeking model. The result is a "four-phase framework that will provide a common structure and terminology for information searching while preserving the distinct features of individual library collections and search mechanisms" (Chowdhury, 2003).

Phase 1: Formulation.

The formulation of a search is triggered by the need for information, and the seeker makes decisions about sources to include, search phrases, fields, and search variants (Chowdhury, 2003). The selection of sources is important to this phase. Users often have access to a multitude of collections, so having an idea of what each collection encompasses is important (Chowdhury, 2003). It can be difficult for information seekers to articulate what they are searching for, and the well-designed user interface of a digital library often plays a key role in properly identifying fields, operators, and search variants.

Phase 2: Action.

When the user has finally settled on a search phrase, he is ready to execute the search query. Traditionally, this has been done by pressing the "search" button, but users may become frustrated while waiting for the search to end (Chowdhury, 2003). Therefore, it is recommended that DL developers consider using the "dynamic queries" method, in which the results are continuously updated as the search progresses (Chowdhury, 2003).

Phase 3: Review of results.

Users synthesize search results in different ways, and require different tools to sort and organize. Successful interfaces provide information seekers with a variety of visualization techniques for the display of search results (Chowdhury, 2003). These techniques may include sorting options (author, title, subject, etc), highlighting options, and "helpful messages to explain results" (Chowdhury, 2003).

Phase 4: Refinement.

The final phase of information searching is refinement of results. Once the search query has been executed, and results reviewed, users sometimes need to reformulate the search phrase and conduct a new search (Chowdhury, 2003). Search interfaces should provide different options for modifying queries and conducting new searches. These options should be embedded onto the results page to avoid user frustration (Chowdhury, 2003).

Marchionini's analytical search strategies (1999)

Analytical strategies are goal oriented, systematic, and meant to maximize retrieval effectiveness. Marchionini's strategies illustrate how electronic environments have changed the information seeking process by allowing the systematic manipulation of large document and source sets. In turn, these strategies have affected the design and development of online systems. These analytical strategies are identified as: *building blocks*, *successive fractions*, *pearl growing*, and *interactive scanning*.

Building blocks

The most widely used online information seeking strategy is the "building blocks" approach. In the initial stages of searching, the information seeker establishes the main concept groups associated with the topic of interest. The individual sets of concepts, or building blocks, are then combined with Boolean operators to produce a set of results related to the original search query. Depending on the information seeker's familiarity with the system, additional "tactical options" will be used (Marchionini, 1999). These options may include using a controlled vocabulary, combining results sets, and limiting the search to specific fields. The building blocks strategy is utilized more than the other four strategies because it simplifies the process by breaking it down into manageable and easily definable parts. This applies to both the "conceptual analysis" of the problem and in the "technical specification" and refinement of Boolean queries (Marchionini, 1999).

Successive fractions

Another popular search strategy is the "successive fractions" approach. Information seekers start with a large subset of the entire database, gradually paring it down with concepts specific to the search topic. This strategy works best with vague or broad topics, and uses backtracking as well as monitoring of sources. There are variations on the main strategy, again, depending on the information seeker's familiarity with the system. As with the building blocks approach, this strategy simplifies the search process by breaking it into a sequence of "systematic and discrete" steps (Marchionini, 1999).

Pearl growing

"Pearl growing" starts with a specific document set, or "pearl," known to be relevant to the search problem, and uses its characteristics to "grow" a set of related documents and sources (Marchionini, 1999). Seekers use the original document set in tandem with assigned index terms (names, citations, publication data, etc.) to formulate search queries that will generate subsequent related sets. Next to locating the initial pearl, the most difficult part of this strategy is determining when to stop "growing" subsequent sets. This approach is highly dependent on "interaction between the searcher and the system" and searcher inferences. Pearl growing is less algorithmic than building blocks and successive fractions, requiring more searcher interactions with the system (Marchionini, 1999).

Interactive scanning

The "interactive scanning" approach takes a comprehensive set of documents loosely related to the search topic, scans them, and notes key features of the problem. These features are then used to "formulate and pose successive queries" that further define the search topic. As a clear picture of the search problem emerges, document sets are saved as part of the final set of sources. Search criteria are altered as more specific sources are retrieved and the topic is better understood. This approach is useful in instances where the information seeker wants to first explore a topic area before applying one of the more "analytical approaches". It is also useful for conducting searches requiring a high recall rate or for exploration of problems in domains unfamiliar to the information seeker (Marchionini, 1999).

Factors Affecting Information Searching

Searching for information occurs in certain places, at certain times, for certain purposes, using certain tools, and is undertaken by people who bring an enormous range of background experience and motivation to the task. All of these things – goals and tasks, user knowledge, user motivation, type of information system, and social or organizational setting - contextualize the information search.

As a general rule, the more ambitious the goal and the more complicated the task, more information is needed and more information "channels" are needed. The complexity of the task determines a whole array of actions, from project conceptualization, brainstorming, initial forays, information gathering, and information presentation. A simple way to picture the process is the searcher moving from general information (topical overviews) to the particular (specific facts) (Bystrom, 2002).

User motivation contributes to searching in a number of ways. Understanding what motivates a person to seek information is fraught with hazard and uncertainty – after all, quite often the information seeker his or herself doesn't have a clear understanding of why she is seeking information. Theories of motivation range from the rational and instrumental, where specific information is needed to solve a specific problem, to the emotional and subjective, where users feel a vague sense of unease, a sense of having a gap in knowledge. While the rational theory of information seeking certainly holds true sometimes, most researchers subscribe to the subjective model, as it emphasizes that when it comes to information seeking behavior people tend to try to "make sense" of the entire situation instead of searching for specific data (Case, p. 77).

The type of information system used by searchers is almost self-explanatory, but it intertwines with user knowledge with profound effect. A university librarian (possessing vast user knowledge) will search the library's OPAC (the information system) very differently than will an incoming freshman. Software interfaces, information objects like metadata, and the various features and functionalities tied to information systems potentially have great effect on one's information searching. User knowledge, or lack thereof, is what unlocks that potential, or not (Lozander, et. al, 2000).

Finally, social or organizational setting impacts searching behavior in myriad ways. Time pressures to complete tasks, filters on computers (at work and home), and even the type of equipment available shape one's searching parameters to some degree (Fidel & Pejterson, 2004).

While early work on information seeking was focused largely on the sources of information and their relative effectiveness for users, over time there has been a gradual shift in focus toward the user himself. Case observes that most researchers tend to frame their work in terms of one of three large categories, centered on the user: his social role, occupation, and demographic characteristics. Knowledge gaps and information poverty, ideas that describe the temporary or chronic lack of knowledge in one demographic of a population with relation to another, may be considered to be related to information seeking within a digital resource insofar as they can affect a user's ability to frame adequate queries, or to decipher the relevance of results (Case, 2007).

When the quantity of information received is simply too great to effectively process, a user may be said to experience "information overload" (Case, 2007). Miller developed a list of potential responses to overload, including "omission," "error," "queuing," "filtering," "approximation," "multiple channels," and "escaping" (as cited in Case, 2007, p. 104). An analysis of these responses by Katz and Kahn labels some of these, like omission (leaving things out), errors (making mistakes), and escape (giving up) as dysfunctional, while others, like queuing (putting off till later) and filtering (selection), are seen as only potentially problematic (Case, 2007).

A great deal of research has been done on the anxiety and stress caused by information overload in many contexts, from education to the workplace. The key idea with anxiety, particularly in the field of information literacy, is that instruction should take steps to ensure that seekers are successful to a minimum degree so that they can complete task (Case, 2007). This goal is of key importance in Kuhlthau's research on information literacy, since her ultimate aim is to offer assistance at those low moments in the research process when students are likely to give up (Kuhlthau, 2005).

Case (2007) describes the tendency we have in our culture to see information and entertainment as occupying two completely separate realms as "artificial and unfair" (p. 111). Looking at the library environment alone, there can exist a component of entertainment even in academic materials, and many educational sources of information, such as documentaries, strive to be both entertaining and informative. When considering information seeking, the need for entertainment will surely be a factor when users decide which resources to use (Case, 2007).

Case studies of the search strategy development in digital libraries

Case Study 1: Information seeking behaviors in databases in digital libraries (2000)

Research purpose.
This study tested the authenticity of the general hypotheses found in information retrieval literature. Information retrieval systems that implement interactions with multiple databases, through a common interface, and with multiple databases as if they were one were tested for usability and effectiveness (Park, 2000). User preferences and searching behaviors were also tested by focusing on how information seekers interact with multiple heterogeneous information resources (Park, 2000).

Research questions.
- *User preferences*: Which system did you like better and find more useful, easier to use, and easier to learn to use?
- *Usability & User satisfaction*: How easy is it to do the search on the topic? How satisfied are you with your search results? Did you have enough time to do an effective search?
- *Effectiveness*: Is there a statistically significant difference in performance (aspectual recall) between systems?
- *Search behaviors*: Is there a statistically significant difference in individual's searching behavior (e.g., the usage of frequency of various system features) between systems?

Methods.
An experiment was conducted to compare a common interface system, HERMES, with an integrated interface system, HERA, using a "within-subjects" design so that each test subject could search and compare the two systems (Park, 2000). The HERMES interface allowed users to interact separately with four different resources (databases) through a common interface, allowing test subjects a user-directed choice of a database (Park, 2000). The HERA interface combined results from different sources, letting users interact with integrated results (Park, 2000). After test subjects submitted a query, the databases were ranked, searched by the system, and the results of the searches were merged according to weighted scores (Park, 2000).

Twenty-eight graduate test subjects were asked to conduct three different searches on each system, which were new to the users. During the three-hour session, users were given tutorials for each system and then required to search three separate topics. After conducting each search, subjects answered questions about familiarity with the search topic, experience with the searching task, and satisfaction with the results (Park, 2000).

At the end of the entire session, users were asked to complete an exit questionnaire to identify demographic characteristics and experience with other information retrieval systems. They were also asked to compare the two systems, supplying comments on their understanding and use of interactive features and different interaction support mechanisms (Park, 2000). An exit interview was also conducted to gain perspective on the overall searching experience.

The searches were conducted using resources from the Text Retrieval Conference (TREC), a major information retrieval conference for evaluating and understanding advanced information retrieval systems and techniques (Park, 2000). TREC is known for its large-scale full text collections and the availability of thousands of relevance judgments for each of its information problems (Park, 2000). The TREC interactive track was designed to investigate and evaluate interactive information retrieval and to investigate searching as an interactive task by examining the process and the outcome (Park, 2000). Topics of resources and search tasks included the Federal Register, Wall Street Journal, Financial Times, and the Congressional Record. (Park, 2000)

Findings.

Users found that the HERA integrated interface was convenient and efficient, taking less time and less physical and behavioral effort to use. HERA was also easier to use, requiring fewer decisions and less effort. It provides a more comprehensive and general overview of search results, and accommodates proven search tactics (starting with a general search and narrowing the topic down). The downside of HERA is the lack of user control, and the presence of irrelevant databases is distracting. (Park, 2000)

The HERMES common interface allowed more control over database selection, giving users an opportunity to concentrate on the database of their choice. Irrelevant and useless databases could be eliminated, but users found the process to be time consuming, inconvenient, and inefficient (Park, 2000).

Overall, users preferred the common interface system (HERMES) over the integrated interface system (HERA), finding HERMES to be more useful than HERA. However, because most system features were shared by the two interfaces, users found that there was no clear distinction between the systems in terms of ease of use and learning how to use the system (Park, 2000).

Some users found HERA easier to use, because they did not have to evaluate and select databases, requiring fewer decisions than with HERMES. Some test subjects found it distracting to make a choice between databases when testing HERMES, whereas HERA made the decision for them (Park, 2000). Additionally, users desired the ability to eliminate irrelevant databases and sources, target and review relevant responses, and continue a search in more depth without being distracted by results from irrelevant databases (Park, 2000).

Case Study 2: Scholars and professionals' information use in digital libraries (2000)

Research purpose

A transaction log analysis was conducted on user activity in the Computer Science Technical Reports Collection of the New Zealand Digital Library. The results include issues with interface design, common mistakes made in searching, and patterns in query structure and refinement (Jones, 2000). User log data was analyzed "automatically" through the calculation of summary statistics, and "manually" through examination of query strings for semantic clues on search motivations and strategies (Jones, 2000).

Methods

Quantitative and qualitative analysis of transaction logs

A quantitative and qualitative analysis of transaction logs was performed, spanning over a year's use of the New Zealand Digital Library (Jones, 2000). The analysis is deemed significant in comparison with other transaction log studies, because of the large span of time studied and the specificity of the collection (Jones, 2000). While the computer science research community could be thought of as "best case" users of search engines, this study indicates that many users from this community encounter the same difficulties with searching and query language as the general public (Jones, 2000).

Target digital library: New Zealand Digital Library (NZDL)

The NZDL, active since 1995, is a publicly accessible digital library. It contains more than 20 collections, comprised of text-based documents for which searchable full-text indexes have been built (Jones, 2000). However, there are collections included in the digital library that deliver multimedia resources, including music, photos and video. One aspect of the research was to evaluate and improve the digital library's user interfaces, through usability studies and analysis of transaction logs (Jones, 2000).

Target collection: Computer Science

Analysis was focused on the (CSTR), which contains more than 46,000 publicly available computing-related technical reports harvested from over 300 research institutions, including a large collection of "grey literature" (Jones, 2000). Two principals of the researcher's digital library architecture are 1) to make minimum assumptions about conventions adopted by document repositories and 2) to avoid manual document processing (Jones, 2000). Therefore, since the CSTR collection is based on a large, diverse set of document repositories, the presence of bibliographic metadata could not be relied upon (Jones, 2000). The collection is not formally cataloged, but the full text of the documents is extracted and indexed (Jones, 2000).

Data collection

All user activity within the NZDL is automatically logged, although user identity remains anonymous. The data used for this study was collected in a 61-week period, from April 1996 – July 1997, and more than 30,000 queries were recorded (Jones, 2000). User activities are time stamped and include: query text and options, documents viewed, and the size of results sets

(Jones, 2000). Query options include types, stemming, case sensitivity, term proximity, and recall (Jones, 2000). The log records the number of resulting documents that the user chooses to view and the locations of said documents on the results list (Jones, 2000).

Findings

Quantitative statistics about query use

The study found that users were generally accepting of the preset query and default settings. This proved to be true, even though the default query type was changed from Boolean to ranked 45 weeks into the study (Jones, 2000). Queries themselves were often kept short. Approximately 80% of queries contained one to three search terms, 18% contained four to six search terms, and the remaining 2% contained more than six search terms (Jones, 2000). Two out of three queries contained no Boolean operators, and fewer than one in 40 queries contained union or negotiation operators (Jones, 2000).

The query logs contained 4993 unique terms, excluding terms appearing in quoted phrases. Seven of these terms are stopwords (and, of, a, the, for, or, in), and examination of the query strings gives the impression that the information seeker intended to conduct a phrase search, but omitted the quotation marks (Jones, 2000). Therefore, in most instances, the use of "and" and "or" appears to be the mistaken use of these words (Jones, 2000). Approximately one in twenty search terms did not match any of the documents in the collection, and upon closer inspection, these terms were most commonly misspelled, consisted of personal or product names, or simply did not appear in the collection (Jones, 2000).

Search failures were measured in terms of precision and recall measures. Over the 61 week period 1020 queries, roughly 10.53% of all queries, generated no hits (Jones, 2000). Of these failed queries, 105 contained no query terms, 411 were ranked queries, and 504 were Boolean queries. The fewer terms in a query, the more likely the query was to fail (Jones, 2000). Approximately one fifth of all user sessions were to NZDL Web pages that did not entail submission of a query, and just over half of the sessions included the submission of one to two queries (Jones, 2000). Slightly more than a fifth included three to six queries, and only a handful included more than six queries. Researchers came to the conclusion that users were unwilling to put forth the effort in query development to research a topic of interest (Jones, 2000).

It was found that the majority of queries issued by users contained at least one search term in common with a previous query. Some queries even contained up to three search terms in common with a previous query, leading to the conclusion that query refinement is a common activity albeit in small, incremental steps (Jones, 2000). In most cases, an average of 50 documents were retrieved and displayed, and in some cases the number reached 100-200 documents. However, almost 65% of users did not review any of the documents, 19% reviewed one document, and the remaining users reviewed two or more documents in the results list (Jones, 2000). It was determined that users who did review documents reviewed those at the top of the results list.

Qualitative analysis of search strategies

The study found that misspellings were rare in the search terms themselves. 240 of the searches contained misspelled words or typographical errors. Most of this was caused by the omission of special characters from product or program names, or users forgetting to take into account the difference between UK and American spelling of words (Jones, 2000). Rather than a single, homogenous DL covering all subjects, the NZDL is a collection of different sub-collections, each focusing on a different area of interest (Jones, 2000). A sub-collection must be selected before submitting a query. A review of the query logs showed that a small percentage of users did not choose a sub-collection related to their query. It was determined that it would be appropriate to include more detailed information for users about each of the sub-collections to facilitate appropriate selections (Jones, 2000).

There was evidence of users attempting to come up with alternate search strategies. Most notably, information seekers tried to search fielded access points such as author, full document title, technical report number, and publication date. However, this would only apply to a cataloged system (NZDL is not cataloged) (Jones, 2000). Some users also attempted to search for content in other languages. Surprisingly, some users attempted to use "graffiti" terms or obscenities in their search queries. The research team felt that this may have been done out of frustration or to exhibit playfulness, but since there is no way to examine the specific mindset of users in this particular search, these claims cannot be proven. A manual examination of Boolean query strings found that, in many cases, Boolean terms were used incorrectly. Specifically, the search engine required the use of (&, -, and !), yet users substituted these symbols with "and," "or," and "not" (Jones, 2000). Also, information seekers used syntax specific to other search engines, and used extraneous parentheses and quotation marks (Jones, 2000).

Implications for digital libraries

What then, have researchers learned from information-seeking research that can be of use in designing digital libraries? Depending on the nature of the digital library, users may visit for any number of reasons, including a personal or academic need, curiosity, or the desire for entertainment. While some digital libraries, such as those that cover highly technical topics, will be limited in the demographics or occupations of their patrons, many others will be of wide interest to the general public. As a result, the interface design and search functions should make resources as accessible as possible.

Within the body of information seeking studies most relevant to digital libraries is some of the research focused on students as a demographic group, since much of this work addresses information seeking using formal sources of information, either print or online, with increasing emphasis on digital sources. Early studies examining how students used bibliographic databases in the 1980s can offer valuable insights into human behavior and processes, yet the greatly increased contact that users across all age demographics have had with web resources has doubtless shifted the baseline of technology experience so far to the positive side that one wonders how valid their specific findings can be for today's user.

"Early" research, conducted using online or CD-ROM databases such as encyclopedias, found that school-aged children were able to effectively navigate these resources by menu, keyword, or browsing (Marchionini, Large et al., as cited in Newman, 1997), though other problems with using the information sometimes arose. Solomon's 1993 study on OPAC use noted key areas, like specific syntactic rules and query formation, in which students needed to have prior knowledge to be successful (as cited in Newman, 1997). In an early study of high school students using an electronic encyclopedia, students who planned their search queries wrote higher-quality final results than their counterparts who relied on browsing. Though the authors ascribe this difference to a better prior "internal organization" of information, it seems just as likely that the more analytical students were simply better at using and writing about information precisely because they were analytical (Liebscheer, & Marcionini, as cited in Newman, 1997, p. 74).

Additional findings in other studies, all done with high-school students, pointed out commonly-observed flaws in searching strategies, like using the wrong database, not having the appropriate subject-specific vocabulary needed to carry out effective queries, or assuming that relevant material would be organized using the same terms students themselves used to approach a topic. This "conceptual naiveté," which seemed frequent among younger users, may still exist in older users of a digital library (Newman, 1997). Indeed, given that searches using keywords are "becoming a more dominant search behavior," understanding the lexicon specific to a digital library's content can mean the difference between success and failure at finding relevant information. Useful and complete metadata is more important than ever, and catalogers of a digital library should consider including keywords that are derived from commonly used terms, in addition to subject-specific vocabulary (Connaway et al, 2010).

Such basic components of searching in electronic databases as "generating search terms, designing effective search strategies, and overcoming mismatches between personal ideas of how information is organized and how information is actually organized in databases" reappear as major stumbling blocks in a 1995 Delphi study (Neuman, as cited in Nahl, 1996, p. 121). Younger students increasingly overestimate the effectiveness of their own information literacy skills, and tend to "power browse," which is to skim results so superficially as to prevent any real understanding (CIBER, as cited in Connaway, et al, 2010).

One may imagine that adults using digital libraries may have become effective and efficient searchers of information, but even a demographic with a fair amount of experience in information seeking, such as undergraduate students, may still have difficulties. User behavior studies, such as those compiled in the 2008 report *The Digital Information Seeker: Report of the Findings from Selected OCLC, RIN, and JISC User Behaviour Projects*, indicate that in general, the information literacy skills of library users have not kept pace with the use of digital resources, in spite of a generalized perception to the contrary *(*Connaway et al, 2010*)*. This same report, a meta-analysis of 12 representative studies of user behaviors, gives us a clear picture of some trends in user behaviors. The research evaluated here was mostly carried out with academic library users, though some address non-academic use of libraries, or the general information behavior of the "Google generation" (CIBER, as cited in Connaway et al, 2010).

Among the "common findings" drawn in the Connaway et al (2010) analysis, several that may be applicable to creators of digital libraries stand out. First, users place great value on resources that are fast and convenient. They also are increasingly demanding "enhanced functionality," which may be anything from advanced search capabilities to communication options. Additionally, although most users display confidence in their own searching ability, the actual level of information literacy has not risen in recent years, which points to the importance of providing high-quality metadata in order to help searchers.

Brenda Dervin, et al (as cited in Connaway et al, 2010) found that academic users are able to adapt their search strategies and level of effort to their specific needs at a given time, quite unconsciously. Young users' tendency to "power browse," or skim results with little real comprehension, often leads to carelessness (CIBER, as cited in Connaway et al, 2010). Hampton-Reeves, et al found that many undergraduates rely on keyword searches (as cited in Connaway et al, 2010). This also suggests that enhanced metadata, such as abstracts and summaries, may be of use in not missing important items, since many users read very little as they search (Connaway et al, 2010).

Among academic researchers, refining results to try to pin down relevance was the search strategy most frequently identified (Research Information Network, as cited in Connaway et al, 2010). Other findings may have important implications for libraries. Since there is a wide range of types of users, systems must be able to accommodate different kinds of behaviors. Search functions need to be styled on the popular search engines and web pages that many users rely on, such as Google and Amazon. Indeed, in both studies of the general public, as well as of college students, approximately 90% of users initiate an information search using a commercial search engine (De

Rosa, 2005; De Rosa, 2006, as cited in Connaway et al, 2010), which gives clear evidence of their preference for their style and functionality.

These results indicate the importance of taking into account the information-seeking behaviors of potential users when designing a digital library. Any difficulties placed in the path of information seekers run the risk of causing a breakdown in the process, making searches less effective. The models to follow are provided by today's most successful search engines, but complete and accurate metadata is also a key. Enhanced functions should be available, but perhaps not overly obtrusive. These observations would suggest that user testing is an important component of building an effective digital service.

7.3 Sharing, Networking, and Interchange (e.g., Social)

Librarians are constantly trying to discover innovative ways to reach patrons beyond library walls. Web 2.0 can help librarians achieve that goal. "In the simplest terms, Web 2.0 is the use of Internet technologies to enhance information sharing and the creative and collaborative development of projects" (Fiehn, 2008). With available technology and so many online services, it seems a natural progression to take note of what these services can offer. Web 2.0, Library 2.0 or Social Networking, by whatever name you call it you can be assured that it all refers to the idea of information input by users for users and with the hope that someone, somewhere, even if it's the one who initiated the information, will find it useful. To that end we will investigate various means of social networking and discover how this trend affects digital libraries.

Types of social networking

Instant messaging

Synchronous messaging, more commonly referred to as instant messaging (IM), allows real-time text communications between individuals (Maness, 2006). Libraries have instated this service to allow patrons to communicate with reference librarians in the same manner they would during a face-to-face encounter (Maness, 2006). IM allows a user presence within the library's Web-presence, as well as collaboration between librarians and patrons (Maness, 2006). The software used by chat reference services is often more robust than ordinary IM applications, allowing co-browsing, file-sharing, screen-capturing, and data mining and sharing (Maness, 2006). Audio and video messaging is becoming more common, and links to chat services are appearing within resources themselves, such as at the article level of online databases (Maness, 2006). With each new improvement made to IM reference services, patrons are provided with a more seamless experience (Maness,

2006). Developments are being made to IM applications to recognize user seeking behaviors, and subsequently prompting a chat session (Maness, 2006). Such instances could occur when a user browses through certain resources, and "repeats steps and moves cyclically through a classification scheme or series of resources," prompting the IM service to offer assistance (Maness, 2006).

A 2007 study conducted by Nahyun Kwon from the School of Information of Library Science at the University of South Florida, examines the type of questions patrons bring to chat reference services and how well they are answered. A seven-question voluntary user-evaluation survey was incorporated into live chat transactions of the IM reference service used by a 33-branch library system in Florida. 415 transactions from a six-month period were evaluated for question type and locality, user satisfaction according to question type, answer validity, and answer quality (Kwon, 2007). The breakdown of question types are as follows: circulation issues 48.9%, subject based resources 25.8%, simple factual information 9.6%, accessing library resources 8.9%, and information about local branches of the library (hours, directions, etc.) 6.8% (Kwon, 2007).

When comparing the completely answered transactions across the five types of questions, factual questions had the highest answer completion rate with 77.5%, followed by subject-based research (70.1%), resource access (56.8%), local library information (53.6%), and circulation-related questions (45.8%) (Kwon, 2007). Each of the question types was also measured for user satisfaction, answer validity, and answer quality. Subject-based research questions had the highest satisfaction rate, followed by factual questions, then local library inquiries, circulation-related questions, and finally resources access questions (Kwon, 2007). Kwon came to the conclusion that while there were high levels of user satisfaction with the IM system, there is room to improve the service (Kwon, 2007). Developers should continue to improve usability of these applications.

Blogs

Blogs are often used in the library profession as a way to communicate and "find, share and offer advice to others in the Library and Information Science profession" (Powers, 2008). A blog is a tool used to write opinion but also to be used as a resource, one of many in the social networking arena.

Blogs should be accountable for ethical and accurate information transfer. Bloggers should show "insight and reflection in their community with a potential for shared knowledge, learning, creation of best practice in their blogs" (Powers, 2008). Sharing best practices can pave the way for others to accomplish similar goals with the knowledge of pitfalls and successes of those who have been there previously.

Learning how to establish a Digital Library through discussion on blogs can help with problems that crop up unexpectedly as well. Asking for advice on a blog will surely result in various answers and opinions.. Seeking advice, learning ways to accomplish tasks, and posting descriptions of processes are ways blogging can be advantageous to librarians embarking on digital library development.

Delicious

Taking advantage of social networking technology, the use of the social bookmarking site delicious.com is another way to engage the user community in the library and provide a 2.0 experience. Delicious.com is a service that allows the user to save and share web pages (bookmarks) online. It is organized and searchable by tagging (Yahoo, 2010). The Vancouver Public Library is using this networking tool to manage their more than 5000 annotated web links (Cahill, p. 153). The site allows the user to create their own collection of sites that are accessible from any computer and to see what others are marking.

Facebook

Libraries' acceptance of Facebook has become more commonplace since the site was launched in 2004. Libraries should use the widely popular networking site to their own advantage. An information services librarian at Georgia Institute of Technology, Brian Mathews, thought it would be a way to connect to most of the students at the school. Mathews was effectively able to "expand the goal of promoting the library [by] using Facebook as an outreach tool to promote library services to 1,700 students in the School of Mechanical Engineering after he discovered that 1,300 of these students were registered on Facebook" (Charnigo, 2007).

A survey performed in 2006 determined that Facebook has a minimal effect on library services such as need for increased bandwidth, library traffic, and noise (Charnigo, 2007). Noting this, as well as the ability of accessing a large amount of people who already enjoy the advantages of Facebook, it only seems natural for a library to use the site to promote its own agenda, or announce new programs or features that the library offers.

New ways to reach patrons depend on the innovative librarian to use as many tools as possible to promote the library and its offerings. Facebook's means of connecting people to library services encompasses both text and photos, making it easy and interesting to view. Facebook is just one more tool to announce those services: "exploring popular new types of Internet services such as Facebook instead of quickly dismissing them as irrelevant to librarianship, we might learn new ways to reach out and communicate better with a larger segment of our users" (Charnigo, 2007).

Flickr

Another way to promote library services and record events is through the use of Flickr, a free Web 2.0 photo-sharing network. Flickr accounts allow for easy storing, indexing, organizing and sharing of photos. When looking at any service of this type, librarians must consider whether to trust in the service's longevity and technical support (Saunders, 2008).

Darren Chase, a librarian at Stony Brook University Health Sciences Library in New York, utilized Flickr's technology to install a carousel of images on his library's website's homepage. Chase mentions that the indexing ability of each photo returns highly relevant results, which is a "testament to the power of tagging, or user indexing" (Chase, 2007).

This site could offer a means for a digital library to allow a community of contributors to add content to the library. If a library "invites the general public to become contributors to an image site by letting them volunteer photographs, then you will have a virtual community in no time" (Saunders, 2008).

Library OPAC

Catalogs are also a way to allow users to tag resources, write reviews, and rate materials. Destiny Quest from Follett Software Co. learned how to provide interface design that appeals to students who were accustomed to using the Internet. Their interface allows "students, teachers and staff to give star ratings to books and submit text, audio, or video reviews [the can] recommend books to each other, suggest items for purchase, and request additional copies" (Fiehn, 2008).

SirisDynix is working on an OPAC that is able to help with spelling errors. Catalogs are traditionally sticklers on spelling, but who hasn't appreciated the Google "Did you mean..." feature? This OPAC will allow "dictionary matching of within plus or minus 3 letters" (Fiehn, 2008), and also help in variations of prefixes and suffixes.

Another company's features will permit "building of favorite author and types of booklists and reader's advisory. They are engaging customers in discussions of how these social networking features will work and how they will affect staff time in monitoring" (Fiehn, 2008). A digital library can use these characteristics to enhance patron use by interesting other patrons in their reviews, lists and discussions. It is also another way to alert patrons of programs and library services.

RSS feeds

Libraries have taken great strides to achieve customized content through really simple syndication (RSS) feeds. Through the RSS process, web content is automatically delivered to registered users through readily available software, allowing for a personalized experience (Benson, 2006). RSS feeds allow patrons to subscribe to Websites, blogs, podcasts, booklists and a number of other tools that libraries use to "quickly push information and news to their users" (Sodt, 2009). RSS feeds can be subscribed to in a multitude of ways. Google Reader and Bloglines are two of the better-known methods for doing so (Sodt, 2009). Feeds may also be used in tandem with other social networking tools. For example, patrons can subscribe to RSS feeds to specific Twitter tags or a whole Twitter account to discover when new sites have been bookmarked (Sodt, 2009).

The library at Georgia State University offers more than twenty RSS feeds to users. Each feed is broken down by academic discipline, giving users the opportunity to view only the information that is relevant to their interests (Benson, 2006). The Hennepin County Library in Kansas uses RSS feeds to keep patrons up to date on library news, booklists, career opportunities, and special events scheduled at the library. Separate feeds are categorized and listed under an appropriate subject heading, including subject areas, library news, library catalog, and special events. While this allows users access to new releases, more importantly, it preserves the community aspect of public libraries.

Twitter

Twitter is a type of Short Message Service (SMS) that allows users to post text messages through a "store and forward best effort delivery system" (Krishnamurthy, 2008). Twitter is an example of a "micro-content Online Social Network (OSN)" limiting individual Twitter messages, or "tweets," to 140 characters (Krishnamurthy, 2008). The relatively simple nature of Twitter offers a high level of interoperability. In addition to accessing messages by logging into one's user account, tweets can be received as a text message on a cell phone, through a third party modification applied to a Facebook account, via email, as an RSS feed, or through instant messaging (Krishnamurthy, 2008). Twitter can be used to communicate, ask questions, ask for directions, and ask for support (Grosseck, 2008). According to Grosseck, Twitter has "mashed up" personal publishing and communications, creating a hybrid social networking tool that provides real-time publishing (Grosseck, 2008).

Libraries are using Twitter to communicate with patrons in a variety of ways, including recommending Web resources, providing library news and the announcement of events, and offering virtual reference resources (Kroski, 2008). The Missouri River Regional Library uses Twitter to promote its blog and share pictures from its Flickr stream. The library director finds that Twitter provides a cheap, easy-to-use, effective infrastructure for a "dedicated alert service" that allows the library to get announcements out to patrons in a variety of formats (Kroski, 2008). The Nebraska Library Commission (NLC) uses Twitter as an extension of their Virtual Reference (VR) service. NLC tweets all of its incoming reference questions, submitted from the Ask a Librarian service, with an accompanying answer (Kroski, 2008). Finally, the Association for Library Service to Children (ALSC) utilizes Twitter for professional development purposes, tweeting regularly about news and events of interest to children's library professionals, such as literature seminars, collection management, and special collections (Kroski, 2008).

YouTube

YouTube was founded in 2005 and was purchased by Google about a year later (YouTube, LLC, 2010). YouTube (2010) describes itself as "the world's most popular online video community, allowing millions of people to discover, watch and share originally created videos." Their purpose, according to the site's About page, is to "provide a forum for people to connect, inform, and inspire others across the globe and act as a distribution platform for original content creators and advertisers large and small" (YouTube, 2010). So what does this mean for libraries and patrons? With its popularity, YouTube offers a library another way to promote itself and engage the community. The Vancouver Public Library posts video content from library events and video tutorials (Cahill, 2009, p. 151). Creating a YouTube account is free, easy to do, and takes just a few minutes. Maintaining the site also takes minimal effort and time. YouTube provides plenty of directions and help articles on the website. Posting video clips does reach out to patrons and while there are risks in using a third party to deliver library content, Vancouver decided the benefits outweighed those risks to create a relevant web presence (2009, p. 154). The benefit to libraries and patrons alike is another way to connect and interact.

7.4 Interaction Design and Usability Assessment

General usability principles

Usability refers to the degree of ease with which something can be used. In interaction design, it refers to users' ability to perform tasks within a system quickly, efficiently, and comfortably. Koohang has developed a listing of 12 items that describe the usability properties of digital libraries. These are simplicity, comfort, user friendliness, control, readability, information adequacy/task match, navigability, recognition, access time, relevancy, consistency, and visual presentation (2005). These properties influence user acceptance and enable users to accomplish their tasks easily.

In the context of a digital library, users are likely to perform searching and browsing tasks in order to retrieve information, though a significant number of other tasks are possible (Zhang, Li, Liu, & Zhang, 2008). These tasks can be greatly improved through Nielsen's five attributes of usability: learnability, efficiency, memorability, error handling, and satisfaction (2003).

Learnability

Learnability relates to first-time user experience. A learnable site requires little effort on the part of the user to accomplish basic tasks. Users are highly unlikely to spend time with manuals and tutorials to perform basic tasks in even the most informative and powerful digital library. To make task performance more intuitive, Nielsen (2000) emphasizes the importance of simplicity, epitomized in Google's famous search interface. Users come to Google primarily for simple keyword search, and the homepage reflects this task admirably through its minimal interface. Links to Google's myriad other services are present, as is a link to advanced search options, but none detract attention from the central search box. Google is an extremely learnable site and requires very little prior knowledge or skill.

Efficiency

The efficiency of an interface is measured in the amount of time it takes for a user to complete a task. Efficiency is improved by good use of navigation systems and labeling, reducing page load time, and providing system feedback. Navigation should adequately reflect the architecture of a site, in language that is immediately comprehensible to users, while answering the following questions: where am I? Where have I been? Where can I go? (Nielsen, 2000).

While a robust navigation system provides users some degree of choice, they are at the mercy of their connection speed with respect to page load time. Ensuring that pages load quickly should be a priority in usable systems design. For example, images and Flash applications should be used with care, as they may cause pages to load too slowly. Some web applications may benefit from AJAX technology, which allows dynamic content to be updated without reloading the entire page. Examples of AJAX programming include many Web 2.0 applications, such as Google Reader, Facebook, and YouTube (W3C, 2010).

Finally, system feedback is especially important in interfaces such as digital libraries, where primary user tasks are concerned with information retrieval. Shneiderman's usability guidelines, cited in Chowdhury, Landoni, and Gibb (2006), advise designers to "reduce short-term memory load" by designing systems that track user actions. A system that remembers active and previous search history aids users performing complex research. For example, EBSCO host displays the user's query at all times, while allowing modification of the query directly from the results page, and keeps track of the user's session search history for reference. These functions allow users to find needed information more quickly by freeing them from the need to trace their own steps.

Memorability

Memorability refers to users' ability to return to a site without needing to relearn how to use it. Memorability is closely related to learnability, in that intuitive interfaces seldom require any relearning. However, Louis (2010) notes that memorability is strengthened when users encounter an unexpected, positive reaction when using a site, or when visual cues are used effectively. Louis cites the example of the "home" icon in most browsers as an instantly memorable visible cue.

Error handling

The way a site notifies users of errors can also be an effective usability tool. Error messages should be clear and concise, and should provide suggestions for correction. For example, 404 Page Not Found errors are produced when users enter a nonexistent URL or click on a broken link. Usable sites should include custom 404 pages that contain a clear description of the problem, links to the home page and site map (if one exists), and a search box (Lloyd, 2004). These considerations give users options for locating desired materials or for reorienting themselves within a site.

Satisfaction

User satisfaction with the "look and feel" of a site is often overlooked by developers. A poorly designed site will produce a negative reaction in users and may immediately drive them away, no matter how carefully organized and feature-rich a site may be. In fact, the Stanford Web Credibility Project, cited in Batley (2007), found appearance to be the primary determination of whether or not users trust a site. Designers should strive for a professional, visually pleasing site in order to retain visitors. Furthermore, good site design and usability often go hand in hand – for example, there should always be contrast between text and backgrounds to prevent eye strain, menus should be attractive and easy to use, and graphics should not distract from the page's main content.

The user-centered systems design process

Usability principles should inform the entire design process. Interaction design's focus on user behavior, needs, and interaction style should also play a major role. User-centered systems design places usability and user needs at the center of every stage of development. The major stages of user-centered systems design process, according to Gulliksen and Göransson (2003), are analysis, design (prototyping), evaluation, and feedback.

Interaction design in digital libraries

Lowgren (2008) defines interaction design as "the shaping of interactive products and services with a specific focus on their use." He elaborates further by explaining that interaction design does not attempt to design interactions themselves, as each interaction is unique to the user and the user's information need, but rather the conditions in which those interactions occur. Interaction design for digital libraries significantly overlaps with web design, graphic design, information architecture, content management, psychology and social science; interaction design should be viewed as a type of "choreography" that brings these elements together in a user-friendly form (Baxley, 2002).

The main points of interaction design in digital libraries include the following according to the work begun by the UNC/VT Project Team in 2009: 1) visualizing what appears on the screen of a digital library, 2) identifying how users manipulate, search, browse and use objects in a digital library, 3) enhancing the effective interaction among components of digital libraries, and 4) interacting design elements of digital libraries (Fox, Yang, Ewers, Wildemuth, Pomerantz, and Oh, 2009). To illustrate these points, Marcia J. Bates's diagram known as *The Cascade of Interactions in the Digital Library Interface* (Bates, 2002) offers insight into the importance of enhancing the effective interactions among components and the interacting design elements.

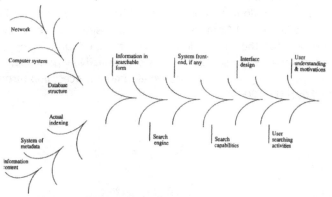

Figure 7.1: The cascade of interactions in the digital library interface.

The diagram in Figure 7.1 presents example layers, even including use patterns and use environment at the right, that determine the overall functional effectiveness of a digital library information retrieval system. Design decisions at each layer have a cascading impact on subsequent layers; poor design at later layers can block products of earlier layers (Bates, p.384).

In designing a digital library there needs to be a structure that allows for cohesive construction. Bates contends that the cascade of interactions model differs from other design models in that it "emphasizes the many design layers that should be considered in relation to each other in the process of designing and implementing an automated information system" (Bates, 2002, p.385). Bates (2002) concludes "digital libraries cannot be fully effective as information sources for users until the entire design process is done in a manner that involves genuine conceptual and practical coordination among the people working on the system layers" (p. 397). Bates' model focuses on four interconnected areas that need to be considered to create an effective interface: technical infrastructure, information/content, the information retrieval system, and the human portion (2002).

The Process of interaction design

Life cycle of interface design

As with any design model it is helpful to have a graphic display of the steps involved to better visualize the process and the interaction of the components. A model that succinctly shows the process of interaction design is the Key Principles for User-Centered Systems Design (UCSD) from Jan Gulliksen and Bengt Göransson. This guides the designer through a thorough design process that analyzes requirements and user needs and keeps the design focused with feedback and evaluation phases. The system is a cyclical model that creates better interactions for users because it allows for continuous evaluation and thus improved iterations of the interface can be created. Gulliksen and Göransson's model is based on several key principles that provide for the foundation for the design process. Top among the principles is that "representative users should actively participate, early and continuously throughout the entire development process and throughout the system life cycle" (2003).

Figure 5: Identifying users' needs and establishing corresponding requirements

DLs' integration of content level and format should be based on users' preference, time frame, subject areas and interest. Users' behavior feedback was an important consideration in the designing of Microsoft's new search engine, *Bing*. *Bing* allows users to quickly view a large amount of data by using a feature called Visual Search. It is commonly accepted that users browse more easily through images than text (Helft, 2009). Cataloging and organizing digital material are important in creating a digital library, but the bottom line is a digital library must be able to offer a site where users can select, retrieve and view its contents effortlessly.

User analysis.

The first stage of user-centered design begins with users themselves. Who are they? What do they need? How will they find it? The answers to these questions can be found through user modeling and task analysis. This stage of the process provides a solid foundation for creating a usable system.

Some digital libraries exist for general audiences. Others target very specific demographics. For example, the World Digital Library (http://www.wdl.org) was designed with a truly global audience in mind. The site is fully translated in seven different languages and includes materials from every UNESCO member nation. In comparison, the Harvard-Smithsonian Digital Video Library (http://www.hsdvl.org) specifically targets United States STEM educators in its collections, terminology, and searching and browsing strategies. In both instances, user demographics have informed major design, content, and technological decisions. Thus, the first stage of analysis should include a demographical user assessment.

Another very important user consideration is varying levels of expertise. Most systems will need to accommodate novice, intermediate, and expert users. Novice users will be most comfortable with a simple system that provides extensive feedback, while expert users might prefer advanced functionality, short cuts, or command interfaces (Batley, 2007). Analyzing the technological proficiency of users will greatly inform developers' design decisions and ensure that sufficient provisions are made for various skill sets.

Knowing who the intended user group is and what their needs are is the first task in creating a functional and usable digital library interface. The categories of information to be aware of are demographics, knowledge and experience, computer/IT experience or knowledge, level of experience with a task, and psychological characteristics. Basic demographic information includes such items as age, gender, perceptual abilities and handicaps, physical disabilities, and motor skills. User knowledge and experience consists of items like education level, reading level, native language, and knowledge of domain-specific language. Computer literacy, level of experience with similar systems, and level of experience with other systems are aspects of users' computer/IT knowledge that effect design decisions. Additionally, the user's experience with a task and psychological characteristics, including attitude and motivation, need to be considered. This data is often gathered through questionnaires, observations, or interviews.

As an example, a study conducted by Kani-Zabihi, Ghinea, and Chen (2006) sought to group users based on IT knowledge backgrounds to help determine expectations for digital libraries' functionality. To that end, the participants were asked to respond to a 10-item questionnaire and were then categorized as novice, intermediate, or advanced based on the number of yes responses (Kani-Zabihi 2006, p.400-401). This user criterion allowed the comparison of task behavior and suggestions across the group. However, designing for every possibility or characteristic that could exist is an unattainable goal, so the use of personas helps to make a more focused project.

Developing user personas

Developing user personas has proven to be an important aspect of designing user-friendly interfaces. A persona is a hypothetical-user archetype, developed for interface design projects and used for guiding decisions about visual design, functionality, navigation and content...interfaces are built to satisfy personas needs and goals" (Head, 2003). User personas are based on an understanding of target users' information needs and information-seeking behaviors. Alison Head (2003) notes three benefits for persona development as "becoming believable constructs for honing design specifications [for the design team].....[...][and they] give design teams a strong sense of what users' goals are and what an interface needs to fulfill them."

Head backs up Cooper's argument in *The Inmates are Running the Asylum* when he argues that interaction design will be far more successful if it meets the goals of one person in mind, rather than trying to decide for the needs of many users. Using personas introduces teams to hypothetical users. Designers then design specifications based on these users, which represent the larger group. By using a persona, the design team is building for typical users' goals and creating an interface that will fulfill those goals (Head). When personas are used in usability testing as discussed below, there is a far greater chance that the interaction design will meet the needs of the user.

To build a persona, Head (2003) suggests starting with interviews with real people to collect demographic data but also information that gives insight into such things as their environment, behaviors and attitudes. It is this anecdotal information gleaned from open-ended questions and careful listening to responses that allows for the creation of a believable and "real" user that helps the design team focus on appropriate product development (Head, 2003). It is also suggested that the number of developed personas be kept between three and seven "so that they are distinct and can be easily remembered by project members" (Head, 2003). Once the personas are built, it is important to categorize the user types as primary or secondary. As Head indicates, this is to keep the focus clear on whose needs are to be met by the design. Secondary persona holds some importance as archetypes, but is not as highly considered. There is a third category that may emerge, known as the "negative persona" or anti-persona, which portrays a group that the interface is not meant to satisfy (Head).

Specifying user tasks

After establishing the demographic and knowledge patterns throughout a system's prospective users, developers must turn their attention to the tasks users must be able to perform. User tasks are the final component to analyzing and identifying user needs and are meant to "identify likely problems so that those problems can be fixed before the system is released, or to assess the current system in order to improve the next version" (Notess, Kouper, Swan, 2005, p.300). Rosenbaum, Glenton, and Cracknell (2008) found that the majority of digital library users preferred to use simple search. Furthermore, those users expected digital library search functions to behave in similar ways to major search engines. They expected spelling suggestions, related terms, and relevance ranking. On the other hand, a digital library designed for information architecture faculty would do well to include highly visible site hierarchies, controlled vocabulary lists, etc.

A typical DL needs to be understood from a variety of angles including frequency or timing, complexity and difficulty, relationship to other user tasks, physical environment of task performance, and the social, organizational and cultural environment. This means that tasks should be authentic and reflects real-world situations (Notess, et al., 2005, introduction). Developing effective tasks for usability tests is not without challenges. In fact, Notess, Kouper, and Swan (2005) set out to explore these challenges. They found that it is necessary to develop and refine tasks iteratively through testing different versions and that real user needs are complex, so it is hard to create representative tasks focusing on testing a particular feature. And finally, unrealistic user tasks can make users hesitant and reluctant to carry them out.

Designing an interface.

Once the basic requirements are established it is time to make design decisions, beginning with applying the empirical evidence from user analysis. The design phase takes the information gathered during analysis and translates it into an interactive system. Hutchins, Hollan, & Norman (1986) contend that design decisions are made in every step of the process. In the planning (vision) phase the decisions are about the interfaces needed in order to achieve user goals. In the translation (analyzing phase) user behavioral intentions are transformed to specific actions. During physical (construction) phase decisions involve representing the planned sequence of actions to interfaces. Evaluating whether users' sense and interpret the interfaces as they are meant to be and evaluating whether the outcomes achieve the user goals are the assessment (evaluation & feedback) decisions.

In user-centered design, prototyping is the major component of the design stage

Prototyping is the next step, when the decisions made and information gathered are put to action for further evaluation by users. According to Rogers and Preece (2007), a prototype is "a limited representation of a design that allows users to interact with it and to explore suitability" (p.241). Prototypes are developed in accordance with previous analysis, and repeatedly evaluated for usability (Usability Professionals' Association, n.d.). Gulliksen and Göransson from the UCSD model explain that prototyping needs to happen "early and continuously" and "should be used to visualize and evaluate ideas and design solutions in cooperation with the end users" (2003). The prototype stage allows for creating a concrete representation of the design decisions. Working from a prototype carries less risk than implementing an entire system before performing usability assessments. When a prototype successfully clears usability tests, it is ready to be constructed and implemented (Gulliksen and Göransson, 2003). However, the process is far from finished when a system goes live. After a site has been constructed, further evaluation should be performed on the final model. Feedback from evaluations using any of the methods discussed below could be used to plan future changes or full redesigns of the site, at which point developers begin the analysis phase all over again.

The interface design must take into consideration universal accessibility. Designers must make sure to take into account users' physical disabilities, cultural differences, language barriers, and computer/network illiteracy. Ben Shneiderman, in an article titled "Universal Usability," states that he "believe[s] that accommodating a broader spectrum of usage situations forces researchers to consider a wider range of designs and often leads to innovations that benefit all users" (Shneiderman 2000, p.87). To this end the W3C Consortium, an international group working to create web standards has as part of its mission to create a "Web for All" that they explain as:

> The social value of the Web is that it enables human communication, commerce, and opportunities to share knowledge. One of W3C's

primary goals is to make these benefits available to all people, whatever their hardware, software, network infrastructure, native language, culture, geographical location, or physical or mental ability (W3C, 2009, mission).

Through their Web Accessibility Initiative (WAI), they have established a set of essential components that web developers should consider in making sites that are more broadly accessible to people with conditions that may limit web accessibility. Another group, Association for Computing Machinery (ACM) has a component called ASSETS which is a

> ...series of conferences whose goal is to provide a forum where researchers and developers, from academia and industry, can meet to exchange ideas and report on new developments relating to computer-based systems to help people. The conference scope spans disabilities and special needs of all kinds, including but not limited to: sensory (hearing, vision); motor (orthopedic); cognitive (learning, speech, mental); and emotional (Association for Computing Machinery, 2010).

Evaluating the design.

Usability issues and lack of evaluation affect users' attitudes towards digital libraries. "A critical facet of digital library usability is the users' views and perceptions....[U]ser's views and experiences are vital and must be taken into consideration in deciding the usability of digital libraries" (Koohang). Unfortunately, evaluation has not kept up with other efforts in terms of developing digital libraries. It is claimed that in this stage of the evolution of digital libraries, formal evaluation is often being bypassed. It is often though that user studies are sufficient in terms of evaluation, but "user studies while useful for understanding how people use systems, by themselves are not evaluation even though they may have evaluative implications and they provide important criteria that can be used in evaluation" (Saracevic, 2001).

At this time, there is no one best approach to evaluation. Library collections were built in relation to a set of standards (Dewey, Library of Congress) but digital libraries are only now developing a set of standards, and often they are not consistent amongst libraries. Additional criteria must emerge beyond the traditional library collection criteria. For many, it is unclear what should be included when evaluating a digital library. Usability assessments vary greatly and there is no form of usability assessment or evaluation that has been agreed upon as the best form for digital library evaluation. Usability testing may involve creating a list of tasks that participants follow when using a digital library, then observing how they complete those tasks. The purpose of this type of usability assessment is to pass the information gathered along to the developers and designers so that a user centered interface design process takes place.

Evaluating a digital library's usability is a critical component of the design process.

Saracevic (2001) believes that a "true" evaluation must meet certain requirements and must involve decisions related to the following: construct of evaluation, context of evaluation, criteria reflecting performance as related to selected objectives, measures reflecting selected criteria to record the performance, and methodology for doing the evaluation. Unfortunately, there is no agreement as to the elements of each of these; therefore the evaluation of digital libraries is still in the formative stage. It is clear, though, that an evaluation must clearly specify what elements are being evaluated. These elements include security, costs, digital collections/resources, access, distribution, interface, etc. (Saracevic, 2001)

It must always be kept in mind that people are central to all libraries. All future efforts to evaluate digital libraries must be based on the information needs of users. It is imperative that evaluation of digital libraries becomes formalized in order to best meet the needs of the users.

Several methods of evaluation have proven useful in determining usability strengths and weaknesses. Since each method has its own strengths and weaknesses, using a combination of the following methods throughout the design process will increase user satisfaction with a digital library interface. Furthermore, ongoing evaluation will ensure that digital libraries continue to be relevant and satisfactory resources in a rapidly changing technological environment. Heuristic evaluation, cognitive walkthroughs, claims analysis, and user testing are core components in the evaluator's toolbox.

Usability criteria applied to DL design

According to Jakob Neilsen, "usability is a quality attribute that assesses how easy user interfaces are to use. The word 'usability' also refers to methods for improving ease-of-use during the design process" (Usability 101, n.d.). The attributes that compose usability (as mentioned earlier) are learnability, efficiency, memorability, errors, and satisfaction (Neilsen, n.d., Usability 101, What). The importance of applying these usability criteria is to get people to use and return to the site. As Neilsen points out, if people have difficulty with the site, they will leave (Usability 101, n.d., Why).

Kling and Elliot look to the concept of "organizational usability." Their work defines this as "a new term that refers to the design of computer-based systems so that they are effectively integrated into the work practices of organizations" (Kling and Elliott, 1994, Abstract). In other words, is the design workable from the standpoint of the group administering it? So, while they acknowledge the importance of the attributes of learnability, efficiency, memorability, and errors for interface usability their research broadens the considerations of usability within an organization. The case study of Legal Research in Civil and Criminal Courts (1997) demonstrates the importance of accessibility, compatibility, and integratability into usability at an organizational level. They concluded three things:

"First, the organization of access points influences whether or not professions integrate LRDLs into their work practices. Those who can access LRDLs close to their normal workplaces use them more often.... Second, there appears to be a strong interplay between computer use at home and the use of computers at work....Third,...training and support are needed." (Elliott and Kling, 1997, p.10)

They also used their data to look at what makes the LRDLs organizationally unusable. Those contributing factors are low levels of training and lack of follow-up consulting, lack of systematic computer use, and disinterest in LRDLs (1997, p.10-11). So, within an organization, DLs must be structured and evaluated on accessibility, compatibility, integrability and organizational expertise to ensure that they will be utilized and meet users 'needs.

User acceptance of digital libraries

Thong, Hong, and Tam continue to look at the organizational level of DLs by studying user acceptance of digital libraries. In summary, their "findings show that both perceived usefulness and perceived ease of use are determinants of user acceptance of digital libraries. In addition, interface characteristics and individual differences affect perceived ease of use, while organizational context influences both perceived ease of use and perceived usefulness of digital libraries" (2002, abstract).

The individual factors--computer self-efficacy (judgment of one's ability to use a computer; quoted by Hong, et al from Compeau & Higgins 1995) and knowledge of search domain (the user's background knowledge related to conducting the search)—do have an impact on the user's acceptance of digital libraries. They conclude that "users who have higher levels of confidence in using computers...are more likely to find digital libraries easy to use... [and that] when users are more familiar with the subject domain they are searching, the search activities become easier for them." (Wong, et al. 2001/2002 p. 105)

The system characteristics of relevance, terminology, and screen design also contribute to user acceptance. Relevance means that the system content that is presented is what the user is expecting to find. Hong, et al. contends that "having more relevant content in the digital library can assist the users in finding the necessary information more easily" (2001/2002, p.117). The words, sentences and abbreviations used in a system make up the terminology and the authors feel that clarity of terminology will positively affect perceived ease of use and usefulness (Hong et al., p.106). The results showed that terminology impacted the perception of ease of use, but not usefulness. Screen design, or user interface, "can create a comfortable virtual environment where users can easily identify functional groups and navigation aids, freely move around and scan search results, and make more efficient searches" (Hong, et al. p.107). Again, they found a connection to perceived ease of use, but not usefulness in relation to screen design. Hong, Thong, Wong & Tam's implications for creating DLs that will be used are twofold. First "attention must be placed in designing user-friendly interfaces, including using student-familiar terminology, well-depicted buttons and icons, consistent interface style, and clear navigation flow" (2001/2002, p.118). And ultimately, the content must be relevant (p.118).

Evaluation methods

Heuristic evaluation

Heuristic evaluation is an evaluation method in which a group of evaluators works through a site and checks for usability errors using a checklist, also known as a set of heuristics (Nielsen, n.d.). Heuristic Evaluation as described by Blanford, et al. (2004) is a widely used tool that has evaluators go through each page or screen and ask a series of questions about the system, concerning such aspects as error prevention and user control & freedom. The heuristics used help to structure the evaluation and provide a somewhat standard approach among the evaluating panel. One of the most commonly used sets of heuristics is Nielsen's own list:

- visibility of system status
- match between the system and the real world
- user control and freedom
- consistency and standards
- error prevention
- recognition rather than recall
- flexibility and efficiency of use
- aesthetic and minimalist design
- help users recognize, diagnose, and recover from errors
- help and documentation. (Aitta, Kaleva, & Kortelainen, 2008).

Nielsen (n.d.) recommends that a group of three to five evaluators examine the interface, prototype, or written description of a system individually and present their findings either as a written report or verbal communication with a session observer. This method is fast and inexpensive, requiring approximately one to two hours per evaluator. Notes can be compared and problems can then be addressed in the ten areas he developed (Nielsen, 1994). While useful in detecting surface usability difficulties, heuristics does have limitations in that it demands some level of expertise in understanding users and uses of DLs (Blandford, et al. 2004, p 29).

Cognitive walkthrough

Cognitive walkthroughs are similar to heuristic evaluations in that they also rely on a three-to-five person panel of experts. However, cognitive walkthroughs do not use any sort of criteria, as in heuristic evaluation. Instead, cognitive walkthrough evaluation requires a concrete list of desirable user actions, which the experts are then asked to perform. Cognitive walkthrough takes a user-centered perspective, and as Blandford (2004) cites Wharton (1994), the recommendation is that a team works through the tasks and agree on these four questions:

- Who will the users be?
- What tasks are to be analyzed?
- What is the correct action sequence for each task?
- How is the interface defined?

The next stage is individual work to answer an additional four questions for each page/screen. Wharton defines these as

- Will the user try to achieve the right effect (goal)?
- Will the user notice the correct action is available?
- Will the user associate the action with the effect (goal)?
- If the correct action is performed, will the user see that progress is being made towards the goal? (Blandford, et al. 2004, pp.29-30).

As the evaluators work through each task, they develop a narrative describing probable user behavior. If the narrative ends in correct task completion, the system may be considered a success. Otherwise, the narratives point to design flaws that warrant correction (Rieman, Franzke, & Redmiles, 1995). Finally, the individuals regroup to compare and analyze findings and revise accordingly. Cognitive walkthroughs' greatest strength is their ability to reflect support of "exploratory learning" (Rieman, Franzke, & Redmiles, 1995). Also, like heuristic evaluation, it can be done quickly and cheaply at any stage of development. Cognitive walkthroughs tend to provide more insight into user behavior than heuristics, though they often produce fewer concrete problems and solutions. However, like heuristic evaluation, they also suffer from the expert bias of evaluators. This type of evaluation does help identify issues and the structured format creates more reproducibility across evaluators. However, it does not help discover deeper user problems like formulating good queries (Blandford et al. 2004, p. 31).

Claims analysis (CA)

Blandford, Keith, and Fields (2006) found that heuristics evaluation, cognitive walkthroughs, and traditional user testing were good tools for superficial usability problems, but rarely revealed deeper issues concerning successful information retrieval. Claims Analysis (CA) as explained by Blandford, et al. (2004) is based on creating a context for the evaluation of the effects of a design on a user. It is less structured than cognitive walkthrough, but more structured than heuristic. The benefit to CA is that it "supports the analyst in thinking about the usability issues for DLs more deeply" by combining the questions of layout and feedback with the why and how (p.32).

Claims analysis uses a semi-structured statement approach to work through a system. First, the evaluation team designs plausible scenarios in which a user interacts in some way with a system. Analysts make positive or negative "claims" statements about the scenario. This psychological approach to expected user behavior and site design results in a set of positive and negative characteristics for designers to work with. If possible, negative characteristics are eliminated, but if not, the claims set can be used to balance a site's strengths and weaknesses according to its priorities.

Claims analysis can take place during initial development, during prototyping, or after deployment. Like previously described methods, it does not require an interface to be in place. Once again, care must be taken to encourage evaluators to think like users. However, the scenarios used in claims analysis allow for the creation of user personas. User personas are fictional characters that represent the most common characteristics of site users (Batley, 2007). For example, an evaluation scenario might include novice, average, and expert user personas. Expert evaluators may find personas useful as filters for approaching a system from a user point of view (Blandford, Keith, & Fields, 2006).

Usability testing

A final means of usability evaluation is user testing. User testing requires actual users, as opposed to experts, and can only be conducted when a working prototype is already in place. User testing typically involves asking users to engage in DL tasks while being monitored, either by a human or a video camera. As Nielsen (2003) points out, "most projects require multiple rounds of testing and redesign to achieve acceptable user-experience quality, and the equally strong finding that it is a hundred times cheaper to fix usability problems discovered early in the project rather than at its end." Mvungi, de Jager, and Underwood (2008) emphasize the importance of making users comfortable by making it clear that it is the system that is under evaluation, not the users' performance.

The *type* of usability testing must be taken into consideration when choosing a pool of test users. If the concern is improving ease of use for users unfamiliar with the system, then the test group should be comprised of primarily novice users. On the other hand, if the goal is to evaluate the system on a deeper, more technical level, then the test users must already have a higher level of understanding of the system (Nielsen). The next step is selecting the test facilitators, and organizing the test itself (including all stages of introduction, execution, and debriefing). Think Aloud Protocols, as explained by Nielsen, "ask users to verbalize their thoughts in a running monologue as they use a design. This think-aloud process tells you how people interpret the design elements, whether any are confusing, and which ones are compelling or repelling." This poses challenges to the test subject who may be unfamiliar or uncomfortable with the process. Tangible evidence is also part of a usability test, and may include videotaping a user and using screen captures. The final phase is to use the results of the testing. Data is interpreted and analyzed, leading to recommendations for changes and improvements. Then the problems need to be prioritized so that the revision of the prototypes can take place to improve usability.

7.5 Information Summarization and Visualization

Information summarization

Summarization defined

Human summarization.

Information summarization is the process of analyzing source material, selecting and condensing key information, and then generating an abstract of these key concepts (Maybury, 1995). When the process has been successful, the information seeker is able to distill the most important concepts from a body of information and produce an abstract useful for a specific task or user (Maybury, 1995). The structure of the source, along with the abstractor's knowledge, plays a large role in the summarization process (Maybury, 1995). The type and depth of mental processing that occurs during summarization is affected by the structure (content, length, and type) of the abstract (Maybury, 1995).

Automatic summarization.

Automatic text summarization (ATS), a subfield of Natural Language Processing (NLP), utilizes computer applications to "produce a cluster of information which is most relevant to the user," through one of three approaches: the shallow approach, the deeper approach, or the hybrid approach (Diola, 2004). The shallow approach, the simplest of the three methods, produces a summary by extracting sentences from the information source (Diola, 2004). This approach is sometimes problematic, as it is difficult to preserve the original context of a source. The deeper approach utilizes template or concept abstractions to produce in-depth abstracts (Diola, 2004). This approach utilizes inferences about the original text, and concepts not explicitly found within the text to create coherent abstracts (Diola, 2004). Finally, the hybrid approach combines extraction techniques with NLP and

Artificial Neural Network techniques to create a summarization that falls somewhere between simple and deep abstracts (Diola, 2004).

Maybury states that ATS includes four distinct types of text processing: 1) analysis of the source text, through the use of word frequencies, clue phrases, layout, syntax, semantics, discourse, and pragmatics; 2) identification of important source elements, through the use of word count, clue phrases, and statistical and structural attributes; 3) condensation of information, through the use of abstraction and aggregation; and 4) generation of the resulting summary presentation, through the use of planning, realization, and layout techniques (Maybury, 1995).

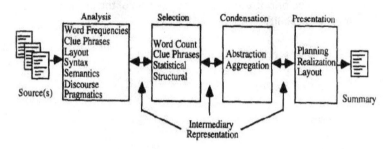

Figure 7.3: Maybury's Summarization Process.

Computational techniques applied in textual summarization

The statistical approach and machine learning

The statistical approach is used in ATS to determine the frequency of words and phrases in the original text as a way to identify key words and phrases that will be included in the abstract (Fung, 2010). Supervised learning, a machine learning technique for "deducing a function from training data" is used to identify these key words and phrases by using a classifier (Fung, 2010). Unsupervised learning, or clustering, may also be used. This method identifies key words and phrases by surveying similar characteristics (Fung, 2010). Finally, any number of statistical and machine learning techniques may be applied to identify main sentences as part of the abstract (Fung, 2010).

Natural language processing

Natural Language Processing (NLP), as discussed in an earlier chapter, is used to produce an abstracted summary by "understanding the context of the original content" (Fung, 2010). This often produces abstracts that do not contain words or phrases from the original source, because this technique sometimes aggregates words and phrases from related sources (Fung, 2010). NLP may be used in tandem with other techniques, such as text summarization, to produce more accurate and authoritative abstracts (Fung, 2010). This combination would evaluate original context through the use of NLP, yet also employ recall and precision through the use of text summarization (Fung, 2010).

Web summarization

Web pages provide users with static and dynamic content. Static content is information on a Web page that is blended with an HTML tag in the file and cannot be changed by the end user unless they have access to the file (Fung, 2010). Dynamic content is information generated using PHP and ASPX, and can be changed based on requests by end users without access to the original file on the server, allowing information to be displayed on demand (Fung, 2010). To create an abstracted summary from the Web, HTML tags and Web programming must be separated from the text (Fung, 2010). Additionally, advertisements and unrelated content must also be removed or filtered out (Fung, 2010). Web summarization techniques are employed for this process, and then text summarization is used to analyze relevant content and create the abstract (Fung, 2010).

Information visualization

Definition, history, and background

The computer is the ultimate way for its users to "see" new ideas and information. Even though great progress has been made in Information Visualization with the computer, it isn't the only form of visualization. Any tools humans "use to amplify their cognition" (Dürsteler, 2002) pertain to Information Visualization. As a result of computer use in Information Visualization, fields that were once thought of as distinctly separate are now cohesive. These fields include graphic representation, data filtering, visual languages, cartography or cognitive psychology (Dürsteler, 2002).

Information Visualization is an interdisciplinary study that has arisen "from research in human-computer interaction, computer science, graphics, visual design, psychology, and business methods. It is increasingly applied as a critical component in scientific research, digital libraries, data mining, financial data analysis, market studies, manufacturing production control, and drug discovery" (Bederson, 2003). The term Information Visualization has been used for over 20 years and is credited to Stuart Card, G.G. Robertson and J.D. Mckinlay from Xerox PARC and Nahum Gershon, a scientist at MITRE Corp for coining the term (Dürsteler, 2002).

The role that the external world plays on thought and reasoning is an important part in starting to understand Information Visualization. The idea of this thought and reasoning is called external cognition. It expresses the way "in which internal and external representations and processes weave together in thought [and] the use of the external world and especially the use of cognitive artifacts or physical inventions to enhance cognition are all around us" (Card, et al, 1999).

Use in the digital library field

When designing visualizations, it is helpful to understand user tasks and needs. "Most information-visualization projects have emphasized three tasks" (Wan, 2006): searching, navigation, and browsing.

Searching

A two-dimensional display, proposed by Shneiderman et al. enabled several thousand results to be viewed all at once. This was a two-pronged approach with two-dimensional visualizations and browsers for hierarchical data sets. Users saw an overview of color coded dots or bar charts on a grid organized and labeled by classification. Users could focus on one classification or change to another hierarchical section. Another search aid for digital libraries was a "language-independent document-classification system, completed by Liu et al., and helped users analyze the search query results visually" (Wan, 2006).

Navigation

With navigation, as with searching, there are a diversified number of information visualization applications. Shneiderman's two-dimensional display also had navigational functions. Another navigation tool dealt with maps: Hascoet produced a map interface which had "summary views in the form of navigational tree and neighbor trees that showed documents related to one focus document" (Wan, 2006). Users could modify the configuration of maps they retrieved by simple cut, paste, move, delete, expand and save operations (Wan, 2006).

Browsing

Film finder is an example of a browsing technique that has been around for years. With Filmfinder, "users can move several sliders to select query parameters, and the search results change with the movement of the sliders. This tool can help users browse movie records more easily and cognitively" (Wan, 2006). Another browsing technique is Query Previews, in which "users are presented with generalized previews if the entire database using only the most salient attributes. When they select rough ranges, they will immediately learn the availability of the data for their proposed query" (Wan, 2006).

Applications for visualization and summarization

As the amount of available information increases, users of information expect to have useful and usable ways in which to access this information. Digital libraries are striving to find ways to meet these needs by applying visualization and summarization technologies. One such application is the Informedia Digital Video Library Project.

Informedia digital video library project

The Informedia Digital Video Library project sets the "foundation for full content indexing and retrieval of video and audio media" (Wactlar, 2001, abstract). The concept is that information from the library, which contains over 2000 hours of video, be retrieved and displayed in a collage. The "collages enable the user to emphasize different aspects or facets of the digital video library" (Wactlar, 2001). The display shows multiple images such as a map depicting the distribution by nation of El Niño effects with overlaid thumbnails. Users could then zoom in on a particular area and see video images of that area. Further collage elements are timelines with key people and events to provide a context for the selected map area (Wactlar, 2001). According to Wactlar (2001), the "overarching long-term goal ...has been to bring to spoken language and visual documentation the same functionality and capability that we have with written communication, including all aspects of search, retrieval, categorization, and summarization."

Cross-language text retrieval

Another application of visualization and summarization technology is the development of Cross-Language Text Retrieval (CLTR) tested by Ogden, Cowie, Davis, Ludovik, Molina-Salgado, & Shin (1999). The purpose of the study was to create access to and translations of works in another language that were relevant to the user's needs using an interface called "document thumbnail visualizations" (Ogden, et al., 1999). This gives users a look at multiple documents with search terms highlighted, as opposed to just titles. In addition, the system sought to improve users' ability to select relevant works through the ability to enter English queries and then be able to refine the context/connotation of the word through a translator in order to determine which documents would be "most consistent with their information needs" (Ogden et al. 1999). What this study showed was the "keeping the human 'in the loop' during query formulation had significant value...[and that thumbnail visualization] can provide advantages to the end user over standard WWW-based retrieval presentation methods..." (Ogden, et al. 1999, conclusion).

Search output

A third example of visualization and summarization concerns search output. In 2002, Cole, Mandelblatt and Stevenson explored the presentation of search output "so that the user is not overwhelmed and can in fact make use of the message about the information or topic space the summarization and visualization attempts to communicate" (p.38). They examined five information science visualization schemes based on work by Lin (1997) and Small (1999), which are hierarchical, network, scatter, map and hybrid (Cole, et al., 2002). Digital library designers must keep in mind that the "efficacy of a visualization scheme is whether or not the graphic representation helps the user understand something about the information space that (i) cannot be said in words, or (ii) that can be better or more quickly understood than if the information space was described in words" (Cole, et al. 2002, p. 44). They concluded by suggesting two-level visualization for the novice user, which allows for associative thinking (Cole, et al. 2002, p. 51). For digital libraries this implies the need to create some stable, predictable designs, but also allow for the associations created by the user.

Applied to digital libraries, these technologies make information available to users in ways that benefit presentation and accessibility. The vast amount of available information must be organized so that is useful, usable, and meets the needs and expectations of the users. Cohesive formats like accessing multiple video clips or viewing thumbnail documents allow for digital libraries to improve and enhance a user's search for information.

Conclusion

Usability is an obviously desirable quality in any interactive system. Nevertheless, Blandford, Keith, and Fields (2006) noted that digital libraries tend to be difficult to use, due to unfamiliar organizational structures, complex results listings, and rationales that do not match the way that users approach information. They also write that user concerns are often overlooked in the face of serious technological challenges (document format, interoperability, indexing, etc.) during digital library development.

In order to remain relevant, digital libraries must begin placing a higher priority on usability and good interaction design. The most recent literature suggests that digital libraries are becoming increasingly "person-centric... [their] goal is now to facilitate communication, collaboration and interactions, and not just providing access to digital information" (Chowdhury, 2010). As the definition of an ideal digital library continues to expand, interaction design must keep pace with new user requirements and expectations. The key to interaction for traditional behaviors such as searching and browsing and to more recent developments such as user-created organization systems, personalization features, collaborative functionality, and communicative tools, lies in basic usability principles and processes associated with usable interaction design. Digital libraries must develop these practices, or their other innovations, while impressive, will only rarely be appreciated by their intended audience.

Study questions for Chapter Seven:

1. Improvements in technology abound, such as the capture and storage of information, but what are some of the greatest challenges of the global infrastructure today? Will libraries be able to meet demands of their

users? Will commercial entities take over the role of libraries in this new environment? Do you believe that user-centered DL systems will lead to generic out-of-the-box DL systems reducing the need for customization? Is this good or bad? Use those most recent studies/literature to support your arguments.

      2. Lesk writes, "If the electronic library comes to pass, there may be, as a result, a greater distance from the real world. People will study more and do less. Will children lose even more touch with the physical world and other people, as computers add to television as an artificially created distraction?" (1997, pp. 264-265). Seven years down the road, is there any hard evidence that these things are happening? If so, is this something librarians should be concerned about? If it is, what do we do? Use examples from your experience or from the most current literature to support.

      3. As Borgman states, "Information can be empowering, but it also can be overwhelming. "How then can future developers build global information infrastructures that empower users without burdening them?

      4. How should digital library projects address the very serious issue of language? Are there any digital library projects that attempt to deliver information in many languages or through translation devices? Because most projects are in English, does this mean that those people who most need the information are not getting it? How does this issue impact that of equal and open Internet access?

      5. Borgman argued, "Though considerable technological progress has been made, true interoperability among languages and forms remains an elusive goal" (p. 223). The problems of multilingual information access must be addressed for any global digital project. Particularly, character encoding issues. The Unicode site provides some information on current characters being worked on at http://www.unicode.org/unicode/alloc/Pipeline.html. Do you think we will see universal character encoding issues resolved soon and can you share any examples where you have seen multilingual coding used effectively? One important area would be multilingual
OPACs.

Chapter Eight: Services

Digital library services is an area growing much more rapidly than other areas of digital library studies, especially in this age where many digital libraries have been fully developed in terms of their technological framework.

8.1: What services may a digital library provide?

Digital libraries have the potential to deliver Vannevar Bush's dream of placing a complete research library on everyone's desk top along with the scholarly collaboration he so coveted. Digital library user services are significantly enhanced due to technological improvements in computer systems. Today we already have remote reference capabilities in many libraries; in Connecticut, for example, Bibliomation provides reference services to member libraries after hours, and Wesleyan University allows access even for non-students. Technological breakthroughs will allow the patron to interact face-to-face with librarians via video conferencing technology, which will become cheaper in the future, and thus accessible for the majority of digital library patrons. The recent trend of technological improvements will reinforce the movement in libraries away from an emphasis on preservation of materials to dissemination of information. This change in emphasis of the role of the library will have ramifications on the structure of the library staff; the hierarchy will change as librarians become technically skilled and as they will work with many other individuals with whom they did not work before, such as computer technicians. There will be areas of overlapping responsibility, as librarians work even more closely than they already do in creating and improving digital libraries with computer experts. The more flexible structure in the library will also lead to enhanced services for the patron.

Digital libraries can potentially provide a number of new services that traditional libraries cannot provide, yet they can also support a range of traditional library services. Although advanced DL research projects explore the possibilities of a digital-only world, working digital libraries support functions that closely resemble their brick-and-mortar library counterparts, in slightly different guises.

The following is the list of services that digital libraries can provide.

Electronic Services

Electronics services are not limited to circulation review, renewals, inter-library loan request, and full-text/document delivery. They include many others as well.

Information Retrieval

All content of a digital library is searchable, whether through direct query entry or through some form of browsing, or both. LC's American Memory project, for example, is one of the more well-developed and complex digital libraries. It offers direct search through the entire collection, or through selected collections, with the same kinds of options (match any words, all words, this exact phrase) as Internet search engines. Users may also browse through collections, and can browse subject and author indexes within a collection.

Reference Services

To fulfill reference queries electronically is a unique service a digital library provides. A recent study found that 99% of 70 academic libraries offer e-mail reference and 29% offer real-time reference service (Tenopir, 2001). There are also ask-an-expert (AskA) services on the Internet that provide reference service with Web-based query forms and e-mail. However, few digital libraries are sufficiently advanced to have incorporated interactive reference services. Most offer an e-mail contact for queries, and one or more frequently asked questions (FAQ) files, which typically focus on either description of the technology or information about the resources. For example, digitized collections at Duke University are listed on the home page of the Rare Book, Manuscript, and Special Collections Library, along with a link to a page that provides e-mail and telephone contact to reference services for those doing research in the collections, whether print or digital. [See extended discussion in Lecture note, Digital Reference Services.]

Digital Reserve

Reserve has been a tradition in college and university libraries in the US. There has been a growing need for libraries and patrons to have reserve materials accessible online. OverDrive developed a software package called Digital Library Reserve that enables libraries to develop, manage and preserve eBook and digital media collections. The purpose is to allow patrons to borrow best-selling eBooks for onscreen reading. Using this technology, Cleveland Public Library has built up a digital book collection, which can be "Accessed-Anytime-Anywhere." The book titles include academic, research and business titles.

Instructional Services

User training, such as bibliographic instruction, can take many forms--guides, tutorials, manuals, pathfinders, workshops, videos, or one-on-one guidance. Some digital libraries have developed user training. In addition to FAQs, many digital libraries carry guides to using the collections. As a typical example, the Lester S. Levy Collection of Sheet Music at Johns Hopkins University includes several useful pages on searching and browsing. The William Blake Archive goes further than most in providing a well-developed virtual tour, extensive help documentation, a history of the project, an FAQ, a bibliography, and information on editorial principles, the editors, and the technology.

Collaborative Learning Services

Public libraries traditionally work closely with local schools, and school and academic libraries are directly involved in the curricula of their instructions. Digital libraries are also concerned with helping educators make the most of electronic resources and services. The University of Michigan Digital Library Teaching and Learning Project has online learning resources in a number of different subject areas for high school and middle school students. The Perseus Project at Tufts University (one of the oldest digital libraries) devotes a section of the site to "Teaching with Perseus," including syllabi and class notes, along with comments from instructors, and teacher and student guides. Similarly, the Colorado Digitization Project includes a section on "Working with Schools," with lesson plans and links to additional tools and resources. Classes using these resources could meet entirely in cyberspace, although it is likely that most of them do not. Digital libraries can, of course, support collaborative research activities among individuals who may be far removed from each other, and from the digital library. This has been a subject of research interest--for example, the University of Michigan Digital Library site illustrates a visual collaborative information space in research on user interfaces, though little has surfaced in actual working demonstrations.

Interface Services

On the other end of these services are users, who may be elderly, or children, or a restricted community (where access is limited to authenticated users), or may be Internet users at large. Through different interface designs, digital libraries can provide different services based on the characteristics of the diverse users, to better fit their different needs.

Such services can also be called Human-Computer Interaction (HCI) Services. Consideration must be given to the primary community in regard to access capabilities. Technology and connectivity at the user end will vary with respect to speed, capacity, device, and graphic display, and these variations should be taken into account during interface design. Users may also face physical challenges, restricting their ability to use a keyboard, or requiring the use of an assertive device that translates information into spoken words. For the most part, digital libraries rely on pointing devices (e.g., mice, styli, etc.) and keyboards for interaction, and are primarily designed for display on desktop or laptop computers, although the huge growth of interest in wireless computing, and the development of standards for transmitting and displaying Web-accessible information on handheld devices, is likely to lead to more work along the lines of Cornell University's Nomadic Digital Libraries.

Direct Search

End users of library online public access catalogs (OPACs) and commercial online secondary services (e.g., SilverPlatter) can usually choose to search by keyword (which normally includes words from title, subject heading, and other content describing fields), or by a particular field (e.g., title, subject, author). Under "advanced" options, such systems offer Boolean searching, truncation, and perhaps proximity functions (i.e., word x must be within so many words of word y). Retrieval is usually based on exact match to the query; that is, the results contain exactly what the user specified. If the system cannot match to a query, either the user is told that nothing exists, or an index of alphabetically close words may be displayed for browsing.

On the other hand, a look at the world of Internet search engines demonstrates almost infinite variations on the theme of "type something and we will try to find the best answer." Many include advanced options similar to those just mentioned, but retrieval is based on primarily statistical algorithms that take into account the amount and distribution of query words in Web page representations (as well as many other factors). Query words are usually stemmed (suffixes are removed, and other transformations may occur), and almost invariably something is retrieved (although in some cases the results may have very little relevance).

Direct search in digital libraries is usually similar to the OPAC or online searching model, employing search templates or index navigation tools. This takes advantage of the fact that digital libraries hold well-structured data and metadata, providing the basis for fielded search and browsing through indexes. Also, many digital libraries contain non-text objects, which do not lend themselves to text-based statistical retrieval algorithms (although some interesting work is being done in image pattern matching). Digital libraries frequently employ one of the prevailing standards for managing search, such as the Z39.50 protocol, structured query language (SQL), and tools developed for Web search engine applications (e.g., Open Text). Experimentation with sophisticated statistical and linguistic algorithms is thus far usually confined to research settings.

Advanced Intellectual Searching

In addition to accommodating technical constraints and special needs in user communities, a digital library should accommodate varying levels of expertise, and should offer flexibility in methods of exploration. Users should be able to find objects directly (analogous to finding a specific author or subject in a library catalog), and should also be able to browse systematically. The interface, together with the underlying infrastructure, interprets digital objects for presentation to the user, manages the relationships among objects, and may have also to negotiate terms and conditions for use of objects.

My Digital Library Services

Customized services may allow users to make their own personalized interface and connections. MyLibrary (http://dewey.library.nd.edu/mylibrary/) is a digital library project allowing patrons to create and manipulate their own individual web pages within the digital library, incorporating links to the resources and services they like the most. MIT and Hewlett-Packard's DSpace is a more flexible example of this kind of personalized service (Tennant, 2002). Open Access is another service that allows authors to share and exchange their primary studies within their communities, in which articles "are immediately and permanently available online" and unrestricted use, distribution and reproduction in any medium is permitted" (http://www.biomedcentral.com/info/about/access).

Indexing of the Internet

Indexing the Internet is a major challenge facing information professionals. In one line of research that focuses on this problem, Thompson, Shafer and Vizine-Goetz (1997) look at the degree of class integrity in the Dewey Decimal Classification system (DDC) and evaluate DDC as a knowledge base for an automatic subject assignment tool.

DDC is a widely used classification scheme, currently used in 135 countries and translated into 30 languages. It is used in 95% of U.S. public and school libraries (Thompson, Shaffer & Vizine-Goetz, 1997). DDC is continuously updated, with updates taking place at the rate of about 10 Library of Congress subject headings (LCSH) per week being incorporated into DDC (Vinize-Goetz, presentation, ACM Digital Libraries T97, July 1997). In one study, the integrity of the DDC was tested by feeding DDC concept definitions into the system to see how well DDC could classify its own concept definitions. The researchers concluded from these tests that DDC is adequate to classify the Web--but not completely.

The major drawback to this work, at least as reported at ACM Digital Libraries T97 and in the associated paper, is that the researchers failed to draw a distinction between classification systems, such as DDC and LoC, and categorization or subject heading systems such as LCSH and Sears. We could say that, for example, DDC and Sears are at 90 of one another: that is, DDC divides knowledge—along the warp—into disciplines and sub-disciplines while Sears weaves the disciplines together—along the woof or weft—by common topic. To add subject headings to a classification scheme would appear to add depth to the divisions within each discipline while defeating, or at least camouflaging the purpose of subject headings (see Sears, Preface). One would think this would also make the classification scheme unnecessarily complex and perhaps awkward.

Nevertheless, the technique used in this research is interesting. Words in the search query were truncated to their stems and then matched to stems in the DDC scheme. Stemming, such as stemming German to germ and matching the query to biological concepts, did improve retrieval overall. It would be interesting to see longer queries, for example "the German people, country, and customs," stemmed and rated on density of match within hierarchies to see if retrieved concepts more closely matched query concepts.

8.2: Digital Reference Services - Trends and Issues

With the advent of digital libraries, there is an increased need for formal methods of remote communication between information seekers and information professionals. Responding to this need is the provision of reference service via the Internet, or digital reference service.
Recent practice of digital reference services relies on much of the technology used in digital libraries.

Common Reference Services

Email services
Early digital reference services primarily used e-mail to receive questions and provide responses. A study conducted in 1999 found that 45% of academic libraries (Janes, Carter, and Memmott, 1999) and 13% of public libraries (Janes, 2001) offered digital reference services through e-mail and the Web. A later study found that 99% of 70 academic libraries offer e-mail reference and 29% offer real-time reference service (Tenopir, 2001).

Ask-an-expert (AskA) services
Based in traditional library environments, hundreds of ask-an-expert (AskA) services on the Internet (some in existence for six years or more) offer information in a variety of subject areas as well as general reference, primarily through Web-based query forms and e-mail.

Commercial reference service
In addition to the many non-profit educational AskA services, a large number of commercial Web sites offer reference service to Internet users (e.g., Abuzz), proving extremely popular and causing concern among those who view use of these services as competition for libraries (Coffman and McGlamery, 2000).

Real-time reference
E-mail service is often criticized for presenting barriers to two important aspects of traditional face-to-face reference service: patrons often do not receive the same immediate response, and librarians cannot as easily conduct the reference interview that is so often necessary to accurately determine and meet users' needs (McGlamery and Coffman, 2000; Oeill, 1999).

Technologies for real-time services

Libraries try to recreate the intimacy found in face-to-face reference interactions in a digital environment through the use of synchronous, real-time technologies:
- chat technologies
- instant messaging software
- Web contact center software
- some combination of the above options

1. Live chat technology is one of the most important real-time reference tools
It enables users to communicate on the Internet with others in real time. It has been used to provide digital reference service as far back as 1995, when the Internet Public Library experimented with a type of text-based chat environment called a MOO (Multi-user Object Oriented) (Shaw, 1996).

More recent efforts include the use of commercially available Web-based products such as Conference Room from Webmaster (Antonelli and Tarlton, 2000) as well as custom-built solutions, as in the case of Temple University Libraries' Interactive Reference Project (Stormont, 2001).

2. Another real-time reference tool is instant messaging software. Products such as WhatsApp and WeChat allow librarians to communicate in real-time with patrons through a series of messages sent back and forth. Instant messaging products enable librarians to indicate their availability on a contact list, share URLs and files with patrons, and record sessions (Yue, 2001). These products are free but must be downloaded on both librarians' and patrons' computers. Instant messaging products offer the option to communicate synchronously in a shared environment.

3. Web contact center software is also a real-time reference tool.

Web contact center software allows live interaction between librarians and patrons, routing mechanisms to transfer queries between institutions, and collaborative browsing (enabling librarians to display specific Web pages on the patron computer screen) (McGlamery and Coffman, 2000).

Examples include:
- Virtual Reference Software from LSSI (Coffman, 2001)
- 24/7 Reference from the Metropolitan Cooperative Library System (Metropolitan Cooperative Library System, 2001)
- LivePerson, commercial products, (Eichler and Halperin, 2000).

Digital reference service trends

Collaborative services and developing standards are two important trends in digital library reference services.

Collaborative services

Many digital libraries have recognized the benefits of providing digital reference service through collaborative services, which share question loads and expertise.

Regional library consortia offer member libraries the opportunity to share reference questions with each other using the Internet and other technologies. The Metropolitan Cooperative Library System, based in the Los Angeles area, offers real-time service for its public and academic libraries using Web contact center software that can be customized for each individual library (McGlamery, 2001). Eight academic libraries in the Alliance Library System in Illinois piloted Ready for Reference, a collaborative 24x7 live reference service (Sloan, 2001).

Digital libraries invite participation from institutions locally and globally who can offer their specialties and their subjects of expertise. The Virtual Reference Desk (VRD) Network consists of almost twenty AskA services (specializing in science, math, education, art, general reference, and other areas) that submit out-of-scope and overflow questions via e-mail to VRD to be redistributed to other member services or answered by librarian volunteers (Bennett, 2001).

The Collaborative Digital Reference Service, operated by the Library of Congress, is an international network of libraries, consortia, museums, and AskA services, that uses a help desk system to route questions to appropriate institutions based on member profiles (Kresh, 2001; Kresh and Arret, 2000).

Developing standards

With the growth of digital reference services and collaborative networks, there is a clear need for defined standards in order to ensure service quality and interoperable technology. A number of efforts have been developed to identify standards in these areas.

The Virtual Reference Desk Project identified a set of quality characteristics for AskA services in 1997, which were later revised as a working set of standards for organizations participating in the VRD Network. The standards, offered at varying levels of membership to accommodate different types of services, are based on eleven quality characteristics (Kasowitz, Bennett, and Lankes, 2000).

Development and assessment of measures and quality standards for digital reference services is the focus of a research study sponsored in part by OCLC (Online Computer Library Center, Inc.) and the Digital Library Federation (McClure and Lankes, 2001).

There are two important digital library services standards recently in practice.

Question Interchange Profile (QuIP) is a threaded data format using metadata to maintain, track, and store digital reference services' questions and answers in a consistent manner. QuIP also allows for the development of a shared knowledge base of services 'question and answer sets, and aids in balancing question loads among services (Lankes, 1999; Lankes, 2001).

KnowledgeBit (KBIT) is a common, standard data format for the management of reference transactions (Butler, 2001).

8.3: Digital libraries and the change in reference services

"The Internet and communication technologies have dissolved the walls of the libraries, and librarians can extend their reach to anywhere in the world" (Hvass &Myer, 2008, p. 531). Virtual reference enables users to access resources when and where they are needed, continually striving to offer better and faster ways to increase access. Bainbridge, Witten, &Nichols (2010) list common tools in virtual reference: telephone, fax, email, web forms, text messaging (i.e., SMS), online chat (i.e. instant messaging), and live video chat to name a few; the many different forms of synchronous and asynchronous reference will be discussed further in this chapter (p.61-62). We will also discuss information retrieval, copyright issues, and data mining in digital libraries.

Reference services in all libraries have traditionally centered on face-to-face interactions held at the Reference Desk inside a physical building. Over the last two decades, the rise in computer technology and the rise in popularity of the Internet allowed librarians to greatly expand how they provided reference services. Libraries have shifted focus from physical reference to virtual reference, finding new ways to reach users online by adapting new and emerging technological resources. Increased use of technologies in libraries has not changed their mission of providing reference; it is only the tools used to deliver reference services that have changed in response to the needs of users.

Synchronous reference services

Synchronous and asynchronous service refers to the time reference services are provided. Synchronous reference is "the occurrence of two or more separate events or actions at the same moment in time...at regular or irregular intervals" (Reitz, 2010), and is better known as 'real time' reference because librarians and users are able to communicate at the same time. Examples of this type of service include telephones, chat, IM, text, live voice and video chat. An early synchronous service, the addition of telephones at Reference Desks, enabled users to receive real time interaction from a librarian, bypassing some traditional barriers to information, such as geographical distance and the need for physical proximity. Many digital libraries offer more than one of the services described below to improve reference services from digital libraries.

Asynchronous reference services

Asynchronous means to occur at different times; in reference, the term refers to a "response that is delayed due to the nature of the transmission medium," and examples of this service include fax, email, and web forms (Reitz, 2010). The time delay allows librarians the choice to research and work on an answer right away or to be able to handle other synchronous reference requests made first. Each library sets a time period for users to reasonably expect a reply. A few negative aspects of asynchronous reference are the time delay from request to answer, or further delay if more information or clarification is needed and librarians cannot immediately ask the user.

Human mediated digital reference services

The reference services discussed below all share a similar feature in that they are reference services staffed by actual humans (normally librarians or trained staff), opposed to automated reference, which refers to service systems set up by humans but run by computer and artificial intelligence; this will be discussed later in the chapter.

Chat reference

Chat reference is a "more feature-rich descendant of simple IM, typically offer[ing] cobrowsing, page-pushing, automatic statistic gathering, and user satisfaction surveys" (Steiner 32). Chat reference is a powerful tool for librarians to deliver high quality service in real time that can meet the immediate need of the user. Chat reference allows librarians to control the web browser and take the user directly to the webpage or source. Librarians also benefit from the software used to track and count reference interactions, as well as the ability to save transcripts to monitor quality of service. Chat reference is usually available on a 24/7 schedule, so that users with questions at 3:00 a.m. have someone to turn to. Chat reference is typically found in public and academic digital libraries.

Manchester Community College, in Manchester, Connecticut, joined a consortium of other libraries to offer 24/7 chat services to students. As seen below in Figure 8.1, students fill out a web form about their information needs and a librarian within the network will pick it up and attempt to answer it, normally within 10 minutes.

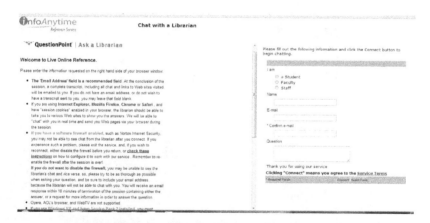

Figure 6: 24/7 Chat Reference from Manchester Community College.

Negative aspects of chat reference

One potential drawback is that it is one of the slower real time services, where it can take a user longer to relay their needs due to natural delays for librarians to type and search. Unfortunately, staffing this service is expensive and time consuming, which forces many libraries to share the cost of this service by devoting staff to man the service on a rotating schedule (Houghton, 2005, p. 27).

Instant messaging reference

Instant messaging (IM) allows "users [to] set up a list of partners who will be able to receive notes that pop up on their screens the moment one of them writes and hits the send button" (de Bakker 143). Grinter and Palen further define IM as "systems support[ing] Internet-based synchronous text chat, with point-to-point communication between users on the same system (de Bakker 144). IM is a text-based communication, though many systems also offer users audio and video options. The software is free and many are already familiar with the format due to personal use. IM is known for speed, the ability to serve multiple users at once, ease of use, and the lack of compatibility delays. Librarians do not have the control of the web browser, as in chat reference, but they are able to send links to users to imitate this service (Houghton, 2005, p. 29).

The New York Public Library (NYPL) offers multiple reference services on their library website (nypl.org), including: phone, text, chat, email. The NYPL recognized the need to provide equal access to reference help for Spanish speaking community members, offering users the option to receive a live reference chat in Spanish at: ¡Información en vivo! In Figure 8.2, a screen shot is shown of the description of services.

Figure 8.2: NYPL IM Reference ¡Información en vivo!

Negative Aspects to IM reference

Some negatives are that if users must install software on their computer, the availability of IM reference may be limited to when the library is open and staffed. Again, the time and expense of staffing forces many libraries to restrict IM reference to traditional physical library hours when staff is available (Hvass & Myer, 2008, p.535). In a digital library, IM is delivered quickly in a real time situation, but in the past service would occasionally be lost with interruptions to the Internet connection.

Presently, most instant message capabilities offered by libraries nowadays rely on an applet (running javascript or similar) that runs in the browser, eliminating the need to download any third-party software.

Small sample of recommended software for IM reference.
- Trillian - Multiple network
- Pidgin - Open Source, multiple network
- Fire - Open Source, multiple network, Mac
- Adium - Open Source, multiple network, Mac
- Meebo - Multiple network & web-based interface, was acquired by Google on June 4, 2012. Meebo me!: widget that lets people chat directly through your web site.

Online Reference at can be a good source for update information.

Example of multiple network IM service.

Libraryh3lp was designed by programmer Eric Sessoms as a collaborative chat service among Duke, North Carolina State University, and University of North Carolina-Chapel Hill. Libraryh3lp was designed to be an integrated web chat platform to enable chat between and for libraries (*Libraryh3lp H3lp, n.d.*). Figure 8.3depicts how multiple librarians are able to receive chats from whatever IM service the user has; the first librarian available to respond is then connected to the user. One great feature is the ability to transfer any chat, IM, or texts between librarians on the same domain. Libraryh3lp was also designed with the user in mind: it is mobile-device friendly and easily allows users to text their questions (*Libraryh3lp H3lp, n.d.*).

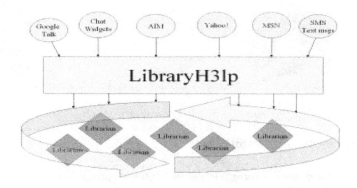

Figure 8.3: How Libraryh3lp works (http://libraryh3lp.com/docs/).

Text a librarian (SMS)

SMS (short message service) "was created when it was incorporated into the Global System for Mobiles (GSM) digital mobile phone standard. The length of a single message can be up to 160 characters, and this limit has forced users to adapt the English language to create an abbreviated language peculiar to SMS" (Hill, Hill, & Sherman, 2007, p. 18). The SMS protocol is extended by MMS", which will send messages in different formats: image, video, and sound content (Hill, Hill, & Sherman, 2007, p. 19). Similar to IM, texting started out as a social means of communication short messages and has continually grown in popularity. This service is a great mobile way to deliver reference service, though again, libraries are limited in hours of availability due to staff costs. This type of reference is best for academic libraries, due to the prevalence of cell phones, though those in high school have increased access to cellphones (Hill, Hill, & Sherman, 2007, p. 18).

Example of a text a librarian service

One library offering a 'Text a Librarian' service is Sims Memorial Library at Southeastern Louisiana University. Figure 8.4 shows Sims Library's information page about their Text a Librarian service. Students are instructed to text the dedicated phone number and will receive assistance from librarians. If a reference response with more than 2 texts long, the full transaction will be emailed to them.

Figure 8.4: Sims Memorial Library Ask a Librarian service

(http://www.selu.edu/library/askref/text/index.html).

Voice over Internet protocol (VoIP)

Voice over Internet Protocol (VoIP) is similar to regular phone reference service: "VoIP services convert your voice into a digital signal that travels over the Internet. If you are calling a regular phone number, the signal is converted to a regular telephone signal before it reaches the destination"

Digital Libraries in Theory and Practices

(Frequently Asked Questions, 2010). Users can make calls directly from a computer or a special VoIP phone, or users can purchase a special adapter for traditional phones (2010). Some VoIP providers do charge a fee for this service or additional features.

Figure 8.5 shows an example of an academic library system, Ohio University Libraries (http://www.library.ohiou.edu/ask/skype.html), using Skype, a VoIP technology. Skype is a free Internet calling service that allows users to ask questions via video call; users need to create a Skype account, then add the library Skype ID, 'ohiolibref,' to their contact list.

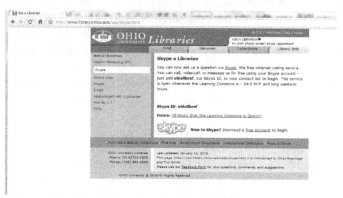

Figure 8.5: Ohio University Libraries Skype Services.

Unmediated reference services

As mentioned before, human-mediated services feature a live person at the other end, whether there is a time delay or not. Unmediated reference services include: reference expert systems, question-answer systems (QA systems), and automated information retrieval systems (IR systems).

Reference expert systems

Reference expert systems were designed to recreate the problem solving process practiced by an expert in any potential field and the ability to retrieve and respond to the user with varying degrees in accuracy. Parrotti (1992) explains the software tool as:

> A system with a knowledge base covering various aspects of the reference process in a library setting. Knowledge bases generally consist of several components (such as databases, rule bases, frames, and semantic nets) that interact with an inference engine, a user interface, and each other (118).

Ultimately, the success of these systems was dependent on the design complexity and structure, as well as the breadth of the knowledge database; a successful system still only retrieves links. Interest in replacing librarian guidance with this automated service peaked in the early 1990s and development fell off due to the high cost of human labor and hardware needed to design and run systems of this size (120).

Question-answer services

Question answer (QA) systems use automated information retrieval to answer a question made in natural language. QA systems search within a structured database or natural language document (like the World Wide Web) (Question answering, 2010). The ability to search natural language queries made QA systems the next evolution of expert systems services. QA systems do not just provide a link, as in IR systems, but instead search and retrieve small pieces of the original documents, the idea being that users do not want to search through links (2010). QA system search results can bring an answer from more than one document or source. Creating a QA system is costly, but once established this type of system is feasible to maintain.

Five milestones of QA roadmap research.
Burger et al. describe the five milestone topics that must be addressed for a successful QA Roadmap research plan:
- Timeliness: QA is not an asynchronous service; answers must be provided speedily and in real time.
- Accuracy: Answers must be correct, as "incorrect answers are worse than no answers" (2001).
- Usability: The main concern of the system must be the users and their needs; systems search various forms of media to provide an answer in whatever format the user specifies must be retrieved (2001).
- Completeness: Systems search multiple databases and documents, but all the parts that comprise the answer must be brought together to create an answer for the user (2001).
- Relevance: Answers must be relevant and provide a specific context to what the
- user asked. Some QA systems allow for further questioning of the user and their initial query to narrow down the context of what they are searching for, and help provide clarity (2001).
- *Example of a QA system.*

START, promoted as the world's first Web-based QA system, is from the InfoLab Group at the MIT Computer Science and Artificial Intelligence Laboratory and has been online since 1993. Below, Figure 8.6 features START's homepage, explanation, and search field. Users can type in factual questions and START will attempt to answer them. Fig. 8.7 illustrates START's reply to "what is the population of Norway?", indicating that the service brought back the needed information. Difficulty arises when users ask questions like "who was the first pope?" or "how high can a human jump?"

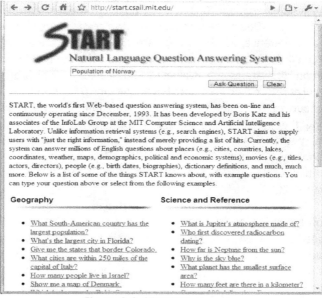

Figure 8.6: START Homepage.

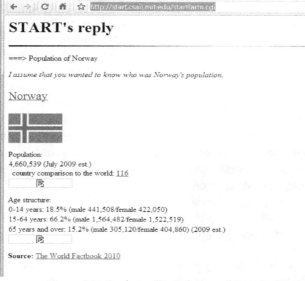

Figure 8.7: Reply to: "Population of Norway?"

Text retrieval conference (TREC)

The Text Retrieval Conference (TREC) is an annual series of workshops on various information retrieval areas (tracks). Since 1992, the National Institute of Standards and Technology (NIST) and the Disruptive Technology Office of the U.S. Department of Defense have co-sponsored this event (Text Retrieval Conference, 2010). Groups are given data sets and test problems, which could be questions, topics, or target extractable features; upon completion all systems are evaluated and scored on which are the most successful at returning correct fact-based questions. "Its purpose is to support and encourage research within the information retrieval community by providing the infrastructure necessary for large-scale evaluation of text retrieval methodologies and to increase the speed of lab-to-product transfer of technology (*Question Answering*, 2010). "The best system of the 2004 competition achieved 77% correct fact-based questions" (Text Retrieval Conference, 2010).

TREC competitions further developed open-domain text-based question answering. An example of this development is that, in 2007, blog text was added to test QA systems; the searchable text contained 'clean' English and noisy text (poorly written English common to actual blogs), which created a more realistic test of this system (*Question Answering*, 2010).

Automated information retrieval

"Information retrieval (IR) deals with the representation, storage, organization of, and access to information items. The representation and organization of the information items should provide the user with easy access to the information in which he is interested" (Baeza-Yates & Ribeiro-Neto, 1999, p.19). Users must think about what information they want and make a query of those terms or keywords, which can then be processed by the search engine (or IR system). "Given the user query, the key goal of an IR system is to retrieve information which might be useful or relevant to the user. The emphasis is on the retrieval of *information* as opposed to the retrieval of *data*" (Baeza-Yates & Ribeiro-Neto, 1999, p.19). IR systems try to retrieve links to documents that have a high precision rate to the original user query, but the user must still scan results and find what is relevant to their information needs. Even though IR allows users to enter their questions in natural language, poorly structured user queries are one barrier to success.

Evaluation of reference services in digital libraries

A lot of literature has been written on libraries considering or preparing to adopt new reference service technologies and the short-term success or failure of the service. Unfortunately, there have been few studies and articles that take a critical look into the long-term feasibility and success rates of digital reference services, like IM and chat reference, which have each been around for almost a decade. Little has been published concerning the evaluation of the quality and impact these technologies have had in a library setting (Steiner 32). There are many potential areas for study in the evaluation of digital reference services for researchers.

Use of content from digital libraries and other sources

Reference services are about finding answers to users' questions, whether the librarian attempts to retrieve an answer by searching the library's collection of material, content from other digital libraries, or any website available online. In a time of great digitization of resources and materials, digital copyright and ownership is becoming an increasingly important topic. There are 3 main methods of creating a digital library: digitize paper and other physical work, acquire original digital work for library's collection, or include links for external materials not held or owned by the library (Cleveland, 1998). Digitizing and acquiring materials is time and cost heavy for libraries trying to create digital libraries, and linking externally helps expand a collection for users; this is an old problem for libraries, access versus ownership, "but in the digital realm [sic] with many of the same concerns such as: local control of collections, long-term access and preservation" (1998). Often libraries will form groups to collaborate and share collections, which is beneficial because it avoids duplicating digitized materials and creates a larger mass of material.

There are potential legal and copyright issues when DLs search material, in any media, owned or created by others. "Many librarians think that already our society is tightening control of information at the expense of digital access...one university-library director complain[ed] that the early 21st century may be characterized as the dawn of the Age of Barricaded Information" (Marcum, 2005, p. B24). In 2005, Marcum optimistically reported that

> the Library of Congress convened a study group to re-examine the exceptions to copyright law applicable to libraries and archives in light of changes in digital media. We hope that ways can be found to meet reasonable needs of copyright holders without unduly restricting the ability of libraries to take advantage of digital technologies to make information widely accessible. (p. B24)

Data mining

Data mining is the process of turning data into information by searching for patterns using statistical, analytical, and visualization tools (Nicholson, 2006, p.5). Data is collected logging all site traffic and by tracking user searches. The data mining process starts with the timely process of 'cleaning' the data, which brings flaws to light. Librarians have ILS systems but they are still inundated with data sources and system logs (2006, p. 2). Methods can be predictive (tools to determine the unknown from the known) or descriptive (compare past and current data patterns) (2006, p. 6).

Digital warehouse

A data warehouse "facilitates the capture of the transaction along with the data about the patron's characteristics at the time...[this] process takes a snapshot of the patron status, attaches it to information about resources used, and brings both into a separate data source" (2006, 4). This data is always ready to be analyzed and it will potentially provide a better idea of library usage (2006, 4). An example to better illustrate:

> a digital reference service in an academic library has one data source about the users and another for the questions and answers. The university maintains the student data with current status information (major, grade level, etc.). The librarian wants to understand who's asking what questions and, more importantly, what resources are useful in providing answers to that cohort. If the librarian only matches the university's current status information to past questions and answers, the query won't reveal what the patron was like while using the service." (p. 4)

Privacy issues

Privacy issues arise when potentially identifiable information is available. Users can access the Internet remotely, creating a feeling of anonymity, when in actuality technologies can track searches, phone calls, ATM visits, etc. Issues arise once libraries make users' questions responses searchable, even if attempts are made to make data anonymous. One well-known example occurred in 2006, when AOL released 20 million user searches to researchers. All personal data was removed from searching, but it was not enough. Researchers studied the queries, geographically and topically, and were able to identify user ID 4417749 as: Thelma Arnold of Lilburn, GA, USA (Bainbridge, Witten, Nichols, 2010, p. 57). The privacy of users was unintentionally violated, even though precautions had been taken.

Collection development in digital libraries

Digital library collections, like traditional library collections, are built and developed to further the mission and goals of the library. As discussed above, if collections are built around user requests this may lead to collections with a few strong areas, while other smaller topics languish without new materials, potentially lowering future interest. An example could be if a digital library for a public library received many questions and requests on children's books, events, and materials and the library decided to expand that area at the expense of books, resources, and materials for non-English speaking users; both are important, but libraries need set guidelines.

Libraries are creating collection development policies for their e-resources. Figure 8.8 shows Wellesley College Library's policy, which includes 10 basic guidelines requiring e-resource materials to conform to traditional physical library policies, and also considers format, vendor and license.

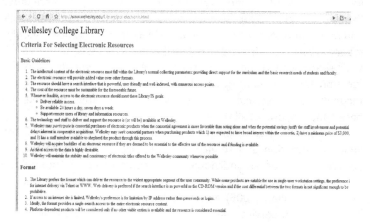

Figure 8.8: E-Resources Collection Development Policy for Wellesley College Library

8.4: Recommender Systems

The number of digital libraries is increasing and the contents and services being offered are becoming more diverse. At the same time, users are becoming more efficient with technology, and as a result digital libraries need to evolve and offer innovative services that will meet their various needs. Traditional search functions alone are no longer able to meet the increasingly complex needs of users faced with vast libraries of information. As a result, digital libraries need to adapt to users and/or communities by personalizing information and services to their needs. It is necessary for digital libraries to take this step in order to provide users and/or communities with the level of service needed to best meet their evolving needs (Smeaton & Callan, 2005).

As the LibRec pointed out "Recommender systems have been well recognized as a typical application of Big Data and Machine Learning." I hope to see more discussion and resources on this hot topic, one top trend in digital library services. A Leading Java Library for Recommender Systems at https://www.librec.net/; and LIBMF: A Matrix-factorization Library for Recommender Systems at https://www.csie.ntu.edu.tw/~cjlin/libmf/, and share your views.

A recommender system, or a recommendation system (sometimes replacing 'system' with a synonym such as platform or engine), is a subclass of information filtering system that seeks to predict the "rating" or "preference" a user would give to an item (Wikipedia, 2021).

Recommender systems were created to sort through the vast information the Internet contains and present a less overwhelming list of possibilities to the user. These systems are so common most users don't even know they are using one. From their introduction, recommender systems have been exploited for recommending books, CDs, movies, news electronics, and many more products and services. E-commerce is not the only area that is benefiting from this system; digital libraries and research sites are improving their search capabilities by incorporating recommendations in their search function by narrowing down the list of results. There are four types of recommender systems: content-based, collaborative filtering, knowledge-based and a hybrid of all three.

Smeaton & Callan (2005) define personalization as"... the ways in which information and services can be tailored to match the unique and specific needs of an individual or a community." The utilization of a recommender system is one way to provide personalization for users. Smeaton & Callan (2005) go on to state that a recommender system is a personalization service that "... learns about a person's or a community's needs and then proactively identifies and recommends information that meets those needs" (Smeaton & Callan 2005). Perugini, Gonzalves, & Fox (2004) further explain that "By selecting a subset of items from a universal set based on user preferences, recommender systems attempt to reduce information overload..." Recommender systems first received attention in the literature as a subtopic in the broader areas of information retrieval and filtering, however, it is now a growing area of research itself (Perugini, Gonzalves, & Fox, 2004).

Recommender support systems act in cooperation with recommender systems. Terveen & Will (2001) explain that "Recommendation support systems do not automate the recommendation process; thus, they do not have to represent preferences or compute recommendations." However, they note that these systems instead aid users who create and seek recommendations by acting as a support tool for the sharing process.

A modern recommendation system is often used in conjunction with an online portal. Pazzani & Billsus (2007) explain that the system commonly "... presents a summary list of items to a user, and the user selects among the items to receive more details on an item or to interact with the item in some way." E-commerce sites frequently use recommendation systems to aid their customers. These sites often display a list of products on a page and a user has the ability to access more details about the product that he/she selects and then purchase the product if desired. Pazzani & Billsusus (2007) clarify the process involved in displaying products tailored to the user or customer:

A web server typically has a database of items and dynamically constructs web pages with a list of items. Because there are often many more items available in a database than would easily fit on a web page, it is necessary to select a subset of items to display to the user or to determine an order in which to display the items, especially those which might be of interest to the user and also possibly result in a purchase or customer retention/satisfaction for the e-commerce portal.

Types of recommendation techniques

Memory based vs. model-based

Common types of recommendation techniques include content-based filtering systems, collaborative filtering systems, and hybrid systems. Typical user-based collaborative filtering and the majority of content-based filtering systems that use "lazy learning algorithms" are representative of the memory-based approach. Item-based and other collaborative filtering approaches that learn models before operation are considered part of the model-based approach (Mobasher, 2007). Hwang and Chuang (2004) explain that the memory-based approach uses "... a rating matrix, with rows being users and columns being items, to represent users' ratings on items. It computes a weighted sum on rows or columns of the rating matrix for predicting the preference of a user to an item." Some of the possible weighting schemes for memory-based approaches include correlation, cosine and regression. Hwang and Chuang (2004) describe the model-based approach as one that "...first structures users' preferences as a probabilistic model, and then applies this model to predict the probability that a user likes an item." Probability models that are often used in conjunction with the model-based approach include Bayesian classifiers, support vector machines, decision trees, and neural networks.

Content based recommenders (CB)

Content-based systems, also called machine-learned research, provide recommendations based on the user's current inquiry and profile. The system has assigned a set of qualifiers, and compares this set to other sets, finding commonalities for recommendations. Because of its nature, content-based systems rely on well-known document modeling techniques with roots of information retrieval and information filtering research (Mobasher, 2). This system is typically individual, built only from features associated with items previously seen or rated by the active user. Users can customize their recommender system by answering questions or checking boxes creating a representation of their own interests.

Content-based filtering systems all share three features in common. They have a set method for describing potential items to be recommended, a process for developing a user profile, and a system in place to compare items to the user profile (Pazzani & Billsus, 2007). Mobasher (2007) describes these concepts in more detail. He explains that "a user profile captures the content descriptions of items in which that user has previously expressed interest," and clarifies that "the content descriptions for an item are represented by a set of features or attributes that characterize that item." In relation to the actual recommendation process, Mobasher (2007) explains:

> In content-based approaches, the user profile databases contain only a single profile, that of the target user, and the prediction of the interest score for the target item is based on its similarity to the user profile or based on the demographic or other personal attributes of the user. Both user profiles, as well as items themselves, are represented as weighted term vectors. Predictions of a user's interest in a particular item can be derived based on the computation of vector similarities (e.g., using the Cosine similarity measure) or by using probabilistic approaches such as Bayesian classification.

Therefore, in purely content-based approaches, profiles are created only from attributes linked to items that a user has seen or rated.

Amazon.com is a hybrid of collaborative filtering and content-based systems. An example of their content-based recommender is a feature called "favorites" that represents the categories of items preferred by users. These favorites are either calculated by keeping track of the categories of items purchased by users, or are set manually by the user. Figure 8.9 is a screen shot of book recommendations.

Figure 8.9: Amazon book recommendations.

There are a few problems with a purely content-based system. The content of items is not analyzed deeply. The computer is simply looking for commonalities, ignoring other factors that might influence the user's idea of what is useful. For example, when searching web pages, the content-based system would ignore things such as loading time, whether images are included, and ease of reading. Another problem is user participation. With users needing to personally customize their likes and dislikes, participation is crucial to providing accurate recommendations. The more data entered, the better the recommender system can work. This is a rule that applies to all recommender systems.

The main problem associated with content-based systems is over specialization. Adomavicius and Tuzhlin (2005) explain "when the system can only recommend items that score highly against a user's profile, the user is limited to being recommended items that are similar to those already rated." As a result, the user does not benefit from being provided with a diverse range of options but instead receives a set of very similar alternatives.

Collaborative filtering

Collaborative filtering (CF) techniques are significantly different from content-based filtering methods. Instead of recommending items solely based on how they compare to previous items that a user has shown interest in, collaborative filtering takes into account the preferences of similar users (Smeaton & Callan, 2005). Mobasher (2007) reports that

> in standard collaborative filtering, the interest scores usually represent rating values from an ordered but discrete scale, and the user databases contain the past ratings of all users of the system. In that case, the prediction or estimation of the interest score for the target user is based on the similarity of that user's profile to other profiles in the user databases.

Just as the name suggests, CF is where a community of users with shared interests work together to produce recommendations based upon information gathered over a period of time. This becomes a natural fit for digital libraries, where it is assumed, the community using the content and services the DL offers will have commonalities. In CF, each member of the community shares their evaluation of any content item they experience. Then each user can tap into the collection of past evaluations by all other members of the community, and use those evaluations to help select new information (Webster, 181).

Sarwar, Karypis, Konstan, & Riedl (2001) outline the recommendation process through the example of a fictitious user: "A new user, Neo, is matched against the database to discover neighbors, which are other users who have historically had similar taste to Neo. Items that the neighbors like are then recommended to Neo." The technique that is most often used to carry out this task is the memory-based k-Nearest-Neighbor (kNN) approach, which compares a target user's profile to the historical profiles of other users with the goal of finding the top k users with similar preferences. Therefore, "the interest score of a user for a target item is estimated based on the interest scores of users who are deemed to have a sufficiently similar profile to the target user" (Mobasher, 2007).

Two common techniques used to carry out the kNN approach are Pearson Correlation Coefficient (PCC) and Cosine Vector Similarity (VS). Zhang and Zhang (2005) describe and differentiate these two approaches by explaining, "PCC is a statistical analysis used to measure how well a linear equation explains the relationship between two variables... [and] VS measures the distance between two vectors by computing the cosine of the angle formed by the two vectors." Furthermore, Zhang & Zhang (2005) explain that due to the fact that different items may have different impacts on determining user preferences, it is important to increase the sway of items that are more likely to discriminate user preferences. Item weighted schemes can be used to carry out this task. Three item weighted schemes commonly used include Inverse User Frequency, the Item-variance Weighing Factor, and Automatic Weighing Scheme.

Item-based techniques are a form of model-based collaborative filtering. Mobasher (2007) explains that in item-based collaborative filtering, an item-to-item similarity matrix is built offline using the user rating profile databases. This matrix is used in the prediction phase in order to generate recommendations. He goes on to explain this process in further detail:

> ...similarity between items is based on user ratings of these items. A vector represents each item, and the similarities are computed using metrics such as cosine similarity and correlation based similarity. The recommendation process predicts the rating for items not previously seen or rated by an active user using a weighted sum of the ratings by that user of items in the item neighborhood of the target item.

Three different approaches used for model-based collaborative filtering include treating collaborative filtering as a classification problem, the Bayesian network, and the rule based approach. Zhang and Zhang (2005) explain that the goal of treating collaborative filtering as a classification problem is to "learn a classifier for each user in the system based on users' existing rating on different items. The learned classifier will then classify each unrated item into two or more classes." They describe the Bayesian network as "a directed acyclic graph of nodes representing variables and arcs representing dependence relations among nodes. In the collaborative filtering domain, each node corresponds to an item and the states of each node correspond to the possible ratings for that item." Sarwar, Karypis, Konstan, and Riedl (2001) explain that the rule based approach "applies association rule discovery algorithms to find association between co-purchased items and then generates item recommendation based on the strength of the association between items."

Many other approaches based on data mining have also been investigated in order to attempt to improve the scalability of collaborative filtering. A particular area of interest has been the context of Web personalization systems, which use click stream or other types of behavioral data. Mobasher (2007) provides a description of these methods:

> In these approaches pattern discovery algorithms, such as association rule mining, sequential pattern discovery, and clustering are applied to the user profile databases containing historical rating or navigational profiles of past users, in order to generate aggregate user models. The user models, in turn, can be used, in conjunction with the profile of an active user, to predict future user behavior or generate recommendations.

An example of CF is a research system called AntWorld. AntWorld is a web search support tool. Figure 8.10 shows how AntWorld works. AntWorld follows the user's Quest, and compares their judgments and evaluations to the database of stored Quests. When it finds related Quests, it examines the pages that were relevant to them (represented by arrows leading out of the stored Quests. When it finds a consensus (shown by the blue arrows) it provides an AntMark and recommendation that lets the user jump directly to that relevant page (shown by the orange link that loops directly from your Quest to the target page in the Web) (http://aplab.rutgers.edu/).

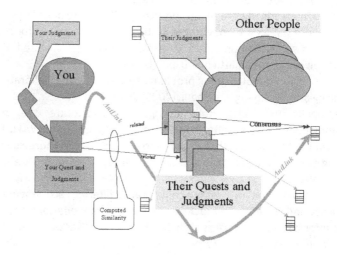

Figure 8.10: AntWorld system map.

The most significant drawback of memory-based collaborative filtering is its lack of scalability. Zhang and Zhang (2005) describe the scalability problem as "the fact that the computational complexity of standard collaborative methods grows exponentially with the increase of numbers of users and items." Item-based approaches, as well as other model-based approaches, have shown to address some of these issues. Sarwar, Karypis, Konstan, and Riedl (2001) point out that item-based techniques have the potential to facilitate collaborative filtering based algorithms to scale large data sets while still producing high quality recommendations.

Another issue associated with memory-based collaborative filtering is the problem of sparse user feedback. When there is a lack of feedback data, it can be very difficult to predict similar users and the results may be unreliable (Huang, Chen, & Zeng, 2004). If the users are not willing to take the time to provide feedback about the items they have used, the collection of recommendable items becomes small compared to the actual information available.

The cold start problem is another concern and is closely correlated with the issue of sparse user feedback. Huang, Chen, & Zeng (2004) delineate the cold start scenario and explain its impact:

> The cold-start problem refers to the situation in which a new user or item has just entered the system. Collaborative filtering cannot generate useful recommendations for the new user because of the lack of sufficient previous ratings or purchases. Similarly, when a new item enters the system, it is unlikely that collaborative filtering systems will recommend it to many users because very few users have yet rated or purchased this item.

This leads to a "ramp up" problem: "Until there are a large number of users whose habits are known, the system cannot be useful for most users, and until a sufficient number of rated items has been collected, the system cannot be useful for a particular user" (Burke, 2).

An additional ongoing problem associated with collaborative filtering is shilling attacks. Zhang and Zhang (2005) describe shills as "...those users who intentionally use false item ratings to deteriorate the quality of recommendations generated by a system." Shafer, Frankowski, Herlocker, and Sen (2007) explains that user based algorithms are more susceptible to shilling than item algorithms and new or rarely rated items are particularly vulnerable.

A final concern linked to collaborative filtering recommender systems is privacy and security. In order to provide recommendations, these systems need information about users. Schafer, Frankowski, Herlocker, and Sen (2007) explain that as more information is stored in a system, users become increasingly worried about what information is collected, where and how it is stored, and how it is used. However, Smeaton and Callan (2005) explain that "[the public] is often willing to give up a degree of privacy in exchange for a specific benefit. The challenge for digital library developers...is to protect peoples' most essential privacy while also ensuring that desirable social effects are supported." They go into further detail on this topic, asserting that "...solutions must allow people to shape and control who they present themselves..., which requires that the solutions be comprehensible and based on informed consent. It also means helping people understand that any sharing of information can bring benefits and losses." It may be the DL's responsibility to shift thought from "how to protect users' privacy" to "how to inform users about privacy concerns" (Webster, 189).

Knowledge-based systems

A knowledge-based recommender system is one that uses knowledge about users and products to pursue a knowledge-based approach to generating a recommendation, reasoning about what products meet the user's requirements (Burke, 1). Because of this, a knowledge-based system does not have to rely on user ratings or gather information entered by the user. The system will be able to learn and draw conclusions by using an artificial intelligence that will accommodate a more diverse selection. For example, if a user has researched flashy, trendy apparel, and then browses for furniture, the system can begin to recommend contemporary, daring furniture (Gahni, 1). Because of these characteristics, knowledge-based recommenders are not only valuable systems on their own but are also highly compatible to the before mentioned recommender systems.

Hybrid systems

Hybrid systems match and combine two or more recommender systems to solve some problems and provide a more accurate response. A variety of hybrid recommender systems have been developed in an attempt to combine elements of different approaches such as content-based and collaborative filtering techniques. Mobasher, Burke, Bhaumik, & Williams (2007) show that hybrid recommender systems, which combine collaborative recommendation with other types of recommendation elements, can result in defensive advantages for recommender systems, protecting them against shilling attacks and providing improved prediction accuracy over the standard item-based algorithm. Adomavicius and Tuzhilin (2005) describe some of the approaches that can be taken when creating a hybrid model:
1. Implementing collaborative and content-based methods separately and combining their predictions
2. Incorporating some content-based characteristics into a collaborative approach

3. Incorporating some collaborative characteristics into a content-based approach
4. Constructing a general unifying model that incorporates both content-based and collaborative characteristics.

Two of the more commonly combined systems are the knowledge-based and the collaborative filtering system. They note "hybrid recommendation systems can be augmented by knowledge-based techniques, such as case based reasoning, in order to improve recommendation accuracy and to address some of the limitations (e.g., new user, new item problems) of traditional recommender systems." A particular benefit of a hybrid is that it gathers preference information without requiring that users make their ratings open. Rather than requiring the user to input his or her preferences as a starting point, the hybrid lets the user browse through a catalog using qualitative ratings as navigation aids. Each navigation step informs the system about the user's preferences at a finer grain of detail than a single decision, and a user is likely to make several such navigation steps while using the system (Burke, 16).

User profiles

Regardless of the algorithmic approach used in the recommendation process, data must be collected either implicitly or explicitly for user profiles. Rao and Talwar (2006) state that "relevance feedback is typically used for query expansion during short term modeling of a user's immediate information needs and for user profiling during long term modeling of a user's persistent interests and preferences." The process of gathering explicit feedback or data requires the user's active participation. Rao and Talwar (2006) observe that three common ways of gathering explicit data are like/dislike, ratings, and provision of text comments. They also point out some of the disadvantages of explicit relevance feedback:
1. The types of numeric scales implemented in the filtering systems are not sufficient for the user to represent the relevance of items.
2. Users are generally reluctant to provide relevance feedback when it is meeting their immediate goals.
3. The relevance feedback must always be relative to the changing information need of a user and the relevance judgments of individual items are assumed to be independent.

Rao and Talwar (2006) also describe and provide examples of implicit feedback techniques. They explain "implicit feedback techniques obtain information about users by intelligently observing their natural interactions with the filtering system." Common behaviors of users that can be used as sources of implicit feedback include document reading time/time spent on a particular web page, links followed by the user, history of purchases, bookmarking a web page, saving a document, printing a document, etc. Other factors that may be considered when investigating user interests include the properties of documents that a user looks at (language), document structure such as format (text, image, audio, video) and document source (URL, publisher, author, etc.). Additional sources of implicit feedback can be replying to or forwarding an email as well as scrolling, maximizing, minimizing or resizing the window containing the document. Mobasher (2007) also explains that heuristic indicators such as the time spent viewing an item or whether an item was purchased are frequently being used in personalized systems. Rao and Talwar (2006) note that an advantage of implicit feedback is the fact that no direct feedback from users is needed. However, they point out that implicit measures are often less accurate than explicit ones. Still, they conclude that implicit feedback measures and explicit ratings can be combined in order to obtain a more accurate user profile.

Emerging trends

One emerging trend in recommender systems is the incorporation of ontological domain knowledge with user profiles. Ferran, Mor, and Minguillon (2005) explain "ontologies are a powerful tool for describing complex scenarios of use such as a digital library, where several concepts and relationships between these concepts can be identified and represented." Mobasher (2007) further explains some of the concepts surrounding this trend:

> In the presence of a domain ontology, the user profiles may actually reflect the structure of the domain, and thus may require a more complex representation than the flat representation used in standard approaches. Such approaches allow recommenders systems to utilize the existing domain knowledge or available ontologies to produce potentially more effective recommendations. In addition, the integration of ontological knowledge may allow such systems to reason about recommendations or to better explain the generated recommendations to users.

Liao, Hsu, Cheng, and Chen (2010) designed a recommender system that adopted the methodology of a personal ontology model and incorporated collaborative filtering techniques with domain specialization. Their system proved to diminish data scarcity, improve accuracy and solve the cold start of new items.

He, Peng, Mao, and Wu (2010) conducted comparative experiments involving DiLight, an interacting e-learning system that integrates digital library and ontology technologies. These authors explain that it is often important for students to gain an understanding of related topics that are taught in different classes and under different circumstances. If the student is unfamiliar or does not understand a topic, he needs to be directed toward relevant resources. In this situation, with a comprehensive understanding of internal connections between different topics, teachers can use the "derived from" relationship that is available from the system's ontology to explicitly markup the connections. These relationships link documents in both topics together across the ontology. As a result, an associated recommendation is provided when a student accesses either topic.

Mobasher (2007) explains, "The recent emergence of ad hoc communities, emanating from social tagging and other social navigation systems, has also provided new opportunities for the use of recommendation technologies." He describes the concept of social tagging as one where "many users add metadata in the form of keywords to shared content resulting in loose semantic structures also known as folksonomies." Mobasher (2007) also explains that although collaborative tagging opens up new opportunities for users to search vast amounts of information and access content of interest, the open nature of these systems also results in considerable noise, which can divert users from sources of interest. He notes that the application of data mining and recommendation technologies to the underlying user-item-tag space can help users to find relevant tags, interesting items, or communities of common interest.

Shepitsen, Gemmell, Mobasher, and Burke (2008) showed that hierarchical agglomerative clustering of tags is an effective means of personalizing navigational recommendations in collaborative tagging systems. They found that clusters of tags can be used to learn about the user's interest and to determine the topic of a resource. As a result, they are able to more efficiently connect users and resources.

Diederich and Iofciu (2006) used the tags from a folksonomy system to build user profiles and provide them to a recommender system, particularly to identify related persons in the community. Their methods were intended to better grasp the interests of users when carrying out the recommendation process and to reduce the problem of sparse user profiles. They found that using tag-based profiles can give more recommendations than standard object-based user profiles.

8.5: Personalization

What is personalization?

Personalization refers to a variety of user-driven accommodations in digital library settings. Just as librarians traditionally help patrons through book recommendations, search advice, and other means, personalization seeks to individualize the digital library experience for the user. Varying definitions for personalization methods exist. Kramer (2000) defines personalization as "a toolbox of technologies and application features; from simple display of the end-user's name on a Web page, to complex catalog navigation and product customization based on deep models of users' needs and behaviors; used in the design of an end-user experience" (as cited in Jeevan & Padhi, 2006, p. 557). Other definitions emphasize the power of the digital library to generate user-driven content, such as Perugini and Ramakrishnan's (2003) view of "personalization as the automatic adjustment of information content, structure and presentation tailored to an individual user" (as cited in Jeevan & Padhi, 2006, p. 557). Though current definitions vary in the types of technology mentioned, all place emphasis on delivery of user-driven content to improve the patron's library experience. Personalization offers digital libraries an opportunity to provide a more meaningful, user-centered experience for patrons to fulfill their information needs.

Current personalization services in digital libraries greatly vary. Personalization may refer to presentation adaptation, such as changing the color scheme of the interface, or altering the page layout. Patrons may be able to organize their favorite resources using bookmarks, comment on an item's quality through the OPAC, or even highlight and annotate materials. Users may sign up for RSS feeds or alerts to notify them of new, relevant resources or receive e-mail updates about the library. Some digital libraries even offer recommender services similar to the Amazon.com model.

Personalization may also refer to accommodations that make the library available to disabled users, such as accessibility features that may be used with switch hardware or other devices, such as eye trackers or Sensecams. In addition, personalization services may allow for preservation migration, or the transference of materials and resources from one digital format to another. Personalization allows digital libraries to virtually provide services that assist patrons in retrieving needed materials.

Goals

As users increasingly turn to the Internet to meet their information needs, personalization services help differentiate digital libraries from popular search engines. Jeevan & Padhi (2006) suggest that "personalization of library resources today is projected as a viable way of helping users cope with the information explosion, enabling them to rededicate their time to more productive intellectual tasks" (p. 557). Since patrons do not always perform adequately complex queries by using Boolean or advanced searching capabilities, personalization services can help users find appropriate resources that search engines might not retrieve. As Ferran, Mor, and Minguillón (2005) state, "personalization is one of the key factors which are directly related to user satisfaction" (p. 207). Thus, the goals of personalization services are to help patrons find useful, appropriate information and to ensure the continued importance of libraries in the digital setting.

User-centered

In order for personalization services to be successful, "the system ... depends on its efficacy in mapping user interests and feedback, continuous interactive support received from beneficiaries to sustain and improve its performance, and a large electronic resource base to work with" (Jeevan & Padhi, 2006, p. 557). Ultimately, if the personalization system cannot quickly deliver relevant resources to the patron, it will fail. Capturing user information in a confidential manner will help the digital library recommend appropriate resources and services to its patrons.

Personalization systems may provide recommendations based on session behavior whereas others may require knowledge of the patron's demographics, search behavior, and interests. As Whitney and Schiff (2006) explain:

> The first strategy, which we will call "patron-neutral," continues along a development path that requires no persistent knowledge of the patron who is viewing the recommendations. The second strategy, which can be labeled "profile-based," investigates the use of persistent patron profiles to facilitate collaborative filtering as well as popular services such as shared lists, annotations and tagging.

Patron-neutral personalization is frequently based on providing general recommendations to users through examination of circulation statistics or search session behavior. For example, the Melvyl Recommender Project used anonymous patron identification numbers to identify similar resources to those that they had viewed during the search session in order to provide "more like this" recommendations for the current users (Whitney & Schiff, 2006).

Ideally, personalization systems follow the second strategy and recommend resources and services to patrons based on their both their browsing history and their current searches. Libraries have traditionally held personal information about their patrons, including "membership files, records of loans or electronic publications/files consulted, lists of requests for information, user profiles for dissemination services, records of online searches, e-mail and Internet searches carried out on public terminals, Web pages visited, and other digital activities" (Sturges et al, 2003, p. 45). Used confidentially, such information may be used to create online profiles that are accessed through passwords or by other secure means, such as eye gaze. Patron privacy must be protected and digital library visitors must be allowed to opt out of inclusion in personalization services. If used appropriately, patron profiles serve as a powerful tool for personalization services.

Whether the digital library chooses patron-neutral or profile-based personalization, individualized services require knowledge of the user's searching behaviors. As Ferran, Mor, and Minguillón (2005) discuss:

> Two different behavior types can be identified, depending on the users' navigation, exploratory navigation and goal-oriented navigation. The exploratory navigation can be mainly oriented to obtain a general vision of the available resources in the library. Depending on user profile, the exploratory navigation would have different implicit intentions. In the case of goal-oriented navigation, it is usually considered that the user is looking for a resource. (p. 211)

Through the use of algorithms that examine the patron's searching behavior, the personalization service can provide appropriate recommendations. For example, when a patron searches for a specific author, the service may recommend other works by that writer that are rated highly in the catalog.

The choice of patron-neutral or profile-based personalization may also affect how the service is distributed to users. If the digital library chooses profile-based personalization, patrons may need to login to password protected accounts to access their recommendations. Digital libraries may also opt to offer a hybrid system that provides recommendations based on patron-neutral information for users that choose to opt out of creating an online profile, while allowing those who have profiles to receive more specialized services.

Digital libraries may also use RSS feeds, alerts, and on-demand services to deliver content to users at their request. Some digital libraries may offer trails or breadcrumbs that summarize the user's search queries and facilitate navigation back to the home page. Other distribution methods may involve an Intelligent Tutoring System, which helps users to form better searches and guides them toward retrieving more relevant resources. Intelligent Tutoring Systems may utilize graphic interfaces and provide tutorial or simulation exercises to assist patrons.

To capture user behavior, digital libraries employ a variety of methods in addition to examining searches. Certain digital libraries gather information using specific technological devices. One such device is an eye tracker, which records the eye movements of a patron to determine his or her gazing behaviors. Digital libraries may use this information to determine which sections of the display catch patron attention and how the patron interacts with the interface. Other devices include Sensecams, which automatically take pictures of patron behaviors.

Since technological devices may be costly, an inexpensive alternative is the creation of patron logs. Since patron logs may be large files, the digital library must determine what information to collect. Smeaton and Callan (2005) suggested that four primary questions must be addressed when creating patron logs:

- What data should (and can) be collected and how can be captured?
- How are anomalous data recognized and filtered out?
- How should the data be analyzed and which parameters need to be set?
- How are data weighted appropriately over time? (as cited in Ferran, et. al, 2007, p. 156).

As the digital library collects data, it must always prioritize patron privacy. The digital library should have a privacy policy that adheres to legal requirements and that is informed by the American Library Association's Code of Ethics (1995). As previously stated, users should be able to opt out of personalization services that collect personally identifiable data.

Once patron logs are created, they must then undergo analysis. According to Ferran et. al (2007), deep log analysis "consists on triangulating and enriching data from all possible sources, namely … navigational logs, library usage logs, socio-demographic data and academic background" (p. 156). In addition to analysis, digital libraries should constantly test the effectiveness of the personalization service by distributing surveys or questionnaires to patrons. By periodically questioning patrons, the library can determine other factors that may contribute to the success of the personalization service.

Information filtering

In order to guide users to relevant resources, personalization services must filter information based on patron profiles or session behaviors. Digital libraries with recommender systems often use collaborative filtering to determine similar relevant resources. As Ferran, Mor, and Minguillón (2005) explain:

… collaborative filtering is selecting content-based on the preferences of people with
similar interests, basically by pooling and ranking informed opinions (or experiences of use) on any particular topic. That is to say, an automatic system collects information about user actions (explicit, such as voting or answering a question; or implicit, such as noticing which offered links are visited and which are not, and how much time) and determines the relative importance of each content by weighting all the collected information among the large amount of users. (p. 210)

Various types of algorithms that use collaborative information filtering exist to recommend appropriate resources, as explained in the Recommender System section.

Information filtering systems may also use circulation or bibliographic data for recommendations. For example, the Melvyl Recommender Project utilized a weighted graph model. In this model, the system used:

> ... the books as nodes, and the edges formed by patrons who have checked out the books in common. The more often the books have been checked out in common, the heavier the weight on that edge of the graph. Recommendations are generated for any node in the graph by following the edges to other items that have been checked out by the same patrons. The recommendations can quickly be ordered by sorting on the weights of the edges. (Whitney & Schiff, 2006)

The weighted graph model resulted in generally relevant recommendations, but also generated some inappropriate ones. The Melvyl Recommender Project also used information filtering by first letter of call number class, bibliographic metadata, and groupings by subject area class number. The filtering methods employed by the Melyvl Project illustrate how libraries that do not use profile-based systems can recommend appropriate resources to users.

Notification

Notification systems are a popular personalization service in digital libraries. As Farooq, Ganoe, Carroll, Councill, and Giles (2007) state, notification systems "can be used as awareness mechanisms to deliver relevant information to users in an efficient and effective manner" (p. 597). Users may sign up for e-mail alerts about item availability, publications, websites that have moved, or other digital library news. Digital libraries also use RSS feeds to deliver information to users. In some digital systems, like EBSCO, users can have the system periodically search terms for new information, which is then sent to the user through e-mail.

Advanced approaches for personalization

Most personalization efforts have focused on improving library services for patrons based on individuals' interest. As Neuhold, Niederée, and Stewart state, "most personalization methods are based on user models, which mainly reflect user interests and skills, i.e., a simplistic representation of users and their information needs that does not take into account other important aspects like tasks, goals, and relationships to other community members" (2003, p. 7). However, newer methods that focus on more specialized needs of the digital library community are emerging in personalization services.

Neuhold, Niederée, and Stewart identified three areas of improvement for personalization services. New systems must consider the personal web context of users, or "the interrelationship of users with their neighborhood of entities in the domain" (2003, p. 7). To effectively utilize personal web context in personalization, one must identify the types of interrelationships in a user's profile. These relationships may be explicit, such as co-authoring a book, or implicit, such as authoring a work related to another in the collection. These interrelationships can connect patrons with both similar resources and library users with like interests.

The second area of improvement is personal reference libraries, which "take into account the individual conceptualization of the information space that differs between users" (p. 7). In this model, users build and annotate personal reference libraries using digital library resources. This model allows users to alter the digital library structure to meet their individualized learning needs. Personal reference libraries may even be cataloged with preexisting reference collections.

Lastly, future personalization services must address cooperative content annotation, which "takes into account the active role that a user of a digital library can play with respect to library content and metadata" (p. 7). In cooperative content annotation, users actively participate in the digital library by composing reviews, ratings, and annotations that are shared with other members of the learning community. Annotations may include formal comments, highlighting, and notes that may be publicly or privately displayed. Cooperative content annotation allows users to actively interact with the library catalog and other patrons.

Social effects of personalization

As individuals increasingly visit digital collections instead of physical libraries, feelings of isolation many increase since online environments may not offer interactive features. However, personalization services may allow for patron collaboration and interaction. As Callan (2003) suggests:
> With regard to social aspects of sharing, there is great potential for community building and interpersonal interaction. Both institutional and community digital libraries can serve as meeting places where people can communicate with each other through the documents, annotations and logs they make available to each other, and through the conversation and discussion around this shared information. (p. 4-5).

Through catalog rating systems, users can write recommendations and respond to each other's comments. Certain personalization systems may allow users to share documents with one another. Others may feature discussion boards or chat features where patrons can talk about library-related topics. According to Callan, some digital libraries even employ "peer-help systems [that] use information about the tasks and knowledge of individuals to suggest collaborators with specific skills" (2003, p. 6).

As digital libraries offer collaborative and interactive personalization features, they must take measures to protect patron privacy and allow users to not participate. In addition, digital libraries must determine if they need policies regarding patron behavior when using interactive features. As Callen explains, "as with all forms of social communication, the same contribution may be considered as useful and novel by one person, and as annoying and offensive by another" (2003, p. 5).

Personalized information environment (PIE)

Personalized Information Environment (PIE) is a personalization model that encourages users to be active learners and consumers of information. PIE divides personalization into two areas, material and collection. As Jayawardana, Hewagamage, and Hirakawa (2001) state, "Material personalization refers to constructing customized views of library materials. Collection personalization describes how to provide a different view of the library organization through personalizing retrieval and filtering facilities" (p. 1). PIE offers users tools that allow them to engage in traditional learning activities while interacting with digital objects.

PIE systems have two tools: a Digital Library Browser that supports collection personalization, and a Personal Document Editor that supports material personalization. Users perform searches on the Digital Library Browser to find resources. As users find relevant materials, they may add them to their Notebook in the Personal Document Editor using a technique called Shallow Copy. Users may add any format type to the Notebook and annotate the resources with underlining, highlighting, and notes. The Notebook also allows users to organize the materials in ways to support active learning.

Each resource added to the Notebook possesses attributes, such as keywords, phrases, and metadata, which the personalization service uses to identify user interests and browsing methods. These interests and activities are added to user profiles. By using information from the profile to determine searching categories, the personalized retrieving tool assists users in finding new relevant resources based on past queries.

Profile information is also used for personalized filtering of results. As Jayawardana, Hewagamage, and Hirakawa (2001) explain, "keywords, phrases, meta information about images, audio and video, and contextual information in the profiles are used to obtain the learner's interests and requirements. The filtering process is performed based on these interests and requirements" (p. 16). These results are displayed at the bottom of the screen for the user. PIE demonstrates how learning environments can effectively utilize personalization services.

Evaluation issues

In order to ensure that personalization meets users' needs, the digital library must evaluate the effectiveness of each service offered. Evaluation of personalization must address both the accessibility and quality of services from the users' perspective. Though user-centered evaluations may be costly, they are necessary to determine the effectiveness of services. Since personalization focuses on delivering specialized content to individuals, evaluations that are not user-centered may deliver invalid results. Before conducting any evaluation, the digital library must determine criteria for the study. As Xie (2008) discusses, "the commonly agreed DL evaluation criteria and variables are related to the usability of interface, the value of collection, and the system performance" (p. 1351). Users must play an active role in evaluating all variables of personalization services. As Xie suggests, "in order to gain a complete picture of users' assessment of DLs, we need to engage users in every aspect of DL evaluation from defining DL evaluation criteria, their uses, and their assessment" (p. 1351).

Once evaluation criteria have been determined, the digital library must decide which approach and methodology to use in the study. The evaluation may follow a systems-centered, human-centered, usability-centered, ethnographic, anthropological, sociological, or economic approach. Methodologies should effectively assess the evaluation criteria and correspond to the approach of the study. Digital libraries may use surveys, questionnaires, simulations, case studies, journals, observations, data analysis, or other methodologies to collect data for the evaluation (Saracevic, 2004).

When evaluating personalization services, most evaluations employ a usability-centered approach. Saracevic (2004) defines the usability-centered approach as an "… assessment of different features, particularly in respect to portals, by users" (p. 5). According to the ISO, usability is "the extent to which a product can be used by specified users to achieve specified goals with effectiveness, efficiency and satisfaction in a specified context of use" (as cited in Saracevic, 2004, p. 6). Usability evaluations focus on content, process, format, and overall assessment. For content assessment, evaluation studies examine the accessibility, clarity, coverage, quality, and other features of the digital library. To assess process, evaluations focus on the ease and support offered when performing tasks such as searching and browsing. Format assessment addresses the consistency, attractiveness, and other features of the interface. Overall assessment collects data on user satisfaction, impact, usefulness, success, and failures of the system (Saracevic, 2004, p. 6). Since individuals interact with personalization services with little to no guidance from librarians, usability-centered studies offer an effective means by which digital libraries can assess the usefulness and performance of the system.

For personalization services to meet the needs of individual users, evaluation must be conducted. As Saracevic suggests, "perceptions of users

and perceptions of designers and operators of a digital library are generally not very close" (2004, p. 8). Since users may have little knowledge of digital libraries and how they function, they may experience usage difficulties that designers do not foresee. Saracevic names four typical failures of digital libraries from the perspective of the user, which are:
- they usually do not fully understand them;
- they hold different conception of a digital library from operators or designers;
- they lack familiarity with the range of capabilities, content and interactions provided by a digital library;
- they often engage in blind alley interactions (2004, p. 8).

Many such failures may be avoided during the development period if designers constantly test personalization services with users and make system changes as needed. Digital libraries should periodically conduct evaluations to ensure that the learning community's needs are still being met, particularly as the user population's needs and abilities may change over time.

User-centered evaluations improve personalization services as users make recommendations for changes. If users actively participate in evaluations, they will likely feel ownership of personalization services as they see their recommendations become reality. Both libraries and users benefit from user-centered evaluation as it helps develop a stronger relationship between the two. Digital libraries exist to help users meet their information needs and user-centered evaluation ensures that this important objective is being met.

Limitations and challenges

While personalization services may greatly improve library experiences for the user, digital libraries face several issues in their implementation. If digital libraries choose profile-based systems, they must develop policies to protect users' privacy. The digital library must decide which information to collect and how to safely store it. Even if digital libraries choose patron-neutral systems, ratings and collaborative features, such as discussion boards, raise similar privacy issues. Collaborative features also require policies to support freedom of speech while ensuring that library patrons are protected. All personalization services must allow users to opt out of the system.

Though recommender systems help connect users with relevant resources, they may also hinder patrons from developing advanced searching techniques to find appropriate items as they become dependent on such services. Recommender systems have limitations and may not always suggest all relevant resources. If personalization services do not offer collaborative features, such as discussion boards and chat options, users may become isolated from both librarians and their peers. In addition, if the digital library does not perform constant evaluation to determine areas for improvement, personalization services may become predictable and not meet users' evolving information needs.

8.6: Web Crawling

Web basics

Invented by Tim Berners-Lee in the 1980s, the World Wide Web today consists of over a billion hypertext documents that are connected to each other by hyperlinks. The World Wide Web works through a client-server design. The client, typically a web browser, uses HyperText Transfer Protocol (HTTP) to communicate with servers, which sends the requested information back to the web browser through payloads. Payloads are packets of information written in hypertext markup language (HTML) that may be text, audio, video, or images. Search engines were developed to assist users in finding relevant information from the billions of available web pages. In order to help users, find desired information, search engines use web crawlers to index pages for quick retrieval. Here we will review what a web crawler is before discussing the inner workings of a crawler, crawler architecture, crawler policies and web page importance.

What is a web crawler?

According to Fox and Khandeparker (2010), "a web crawler is an automated computer program that browses the World Wide Web by following certain policies as mentioned by its creator. Its main purpose is to create a copy of all the web pages visited by it for later analysis by a search engine." Web crawlers may also be referred to as spiders, ants, bots, worms, or indexers. While web crawlers primarily exist to quickly retrieve web pages for search engines, they may serve other functions. Web crawlers may be used for website maintenance, such as checking for broken links. In addition, one may use web crawlers maliciously, such as collecting e-mail addresses for spamming.

Inner workings of a crawler

Crawlers begin searching the Internet by using seeds, which are URLs that are chosen by the creators. When the crawler visits a seed page, it processes its digital information and stores it into an indexer. The crawler also extracts links from the page, which are placed in a URL frontier. The URL frontier contains links to pages that have not been visited by the crawler. The crawler continuously repeats this process until it has visited either a designated number of pages or all links in the URL frontier. Pant, Srinivasan, and Menczer (2004) refer to this as a crawling loop, which "involves picking the next URL to crawl from the frontier, fetching the page corresponding to the URL through HTTP, parsing the retrieved page to extract the URLs and application specific information, and finally adding the unvisited URLs to the frontier" (p. 3).

Crawler architecture

Crawlers must consist of several important components in order to function properly: a URL frontier, a DNS resolution module, a fetch module, a parsing module, and a duplicate elimination module. As previously mentioned, the URL frontier contains links that have not been visited by the crawler and is often referred to as its to-do list. Since URL frontiers may have limited memory, the crawler's designers must determine the maximum number of pages that it may store and when to ignore other URLs. In addition, the crawler must perform several tests before adding a link to the URL frontier. First, the crawler must determine if the content is already contained in another URL by checking fingerprints. The crawler then uses a URL filter before adding links to the frontier. The URL filter may be exclusive, such as only allowing certain domains, or inclusive. Lastly, the links must be normalized so that all follow the same HTML format.

The Domain Name Service (DNS) resolution module contacts DNS servers to determine the IP address of the page. Since locating IP addresses may require multiple attempts, the DNS resolution module is often a time-consuming aspect of web crawling. Crawlers frequently use cached pages to avoid this issue.

The fetch module retrieves the web page using HTTP when requested by the crawler. Since certain pages may have lengthy downloads or the crawler may encounter server problems, fetch modules need timeouts to maintain quick retrievals. In addition, fetch modules must have error-checking capabilities to ensure that the correct page is retrieved.

The parsing module is composed of two components that extract digital information and links from the page. The URL extraction component scans the coding of the page to remove links from the page. The canonicalization component ensures that the URLs follow similar formats to avoid fetching the same page multiple times. Canonicalization may involve converting URLs to lowercase letters, removing anchors, encoding special characters, and using heuristics to ensure consistent format (Pant, Srinivasan, & Menczer, 2004, p. 7-8). Parsing also involves removing stopwords, such as the, and stemming, or using one root form for similar words.

The duplicate elimination module determines whether the crawler has already visited or recently viewed a page. If so, the duplicate elimination module prevents the link from being added to the URL frontier. The duplicate elimination module ensures that no unnecessary repetition occurs to save time and money.

Crawling policies

Though crawlers index web pages quickly, an entire crawl of the Web could take months. According to Fox and Khandeparker (2010), three aspects of the World Wide Web create obstacles for web crawlers: "its very large volume, it's really fast rate of change, and its dynamic page generation." New pages are added every day and existing pages frequently change or are deleted. In addition, crawlers have difficulty obtaining truly unique content since many pages today are dynamically generated based on user requests, such as through shopping websites. To maintain an updated and relevant index of sites, crawlers must consistently search the Web. However, crawling is not only time-consuming, but also costly.

Given the vast size and ever-changing nature of the World Wide Web, crawlers must have at least four policies to ensure the quality of the process: a selection policy, a re-visit policy, a politeness policy, and a parallelization policy. Each of these policies helps the crawler retrieve relevant, unique content in a timely, cost-effective manner.

The selection policy tells the crawler what to download by determining the importance of a web page. Since no crawler can quickly index the entire Web, the selection policy ensures that it only retrieves relevant pages. Three basic types of selection policies exist: restricting followed links, path-ascending crawling, and focused crawling. When the selection policy restricts followed links, the crawler may only extract information from certain page extensions, such as .html or .htm, or certain media types, such as text. The crawler may determine whether or not it will download the page by examining the URL or performing a HEAD request. By restricting followed links, the crawler may avoid spider traps, which cause it to download "an infinite number of URLs from a website" (Fox & Khandeparker, 2010). One disadvantage to restricting followed links is the omission of possibly relevant information from the index.

Path-ascended crawling, or harvesting, extracts all information from a web page without restrictions. The crawler visits every URL path in an address to ensure that it has extracted all possibly pertinent information. Path-ascended crawling assists the crawler in indexing hard to find websites, but may be too inclusive.

Focused crawling downloads pages based on a predetermined set of topics and categories. The focused crawler determines if the page is relevant by comparing it to other pages on the topic. If the content is similar, the focused crawler then extracts information from the web page. For pages in the Deep Web, a focused crawler may download the page and then determine its relevance before indexing it.

Re-visiting policies help the crawler maintain an updated index by checking pages for updates or changes. To determine if the page should be re-visited, the crawler checks its freshness, or accuracy, and age. Re-visiting policies may be uniform and visit each page at a specified time to look for changes. Policies may also be proportional and may focus on only re-visiting pages that change often. The re-visit policy aims to keep the age of the index as low as possible to maintain relevancy.

Politeness policies respect the rate request regulations that web servers have to keep crawlers from overloading websites. Since crawlers work faster than human rates of speed, they may visit multiple pages on a website so quickly that it may crash. As Koster explains, poorly written and personal crawlers can negatively impact network resources and cause server overload (as cited in Fox & Khandeparker, 2010). Web servers have developed rate policies to prevent crawlers from causing disruptions in the network. The most common rate policy is the Robots Exclusion Protocol, which prevents crawlers from visiting specific pages. As Manning, Raghavan, and Schutze (2009) explain, "this is done by placing file with the name robots.txt at the root of the URL hierarchy at the site" (p. 47). Crawlers must respect the rate policies developed by the web servers.

Since web crawling is time-consuming, developers frequently create multiple web crawlers that work together to complete downloads. Parallelization policies exist for such crawlers to ensure that duplication of downloads does not occur. Multithreading is an example of a parallelization policy. As Fox and Khandeparker (2010) explain, "in a multithreaded crawler, each thread locks the URL Frontier while selecting a URL that it will crawl. After it has picked a URL, it unlocks the frontier so that other threads can access it and pick a URL. While a URL is added the frontier, the frontier is again locked to maintain consistency." Locking the URL frontier prevents the duplication of content and helps each crawler retrieve unique content.

Web page importance

In order for crawlers to be effective, they must retrieve relevant, useful content. To determine the importance of the page, crawlers use several methods. Many crawlers search for specific keywords within web pages to decide if it should be added to the index. When using keywords, crawlers may base inclusion on the occurrence or the frequency of terms. Some crawlers use information from user queries to determine the importance of a web page. The crawler compares the search terms to the retrieved pages to decide if the page should be indexed.

Certain crawlers use mathematical calculations or algorithms to determine the relevance of a page. Crawlers may compare the web page to the seed URL by assigning new pages a relevance score based on a cosine similarity calculation. Other crawlers use classifier bots, which are programmed to give pages automated classifier scores based on comparing new pages to example pages. For Retrieval System Rank, "N different crawlers are started from the same seed and allowed to run till each crawler gathers P pages. The entire set of N*P pages collected from the crawler are ranked against the initiating query or description using a retrieval system such as SMART" (Fox & Khandeparker, 2010). Lastly, crawlers may base relevancy on link-based popularity, such as Google. The crawler bases the page's relevance on how many other pages link to it by using algorithms such as Page Rank.

Crawlers may use any method to determine the importance of web pages, but in order to be effective, they must retrieve relevant results. To evaluate crawlers, one must examine the recall and precision of the results. One may also use the acquisition rate to determine the effectiveness of the web crawler. In order to deliver relevant content to patrons, digital libraries must constantly test and adjust their web crawlers.

8.7: Image Retrieval

Digital images are a significant component of Digital Libraries. The Internet makes the development of an efficient image retrieval technique imperative. Today the growth of digital images is made widespread through the popularization of computers and the Internet. The key to a successful retrieval system is to match the right features that represent the image to be searched. Most retrieval systems will combine features for optimum results.

"Information seeking behavior focusing on different groups of users has been studied extensively from time to time. There are recent studies of ISB of children, young people, undergraduates, astronomers, chemists, mathematicians, physicists, and social scientists" (Yang, 2004). Content-based image retrieval is one of the chief advances of image retrieval in the past ten years. Relevant images are retrieved based on the similarity of their image features as seen in such systems as QBIC, Photobook, NETRA.

The basic image retrieval types are text based and content-based. Since 1970 text based retrieval has been used to interpret images. Keywords are use to describe the image, caption of an image, text surrounding/embedded in it, and its filename. Use of these descriptors requires a high level of relevance of the text with the image.

Textual descriptors are annotations based on semantic reasoning done in two ways: 1) manually with the aid of tools and 2) automatically relating the semantics of the terms with relevant descriptions. After annotation, the various categories and images are indexed for easy retrieval. A noteworthy drawback to text-based image retrieval is the significant number of man-hours required to add interpretation and textual characteristics of images.

The original features in images that are important to image retrieval are color, shape and texture. Throughout most literature, these features are a fundamental to content-based image retrieval. The color histogram is a commonly used color feature representation. A color histogram calculates the intensity levels of the primary colors (red, green and blue) and represents their joint probability.

Shape-based image retrieval is a further feature that should be used if the colors of the images are the same throughout. And the last content-based technique evaluated is texture-based image retrieval.

Indexing techniques are functional when images are stored in large databases and size of the images stored grows exponentially.

Tiltomo is a Content Based Image Search Engine in Beta format.

This Visual Search uses proprietary algorithms to analyze the similarity and relationship between images. You can search a keyword or you may search the default show random images. This method of searching allows you to search making use of your own creative path. Make a broad search and narrow the search to the types of images you like. Tiltomo utilizes a visual image search. The purpose of visual image search is to make finding images easier. This system allows the user to make a broad search and narrow the types of desired images. Below is an image keyword search for coral reef. There are two options. First, click below the image to narrow the search by similar type or second, by color/texture.

Figure 8.11: TILTOMO Visual Search Keyword Coral Reef.

The CBIR (content-based image retrieval) system used by Tiltomo is an advanced proprietary Subject, Color & Texture recognition algorithm to analyze image composition. It can process the relationship between several million images on a single medium specification machine in one day. Content-based image retrieval (CBIR) pulls out several features that describe the content of the image, mapping the visual content of the images into a new space called the feature space. The feature space values for a given image are stored in a descriptor that can be used for retrieving similar images. CBIR also provides a way to index, search and retrieve images.

Descriptors are CEDD (Color and Edge Directivity Descriptor). FCTH (Fuzzy Color and Texture Histogram) is an extraction of a new low-level feature that combines color and texture information. C.CEDD (Compact.CEDD), C.FCTH (.FCTH) and JCD. The descriptor incorporates color and texture information into the histogram. Another feature of these descriptors is size and storage requirements. That is keeping the size small as possible without compromising their discriminating facility.

Tiltomo uses Flickr as its playground. Flickr is the perfect match for their technology. Flickr offers tag searching, group and cluster browsing. Tiltomo has created two test image databases that work independently of each other. To test the theme aspect, they have uploaded 140,000 general images to Flickr. This is a great place to test theme aspect of searching. If your image subject is important, you will search by theme: analysis of subject, color and texture. If you are searching images with similar color/texture, you will search color/texture: analysis of (100% color/texture).

Figure 8.12: Flickr Image retrieval: Tall Buildings.

Img(Anaktisi) is another example of a Content Based Image Search Engine. It is an image retrieval system that employs three steps. First, select a dataset, second select a descriptor, and third select query. Action choices allow you to modify your searched results. You may start another search, search another descriptor, show or clear search history.

Digital Libraries in Theory and Practices

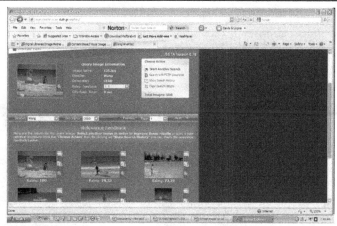

Figure 8.13: Img(Anaktisi) Visual Search: Image Retrieval in 3 Steps.

Image retrieval systems have evolved over a period of time. The need for image retrieval systems has been put in place by the various groups of individuals such as artists, designers, teachers, historians, advertising agencies, photographers, engineers and journalists. Each group has its unique requirements for images.

The most common features a user looks for when searching images are color, shape or texture. Most users would like the retrieval and searching for images to have ease of access. Google has made searching for images easier with better thumbnails, more images, easier navigation and better controls; for example, you can hover the mouse over an image and see more information about that image. You can search for like images by clicking on the "similar" link. You can also browse images on the go using your cell phone with a full-featured browser.

In the left hand side bar of the Google image search, you will see how to refine your search. The any size option allows you to choose large, medium, icon or the exact pixel size. This option is very convenient as the size and resolution of a picture can be problematic. Pictures take up a significant amount of space on the web. To narrow the search by type you may search all or one of the following: face, photo, clip art, or line drawing. The last is a search by color. This is a great tool with lots of choices and typically accurate retrieval of subject searched. Once you made your keyword search and the pictures are retrieved, you can simply narrow your search by clicking below the image. The new Google image can be seen below. This is a clear, easy-to-navigate search.

317

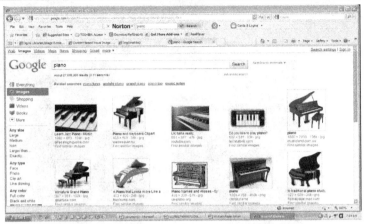

Figure 8.14: Google image search using Keyword piano.

A survey of image retrieval systems for searching images available on the Internet may be found in JISC (2008). Out of these image search engines, Google consists of simple search options with a good advanced search facility. It provides quick and reasonably good search results. Similar to Google, the search options at Yahoo are also simple. In addition, the retrieval process is quick and retrieved images are relevant, without dead links and duplicates. However, the size of the search scoped is unspecified. A few other image search engines have been developed during the last few years. However, none of these search engines can dynamically combine text keyword and image features at the time of retrieval. (Vadivel et al., 2009)

Relevance Feedback Algorithm (RFA) refers to high retrieval scores in content-based image retrieval. This requires the user to evaluate the quality of the inquiry of results by marking the retrieved images as relevant or not. The search engine will then use the results to better serve users' needs. The majority of feedback is based on modification of search parameters.

Currently, most retrieval techniques take on methods using more than one feature type. Color, texture and shape features are used in both IBM's QBIC and MIT'S Photobook. Other CBIR systems include SIMBA, CIRES, SIMPLIcity, IRMA (Image Retrieval in Medical Applications), FIRE and MIRROR.

There are two major research areas related to image retrieval: keyword-based and content-based image retrieval. The disadvantage is that users search high-level concepts rather than low-level features as used by CBIR technique. Few studies have examined user image searching behavior.

Due to the continuous growth in the number of users searching digital images and the increased access to digital image archives, it is critical to understand users' image requests and to create viable solutions to accommodate the varied needs of every growing user population.

The obtained 28 refined types provide a glimpse of the variety of failed queries, and show that such queries have far more conceptual than perceptual refined types. This suggests that the prevalent CBIR techniques can only deal with a small portion of failed queries, and appropriate integration of concept-based techniques is needed. Since users often, request information not provided in the image itself or the information provided is not in accordance with users' representations, there are gaps between users' requests and retrieval technologies. (Vadivel, et al., 2009)

In summary, it is noteworthy to state that image retrieval is continuously evolving and that there will be trends and continued improvements. To be developed are suitable indexing schemes to match the needs of the user. Interaction and feedback in image retrieval will continue to cause major changes in the way image retrieval systems are developed. The World Wide Web will be a source for image storage and web-oriented search engines.

8.8: Location Based Services

Location-based Services, or LBS, refers to the use of real-time geo-data from a mobile device or smart phone to offer information to people who have enabled the LBS on their devices (Goodrich 2018). This is accomplished through the use of an app that uses the GPS in mobile devices to determine your location and suggest things in your neighborhood that may be of interest to you.

"Target locations New Haven, Connecticut" is an example of a search history that refers to location information. Place-based services collect data analytics or gather and recommend information based on a certain location. Targeted advertising is one of the most common instances. Waze, a GPS program that advertises restaurants or businesses depending on a user's location while driving, is one such example. Waze will re-route a user to that business if they click on the ad. To better recommend adverts and information, Google employs location-based services such as an IP address or search history.

Location-based service was first introduced as a Global Positioning System by the United States Department of Defense in the 1970s and was later made available for use by civilians in the 1980s (Schiller & Voisard, 2004). The president of Location Based Marketing Association (LBMA) described LBS as a bridge that closed gaps among all forms of media, inclusive of social media, the Internet, and real-life interaction.

Pereira (2011) indicate that LBS is the outcome of the convergence of three technologies in one device: mobile internet access, positioning, and rich user interfaces. In the late 1990s, LBS was first available on mobile devices that supported voice and SMS but had limited user interface capabilities, according to Pereira (2011). In 1999, the first mobile LBS was launched as a result of the development of Wireless Connectivity Point (WAP) and internet access in mobile phones (Sharma & Nakamura, 2003). Because of advancements in user interfaces and the availability of mobile phones with high-resolution touchscreens, applications with richer interfaces may now do activities that are comparable to those performed by desktop computers.

Location-based services are "social, entertainment, or information services that allow a corporation to reach and engage with its audience using tools and platforms that capture the audience's geographic location" (DiStaso & Khan, 2015). LBS's services transfer information to users through mechanisms such as mobile internet, mobile applications, short message service, text messaging, multimedia messaging service, GPS-based services, indoor location services, digital out-of-home, digital signs, print media, and television (DiStaso & Khan, 2015). Consumers', products', and services' locations can be linked to their interests using LBS to provide relevant data that can forecast intent at any given time.

Other capable smart applications and equipment, such as mobile apps for navigation, personal tracking, emergency calling, gaming, advertising, social engagement, and general well-being, were expected to expand their use of LBS (EGNOS & Galileo LBS Brochure, 2014). These events are now commonplace.

Usefulness of LBS for digital libraries

Location-based services can be used to connect all types of media, including social media, the Internet, and in-person engagement. The capacity to identify consumers, nearby retailers and restaurants, and navigate to desired areas are just a few of the applications of LBS. Consumers are reached and engaged via LBS based on their location. More than just sales can be done with an LBS. By partnering with charity and delivering social good through LBS, you can make a great influence for your brand (DiStaso & Khan, 2015). The Pennies for Life Campaign, for example, launched an SMS campaign to increase donor engagement by allowing them to see the impact of their donation thanks to location-based technologies.

If a digital library produces an app that leverages LBS, they can target people in their neighborhood who are interested in learning more about the library. When consumers start seeing adverts for their local library or museum's digital collection, they are likely to be irritated at first because they are being targeted, but then they will be curious to see what exceptional collection or archive has been advertised. If digital libraries are to grow in popularity in the future, they must begin to use the tools available to them to spread the word, and what better way to do so than by providing a direct link to their collection via an LBS.

Libraries are already benefiting from LBS in a variety of ways. Staff at the Southern Connecticut State University Library, for example, can categorize and group literature works by department, study level, and courses. When materials need to be located in the library, these layouts enable for quick service. The web-based library also serves as a resource for students and researchers by directing them to relevant topics and, in certain circumstances, other cooperating libraries to meet their needs.

Smart libraries, described by Gul and Bano as "a developing and novel technological environment of the twenty-first century," make use of location-based services to imagine new and exciting technologies that might be used to establish a smart library. The "magic mirror" is one such gadget that the authors anticipate. Location recognition, a type of location-based service, is one of the features of the "magic mirror." Through the use of RFID (radio frequency identification) technology, a mix of cameras, speech recognition, and location-based services can be used to sense and report the status of the library's collection in real time (Gul & Bano, 2019).

By tracking active RFID chips in proximity to the sensors, RFID can be used as a local location-based service. Internal batteries in active RFID chips broadcast to the sensors. There are no batteries in passive RFID chips, therefore they must be scanned by a sensor (Schatz, 2021). For a more convenient check-out experience, my local library has passive RFID chips implanted in all of its materials. RFID chips that are passive cannot be utilized for tracking (Schatz, 2021). Within Disney World, the RF tracking technology is used. The Disney wristbands have RF trackers that are detected by park sensors and used to track a person's location (Disney, n.d.).

Patron's tracking isn't the only use case for location-based services. It's also useful for keeping track of materials. Personally, I'd want to see a "magic mirror" system that reflects the genuine state of books. My local library has a large number of lost and missing books that are not included in the catalog. It's quite aggravating. With this technology, incorrect item statuses and misplaced materials in the library would be a thing of the past. As Disney already utilizes this technology in its Florida park, a version of the "magic mirror" is a very conceivable device that can be implemented in libraries today.

The combination of augmented reality and location-based services offers up a world of possibilities. Location-based services and augmented reality can be combined in a library setting to create information bulletins depending on being in a specific library department or visual guidance to find a book within the library. Augmented reality in conjunction with location-based services has a lot of potential. Both the "magic mirror" and augmented reality combined with location-based services are very feasible technologies that can be used in the library provided the library is prepared to invest the necessary funds.

LBS and QR codes

Quick Response is abbreviated as QR. The Japanese car sector was the first to design and use QR codes for inventory tracking in the 1990s. Due to its faster readability and larger storage capacity than typical UPC barcodes, the QR code became popular outside of the automobile industry (QR code, n.d.) and is currently utilized in a far broader context. A single two-dimensional QR code may carry up to 7089 digits or 4296 characters, but a one-dimensional bar code can only hold up to 20 characters. Words and site addresses can be encoded in addition to numbers and letters (Parabhoi, Bhattacharjya & Dhar, 2017).

QR codes can be a valuable tool for libraries and/or memory institutions with non-book artifacts because they are regularly used to connect mobile device users to specific bits of web-based information. Many smartphones and tablets now have the capacity to scan a QR code and be sent to the exact URL you want to promote using the device's camera. The minimal upfront cost is a big benefit: Because QR code generators are freely available from a variety of web-based organizations, there are virtually no costs connected with creating and linking them other from staff time.

QR codes can be utilized in a variety of ways in libraries, including advertising materials, links to online reading material, maps, blogs, and YouTube instructional videos; some libraries have even used them in scavenger hunts (Lamb & Johnson, 2013). I intend to create QR codes to be placed on/near things in my library that will link to photographs in my digital project.

However, QR codes have drawbacks, including the following, as revealed in the research by Parabhoi, Bhattacharjya & Dhar (2017):
- Patrons may not know what a QR code is.
- The patron needs a scanning device, and it must be enabled with the scanning software.
- An internet connection is needed.
- QR codes linking to websites need to have the links monitored.
- The cost of QR code maintenance with respect to staff time has the potential to be significant.

Awareness of use of location-based services

For the most part, location-based services are only useful when consumers, products, and services want to participate. This feature of opt-in is the most important in terms of LBS efficacy. According to DiStaso and Khan (2015), encouraging people to opt-in to a location-based service, even through incentives, is worth every penny because it allows for the collection of information such as demographics, preferences, and purchase habits, which can then be used to deliver more relevant value-added messages and offers to generate profit. Researchers in the field of academia could profit from LBS by receiving customized messages and results summaries as a consequence of subscriptions to specific themes.

Location-based services could be a wonderful way for DL to expand its user base in the future. By providing a direct service to a library, it gives the customer what they want while also providing the library with a user base that allows it to survive. While LBS has many advantages and features, it may fall short when it comes to securing patrons information. Most LBS services acquire and use user information in ways that may not comply with consumer privacy safeguards and expectations, posing a security risk to customers. The issue that may arise is that some individuals are uncomfortable with these LBS being used to target them in marketing. People may perceive it as a breach of privacy and protest the companies responsible, resulting in a negative image.

The use of LBS to advertise to individuals is a relatively recent issue that will likely take a long time to rectify if action is taken. However, if a library advertises its collection in order to attract new customers, I see no problem with it and believe it could be helpful to both sides.

8.9: Mobile apps developed for digital library services

Hoopla is an all-in-one digital library app, a division of Midwest Tape (https://www.midwesttape.com/). It's a media streaming platform for audio books, comics, e-books, movies, music, and television that's available on the web and on mobile devices. Patrons of Hoopla-supported libraries have unrestricted access to the service's digital media collection.

Sonoma County Library is one of examples using Hoopla as an app for their mobile users. Hoopla is a one-stop shop for streaming digital material for library patrons. Comics, music, television, movies, audiobooks, and eBooks in all genres and age groups are available through this app. In both English and Spanish, eBooks and audiobooks are accessible. There are never any late penalties because all checked items return themselves. There are almost 980,000 fiction and nonfiction titles available.

Hoopla gives libraries the option of offering certain digital formats to their patrons, and the controls offered by the service include:
- Allowing checkouts only to the library's patrons;
- Limiting the number of checkouts per month per patron account to a certain number usually somewhere between 2 – 6 checkouts per month;
- Establishing a daily/monthly budgeted maximum spend for the library's account, which can work in tandem with control #2;
- Manually blocking specific titles by price/format.

Shoutbomb, used in Guilford Free Library in Connecticut, is a service that sends patrons SMS with information such as when their holds are ready to be picked up and when their loaned items are due (GFL, nd). Shoutbomb also allows patrons to send texts to the library to renew things, and families with young cardholders or adult offspring of elderly cardholders can receive text notices on several cards (GFL, nd). Signing up is completely free; the patron is solely responsible for any applicable texting fees charged by their telecommunications carrier. This service can also be linked to an email account.

Shoutbomb does not require extra support staff to maintenance, it is fully automated. It is also accessible using a smart phone or any text capable mobile phone (2020); so even flip phones can use this service. Shoutbomb can be configured into Spanish and English; other various languages are upon request (http://www.shoutbomb.com/).

Libby, a free smartphone app "where you may borrow ebooks and digital audiobooks from your public library." Simply enter your library card number into the app, and it will take you to your library's catalog, where you can borrow digital copies (e-books or audiobooks) to your phone if they haven't been borrowed by another patron. One of the biggest advantages of Libby is that you can borrow materials from your phone and get them without ever having to go to the library. Libby is similar to Audible; however it offers free content. (What is Libby?, 2020.)

Another useful feature of Libby is that if you prefer reading e-books on your Kindle device or app, Libby can transmit the books you borrow to your Kindle device or app. According to the Atlantic County Library System website, if the books downloaded are in Kindle format, clicking the "I Read on Another Device" option in Libby's download options will "ask one to send it to ones Kindle or Kindle eReader app, rather than uploading the book to Libby" (Atlantic County Library System, 2018.)

The digital shelf is a component of this software where you may organize all of your loans, holds, and tags in one place. The tags tool is useful since it allows you to categorize books into different categories, such as books you don't want to read or books you want to read after bedtime. It's a no-brainer for folks who have cards at multiple libraries to use Libby for digital books. "Libby makes it easy to swap between library cards or between various libraries," according to the Atlantic County Library System website. All you have to do is click on the menu in the top right corner, and click "See Library Cards" or "Add Library" if you have not already done so. When you check out materials from different libraries, "all your digital checkouts from different cards and libraries are on the same shelf, so there is no need to switch between libraries or cards to read a book (Atlantic County Library System, 2018.)

The main downside of Libby is that you cannot borrow materials if they are checked out by someone else. For example, Michelle Obama's book Becoming is currently checked out, which means I won't be able to listen to it while it's checked out to someone else, which can be inconvenient. I may, however, place it on hold in the same way that a physical copy of the book would be. By clicking on the calendar sign above the title, you can see how long you'll have to wait to borrow the book, as well as how many other people have placed it on hold.

Conclusion

Digital libraries continue to evolve and offer new services that will help them to better meet the needs of users. One topic addressed in the literature is the need for digital libraries to adapt to users and/or communities by providing personalized information and services that will meet their increasingly complex needs. Librarians are quickly finding ways to adapt Web 2.0 technologies to better serve users. The utilization of recommender services is one way digital library creators are attempting to provide personalization to their users. An emerging field, personalization services hold the potential to ensure the continued relevance and importance of libraries in the digital age. By creating and delivering effective personalization services, digital libraries can truly become a learning hub for users. Recommender systems are a great tool for digital libraries to provide a better way to search and discover information on their web site and other sites. As digital collections grow, so should the ability to provide a coherent and efficient way to search all the information available. A successful search system may incorporate different systems but it should be fast, reliable, and user friendly. As a result, recommendation systems have become a growing and increasingly important area of research. Libraries must balance getting information in the hands of their users and respecting copyrighted materials. Libraries are all about service to their community and their users; with the spread of digital libraries this mission is still intact, but the potential community of users has gone worldwide.

Study Questions for Chapter Eight:

1. Chowdhury many times referred to the archiving of digital information as a complex and resource intensive process. How do we balance the long-term maintenance costs with the value of the data preserved? How do we determine what data should be archived? Should there be an international entity to create standards for archiving data? What do you think should be included in these standards?

2. Whether or not we ever build a digital library in our careers, we will all USE some sort of digital library. As we have already learned, many items held by digital libraries cannot be found by using a search engine. How do we, as librarians, know what digital libraries are out there now, and in the future, and how can we help our clientele find and use these valuable resources?

3. The proliferation of digital libraries potentially makes much of the world's information accessible. However, the language barrier can still prevent users from accessing important information. To what extent do we need to be concerned about making our digital libraries accessible to people who speak languages other than English? What would be the criteria for deciding whether a particular digital library should be accessible in more than one language? The following link takes you to an article that can give you an idea of what such a project may entail: http://www.iei.pi.cnr.it/ErcimDL/third-DELOS-workshop/Sheridan/sheridan-delos/eurodlib.ps.gz

4. Many see striving for a global digital library as a lofty and worthwhile goal. Others regard it as the equivalent of giving a box of fancy chocolates to a starving orphan. The chocolates are an extravagance whose price could have bought something more useful and it's possible that the gift will be misappropriated and used to benefit someone other than the recipient. What do you think? Would the energy, resources and creativity required to bring about a global digital library be better directed elsewhere? Would/could a so-called global digital library actually be "global?"

Chapter Nine: Preservation

One of the central roles of libraries throughout history has been to work to maintain their collections for future generations. The preservation of valuable and useful information is essential for the continuation of knowledge and learning. Traditional libraries containing books and other physical materials must work constantly to fight against encroaching decay in the form of brittle paper, fading ink, and broken bindings. Those libraries with the requisite desire and funding to begin such an undertaking have started digitizing at-risk materials in order to protect them from the harmful effects of regular use. Still other organizations are creating new work exclusively in the digital environment, free from the perils associated with older information storage technologies.

Unfortunately, digital libraries come with their own set of problems. Digital librarians must be aware of the ways in which digital information can decay and even be lost in order to combat these problems and preserve their collections for the future. Digital data preservation is a key issue that has come about with the boom of the technology age that we live in.

9.1: Preservation

The move of libraries to the digital arena has uncovered a number of unique challenges related to preservation. Digital libraries have been used to preserve materials, but now they themselves need to be preserved. This is especially important because so much information is originating in digital form as opposed to moving from paper to digital; it only exists in bits and bytes.

In the past, "benign neglect," a mainly do-nothing approach, has often been enough to ensure the survival and usability of physical data. However, computer systems and software applications change so rapidly there is no guarantee that existing data sources will be accessible and useable on future computing platforms or software versions (Wilson, 2007).

Preservation, particularly digital preservation, leaves many questions to be answered. How does one correctly preserve, and what exactly does one preserve? The purpose of preservation is to protect information of enduring value for access by present and future generations (Conway, 1990, p. 206). Knowing this, there is not just one way of preservation for the digital age. The concept of digital preservation encompasses material that begins its life in digital form as well as material that is converted from traditional to digital formats (Hedstrom, 1998).

Nature of digital objects

The nature of digital objects is changing due to the increasing number of digital formats in use. As a result, the field of digital preservation must be flexible and always vigilant for the next "big thing." Digital objects are photos, audio files, written documents, web pages, blogs, emails, message boards, and more. It is now quite simple for people with very little technical knowledge to create digital objects. Preservation of digital objects is as varied as the objects themselves. Simply saving a digital object, however, does not mean the job is done: "It is not only about the ability to find and retrieve an item, but also the ability to use, view, listen to, interact with, display or run the digital item in such a way that users can be assured that what they are viewing satisfies their needs" (Bradley, 2007, p. 154). To be valuable, according to Abby Smith (2007, p. 11), content must be useful. Bollacker notes that "in order to survive, digital data must be understandable" (2010, p. 109).

The immense amount of digital data continues to increase, and "it seems unavoidable that most of the data in our future will be digital, so it behooves us to understand how to manage and preserve digital data so we can avoid what some have called the 'digital dark age'" (Bollacker, 2010, p. 106). Our world is increasingly defined by digital data. "A 2008 International Data Corporation (IDC) white paper sponsored by EMC Corporation described the world we live in as awash in digital data--an estimated 281 exabytes in 2007...storing, accessing, managing, preserving, and dealing with digital data is clearly a fundamental need and an immense challenge" (Berman, 2008, p. 51).

> Bollacker (2010) states that:
> The general problem of data preservation is twofold. The first matter is preservation of the data itself: The physical media on which data are written must be preserved, and this media must continue to accurately hold the data that are entrusted to it. The problem is the same for analog and digital media, but unless we are careful, digital media can be more fragile (p. 106).

Digital media is more fragile than analog media due to a fundamental difference in their data representation design. Analog data is exactly that—a segment of the actual data that was recorded. If an analog tape is damaged, there is distortion in the data. Generally, the worse the damage, the worse the distortion. Yet "it is a smooth transition known as graceful degradation....so that partial failure of a system does not mean total failure" (Bollacker, 2010, p. 108).

Digital data, on the other hand, do not degrade gracefully. This is due to the fact that digital encoding methods are represented by a string of binary digits ("bits"). "A bit, the lowest level of information, is meaningful only in relation to other bits with which it is associated" (Bradley, 2007, p. 149). Damage to a bit "causes an unpredictable amount of actual damage to the signal" (Bollacker, 2010, p. 108). Anyone who has tried to watch a digital television station that does not come in well knows this phenomenon. You either see the channel well or you don't see it at all. This is in contrast to analog television where the viewer could sometimes see the channel, even if it didn't come in very well. Bollacker (2010) notes: "that does not mean that digital encodings are worse; rather, it's just that we have to do more work to build a better system" (p. 109).

Why should we preserve digital information?

We live in an information society where virtually anyone can access information at any time. Furthermore, as Witten, Bainbridge, and Nichols (2010) note, digital libraries are helping rural organizations, creating a repository for scholarly research, and collecting traditions of a dwindling tribe (p. 3-5). Knowledge is no longer reserved for the few. With digital technology, it is the right of many.

Doyle, Viktor, and Paquet (2009) identify a handful of organizations that digital preservation is most important to: e-government, e-commerce, e-health, digital libraries, and digital cultural heritage are at the top of their list (p. 33). However, it can be argued that digital preservation is important to more than just organizations; it is also important to individuals. When is the last time you sent a letter through the Postal Service or went to get film developed? Instead, you probably send emails or take digital photos. If there are not strategies in place to preserve digital information, all of this information may be lost. This is bigger than keeping records for corporations or the government. It comes down to collective memories of people.

In addition, how will future generations find out about who came before them if digital information is lost? We no longer carve words and images into stone or make goods by hand that will last thousands of years. If there was any question about digital preservation being important, it was quelled by the announcement in April 2010 that the social networking site Twitter donated its entire archive of tweets to the Library of Congress. Librarian of Congress James Billington said it was important to have this archive in order to record our contemporary way of life and how we use social media in discussing societal issues (*cited in* Raymond & Garrett, 2010). As Ross and Hedstrom (2005) state, "we use, trust and create e-content, and expect that this content will remain accessible to allow us to validate claims, trace what we have done, or pass a record to future generations" (p. 317).

"Planning and Implementing a Sustainable Digital Preservation Program" discusses how libraries may ensure that their digital content is not lost due to issues such as hardware failure, memory loss, or internal priority shifts (Baucom, 2019). Keeping in mind that all of these things could happen at any time and committing to safeguarding digital data should be high on librarians' priority list.

What needs to be preserved?

There is more to preserving digital information than the information itself. The means for viewing the information must be preserved as well. This is a challenge because digital materials rely on software to make them viewable, and the software relies on hardware to run it. If the hardware or the software becomes obsolete, the digital data may be lost (Doyle, Viktor, & Paquet, 2009, p. 34).

In addition, the means for discovering digital information needs to be preserved. Doyle, Viktor, and Paquet (2009) call this "preservation metadata," which "plays a vital role in increasing the usability of a preserved digital object and its preservation environment as it provides future users with all the necessary information they need to open, render and interact with the preserved digital object, in addition to providing its preservation history" (p. 34).

Digital preservation approaches and strategies

"Meaning does not reside in the technology, and data streams cannot sustain themselves" (Bradley, 2007, p. 151). It is people who must define approaches to digital preservation and construct effective strategies. The strategies for digital preservation are not uniform. In fact, "different types of digital objects have varying preservation and authenticity requirements...depending upon the contexts of their creation and use. Furthermore, these requirements are also subject to differing degrees of stringency" (Gilliland-Swetland & Eppard, 2000). Yet the basic goal remains the same: "establishing the who, what, when, where, how, and why associated with that information" (Gilliland-Swetland & Eppard, 2000). The methods involved in digital preservation have changed over time as digital media formats have evolved. Bradley (2007) states that "digital preservation, a significant and integral part of digital sustainability, is shown to have changed its focus from one technical concern to another as issues and fashions have shifted" (p. 151).

Before the preservation process begins, the library has to decide what is worth keeping. Digital files must physically exist on a disk or a hard drive that is kept somewhere safe. Along with the files of data, the library also needs to store the proper hardware and software to be able to read these files. As such, a digital library has a limited amount of space at its disposal for storage and cannot house every piece of data indiscriminately. An agreed upon rubric to judge the value of each item is essential. Next, the library must create and enact a detailed preservation policy. It is important to firmly articulate the need for action and explain the principles and practices utilized in that action.

The goal in digital preservation is to have a preservation plan in place before the information needs to be archived. To this end, Doyle, Viktor, and Paquet (2009) state that the information should be preserved in order to fulfill potential requirements of end users, including accessibility, executable and understandable content without errors, authenticity, accompanying metadata, and durability (p. 34-35). Thinking about what users may need in the future will help formulate a plan.

In their "Long Definition" of web archiving, the American Library Association offers guidance in developing digital preservation standards and strategies, addressing creation, integrity and maintenance:

Content creation:
- Clear and complete technical specifications
- Production of reliable master files
- Sufficient descriptive, administrative and structural metadata to ensure future access
- Detailed quality control of processes

Content integrity:
- Documentation of all policies, strategies and procedures
- Use of persistent identifiers
- Recorded provenance and change history for all objects
- Verification mechanisms
- Attention to security requirements
- Routine audits

Content maintenance:
- A robust computing and networking infrastructure
- Storage and synchronization of files at multiple sites
- Continuous monitoring and management of files
- Programs for refreshing, migration and emulation
- Creation and testing of disaster prevention and recovery plans
- Periodic review and updating of policies and procedures"

(ALA, 2007b).

Decision making process

In order to preserve data, one must determine what exactly to preserve. One must consider all the various requirements of data preservation, including legal and technical requirements, because "preservation is a collection management...activity with a technology component but also associated policies and procedures" (A. Smith, 2005, p. 10). There are:

things that must be kept by law; things that must be destroyed by law; things that we choose to keep; things that we are certain can be thrown away; things that we would like to keep if we have room; things that we would like to throw away, but are not sure about;

things that we think we have kept but cannot find; things that we have kept but now cannot decipher; things that we have not kept, but now wish that we had. (Future-proof digital storage, 2007, p. 32)

It is unnecessary to save everything and not "all data will, or should, be sustained in perpetuity" (Bradley, 2007, p. 159).

Concerning the preservation of each file containing digital data, the library has three options: save the entire file, save only some of the data it contains, or discard the entire file. To make this decision, digital preservationists consider not only the value of the information presented in the file, but also the continuing interest in the form in which it is kept.

Obsolescence is a serious concern. The world of computer programs is in a continual state of flux. Old programs and coding languages fall out of favor as newer, more powerful (or sometimes just more popular) ones take their place. Modern machines do not all come equipped to work with outdated devices. For example, many new computers do not come with floppy disk drives and as a result cannot read floppy disks. If users want to access information stored on a floppy disk, they must first obtain the proper drive. Further, they need to be sure that their computer has software capable of reading the data present on the disk.

Some obsolete hardware and software were once very popular and there may be a great deal of data stored in that way. If this is the case, the library may choose to maintain equipment capable of reading the files in their original form. Often times, though, this is not a feasible solution. Maintaining many machines can get expensive, not to mention crowded. The organization would need to employ staff with specialized knowledge of the antiquated technology, use valuable storage space to house the machines, and purchase increasingly rare parts when problems arise.

Another option, particularly when considering cases involving less widely used technology, is conversion. The organization could decide to use a limited number of kinds of files. Information stored in any other file type or storage device would then be transferred to one of the acceptable types. An important fact to consider about this process is that whenever file conversion takes place, there is a chance for a loss of information. It is like interpreting a text from one language to another. Slight changes must be made to accommodate the new language, making the interpretation slightly different from the original and sometimes subtly altering meaning. For computer files, there is more risk because conversion is done by computer programs that would create nonsense if there were an error. Digital preservationists would be wise to be wary of easy file conversions and perform quality control on all conversions.

It should be noted that future researchers might be interested in antiquated file types themselves, much like the way some scholars pay close attention to the kind of paper or binding used in old books. A library associated with a computer science school, for example, might find them useful for the study of the evolution of computer resources. This should be considered before marking material for conversion.

Digital preservationists converting materials to a new medium have to make important decisions about what parts of the item are necessary to preserve unchanged. Those items that must be kept are known as significant properties. For a book, properties to consider include ink color, font, typesetting, and images. For some books, the words may be the only significant property and it can be converted to a plain text file for storage and online access. For others, it may not be so simple. Take for example, the novel *Extremely Loud and Incredibly Close* by Jonathan Safran Foer. In it, there is a chapter with markings meant to represent the red pen corrections that the father character likes to make in the newspaper. The markings are mentioned later in the text (Foer, 2005). The novel would be something less than how it was originally published if it were digitized into plain text without the markings and pictures that contribute to the narrative. A digital library concerned with preserving the work as it was conceived would consider such markings significant properties.

Aesthetics are not the only issue governing the question of significant property. Preservationists must also consider legal issues. "Courts, for example, might challenge the admissibility of copies of original documents as evidence in legal proceedings if the reasons for and processes used to produce surrogates were not well documented" (Hedstrom & Lee, 2002). Whenever creating a copy or a change of format, the authenticity of the item can be called into question. It is the job of the preservationist to preserve authenticity as well, by noting important data documenting any changes that may have been made as well as who performed the change and when.

Another factor in determining digital preservation policy is to define a retention period for the digital objects. Some objects or datasets have only a short period of usefulness for academic or intellectual pursuits, whereas other materials might be considered valuable for a very long time. Some, like significant historical artifacts, may be considered valuable enough to preserve for perpetuity. Yet "value" is subjective. While there is general agreement that official digital government records (such as presidential email and videos of congressional hearings in the U.S.) are preservation-worthy and of great political and historic value to society, the video of your niece's voice recital is likely to be of value to a much smaller family group (Berman, 2008, p. 54).

It is not easy to anticipate the needs of future generations. Libraries looking to preserve a digital collection have to consider more than just the obvious when they formulate their preservation plan.

Cost-benefit analysis of preservation approaches

The cost-benefit analysis of different preservation approaches is an important step in choosing what to preserve and how to preserve it. Bradley

(2007) notes that "digital preservation, if it is to be sustainable, is an economic issue, one that advocates investment in the present to ensure access in the future...it is not too strong to say the biggest single risk to sustained access to digital preservation is economic" (p. 158). Therefore, in order to successfully advocate for the importance of digital preservation, one must do a cost-benefit analysis. Access to accurate information in the future is the primary benefit of digital preservation. Abby Smith argues that appropriate digital preservation is essential to the "well-being of the population and the survival of our society, and indeed, our species" (2007, p. 17). Information is literally power in this technological age. Preservation is also "insurance against loss of value...protects against loss of business continuity in the event of disruptions and catastrophes... protects our critical information-based dependencies...and adds value to content by maximizing its potential for reuse" (Smith, 2007, p. 17).

Smith (2007) also argues that "logic would tell us that increased demand for content would naturally increase demand for preservation of that content. But logic would be wrong. Paradoxically, the proliferation of digital content, in high demand today, can make it harder to argue compellingly for preservation. Its sheer abundance and ubiquity make digital content appear perdurable" (2007, p. 7). If all information appears to be free on the web, why pay to digitize anything? It is this issue that demands a cost-benefit analysis of digital preservation.

The primary difference in considering the cost-benefit of digital preservation, as opposed to analog preservation, is one of managing abundance instead of scarcity. Three factors must be considered in assessing the value of digital preservation: our increasing dependence on technologies that change and become obsolete, the time-scales of digital content, and the low-to-no barriers to digital content creation, which have resulted in the elimination of scarcity as a preservation value (A. Smith, 2007, p. 9). Technologies that become obsolete are cause for a major increase in the cost of digital technologies. Chen (2001) notes that "private companies facing discovery orders for their digital information in connection with lawsuits often find that recovering this information costs more than the computer system itself" (p. 3). There is no proven method for determining the cost-benefit of digital preservation. Even the technologies we use to determine the cost-benefits will evolve. As a result, we must project the costs as best we can, estimate the benefits and make the best choices possible, since "preservation is not an exact science, only probabilistic" (Chen, 2001, p. 5).

One method to help determine the cost-benefits of digital preservation is to establish policies based on best practices. The creation of metadata policies and standards is an important factor in determining digital preservation policy. While "short media life and obsolete hardware are factors that are beyond our control...sound metadata policies will alleviate these critical issues" (Chen, 2001, p. 4). In addition to metadata policies, Bradley

Digital Libraries in Theory and Practices

(2007) argued that we must use a sustainable approach to our digital preservation policies. Sustainability must take into account "accurate and informed risk identification and assessment, drawing on highly skilled or informed experts" (p. 159). Another factor in weighing the cost-benefits of digital preservation is making a timeline for various data. Not all data can, or should, be kept in perpetuity. Organizations and individuals should decide how long to keep digital data and when to reevaluate this decision.

Preservation policy

Digital libraries are a relatively new phenomenon. The policies that govern their actions are not yet codified. Organizers of digital libraries need to clearly articulate the policies they choose to uphold in order to state their intentions and make their work uniform. These policy statements outline preservation principles as well as the value of the work done. In the time of analog data, written preservation policies were common but many have been slow to adopt a digital policy equivalent:

> Written archives policies, spelling out what is archived and how other material is expired, were fairly common in the paper world but have gone the way of the clipping files in born-digital workflows...Even those with written statements overlooked one of the most crucial elements of a digital archives policy: the long-term expectations for problematic format. (McCargar, 2007, p. 6)

There are, of course, exceptions, and some corporations and groups, such as the DSpace Federation, have been forward thinking in their policies for digital preservation. DSpace explicitly confronts this scenario when it states, "it is an overt expectation that information assets managed by DSpace system will outlive the current system, the current implementation components with the architecture, as well as external implemented services that access and/or add value to the corpus" (Bass et al. as cited in Bradley, 2007 p. 157).

Interestingly, McCargar (2007) argued "responsibility for digital preservation, such as it is, usually lies outside the domain best equipped to deal with it--the librarians and archivist. IT departments are overwhelmingly responsible for hardware and software with other groups, including vendors and creators like photographers and artists, also having a piece" (p. 6). McCargar (2007) also stated that "best practices like a written preservation policy...tend to fell into a no-man's land between domains, and where lots of groups are assumed to have responsibility, no one has responsibility."

Some of the guidelines for digital preservation are common sense. For instance, Bollacker suggested:

> First and foremost, make regular backup copies onto easily copied media (such as hard drives) and place these copies in different locations. Try reading documents, photos and other media whenever upgrading software or hardware, and convert them to new formats if

335

needed. Lastly, if possible, print out highly important items and store them safely--there seems to be no getting away from occasionally reverting to this 'outdated' media type (2010, p. 110).

In making a preservation policy, the first step is to lay out the basic principles. A guiding philosophy, giving meaning and purpose to the enterprise, will lay the foundation for all the work to come. For most libraries, the philosophy will have something to do with the continuing need of patrons to use the materials and the usefulness of presenting those materials in a digital form. All decisions made regarding what to preserve and how to preserve it will reflect that philosophy. The need for a high level of transparency is made clear by explaining the purpose of extensive metadata that includes data regarding the provenance of the material. Measures to ensure the sustainability of the work are also among the basic principles. What efforts will the organization take that mean the information will still be available decades in the future?

Next, a cost-benefit analysis is performed. In order to best perform its duties, the organization conducting the preservation project will need to have the full support of its financial backing. To gain this, they have to convince those powers that the benefits of the work outweigh the costs. The costs for a normal digital preservation project consist of all of the resources needed to perform the task: the computers, hardware and software needed to convert items into an acceptable format, the space in which to do the work, and the staff to perform the tasks. The benefit value is derived from the value of the material preserved and its usefulness for users. Because the true value of future work is very difficult to determine, preservationists have to be careful to make only the most educated predictions. This section is as much about persuasion as it is about presenting information. The ill effects of charting a different course of action must also be considered at this point.

The most important question to answer is the agreed-upon manner in which a digital library incorporates items into its collection. There are two ways to introduce an item to a digital collection: emulation and migration (Hedstrom & Lee, 2002). Emulation is the practice of creating computer programs that mimic the workings of antiquated hardware and outdated software. A file created for an old program might be unreadable with modern equipment. An emulation program tricks the file into thinking it is running on an old system, allowing it to be read properly. The information is presented just as it would in the old system, but no extra machinery is needed and the file can exist in its original form. The other option is migration. This involves moving the significant properties of an item from one format to another. All digitization projects are a form of migration: taking the material from book form to some digital form. It can also mean conversion from one computer file format to another. Each process has its place in the digital library. Deciding which process to use in a given situation is one of the most important decisions a preservationist will have to make, so there ought to be a clear set of guidelines to follow to help make those decisions uniform across an organization.

Digital preservation projects must work on two fronts to create the most complete and secure collection possible: active and passive (Hedstrom & Lee, 2002). Passive preservation is performed every time a digital item is created, either with a born digital item or through the conversion of a physical item. Embedding the proper metadata within a digital item upon its creation does a great deal to ensure its continuing value to users. Data concerning the item's provenance, its subject content, and its creator are useful tools to keep the item in regular use by helping researchers locate the item a large collection. Protecting the item with powerful encryption keeps it safe from forces that may want to harm its integrity. The simple act of saving the digital item in an organized manner and in a secure place is an important step in loss prevention. Active preservation is the act of going back into the collection to check for any issues that may put items at risk. Regular checks and tests will help to root out problems and ensure the continued safety of the materials. Should a problem arise, files may have to be altered in some way, perhaps even converted to another format, for their protection. The preservation policy document will also describe the plan to enact both kinds of preservation. The passive policy will state what kind of data will be coupled with every item processed, while the active policy will implement a schedule for regular audits of the collection. Digital preservation policies should also provide a way to measure success and revise policies as changes in technology emerge (Horrell, 2007, p. 31).

Methods and approaches to preservation

With Doyle et. al.'s requirements of end users and the potential unreliability of magnetic and optical media, how does one go about preserving digital information? Witten, Bainbridge, and Nichols (2010) suggested five strategies: printing to paper or microfilm, preserving hardware and software in museums, duplicating content, migrating to new systems, or emulating hardware and software (p. 416).

Printing to paper or microfilm provides a hard copy of the information and may be useful if the item is printed to archival material (acid-free paper or film) and stored in a controlled environment. However, considering the sheer amount of digital information, this would be costly and time consuming. Also, how would the material be stored or cataloged?

Preserving hardware and software in a museum would definitely be a window to the past for future generations, but this method also strips away all functionality. It is interesting to see the objects, but in archives, they are not being used to access the digital information and there is also no guarantee. Similarly, one could go to a museum and look at an antique sewing machine, but that does not help one sew a pair of pants.

Witten, Bainbridge, and Nichols (2010) used the slogan "lots of copies keep stuff safe" for the content duplication strategy (p. 416). Having multiple copies of information ensures that if one becomes lost or damaged, there is another to replace it. The slogan's acronym LOCKSS, is the name of an open-source software application that helps libraries collect and preserve digital documents through a special Web crawler that verifies permissions and repairs damaged documents by matching it against others in the network and finding inconsistencies (p. 416). There is no indication that LOCKSS is hardware-specific, but steps should be taken to make sure that it does not fall prey to obsolescence.

Emulation is essentially keeping documents in their current digital form and emulating the obsolete software on which it was originally run. However, this requires copying the information to new media and checking for errors to make sure the copy is a replica of the original (Witten, Bainbridge & Nichols, 2010, p. 416-417). It is very important that any software used for the emulation strategy is open for others to build upon in order to run the obsolete software (Witten, Bainbridge & Nichols, 2010, p. 417). Those who advocate emulation say it better supports the notion of preserving an original along with its look and feel, and it can be more cost-effective than repeated transformations of digital objects. Rothenberg notes that by always operating with the original bits of a file, the "intentions of the document's creator would be better preserved by leaving the byte stream unaltered and introducing software instead to make the old formats accessible on new technologies" (Rothenberg as cited in Bradley, 2007, p. 153). Open ended problems in emulation include determining at what point in time to create the emulator, how to develop emulators including what language and platform to use, and how to deal with intellectual property rights.

According to Doyle, Viktor, and Paquet (2009), migration was the most widely used preservation strategy, but also the most criticized. It involves copying files into a new format after the previous format can no longer be viewed on hardware or software. Elaborate transformations to retain the legitimate representation of the original must be intact for further user analysis. In addition to being costly, time-consuming, and error-prone, it also compromises the integrity of the original digital object because it is no longer in its original format (p. 35). This raises questions of validity—is the item still the same item once it's been written into a new format? Emulation seems to be the best option of these preservation strategies because the behavior of the document and its content can be preserved and run on an emulator that mimics the environment of the original (Doyle, Viktor & Paquet, 2009, p. 35).

The debate between data migration and data emulation has evolved. Bradley (2007) states that "the issues of migration and emulation no longer dominate the agendas of meetings and conferences. Most people involved in making decisions about digital collections are comfortable with the notion that it will be necessary to take one approach or the other, and they are content to make that decision when the time comes" (p. 154). There is now a general consensus to keep the original bits in a file. The transformation of the file can be limited or extensive and the decision to transform or emulate can be made now or later. The discussion of "look and feel" of files has waned because "there has yet to be found a way to automate and make this information machine-readable" (Bradley, 2007, p. 154). The underlying issue in the debate between migration and emulation is permanence of access to anyone who needs the information included within the file.

There is also the use of microfilm. Archival quality microfilm is projected to last 500 years or more (Hedstrom, 1998). Paper and microfilm have an advantage in not needing frequently-changing hardware, or any software, in order to view the information stored upon them.

Collection sharing is another method of preservation. By connecting to different users' software, the collection that may have been originally processed at Boston College is now available for retrieval at Yale University. This collaboration brings down cost and maximizes efficiency. This linking enables the physical object to be at a library, and other libraries to access this same digitized material.

This brings us to the Open Archival Information System (OAIS), whose framework was created by the National Aeronautics and Space Administration (NASA). Breeding (2002a) said it is the most definitive model for long-lasting digital archives because it has strategies for dealing with changing technology and it is not wedded to any specific hardware or software. Furthermore, "it provides a comprehensive and well-accepted methodology for creating digital collections in a way that ensures permanence" and it is a good blueprint for future, permanent digital collections.

Digital libraries are an ongoing process, as the future of libraries and accessing information from everywhere expands across the globe. However, not all digital libraries are built the same. Each one is different in mission, layout, and what information has been cataloged. Not all digital libraries carry the same information because the selection process for contribution is different depending on the library's intended user. The Baseball Hall of Fame, for instance, wouldn't want information on Superman or Alan Moore's "The Watchmen."

A method that can be implemented is using a "shearing layers" model, as described in Stewart Brand's book *How Buildings Learn*. Brand's six shearing layers for buildings are Site, Structure, Skin, Services, Space and Stuff, with each of the layers being handled by an expert for that layer (Library of Congress, 2006b). These shearing layers take apart what could be constructed as an intense website, and break it down so others can collaborate. Suddenly, a very huge project has now been brought down to a different speed and look, because multiple partners have had a hand in it. This is one method that could be used, rather than just a mess of websites that have been designed to carry information.

The biggest idea to this method is long-term preservation. Digital preservation combines policies, strategies and actions to ensure access to reformatted and reborn digital content regardless of the challenges of media failure and technological change. The goal of digital preservation is the accurate rendering of authenticated content over time (ALA, 2007b, p. 2). This requires long-term maintenance, mass storage, and software for retrieval of information. Most common commercial products today provide utilities for backward compatibility and for swapping documents, databases, and more complex objects between software systems (Hedstrom, 1998).

None of these methods and approaches is standardized, but they are accepted, as well as many others in the preservation field that have not been discussed. The goal of preservation is to ensure the long-term availability of objects that may not exist anymore. Having items such as backwards-compatible hardware, or even microfilm ready for retrieval, ensures that another generation will have information from a past era.

Digital preservation challenges

Digital preservation adds a new set of challenges to the existing task of preserving a legacy of materials in traditional formats (Hedstrom, 1998). There are multiple problems and challenges in digital preservation. While there are different methods of preservation above, not every library follows those same guidelines. This lack of standardization slows library progress in the digital world. Libraries can't make sufficient headway because they do not have a collection of rules and definitions. Digital preservation is constrained by the absence of established standards, protocols, and proven methods for preserving digital information, as well as by the tendency to consider preservation issues only at the end of a project or after a sensational loss (Hedstrom, 1998).

The problem is severe because of the very short lifespan of digital information compared to printed information (DELOS, 2010). The average web site life span is between 44 days and two years (Kenney, et al., 2002). Though we may have advanced to digitize tablets the first humans wrote on, born-digital information dies without an analog counterpart. Born-digital is information that is only found online, with no analog counterpart to back up the information. Born-digital content faces extinction if we enter a Dark Digital Age.

More insidious and challenging than media deterioration is the problem of obsolescence in retrieval and playback technologies (Hedstrom, 1998). Devices, processes, and software for recording and storing information are being replaced by new products and methods on a regular three- to five-year cycle, driven primarily by market forces (Hedstrom, 1998). Digital preservation will add little value to the research process if it serves only as an alternative form of storage from which analog replicas are produced for use with conventional analytical methods (Hedstrom, 1998). Should libraries upgrade constantly, facing budgetary problems, or continue to store information on outdated hardware and software? Though new software is being developed, who will have the time or money to explore those methods? Records created in digital form and those converted retrospectively from paper or microfilm to digital form are equally vulnerable to technological obsolescence. As a consequence, digital preservation remains largely experimental and replete with the risks associated with untested methods (Hedstrom, 1998). As limited as those methods are, should libraries take the risk to further test those elements on their digital library, thus risking losing all information due to incompatibility? The Digital Preservation Europe group suggests preventing format obsolescence problem by moving the content from one format to another as each is updated. In addition to this every time you changed your software you could have kept a copy of the software with which you created the file.

Their method for preservation is a logical one, but who can easily access such old formats if suddenly the library removes the physical hardware? Hedstrom's 1998 article "Digital Preservation: a Time-Bomb for Libraries," mentions that the "technologies and methods for long-term preservation of the vast and growing store of digital information lag far behind." All these years later, the problems are eerily similar. While bits of data have come down in storage prices, the price tag is simply too high for some libraries to feasibly grasp the storage space for their own consumption.

There is also the fact that not all libraries have the money to contribute to a digital library specific for their user's needs. The multiple subject areas to contribute to in an attempt to build a digital library need to avoid any generalizations. Even if the subject area is restricted to one community of users such as humanities scholars, the digital preservation team runs the risk of overlooking or misunderstanding potential user needs (Hedstrom, 1998). Libraries can write for grants, but the money is still limited. For the more ambitious types, the digital library process is not concrete for every library, which allows for some creative working with the preservation of materials. To make digital preservation affordable to the widest possible range of organizations and individuals, equipment, media, and maintenance costs must be modest (Hedstrom, 1998).

Another challenge involves the state governments of the United States: "Each [state] government [is] increasingly producing records digitally with no methodologies for ensuring their preservation and access in the long term" (Library of Congress, 2006b). The Library of Congress does not note how many states have this particular method, and also lack the knowledge of what is preserved and what has been lost. A digital preservation movement is needed to help ensure nothing more is lost, and this process has already begun: Europe has the Digital Preservation Europe group (DPE), and America has the NDIIPP (National Digital Information Infrastructure and Preservation Program). This is the challenge for the Library of Congress and any library contemplating inclusion of digital content: In choosing what goes into digital libraries, what should and shouldn't be included? Each library is in danger of isolating a user's needs, simply because staff decided not to include an item in their collection. The importance of selection, therefore, cannot be overemphasized.

9.2: Web Archiving

Creating an archive of information found on the worldwide web is an important and increasingly urgent aspect of preservation as it pertains to digital libraries. As websites have become ever more prevalent in the delivery and dissemination of all types of information, including information that exists only in an electronic format, the need for meaningful preservation has increased (Hswe et al., 2009). From the birth of the worldwide web in 1991 through its present day status as the predominant channel of communication, the need to collect data by creating archives of web-based resources has been recognized by a wide-range of organizations (Brown, 2006).

By 2005 the world-wide web was estimated to be comprised of over 11.5 billion publicly accessible web pages, with the deep-web portion of privately held web-based information estimated to be over 500 times larger (Brown, 2006). The rate of expansion is illustrated by the size estimate from a 2002 report that estimated the size of the web at just 4 billion public pages and 550 billion privately held deep web documents (Lyman, 2002). The web is said to increase by over 7 million new pages per day since then. The enormous amount of data generated in the form of web-based information along with its highly unstable nature, specifically when compared to print and hard-copy resources, requires that great care and effort go into to creating a meaningful and useable archive in a timely and efficient manner.

Even the most stable web pages change a great deal from year to year (Kenney, et al., 2002). Once pages are gone, it may be impossible to recover them unless the effort has been made to archive them. Many organizations, such as the Internet Archive (http://www.archive.org/) in partnership with the Smithsonian Institution and the Library of Congress, are attempting to preserve the Internet as a cultural record for future researchers. Any institution can create an archive of Web sites based on its research focus.

Web archiving aims to preserve selected sets of Internet pages (Guide to Web Archiving, 2009). According to the director of the Library of Congress' National Digital Information Infrastructure and Preservation Program (NDIIPP), the estimated life span of a web site is only 44 days (Library of Congress, 2008). Knowing this allows librarians to begin the next step in digital preservation: web archiving. By replicating what a site originally looked like, a user can look back in the Internet to search the copy of the original site, which may no longer be a valid link. One group, the Internet Archive (http://www.archive.org/), is working entirely on this problem. This includes graphics, color, text, and hyperlinks the original website held. Whether or not the copied links will work in the web-archived copy depends on what the archivists want to preserve.

The archiving of all types of web resources is needed as preservation and ongoing access to cultural artifacts is cited as essential to a robust cultural landscape. The need for a historical collective memory that affects the values, traditions, and self-image of a society must be partially fulfilled by web archiving (Knutson, 2009).

As libraries continue to acquire digital content at a rapid pace through the digitization of print-based and other materials and the collection and preservation of born-digital resources, there is a growing need for archiving those materials. *Web archiving* is used to describe (1) the archiving of digitized (re-formatted) materials using the web as a repository, and (2) the archiving of the (often highly volatile) content of web pages. The American Library Association defines web archiving as digital preservation that "combines policies, strategies and actions to ensure access to reformatted and born digital content regardless of the challenges of media failure and technological change. The goal of digital preservation is the accurate rendering of authenticated content over time" (ALA, 2007b).

> "Libraries and archives are just beginning to grapple with the problem of capturing, managing, distributing, and preserving the digital material that their constituents are producing, and to effectively deal with this content requires not only new technological infrastructure but ...significant transformation of the current models of institutional scholarly content management. Preserving this digital material is one of the most challenging components... [it is] extremely varied in subject and purpose; exists in a wide range of technical formats, with and without software dependencies; arrives at different distances from the time of creation; and requires very different metadata to describe it both functionally and technically" (Smith 2005).

Policies

Digital preservation policies address documentation, specifications, and compliance. Developing and adhering to standards is an important component of a long-term digital preservation strategy for libraries and other repositories. Not only does it assure that the content will be preserved, but it will reduce costs over the long term. The curation or stewardship of digital information over time is the primary concern in developing policies, including preservation standards. Preservation standards are being developed even as they are in use, also "many participating libraries still have limited experience in data management" (Ogburn 2010). He goes so far as to describe an "imperative" in digital data management: "By the time knowledge in digital form makes its way to a safe and sustainable repository, it may be unreadable, corrupted, erased, or otherwise impossible to recover and use." Digital preservation strategies and actions must address content creation, integrity, technical specifications, and storage/maintenance in highly variable environments. An organization's commitment to preserving digital content for future use is detailed by its choice of file formats, the level of preservation, and standards for best practices.

Selection

Careful planning is essential to the success of any web archiving effort, and one aspect of planning is choosing how resources will be selected. Considering that the size of the web is 50 times larger than all the texts collected in the Library of Congress, the issue of selection must be a foremost consideration when creating and/or adding to an archive of web documents (Lyman, 2002). The enormous amount of information being distributed by web servers makes the selection of what information to preserve a difficult task (Hswe et al., 2009).

In selecting resources for archiving, the Library of Congress considers the "usefulness in serving the current or future informational needs of Congress and researchers, unique information provided, scholarly content, at risk of loss (due to ephemeral nature of web sites), and currency of the information" (Supplementary guidelines, 2008, p. 2). From this example, one can see that selection for web archiving is similar to the selection of print resources in some ways (such as evaluating the item's possible usefulness to the collection), and different in others (such as attempting to determine the risk of loss).

Other considerations can be taken into account depending on the particular organization, such as whether the web site might be needed in the future for a specific task or whether there is another way to access the content. Different types of libraries have different web archiving needs; for instance, Sweden's national library developed algorithms to capture sites created in Sweden's domain (Senserini et al., 2004). In planning how to select resources for web archiving, it might be helpful to examine some different approaches to selection: unselective, thematic, and selective.

An unselective approach aims to preserve all web sites. The drawbacks of this method are a large amount of unsorted data and a large amount of material needing storage. Some examples of the wide range of web archiving activities include: the Library of Congress archiving every tweet; the Internet Archive, whose Wayback Machine strives to maintain an archive of the entire published web; Digital Libraries; Institutional Repositories. The

Internet Archive Wayback Machine, creates archives by browsing the entire web and making a copy of all public content (Knutson, 2009).

The unselective method, exemplified by the Internet Archive, provides an objective archive of information allowing for each interconnected website to exist in context of the rest of the web. Archiving the entire web will not constrain future researchers by the boundaries of a collection policy. Despite these positive attributes, unselective web archiving tends to miss information that is not readily available on the surface and is not able to be performed quickly enough to capture all information while it exists on the web (Brown, 2006).

Others seek to create focused, selective collections archiving only a single site or subject matter. A selective collection preserves the most important contextual information by collecting resources that are specifically linked based on the criteria of selection (Brown, 2006). The thematic approach aims to preserve all sites within a predefined set of themes. The selective approach aims to preserve the material that meets a narrow set of criteria defined by the organization (Selection for web resource preservation, 2009). The deposit method, in which "publishers deposit online material based on legal or voluntary deposit codes" (Web archiving models, 2010), is still in an experimental stage. The Netherlands, for example, operates a voluntary deposit system for e-journals. Sweden has the deposit of Web resources as a legislative requirement. Most libraries will find that a combination of the first three methods will meet their needs most effectively (Web archiving models, 2010).

Once the criteria for selection have been determined, decisions should be made about the particular methods to be used in discovering pages for archiving. Extremely specific projects can incorporate manual selection (such as NASA's Goddard Space Flight Center Library, discussed in Senserini et al., 2004), but effective web archiving requires the use of crawlers. Crawlers are subject to some technical limitations, one being the massive size of the web. It can take six months to crawl the entire web, by which time some links will have become obsolete (this is also called link rot). There are also instructions that web site creators can place in their web documents that instruct crawlers not to search them. These instructions are contained in a file titled robots.txt. According to the Internet Archive Wayback Machine, most web sites do not contain such a file, and compliance with its instructions is voluntary. Nevertheless, project designers should be aware of the Standard for Robot Exclusion because depending on the software program used to crawl the web, any content instructing robots not to enter may be inaccessible.

There are other limitations that should be kept in mind when archiving web sites. Some dynamic content is impossible to archive (such as most content that uses forms or JavaScript as opposed to HTML), as is any content that needs to contact the original host server in order to work. Since robots follow links to travel the web rather than entering queries, a page will not be found if it is an "orphan," that is, if there are no links to it (Wayback Machine FAQ, n. d.).

There are two kinds of pages of interest to web archivists: hubs and targets. A hub may contain content but is primarily a portal to various targets, which are sites with content. Hubs should be considered for archiving because they record the relationships between targets at a particular point in time. Hubs can also be termed "seeds" or "entry points," because they are the initiation point for a crawler to begin searching through pages. The selection of entry points is an important step in the web archiving process, so that the likelihood of missing content relevant to the project (as well as the retrieval of too much information) is minimized. This discovery of entry points can be endogenous (from within, or automatic), via instructions contained in the crawler program's software. It can also be exogenous (from without, or manual) via the exploration of various electronic sources. After the discovery of content, the next phase filters the content so that it meets the needs set by the selection policy. This too can be automatic or manual; it is necessary to filter manually when the selection policy cannot be reliably interpreted by software.

The issue of stability is an important consideration in the selection of web resources to be archived. As content on the web can be updated, edited, or deleted altogether without any notice, the need to capture information as it exists at one moment in time is an important consideration (Masanes, 2005). Web pages have been found to have an average lifespan of 44 days illustrating the need for timely preservation before the information disappears (Lyman, 2002). The item must be archived as quickly as possible after it has been selected to be part of the collection to avoid missing any important information. Several factors contribute to determining the frequency with which a specific web resource must be archived. These include whether a site will be indefinitely updated or become fixed at some point, whether there is a typical schedule for updates, and if there is a risk for the website to shutdown because of financial or other complications. While resources such as websites with a predetermined lifespan may only need to be archived once, many others must be archived repeatedly in order to create a complete picture (Brown, 2006).

Web archiving and libraries

To librarians, the need to preserve historically important information and make it available to future generations for educational purposes is often the driving factor (Lyman, 2002). With traditional archives the decision not to include an item likely means that the physical item still exists, however, with web archives the decision not to include an item may mean that it will cease to exist completely given the volatility and rapidly changing nature of the web

(Moghaddam, 2010). This illustrates the importance and urgency involved with creating a focused selection policy.

A written selection policy acts to guard the library from falling victim to personal biases or individual penchants and provides staff with guidance in selecting appropriate resources (Biblarz et al, 2001). The selection of information is dependent on the scope and mission of the web archive being created. If tied to a larger collection, the selection policy of the web archive should be created in harmony with the collection policies of the larger collection. Selection may be based on a specific subject matter, a specific creator or organization responsible for the creation of the website, type or genre of resource such as government records or blogs, or even a single specific domain (Brown, 2006). Subject matter or topic archiving is most often motivated by research and scholarship needs. Site-specific archiving includes materials from a specific creator and is most often performed by institutions and corporate bodies. Domain specific archiving is performed based on location of the content rather than the content itself (Masanes, 2005).

Methods

Web archiving includes the selection and acquisition of information, as it exists on the web. The process of acquiring information encompasses several different techniques including direct transfers, remote harvesting, and database harvesting. Depending on the specific information needs of the web archive being created, each technique has different strengths and weaknesses, making one more useful for a specific application.

Direct transfer

Direct transfers are the simplest and most direct technique of acquiring web data to preserve. Direct transfers depend on the author organization copying relevant files and transferring them to the archive. This method is best for static websites that are easily reproducible. While this method provides for the highest degree of authenticity and completeness, there are complications involved with the direct transfer of dynamic websites. Dynamic database driven websites present some difficulty as the data often depends on a host of software and hardware in order to serve the data as originally experienced by users through the web interface. The wide diversity in different software and hardware architectures and systems make emulation of the original interface and access of dynamic content challenging (Brown, 2006).

Copying websites

To copy websites, it is necessary for the language contained within the websites to be understood by software so that it will be searchable. This is accomplished by a computer program called a parser. The parser "analyzes a text into meaningful units, according to the rules of some language syntax" (Pountain, 2003, p. 324). This can be a natural language or a programming language. There are two kinds of parsers in web copying: an HTML parser and a script parser. An HTML parser scans links and passes them to the crawler, recognizing tag names (such as "img," telling the parser that the element is an embedded image) and tag properties (such as "href," which alerts the parser that the element is a link to another location). Tags can be divided into two groups: those that allow the embedding of resources, like image tags, and those that allow navigation to another resource, such as link tags. There are also files "containing stored commands that...are often used to automate the operation of another program...by executing a sequence of commands" (Pountain, 2003, p. 387). These files are called scripts. A script parser scans these files, separates them into units, and extracts meaning.

Once the mechanics of copying websites is accomplished, the remaining decision is how often to copy sites for the purpose of archiving them. It is inefficient to repeat the entire archiving process every time a website is crawled, particularly if the site contains large files. A reasonable solution is for the crawler to access a data cache, only downloading data that was not present before. The schedule at which this is done depends on whether the particular institution's goals include archiving a site if, for example, "it includes more than 10 new files, or [whether] any change at all represents a new version that should be kept" (Dunn and Szydlowski, 2009, p. 17).

Technical metadata from the server and the crawler should be preserved in order to identify the different versions, such as the http header from the server and the date and time stamp from the crawler (Guidelines for the web archiving process, n. d.). Sites can be downloaded automatically on a schedule and stored on an external drive, allowing archival decisions to be batched, "creating a more flexible and efficient workflow" (Dunn and Szydlowski, 2009, p. 16).

Remote harvesting

Remote harvesting is a technique that involves the use of a web crawler. Web crawlers automatically traverse the web by systematically discovering new information through the hyperlinks that exist on each site they crawl. Using this technique a single crawler can acquire millions of sites automatically (Masanes, 2005). Web crawlers can be configured to follow a limited number of hyperlinks from the initial entry point. This method can be implemented quickly, gather a large amount of data, and has a relatively low cost (Brown, 2006).

Despite the strengths of web crawlers, there are a number of weaknesses that may need to be overcome depending on the intended application. The massive amount of data that can be easily acquired can also be a liability by creating a mass of data that must be evaluated to determine relevancy to the collection. The inability to access dynamic content is greatest drawback of the web crawler method. Dynamic content includes information contained in Flash objects or retrievable only though searching; crawlers fail to archive data or follow links that are generated in this way (Brown, 2006). The speed with which crawlers gather data must be considered, as they are likely to miss ephemeral sites, which only exist for a short time (Masanes, 2005).

Focused crawl

In order to utilize the positive attributes of the crawler method and minimize the negative, a technique called a focused crawl may be employed. Focused crawling begins with a set of topic descriptions with which to target. This method attempts to discover web resources of highest relevance to the list of descriptors rather than prioritizing the breadth of data acquired (Bergmark, Lagoze, & Sbityakov, 2002). Evaluation of focused crawl results could be used to target specific sections of the web to build coherent subject or theme based collections (Masanes, 2002). One potential drawback of this technique is that relevant information may be located on pages that are not directly linked but connected through seemingly off-topic pages (Bergmark, Lagoze, & Sbityakov, 2002).

Database archiving

The proliferation of dynamic web content and the failure of web crawler based technology to collect it necessitate the implementation of database archiving. Database archiving involves the use of software tools to convert the targeted database into a standard archival format to avoid the need for site specific and possibly proprietary database technology to access the archived data. The raw data is downloaded in text format and an XML document is used to store a map of the relational data model used in the original database. While this method provides a technique for archiving dynamic content in a generic and accessible format, it requires advanced knowledge of relational database design and XML to be implemented. Failing to archive the look and feel of the original source, these tools do not preserve the interface of the original site (Brown, 2006).

Twitter Archiving

For decades, if not centuries, the United States Library of Congress has been conserving written items, newspapers, pictures, movies, and even websites. After seven years, the project to create a Twitter Archive came to a standstill in late 2017. Fondren & Menard McCune (2018) highlighted the social, cultural, and symbolic challenges of institutional archiving of digital media through a textual analysis of policy papers, preservation theories, and press releases in their study, "Archiving and Preserving Social Media at the Library of Congress: Institutional and Cultural Challenges to Build a Twitter Archive."

There are an estimated 500 billion tweets sent every day, and archiving all of them would be a monumental task. Not necessarily because of the number of people required to complete it, but simply because of the amount of gear or cloud space required.

Case study: Lost websites

A 2009 article by McCown, Marshall, and Nelson explores the use of web-archives to help restore lost websites. As two percent of websites disappear from their present location each week, there exists a consistently large amount of data potentially lost each passing day. The tool explored in the article is a web-repository crawler called Warrick. The Warrick tool uses the Internet Archive and the commercially created web archives from Google, Microsoft Live (re-branded as Bing), and Yahoo to find data that has been recently lost and deleted from the web, which would severely inhibit a library's ability to store and provide access to the file. The final factor, technical protection mechanisms, concerns restrictions placed on material by its creator or owner. The Library of Congress page states that "custodians of digital content] must be able to replicate the content on new media, migrate and normalize it in the face of changing technology, and disseminate it to users" (Sustainability factors, 2007). Limiting the use of a file to a particular format, preventing the creation of backup copies, restricting use to a particular time period or hardware system, or requiring a password for use are all incompatible with the goals of preservation. Adopting some or all of these factors may assist organizations in making difficult preservation decisions.

Sustainability of hardware and software

Hardware and software are the backbone of any computerized project, especially a digital library. Hardware may include computers, scanners, digital cameras, video cameras, servers, and back-up utilities. Software allows storage, management, security, and deliverability of digital collections containing documents, photos, audio, and video. "Anyone who has ever used...a 5.25" floppy disk knows the life spans of media, hardware [and] software platforms...are notoriously short" (NISO, 2007, p. 48). Technology progresses rapidly, and guardians of digital libraries must keep abreast of changing technology to ensure that digital data can be accessed by future generations.

Aside from the sustainability of file formats, which can be aided by choosing widely adopted formats and migrating to new media in a timely fashion, there is the sustainability of the hardware used to store files. There are several kinds of computer memory in wide usage with varying estimated life spans. None have threatened the hard disk drive so far, including solid-state memory (such as flash memory) or optical disks (such as CD-ROM). According to Coughlin, Waid, and Porter (2004), "none of these technologies have been able to duplicate the momentum behind disk drive technology, and the dedicated, relentless striving for higher performance and lower cost" (p. 5). As Pinheiro, Weber and Barroso (2007) discuss, an "estimated...90 percent of all new information produced in the world is being stored on magnetic media, most of it on hard disk drives" (p. 1). The longevity of this storage medium is necessarily a concern to web archivists. The possibility of predicting disk drive failure, thus enabling preventive steps, is a study still in its early stages. Those archiving web pages should be aware of the fragility not only of media on its original storage device, but of the archived copies as well.

The storage of digital data is another important factor relating to sustainability. The amount of necessary storage space is dependent on the number of objects and the size of the files contained in the digital library. Large files require more storage space. Storage entails both online (hard drives and cyber-lockers) and offline (DVDs and back-up tapes) solutions (JISC, 2009). Environmental conditions can be unpredictable; for example, floods or fires can occur and damage digital files in storage. Digital files may also be damaged or altered—intentionally or unintentionally—by users. As the Joint Information Systems Committee cautions, "the greatest asset of digital information—the ease with which it can be copied or transferred—is paralleled by the ease with which the information can be corrupted or deleted" (JISC, 2009, conclusion section).

Preventing the loss of data due to disk failure can be accomplished in two ways: backing up data and storing it in more than one place. For example, the Internet Archive stores data not only on its hard drives, but on Quantum DLT tape drives capable of storing 600 gigabytes and lasting as long as 30 years. It also maintains collections in multiple locations (Storage and preservation, 2001).

Conclusion

As with most endeavors, the most important part of the digital preservation process is the planning stage. With a carefully constructed policy, the work of preservation is not only easier but also more accurate. The important decisions that need to be made regarding what is kept and the form in which those things are saved must be considered carefully. This will increase the likelihood of the digital library being maintained, available, useful, and accessible for years to come. Strategies and tactics for sustainability should be reevaluated and modified as necessary throughout the life of the digital library. In applying established standards and protocols of archival preservation to the web, libraries must develop policies and put into action long-term strategies for data curation, preservation, storage needs, costs, and best practices for the creation, integrity, and maintenance of web archives.

If plans are not in place to ensure the sustainability of the digital library's finances, file formats, and hardware and software, the digital library could cease to exist or become outdated and useless. Then all of the time, effort, and money spent to create it would have been spent in vain. Having a framework to help digital preservationists make correct and uniform decisions is necessary for the creation of a lasting digital library. To prevent a Digital Dark Age, the ideas of preservation need to be organized and thoughtfully planned. Standardizing what the library feels should be preserved online, and how to access the material, further promotes collaboration. As more and more of the human record is produced and stored digitally, preservation is becoming more vital to every library in the world.

Study questions for Chapter Nine:

1. There are many barriers to global collaboration on digital libraries among different countries. This article discusses those barriers: Toward a Global Digital Library: Generalizing US-Korea Collaboration on Digital Libraries by Fox, E., Moore R., Larsen, R., Myaeng, S., Sung-Hyuk Kim. S.-H., (2002), published in, D-Lib Magazine, October 2002, vol. 8, no.10. Accessed 5 November 2004 at http://www.dlib.org/dlib/october02/fox/10fox.html. What are the challenges and issues to Global Digital Library Collaborations, such as collection infrastructure issues, architecture issues, policy issues, technological challenges, and multilingual challenges? Provide examples from relevant readings, personal knowledge, or examples from the most current literature on the Web to support your arguments.

2. Borgman states: "One of the promises of a global information infrastructure is for individuals to have direct access to information resources located anywhere on the network, so that they can see and use information on their own and can create new resources for others to use." On a global scale how do we deal with giving access? Do we allow free access to all digital libraries? For example, some museums you need to pay to see their collections when you actually go to the museum, should you pay to see their digital collections online? Should EVERYONE have access to all digital library collections?

Chapter Ten: Management and Evaluation

Many believe that the quality of a digital library, including its effectiveness and usefulness, cannot be ensured until after an evaluation is carefully conducted. Both management and evaluation are important components of digital library development. The knowledge and skills of DL management and evaluation should be useful for building your own digital library, as well as for assessing the digital libraries you review and/or encounter.

10.1: Project management

Creating a digital collection project takes more than assigning the project to a willing staff member and hoping it all turns out well in the end. For a project to be successful, it must accomplish set goals by a defined date using the resources (time, people, funds) available. Project development occurs in six stages: 1) Identifying; 2) Planning; 3) Implementing; 4) Managing; 5) Achieving; and 6) Maintaining.

Identifying

In stage one, identifying, the group sponsoring the project must a) analyze the purpose and need for the collection to be digitally available; b) consider the resources needed to achieve the purpose; and c) determine alternative ways of achieving the purposes set out for the project, if necessary. Some of the questions that need to be explored are: what opportunity or need will this collection fill? What will be the benefits of the completed project? Who will benefit from the completed project? What are the consequences if the project is not done?

At this point, the group sponsoring the project needs to come to terms with how well the project aligns with the mission and focus of the organization and with the organization's current strategic goals and performance measure. Then, a strategic value needs to be determined for the project's potential benefits. The project needs to be prioritized based on its strategic value, and the organizers should develop a definition of what constitutes success of the project in terms of the organization's strategic goals. Without this alignment, the project is in danger of being classified as of high importance or urgency without the appropriate resources being allocated or the appropriate measure of outcome when the project is deemed complete.

The organization also needs to conduct a needs assessment in terms of what is needed to accomplish the project. Some questions to consider are: What do we need to know? From where or from whom do we obtain this information? How do we go about obtaining this information: data mining, focus groups, and questionnaires?

The organization should include a stakeholder analysis within the needs analysis. Who has an interest in this project and how are they affected by the project's objectives? Who can influence the project? What are each stakeholder's interests and how are these interests going to be addressed by this project?

Planning

Once the organization commits to going forward with project, it is time to begin planning. Here, the sponsoring group needs to clarify project objectives and develop a sequence of activities or actions needed to achieve the project's intended purpose. Decisions need to be made as to who will be responsible for each action item in the sequence. Specific and realistic budgets (for funding and staff allocations of time) need to be drafted. A project manager needs to be appointed and made responsible for overseeing the successful running of the project.

Before the project is turned over to the project manager, the organization needs to take another look at the goals and plans to assess if the project is worthwhile, at this point, and what the organization and its constituents stand to gain from this investment of resources. The organization needs to understand and acknowledge that once the project is undertaken, the project manager will need to continually assess its progress and make decisions about the balance between what can be achieved and the resources available to accomplish it.

Implementing

In stage three, implementing, the planned project is carried out. During the implementation stage, information is collected to monitor how activities are proceeding, and to identify any problems that were encountered and how they were resolved. The activities during the implementing stage must be documented continually with periodic reports prepared to keep constituents informed on the progress.

Managing

In stage four, managing, the project is continually monitored and assessed against the original plan, goals, and objectives. Two considerations that must be planned in advance are 1) the mechanisms that will be used to effectively monitor the activities, and 2) the data or information that needs to be collected (and their sources) to document and assess the activities. Communication is a key element in managing a project; therefore, good communication skills, both oral and written, are essential.

Good communication begins from the perspective of those to whom the communication will be directed: how do they best receive and understand information? It may be helpful to understand the communication style of each person involved in the project, including the manager. One test, the Communications Style Inventory found at http://occonline.occ.cccd.edu/online/klee/CommunicationsStyleInventory.pdf (from The Platinum Rule by Tony Alessandra, Ph.D. and Michael J. O'Connor Ph.D., New York, New York, Warner Brooks 1996) identifies each person as one of these four types of communicators: Controller/Director, Promoter/Socializer, Supporter/Relater, or Analyzer/Thinker.

It may also be helpful to understand the learning style of each person involved in the project, including the manager. Another test, the Index of Learning Styles Questionnaire—found at http://www.engr.ncsu.edu/learningstyles/ilsweb.html (from Barbara A. Soloman and Richard M. Felder, North Carolina State University), identifies each person as one of these four scales of learners: active/reflective, sensing/intuitive, visual/verbal, and sequential/global. Soloman and Felder also include suggestions on how learners can assist themselves, based on their learning styles.

Put together, the communication and learning styles for each project member will provide a good roadmap for the kinds of communication needed for effective management of the project.

Achieving

In stage five, achieving, the strategic objectives have been attained and the objectives of the project have been achieved. An evaluation needs to be conducted to assess what was learned about the process (which will assist in planning and managing future projects), the impact of the completed project on the organization and user base, and the sustainability of the project now that it is considered completed. At this point those who have participated in the project should be given recognition for their work and achievements.

Maintaining

Few completed projects can be declared finished and sit on a shelf unattended. In stage six, maintaining, a staff member or team of staff members needs to be responsible for maintaining a review and update schedule, hopefully already drafted during the planning and implementing stages. During periodic reviews, the purpose and philosophy of the project are assessed through user satisfaction data to determine if established user outcomes are being met.

Access management

An important issue to consider when creating or reviewing a digital library is access management. For starters, from a management perspective, you must decide whether this library is open to the public for viewing only or, like a wiki, the public can make changes to the content. A library may also restrict access to only individuals within a specific institution or organization. If access is open to the public for viewing, but not for making changes, then you must decide who will be allowed to change the content and how these people will have editing access to the library.

If the digital library has restricted access, this means that the content is only available to specific users, such as the employees at a particular company, the students enrolled in a school, or even the students enrolled in a particular course at a school. In this case you need to decide how these specific people can view the content and who will have control over user names and passwords. A manager also must decide whether users should be able to access the library from any computer or just from computer terminals at a specific site. For example, will a clerk in a law library have to access a case file that is part of a digital library from an office computer or can she also have access from her home computer?

The conclusions of a 1996 workshop on digital library management indicate that users must be consulted in the creation and testing of a digital library because their attitude is crucial to its success (Arms, 1999). It ought to be kept in mind that if the library is too difficult to access, patrons will not use it.

10.2: Evaluation and evaluation studies

Another important issue to consider is evaluation of the digital library. Once a digital library is built, will anyone use it? And will anyone check if it is used and why it is or is not used? It is essential that a digital library meet the needs of its users. What users are looking for and whether your digital library can satisfy the user needs has to be addressed by serious investigations. Usability is a hot study topic in digital library research. The interested parties include information professionals, system programmers, computer technology experts and decision-makers across borders. Many approaches have been explored on digital library or website usability toward the system and program evolution.

Digital Libraries Evaluation-What should we evaluate?

What are some challenges for the evaluation of digital libraries?

First, we need to know, what is evaluation? An evaluation can be a study of questions about performance. The purpose usually is to test, validate, compare, and/or appraise operations to gain insight into the system's behavior and quality. There are many approaches and types of measurements for evaluation. Before conducting an evaluation, one needs to make a choice. For example, for a system approach, the evaluation usually should focus on the system's effectiveness: how well does a system, or part, perform that for which it was designed; and efficiency: at what cost, time, and effort.

What should be covered by digital library evaluation? Evaluations may cover:

- Collection policy and selection criteria
- Organization of collection
- Metadata tools
- Resources and process procedures
- Service scope
- Accessibility and usability, including search features
- Multilingual capabilities
- Source updating currency
- Interface design
- System technologies
- Connection and interoperability
- Security and legality, and
- Management and maintenance.

The digital library evaluation is an important research area, many projects, workshops and discussions have devoted to it.

The Fourth DELOS Workshop: Evaluation of Digital Libraries: Testbeds, Measurements, and Metrics was held on 6-7 June 2002 in Budapest, Hungary, and "aim[ed] at providing a Digital Library Evaluation Forum and a Digital Library Test Suite which will provide researchers with information for the selection of potential digital library testbeds and new research or evaluation targets." Detailed information can be seen at http://www.sztaki.hu/conferences/deval/.

D-Lib Working Group on Digital Library Metrics "is aimed at developing a consensus on an appropriate set of metrics to evaluate and compare the effectiveness of digital libraries and component technologies in a distributed environment. Initial emphasis will be on (a) information discovery with a human in the loop, and (b) retrieval in a heterogeneous world." Detailed information can be seen at http://www.dlib.org/metrics/public/, including proposed overall definitions, frameworks, criteria, standards as well as scenarios have been significant in this study area.

Although many evaluations have been focusing on the six digital library research projects established in Digital library Initiative I (1994-1998), the project results as a whole have not been evaluated, and there is not a full report on what they have actually accomplished. Current interest in digital library evaluation is centered on those projects founded in Digital library Initiative II (1999-2004), which include 36 digital library projects. Half of these projects mentioned in the literature have been evaluated to some extent, but again, there are no detailed results on evaluation as a whole on all these projects. The current state of digital library evaluation seems insufficient to justify action and is still in the beginning stage of development.

What do we need that is lacking in the current practice of digital library evaluation?

Based on the information from the workshops and discussions mentioned above, objectives of the current evaluation research that researchers suggested and should be required for conducting a digital library evaluation include:

1. Establishing an overall conceptual framework to study what construct a digital library, its objects and elements to be evaluated.
2. Clarifying the evaluation approach, to determine what its context is? What approach should be used, and what to concentrate on?
3. Setting up criteria for evaluation, to explore what to evaluate in that context, what to reflect, and what parameters and metrics to select for evaluation.
4. Building a set of procedures, to determine what measures you can apply to various criteria.
5. Choosing appropriate research methods and procedures that can be properly used in the evaluation.

The above objectives should also be elements required for conducting a digital library evaluation.

Conceptually, a digital library includes two systems. One is the operational system, including digitized objects in various forms, organization and representation of the digital objects/collections, software and hardware technologies, interoperability and distributed access and services. Another is the organization system, which includes personnel and institutions that manage the operational system.

Operationally, a digital library evaluation can be performed from two different angles. From a research perspective, the focus of the evaluation could be a range of research problems around the operational system, digital and distributed objects.

The concept supporting the research perspective could be one Lesk stated. "Digital libraries are organized collections of digital information. They combine the structuring and gathering of information, which libraries and archives have always done, with the digital representation that computers have made possible" (1977). From a library management perspective, the focus could be on the practical problems of transforming library institutions and services.

The concept supporting the evaluation from library management perspective could be one from the Digital Libraries Federation (DLF) website: "Digital libraries are organizations that provide the resources, including the specialized staff, to select, structure, offer intellectual access to, interpret, distribute, preserve the integrity of, and ensure the persistence over time of collections of digital works so that they are readily and economically available for use by a defined community or set of communities." (2002)

Two concentrations on digital library evaluation are use-oriented and system-oriented evaluation.

A use-oriented evaluation would study the social aspects of the evaluated digital library, including use, users, and activities of the digital library. Research questions should deal with how well the digital libraries support their users' information demands, community needs and activities, and how well digital libraries support their institutional and organizational mission and objectives.

A system-oriented evaluation should study the digital objects, interface, and technological issues. Research questions should consider how well the given interface provides access, how well the hardware, networks, and configurations perform, how well procedures, techniques, operations, algorithms, and search engines work, how well the collection is selected, organized, structured, represented, preserved and retrieved, and finally if the technology used has resulted in a user-friendly design.

A combination of both user and system-oriented evaluation should study both users and the system. Research questions could include:

- How well does the digital library support the activities of the users?
- How well do the hardware, network and interface work for the average user?
- Is the content organized in a useable way?
- Is the technology used for the DL appropriate for the content?
- Does the DL have a storage method that creates archives and preserves the document?
- Can the data be transferred to a new format from time to time as technology improves?

Accessibility

Bishop summarizes the literature on accessibility by stating "accessibility of an information resource is widely accepted as a primary determinant of the extent of its use" (Baker and Lancaster 1991, 27-38; Lancaster 1995b). Poole (1985) did a meta-analysis of empirical work on the relationship of accessibility to use and found that the propositions on information use most commonly validated in empirical studies were that information-channel use is a function of channel accessibility, perceived cost, and user awareness (119-122).

Accessibility of information resources is usually assumed to depend on a range of cognitive, social, and physical factors, such as whether a person is aware of a resource, has the knowledge and skills needed to access it, and has the resource close at hand. Peterson (1998) explored dimensions of accessibility and, in analyzing people's perceptions of physical access to information resources in different venues, equated the ability to enter a library with the ability to gain access to a computer system. In addition to the availability of a working system, however, people need special knowledge about how to use computer-based information systems. Borgman (1996) concludes that online public-access information-retrieval systems are hard for people to use because they require a combination of basic computing skills and knowledge of how to formulate and execute searches. (1998)

Evaluation Examples

A digital library may contain valuable information but be organized so poorly that few take the time to see if it might be useful to them. And so the question becomes, how do digital library managers evaluate digital libraries? Cullen (2003) lists the evaluation methods of academic librarians. She writes:

> A recent survey of libraries in the higher education sector in the UK conducted by the eVALUEd Project 20 showed library managers employing a wide range of methods to evaluate their electronic information services. The most-used evaluation methods included: management information data (usage/transaction logs); online feedback (queries and comments); questionnaires (when printed and online are combined this is the most-used method); observations; cost-benefit analysis; and printed feedback (general). Considerably less widely used were: focus groups; interviews; and other less-well-established approaches to evaluation such as monitoring workflow, impact analysis, and document analysis. Cullen, 2003)

Judy Jeng, a Ph.D. candidate at the School of Communication, Information, and Library Studies at Rutgers University, takes a more holistic approach to digital library evaluation. Jeng (2005) wrote about the concept of measuring usability as a means of evaluating digital libraries, explaining usability: "The term usability has been used broadly and means different things to different people. Some relate usability to ease of use and consider from an interface effectiveness point-of-view. This view makes sense, as usability has theoretical base on human-computer interaction." She lists usability evaluation methods, such as, "formal usability testing; usability inspection; card sort; category membership expectation; focus groups; questionnaires; think-aloud; analysis of site usage logs; cognitive walkthrough; heuristic evaluation; claims analysis; concept-based analysis of surface and structural misfits (CASSM); and paper prototyping" (Jeng, 2005). She also describes the usability evaluation methods of digital library collections from the following ten universities and scientific organizations.

The National Taiwan University Library used questionnaires to survey 1,784 users on usability (Lan, 2001). The study of CUNY+ (Oulanov and Pajarillo 2002) also employed a questionnaire as the primary method of usability assessment. The authors conducted a two-phase study to compare usability of text-based and Web-based CUNY Web sites. Adams and Blandford (2002) reported on their study of accessibility on a large London-based hospital. They conducted focus groups and in-depth interviews with seventy-three hospital clinicians.

Theng, Mohd-Nasir, and Thimbleby (2000a) utilized questionnaires and heuristic evaluation to measure usability of the ACM Digital Library, the Networked Computer Science Technical Reference Library, and the New Zealand Digital Library.

Sumner et al. (2003) again used DLESE to study usability in addition to National Science Digital Library (NSDL). The purpose of this study was to identify educators' expectations and requirements for the design of educational digital collections for classroom use. A series of five focus groups was conducted with a total of thirty-six teachers and two librarians to review eighteen Web sites.

The evaluation of the University of Illinois DeLIver service applied a mix of methods, including transaction log analysis, surveys, interviews, focus groups, and formal usability testing to measure accessibility (Bishop 2001; Neumann and Bishop 1998).

The University of Arizona Library applied a number of methods to evaluate the usability of the library Web site, SABIO, including heuristic evaluation, walk-through, card sorting, and formal usability testing (Dickstein and Mills 2000).

Dorward, Reinke, and Recker (2002) evaluated Instructional Architect, which aims to increase the utility of NSDL resources for classroom teachers. The methods they employed included formal usability testing and focus groups.

University of the Pacific applied the formal usability testing technique to measure students' awareness of library resources (Krueger, Ray, and Knight 2004). They recruited 134 students to perform eight tasks, including locating an article, locating a journal, finding call number of a book, finding overdue information, finding a biography, and how to connect from home.

Usability Evaluation Methods

When taking a comprehensive evaluative approach, one that considers usability and multiple evaluation methods, information is gathered that can be useful to digital library managers in the long term. The most common usability evaluation methods utilized at the universities and scientific organizations studied by Jeng were questionnaires, focus groups, interviews, and formal usability tests.

Jeng conducted another study in 2008 to evaluate the usefulness of the New Jersey Digital Highway and its portal structure. Jeng defines the project and her evaluation methods: "The NJDH intends to provide an immersive and user-centered portal for New Jersey history and culture. The research recruited 145 participants and used a Web-based questionnaire that contained three sections: for everyone, for educators, and or curators. The feedback on the usefulness of the NJDH was positive and the portal structure was favorable" (2008). Using her comprehensive usability evaluation methods, Jeng was able to collect information that was valuable to the management of the NJDH for the long term and that affected the organization of the digital library: "After eighteen months of the study, the NJDH Governance Planning Committee still uses the evaluation report to address more complex and fundamental changes and the reorganization of the digital library."

What about the problems with digital library evaluation methods? What if the digital library managers don't have the time or money to conduct studies using a comprehensive approach? What if the digital library managers don't have access to digital library software evaluation tools? If the digital library managers don't have access to software tools that report and analyze performance, they rely on the information that they are provided, which sometimes is biased information from vendors.

For example, in 2002, academic librarians in the United Kingdom claimed that they lacked the tools to evaluate digital library services. A 24-month initiative was developed, the eVALUEd Project, sponsored in part by the Higher Education Funding Council for England. Twenty academic librarians completed preliminary questionnaires about how they evaluated digital libraries. These questionnaires revealed that the librarians relied on vendor usage statistics to evaluate the digital libraries followed by questionnaires, database trials, and focus groups. This strategy may be flawed, as "there are problems with vendor usage statistics. The librarians said that data—what is collected, how it is collected, and how it is reported--vary widely among vendors. Lack of time and money to conduct evaluations was also cited" (Albanese, 2003).

The company Outsell conducted a study in the United States similar to the preliminary eVALUEd Project questionnaires and found that "American academic librarians relied most often on user statistics (83%), user testimonies (57%), or ad hoc interviews (56%) for evaluation" (Albanese, 2003). For academic librarians looking to save time and money, the answer might be a more business-like approach to evaluation. Albanese (2003) describes the possible evaluation solutions of the eVALUEd Project: "Business assessments are an aim of the eVALUEd Project and include creating tools for benchmarking and cost-benefit analysis, collecting usage information, and performing online analyses." New software tools that report and analyze performance will hopefully provide digital library managers with more useful tools to evaluate their services and collections when more comprehensive usability evaluation methods are not feasible.

Different types of libraries (public, academic, school or special) require different evaluation methods. More comprehensive usability methods (numerous and more in-depth methods) render information that is valuable to the digital library managers in the long term. Software is available to report and analyze the performance of digital libraries. When deciding on the methods that will be used to evaluate digital libraries, it is important to consider the type of changes that the digital managers are ready to make (small or drastic, change for the short or long term), and how much time and money are available for the evaluations (time to conduct studies and money to buy software).

Evaluation is one of the more important components of a project, and yet it is the one frequently overlooked. Evaluations should be an ongoing process, following every step of the project, yet a more common practice is to leave them to the end, when most projects are out of money, manpower, and enthusiasm. Evaluations should be continuous so that the effectiveness of the system can be tested and fine-tuned.

10.3: Bibliometrics & Webometrics

Bibliometrics is the measurement of properties in documents, with an expanded definition to cover the properties of digital documents, including usage statistics. In the past bibliometrics was used to determine information about print documents, but today is also used for digital libraries. In fact, the growth of digital libraries took the field into the direction of measuring usage: "Perhaps the most significant challenge for bibliometrics in the long run is that the new digital libraries are producing large-scale evidence of the usage patterns of academic articles for the first time" (Thelwell, 2008). Technological advances have enabled the determination of not only how often an item is accessed but also the amount of time spent on a site and whether it is cited in some other work. As the study of bibliometrics and digital libraries develops and the range of tasks increases, it could pull even more information about usage and the type of usage.

Webometrics is an offshoot of bibliometrics involving statistics about links, the effectiveness of search engines and general use of the web. It has expanded from a computer science-based field into more of a social sciences based field. For example, link analysis deals with how often a link is accessed from a web page or site. Search engines are evaluated for how much web content they actually search in response to a query and whether the results are what the user wanted. With the web containing everything from scholarly documents to trash, it has made the webometrics field more complicated. But because it is such a young field, these complications may be solved with time. Through webometrics one can determine the importance and usage of their digital library.

10.4: Cost/economic issues

Physical libraries are faced with the challenge of paying for digital libraries, whether it be setting them up, managing them or maintaining them. Digital libraries offer an alternative to print formats that are becoming more expensive to publish such as scholarly journals, which are becoming more expensive to publish, (Lesk, 2005). Various print sources are on a never-ending cycle of cost and demand. As the cost to publish print materials increase, purchase cost increases, which often results in a decrease in sales, which increases publication costs, and so on.

Digital libraries involve several potential cost factors including administrative costs, digitization/conversion, maintenance, cataloging, and other fees. Libraries may not own the content of digital libraries in the same way they owned their physical books and may have to pay license fees for their digital items. This means that unlike a one-time purchase, as in the case of physical books, digital libraries may have to pay ongoing fees for continued access to material.

Much of the budgetary concerns surrounding digital library costs tend to revolve around collections development, specifically in the move to digitally house e-journals and e-books and push away from physical sources. For the public library, this includes the use of downloadable books in mp3 format, whereas in academic institutions, studies have found that most users prefer e-journal to e-book formats. In his article, *Inside Every Fat Man: Balancing the Digital Library Budget*, David Baker (2008) makes note of the preference given to student usage of e-journals as compared to e-books and writes of students' preference to the journals' "ease-of-use" as compared to their hardcopy counterparts. Similarly, Gregory A Crawford (1999) writes in his piece, *Issues for the Digital Library*, on the apparentness of libraries no longer being able to afford their development of print based collections. More and more institutions are making the move to archive their sources electronically, from books and journals to rare book collections. Jackie Dooley (2009) addresses the digitization of rare books specifically in her article, *Ten Commandments for Special Libraries in the Digital Age*. Dooley (2009) finds digitization of rare book collections necessary, as users increasingly want remote access to such materials. Dooley (2009) states that such advances in technology are "nothing new," and suggests that from the stone clay tablet to the scroll and the codex, libraries have always worked with the innovation of information to provide more accessibility and to consume less space, citing that such changes "resulted in improvements in both the accessibility of rare materials and the economic sustainability of the production enterprise."

Baker (2008) makes note that "detailed comparisons of the cost of providing e-resources suggest that they cost less than paper when all the relative costs are taken into account, and that the relative cost of e-resources is falling." Furthermore, Baker (2008) cites publisher resistance in the licensing of core e-books in libraries as one of the reasons the United Kingdom established the national Joint Information Systems Committee's (JISC) e-book observation project. In the United Staes, Kate Thomes (2002) discusses the ongoing issue of e-serials purchasing after attending a conference in Ann Arbor Michigan. Thomes (2002) suggests a growing awareness in users who want collections of articles rather than journal collections. Looking at the findings of studies from usage patterns and the PEAK project studying title pricing and subscription models, Thomes is able to ascertain which journal articles are repeatedly used as well as how many books were downloaded and the number of times an item was checked out of the library:

> Looking to Mark McCabe's economist view during the conference, Thomes (2002) found that, as commercial publishers analyzed the demand structure of libraries, they came to understand the profitability of acquiring more titles through mergers. As a few publishers gained greater market power they were able to increase the price of individual titles within the portfolios they had to offer.

Thomes (2002) further cites McCabe's three factors, inelasticity of demand, library acquisition by portfolio within broad subject areas, and publisher mergers, as cause of a higher a rate of "journal price inflation, and that this can be explained by the improved quality or increased publishing costs of journals themselves" (Thomes, 2002). She emphasizes that "libraries must communicate the actual costs of digitizing collections to a wider audience" and that "digitalization must be understood not as a cost saver but as a value-added service." Still, when faced with the decision in e-serial purchasing, Crawford (1999) echoes Thomes' notion of purchasing based on user statistics. Crawford (1999) explains that paying for a subscription or unlimited use may not always prove "economically justifiable." "For example," Crawford (1999) writes, "if a database will receive very limited use, it may be more economical to pay only for the actual searches or online time..."

Equally as important as a digital library's collections development is its reference service. R. David Lankes, Melissa Gross, and Charles R. McClure (2003) explore the budgetary and standards concerns of online referencing in their article, *Cost, Statistics, Measures, and Standards for Digital Reference Services: A Preliminary View*. In their piece, Lankes et al. (2003) focus on two key points of online referencing: 1) utilization of the service being provided, and 2) its technical aspects, such as hardware, software and soft tools, including metadata and organizational scheme. Lankes et al (2003) explain that online referencing may lead to a more precise cost analysis as its documentation trail can easily be examined. The authors cite that it is here in which a strong connection between the e-references utilization and technical standards become important (Lankers et al, 2003). They write:

> "If technical standards record the cost of individual reference interactions, then digital reference software can easily report total cost of service with little or no data gathering on the part of the organization." (Lankers et al, 2003)

By looking to a sessions XML or URL, the authors claim that online referencing services can save the significant time and tedium "of trolling through transcripts and/or e-mail records" (Lankers et al. 2003). The authors also predict that although the current online reference software market has been created without a set of technical standards, a minimal threshold will need to be established. They cite for now that the online referencing software market currently consists of real-time vendors, e-mail solutions, and home-grown solutions. They further state, "Since this software market has developed in the absence of technical standards, any introduction and adoption of standards will force new costs in software development and migration of internal data representations to a new standard" be it minimal or substantial (Lankers et al, 2003).

Administrative cost

Administrative costs may be the most difficult to determine. Administrative costs include obtaining copyright permissions, which not only involves the actual fee to get copyright permissions, but the time and effort it may take to locate the copyright holder (Lee, 2001). Obtaining copyright permission can be very difficult. Copyright holders may be difficult to find, may not respond to requests in a timely manner, may desire so much control of the copyright that the price is outrageous, or may narrowly limit how the work may be used (Lesk, 2005). One option to keep these costs to a minimum is to go through a clearinghouse such as ASCAP (the American Society of Composers, Authors, and Publishers), BMI (Broadcast Music, Inc.) or the Copyright Clearance Center (Lesk, 2005).

Digitization costs

Digitization costs involve the cost of creating the digital files (Lee, 2001). There are two ways that digital files can be created: in-house or outsourcing. The in-house cost includes the hardware, software, and staff needed for the conversion. Out-sourcing is using a conversion vendor. Both involve careful evaluation of what is to be converted, the preparation needed for the conversion, the desired quality of the file, and the time involved (Lee, 2001).

Funding

As with physical libraries, digital libraries need to examine funding options. The nature of the digital library may dictate what manner of funding is available. The first step is to establish if the digital library would be eligible for a grant to offset some of the costs involved. Local, national, and subject specific grants are available. Seeking institutional support is another viable option, depending on the nature of the digital library.

Two of the most difficult funding decisions to make are whether to use advertisers and whether to charge users. Both could have adverse consequences to the use of the digital library. Advertisers would help offset the costs of a digital library; however, digital library users, who may find them distracting, often view advertisements negatively. The option of charging users could be a delicate one to choose. Again, the nature of the digital library would have a significant impact on the decision to charge.

There are two options for charging users: 1) fees could be charged for selected services or specific products, or 2) the library could charge for everything (Lee, 2001). The value of the digital library would be a factor in whether or not users would be willing to pay. Another factor would be the fee amount. The amount would need to be affordable for the users while still providing the necessary funding to cover expenses.

Price negotiations with vendors are important in this regard and thus the possibility of entering a consortium of libraries that can bargain for fair prices is an important consideration for a digital library.

As digital libraries are evaluated, managers may find the need to hire technical consultants to set up a system to monitor usage of a digital library and decide whether it is being used enough to justify the cost: "The bottom line to most libraries will be the cost associated with the acquisition and management of electronic resources" (Koehn, 2010). In a study at the Tulsa City-County Library, the cost-per-search was used to evaluate whether a database was worth its cost, but a library would have to decide whether this is the best measure for a resource's value. License fees and many other costs, such as staffing and maintenance, make cost/benefit analysis studies crucial for digital libraries.

10.5: Social Issues

The social issues with the management and evaluation of digital libraries are not easily separated from other areas. Societal information needs are met by different sources; therefore, there are many different types of physical libraries with different types of materials. These different physical libraries each serve a specific clientele. As with these physical libraries, digital libraries also serve specific clientele with specific needs, thereby creating the need for a variety of digital libraries. There are many issues that affect the digital library's role in society.

Some of the social issues already discussed include ensuring intellectual property rights and the myriad cost factors. Copyright compliance can be time-consuming and costly depending on the copyright holder. Additional cost factors such as conversion and maintenance fees also could be expensive, depending on how much material is included in the digital library.

Another social issue involved is determining the clientele and their needs. A digital library may be created with a specific clientele in mind, only to find out that a different set of clienteles is using the digital library and not all their needs are being met. Determining the clientele is difficult for a digital library since they could include members from around the world. An evaluation of the digital library's purpose needs to be made not only from a local perspective but also from a global perspective. If the digital library has potential users from other countries, then language translation needs to be addressed in the digital library. In addition to language awareness, there also needs to be an awareness of the cultural and ethical viewpoints of the digital libraries. In a global community, local bias must be avoided which would offend potential users.

As technology plays an increasing role in the world of information services, it is only natural that it will have a large societal impact on the way users perceive, access and dismantle information, as well as the types of resources users' access. In providing service to such a demographic, Crawford (1999) states that "since patrons want access to whatever information they need--whenever they need it, and wherever they need it" that "the concepts of access, place, and time become very important." John A Shuler (2004) writes on the growing concern of the quality of information retrieved by users who want access to information at ever increasing rates. Baker (2008) also alludes to the "dumbing down" of students who use "marginally relevant electronic resources." In terms of government information, Shuler (2004) writes, "…many depositories are sliding from being active collections of vital government information and into archives of an earlier technology." He suggests that "librarians need to worry less about individual government information sources and more about the processes/policies that lead to their creation and frame their relationships" (Shuler, 2004).

Julie Hersberger (2002) explores how lack of access may lead to a lack of information for underserved populations. In her article, *Are the Economically Poor Information Poor? Does the Digital Divide Affect the Homeless and Access to Information?* Hersberger (2002) found that although information is increasingly being added to and accessed by means of the Internet, according to a study by Amanda Lenhart, many homeless reports that "they are not missing out anything." Hersberger (2002) also found that some Americans are "opting out" of using the Internet all together. She explains that most homeless individuals find out about resources from social service agency staff members and although some agencies do have information found on the web, many in this underserved population find such information by means of case workers or other personnel. Furthermore, due to the demand for aid, some non-profit agencies, mostly local, attempt to not "overly publicize availability of resources in fear of being overrun with requests" (Hersberger, 2002). Still, as she writes in her findings, many did state that their children are learning to use computers at school, and Hersberger estimates that there may be a higher demand for technologies among future homeless populations as the globe becomes increasingly "computer-literate". For now, many consider Internet access to be a luxury though not a necessity (Hersberg, 2002).

How a digital library is managed, whether it is can be accessed by all or requires some sort of membership will determine who has use of it. The need for a computer with Internet access also determines who can use it, possibly keeping the information away from someone who cannot afford a computer. Additionally, if such a person can get access through a public library, he is still restricted to having access only during library hours when there is a computer available and for only the length of time allowed. The digital divide, the gap between people who can afford access to a digital environment and those who can't, is particularly acute when it comes to digital libraries.

In their piece, *The Unseen and Unacceptable Face of Digital Libraries*, Anne Adams and Ann Blandford (2004) find that in certain medical establishments, power struggles exist among clinicians and other staff members in regard to access of information within the institution's digital library reserve. Adams et al. (2004) explain that "many senior staff members perceived DLs stored on an intranet and accessed by junior staff as less politically sensitive than web-accessible DLs." The article finds that while nursing staff, students in particular, find DLs to be empowering, senior clinicians question the junior staff members' ability to interpret the quality of the potential information available through use of the Internet (Adams et al, 2004). Adams et al (2004) cite interaction between training and social status as a major impact in DL awareness, writing that, "ultimately, DLs must be designed carefully to reflect [organizational] social structure needs" (Adams et al, 2004). They emphasize the need in facilitating two key principals in doing so:

> (1) DL users require more communication support (i.e., for collaboration and consultation) in their information searching and usage activities and (2) the importance of social context must be understood in DL design and implementation (Adams et al, 2004).

Crawford (1999) writes that

> Determining the needs of library users can be as simple as asking patrons what they think they need. Or it can be as complicated as doing research on the usage of current systems; analyzing assignments for which library information is sought; examining

interlibrary loan records; or doing content analyses of previous papers, reports, etc., that resulted from library research.

Crawford (1999) further writes that "training has become a major issue," citing the variety of interfaces that the librarian must be familiar with both within the library and on the web. Knowing the social background of the clients being served is also critical, as demonstrated by Adams et al (2004). In serving the public, it may be beneficial for even a digital library to have multiple ways to contact librarians associated with the digital library. These aforementioned considerations must be taken into account in order to meet the needs of users from a variety of social backgrounds.

The digital library environment also raises new issues in terms of social interaction. While a digital environment may lessen the effectiveness of interaction between librarians and users, as well as between users themselves, this need not be the case. Indeed, digital libraries mean that librarians and users are physically separated across sometimes very wide spaces. But users nonetheless value online communication. Kraut (2002) reveals that "surveys of the general public continually reveal that most people using the Internet value electronic mail and other forms of online social interaction. Even in the age of the Web and electronic commerce, online social interaction is still the most important use of the Internet."

The environment of a digital library can potentially lead to new types of interactions, some which were not possible before. New tools are being developed that enhance the social functionality of digital libraries. Ackerman explains how one such tool for digital libraries, the Café ConstructionKit, "provides a set of reusable objects that include message transport for asynchronous and synchronous communication [...] private and public channels for narrowcast communication, message filters, and message retrieval by a variety of semi-structured methods." This tool allows for simultaneous as well as non-simultaneous messaging, communication with one or more selected users, and storage of communication. New tools such as Café ConstructionKit mean that while face-to-face communication may be unavailable in a digital library, users may communicate in larger numbers and in a larger variety of ways.

10.6: Evaluation Resources

In a review of the literature on evaluation criteria of DLs, Heradio, Fernandez-Amoros, Cabrerizo, and Herrera-Viedma (2012) summarize the most important criteria in evaluating DLs from users' perspectives, although they admit that there is no consensus on the relative importance of each criterion. Indeed, current research provides conflicting answers. For example, according to a study by Kani-Zabihi, Ghinuea, and Chen (2006), users identified the two most important requirements for DLs as being 1) "finding information quickly and easily in DLs," and 2) "being able to be easily familiarized with DLs"

(p. 405). In Xie's 2008 study, however, users reported that the most important requirements were "interface usability in general" and "system performance in general." (p. 1357). What these studies have in common, and what Heradio, Fernandez-Amoros, Cabrerizo, and Herrera-Viedma (2012) focus on, is a user-centered approach to quality assessment. Xie (2008) and Kani-Zabihi, Ghuinea, and Chen (2006) rely on users to identify the most important requirements for DLs, thereby giving researchers criteria to use in evaluation.

Digital Libraries Evaluation Resources

At the time written, the list of resources below contains links to evaluation information and strategies aimed at assessing quality and usefulness of digital libraries.

Assessing Digital Library Services
> Library Trends 49(2), Fall 2000 is a special issue focusing on digital library evaluation. It contains these titles: "Evaluating Digital Libraries for Teaching and Learning in Undergraduate Education: A Case Study of the Alexandria Digital Earth ProtoType (ADEPT)," "Evaluating Digital Libraries: A Longitudinal and Multifaceted View," and "Digital Library Evaluation: Toward an Evolution of Concepts."

Digital Libraries: A Generic Classification and Evaluation Scheme
> This paper provides a new description scheme using four major dimensions: data/collection, system/technology, users, and usage. For each of these dimensions, we describe the major attributes. Using this scheme, existing DL test beds can be characterized.

Digital libraries: Challenges for Evaluation
> State of evaluation of digital libraries

Digital Library Evaluation as Participative Inquiry
> Discussion of how can digital library evaluation account more fully for the practices and consequences of use for marginalized members of society, such as the poor and people of color. Can be found at http://www.ideals.illinois.edu/bitstream/handle/2142/13394/02delos.pdf?sequence=2
>
> Northwestern University's (2003). Digital Library Project Evaluation Form. Retrieved online October 21, 2004 from: http://staffweb.library.northwestern.edu/dl/pmg/phase3DLCfirstreview/dlc_project_eval.pdf

Challenges for Digital Library Evaluation
> While there were many efforts in research and practice of digital libraries, evaluation was not a conspicuous activity, but rather a complex and difficult undertaking. We enumerate the challenges facing digital library evaluation and suggest a conceptual framework for evaluation, a review of evaluation efforts in research and practice concentrates on derivation of criteria used in evaluation. Essential

requirements for evaluation are stated. Discussed are constructs, context and criteria of digital libraries: What should we evaluate? For what purpose do we evaluate? Who should evaluate? At what level do we evaluate? Upon what criteria do we evaluate? In addition, we include suggestions for adaptation of criteria from related activities. The paper is considered as a part of the evolution of concepts for digital library evaluation.

Realist Activity Theory for Digital Library Evaluation

Realist Activity Theory for Digital Library Evaluation: Conceptual Framework and Case Study, a study and review of the Flora of North America DL and of its context of development and use. A unified conspectus for plant. See http://www.ics.uci.edu/~redmiles/activity/final-issue/Spasser/Spasser.pdf

User Needs Assessment and Evaluation of Digital Libraries (DLs)

Provides and example of digital library evaluation. See http://glcf.umd.edu/library/pdf/evaluation_resources.pdf

Electronic Library Evaluation

The eVALUEd Project Team writes, "eVALUEd is a HEFCE (Higher Education Funding Council for England) funded project, based at the University of Central England. It has been set-up to develop a transferable model for e-library evaluation and to provide dissemination and training in electronic library evaluation. The project commenced in December 2001.

Evaluating Digital Libraries: A Longitudinal and Multifaceted View at http://ils.unc.edu/~march/perseus/lib-trends-final.pdf

Contains Web CyberGuide Ratings for both content evaluation and web site design.

User Evaluation: Summary of the Methodologies and Results for the Alexandria Digital Library

The Alexandria Digital Library (ADL) is one of the six digital library projects funded by NSF, DARPA, and NASA. ADL's collection and services focus on geospatial information: maps, images, georeferenced data sets and text, and other information sources with links to geographic locations. Throughout the project, user feedback has been collected through various formal and informal methods. These include online surveys, beta tester registration, ethnographic studies of ADL users and potential users, target user group focus sessions, and user feedback comments while using the interfaces. This paper briefly describes the evaluation studies conducted and what was learned about user characteristics and about the study approaches themselves. User reactions to the ADL interface and to the functionality and content of ADL are summarized. Finally, the value of these findings to design and implementation decisions is considered.

A User-Centered Design and Evaluation of Digital Libraries [PowerPoint presentation]

Description: The Cognitive Work Analysis is the specific framework we propose to use. It was developed by Jens Rasmussen and Annelise Mark Pejtersen from Risoe National Laboratory in Denmark.

Access Evaluation of Digital Libraries

Characteristics and Performance of Web OPACs Bethina Schmitt and Sven Oberländer Institute for Program Structures. *See it at* http://citeseerx.ist.psu.edu/viewdoc/download?doi=10.1.1.16.8227&rep=rep1&type=pdf

Lessons in Evaluation of Digital Libraries and Their Application

Evaluation of the CITIDEL Project provides easy access to digital collections in computer science, information systems, information science, software engineering, computer engineering, and related disciplines among them the digital libraries of ACM and IEEE-CS. See it *at*

www.csc.villanova.edu/.../Lessons_in_Evaluation_Digital_Libraries.doc

DELOS Workshop on Evaluation of Digital Libraries: Testbeds, Measurements, and Metrics

The DELOS Working Group of the ERCIM DELOS Network of Excellence on Digital Libraries aims at providing a Digital Library Evaluation Forum and a Digital Library Test Suite, which will provide researchers with information for the selection of potential digital library testbeds and new research or evaluation targets.

Digital Best Practice on Current Trend of Research in Image Quality

The current trend of research in image quality by the Washington State Library. The digital object exists as a whole image. The digital object can be displayed in various measures of resolution, such as pixels per inch or dots per inch. Decisions relating to image quality will depend on the desired outcome. If the outcome is to serve preservation purposes as well as access needs the standard will necessarily be high. Images can be modified or enhanced. The decision to do this depends upon the desire to reproduce the original faithfully or to reproduce it in such a way to make it very readable. If an image is modified the change should be noted in the documentation for the project.

Bibliography of Digital Library Evaluations:

- Cummins, J. (2004). Accessing the International Children's Digital Library. Horn Book Magazine, 80(2), 145-151. Retrieved October 18, 2004, from, Academic Search Premier

- McLachlan, K. (2002). WWW Cyberguide Ratings for Web Site Design. Retrieved October 21, 2004 from http://www.cyberbee.com/design.pdf

Web Resources and Tools for Website Evaluations

Below are web resources or tools for website evaluation, listed alphabetically that are aimed at assessing accessibility and quality of websites, some of which can be used as evaluation criteria for digital library evaluation.

Critically Analyze Information Sources at
http://www.library.cornell.edu/okuref/research/skill26.htm
> A general resource paper from Cornell University Library covers initial appraisal and content analysis.

Evaluating Web Resources at
http://www.umuc.edu/library/libhow/webresources.cfm
> This full text paper provides a number of resources for evaluating web resources including evaluation checklists and techniques.

Evaluating Quality on the Net at http://www.hopetillman.com/findqual.html
> This is a full text paper describing relevance of existing criteria, generic criteria for evaluation, current state of evaluation tools, key indicators of quality.

Evaluating Web Resources: Bibliography at
http://www.asha.org/sitehelp/websites.htm
> Contains a number of literature and links to related resources for web site evaluation. Covers print and online resources from Widener University Wolfgram Memorial Library.

Evaluating Quality on the Net at http://www.hopetillman.com/findqual.html
> Covers relevance of existing criteria, generic criteria for evaluation tools, key indicators of quality by Hope N. Tillman from Babson College, MA

Internet Detective at http://www.ariadne.ac.uk/issue18/internet-detective
> This web site contains an interactive tutorial on evaluating the quality of Internet resources. The project is funded by the European Union.

Top Ten Mistakes in Web Design at
http://www.useit.com/alertbox/990502.html
> This is an informative section within Jakob Nielsen's website (noted designer for SunSite). This was written in '97, but he's updated in '99 and has found that not too much has improved.

The Web as a Research Tool at
http://www3.widener.edu/Academics/Libraries/Wolfgram_Memorial_Library/Evaluate_Web_Pages/659/

Evaluation Techniques [Widener University] Covers need for evaluation, review and adapting of traditional print evaluation criteria.

Web CyberGuide Ratings at http://www.cyberbee.com/design.pdf
Contains Web CyberGuide Ratings for both content evaluation and web site design: WWW CyberGuide Ratings for Content Evaluation -- A guide for rating the curriculum content on web sites; WWW CyberGuide Ratings for Web Site Design -- A guide for rating the design of a web site.

Conclusion

The management and evaluation of all digital libraries includes the topics of access management, evaluation methods, bibliometrics, webometrics, intellectual property, cost/economic issues, and social issues. The topics mentioned affect digital libraries according to the needs of their users and the resources available to the digital library managers.

Study questions for Chapter Ten:

1. Chowdhury in Chapter 13 discusses three methods of evaluating digital libraries: TIME, EQUINOX and Saracevic's criteria. Which of these systems do you think would be the most effective and why? Are there are other criteria you think should be considered that are not covered by these systems?

2. In evaluating digital libraries, one of the key areas of focus is search engine effectiveness. One type of search engine discussed by Lesk is the Rabbit system, or retrieval by criticism, in which the computer retrieves random records subject to constraints to which the user replies and the computer returns another choice subject to this new constraint to which the user responds and this process continues until acceptable answers are converged upon. What is your evaluation of a Rabbit system? For more information on the Rabbit system, the following links may be helpful: http://www.ischool.berkeley.edu/~hearst/irbook/10/node5.html#SECTION0 0143000000000000000

http://209.85.165.104/search?q=cache:2icii Av_xNYJ:www.cs.mu.oz.au/~egemen/bitj00.pdf+%22Rabbit+system%22+sea rch+engine&hl=en&ct=clnk&cd=9&gl=us

http://ist.psu.edu/faculty_pages/jjansen/academic/pubs/cais99.html (Rabbit system discussion begins on page 16)

3. Borgman suggests that the "overarching goal in constructing a global digital library is to act locally while thinking globally." Why should there be a concern for a broader audience if something is created especially to cater to a given audience?

Chapter Eleven: Legal Issues

Legal issues are an important consideration for digital library developers. One major challenge facing digital libraries involves copyright and licensing problems. Rules and regulations regarding intellectual property issues may differ between traditional and digital libraries. There are many new policies and legal issues in existence that challenge not only policy-makers but also digital librarians. In this unit we focus on this study area, policies and legal issues in the digital environment.

Digital materials pose unique challenges that traditional print sources may not face. Prior to acquiring and posting content, developers must become informed about the laws surrounding materials posted. Copyright laws vary by country, although efforts have been made to establish international agreements. Control of materials made available online is more difficult. Privacy, security, and authenticity for both the digital materials and for the users of those materials will be discussed.

11.1: Intellectual Property and Intellectual Property Rights

Intellectual property

Ownership is a valuable right granted for not only physical property, but also for intellectual property. Established laws protect ownership rights from being claimed or changed by others. The laws governing physical property are more concrete than those governing intellectual property. Intellectual property is defined as "intangible property that is the result of creativity." (Soanes & Stevenson, 2008) That intangibility often is coupled with the struggle to ensure its protection.

Intellectual property refers to inventions and trademarks, known as industrial property, and literary and artistic works, known as copyright (What is Intellectual Property, 2010). The World Intellectual Property Organization states: "intellectual property plays an important role in an increasingly broad range of areas, ranging from the Internet to health care to nearly all aspects of science and technology and literature and the arts" (What is Intellectual Property, 2010). With the increasing range of intellectual property, the difficulty of protecting that property increases. New laws such as the Digital Millennium Copyright Act have been created to try to protect the ownership rights of intellectual property. One of the primary concerns is copyright infringement.

There are three types of intellectual property: trademarks, patents and copyrights. Trademarks are commerce related; they protect words, names, symbols, sounds, or colors that distinguish commercial items. Patents are property rights of inventors that may be enforced to prevent others from making, using, selling, or importing an invention in the United States.

Copyrights protect works of authorship and are the main area of intellectual property with which libraries are concerned (United States, n.d.).

Intellectual Property Rights

Intellectual property rights serve as an umbrella for other crucial topics, such as public domain, licensing, determining ownership for digital items, and fair use (Chowdhury & Chowdhury, 2003, p.285). According to Lesk (2005), "there are three basic forms of intellectual property protection ... copyright, patent, and trade secrecy" (p.295). Of the three forms, Lesk states that copyright laws are of primary importance to digital libraries (2005, p.295). Certain challenges are unique to digital formats. In his discussion of the report, *The digital dilemma: intellectual property in the information age*, Gladney noted some key features of these differences:

- Licensing versus ownership;
- Private versus public distribution online;
- Need to redefine access for digital content;
- The "widespread and incorrect belief that copying for private use is almost always lawful;"
- "Fair use and other exceptions to copyright should continue to play a role in the digital environment;" and
- Difficulties with digital repositories (Chowdhury & Chowdhury, 2003, pp.259-260)

Digital libraries must consider materials to which they provide links, in addition to the content contained within their collections. Although the linked materials are not directly under the control of the linking library, Oppenheim (1997) cautions that one should be very careful in creating such links as they may involve questions of copyright and moral rights (Chowdhury & Chowdhury, p.258, 2003). Recently proposed legislation, such as the Stop Online Piracy Act (SOPA) and the PROTECT IP Act (PIPA), has attempted to restrict access and the ability of users to share information online. While those laws were not enacted, they are a reminder of the importance of staying abreast of changes in the law. The American Library Association provides several ways for users to keep current: the Copyright Advisory Network, District Dispatch, and the Library Copyright Alliance.

Intellectual Property and Digital Libraries.

The legality of using information by others in a digital library is a murky area (Witten, 2003). The law says the creators, or whomever creators assign rights to, own the material they created whether it be words, photographs, music or video images. This means they own the copyright, or the rights as to who can copy the material. If material is used without permission, the user could be sued for copyright infringement. For an example, think of the George Harrison 1970s hit song "My Sweet Lord," for which he was sued because of its similarity to the 1960s hit song "He's So Fine" written by Ronald Mack and recorded by The Chiffons. The lawsuit lasted for years and cost hundreds of thousands of dollars.

Physical libraries have the right to share their books and other items with patrons but only on a one-to-one basis. Likewise, users have the right to read a book or even sell it but they cannot distribute the information, or any part of the information, contained in it without permission of the owner of the book's copyright. A library cannot even show a DVD that it has unless it has the right from the owner of the film's copyright to do so. When the rights expire, the items can be used with no problem. However, "copyright protection begins and ends at different times, depending on when the work was created," (Witten, 2003). Copyright laws also vary from country to country.

While the idea of wanting to share information can be a noble gesture, it often entails giving away something that is not yours to give. If an author works two years to research and write a book, she does not want it given away without receiving some benefit for all her work. A copyright owner typically would agree to have her works included in a digital library as long as users agree not to duplicate that work, usually by way of agreeing to a posted copyright statement. However, how can the creator of the library police know what abusers of the agreement do?

The easiest and perhaps best way to handle (or perhaps avoid) the issue is to digitize material that is in the public domain. If the author of a work does not want to copyright it or declares that it is in the public domain, the material can be used without fear of a lawsuit. Otherwise, items that are more than 100 years old are generally in the public domain in the United States. However, if a writer produced a work in 2000 when he/she was 20 years old and that writer lives till the year 2070, the work does not become public domain until 70 years after the author's death, or 2140. Content in digital libraries is affected by copyright law, and the laws will affect digital libraries in a different way, as the format of the content is different than print books.

With the dawn of the digital age, new formats of intellectual property developed as well as new ways to publish and access it. Intellectual property also has become more difficult to protect. With the copy and paste feature, it is extremely easy to capture another's intellectual property and transfer it to a blog entry, wiki, or even email. Even though laws are in place to protect intellectual property, the ways to enforce these laws are not always evident.

Digital libraries are one of the new formats, which must adhere to the protection of intellectual property. Legal issues are the most serious problems facing digital libraries (Lesk, 2005).

Digital libraries pose unique intellectual property issues because their content is readily accessible to users all over the world. Technology has also made it possible to copy digital content on a large scale quickly and easily, and without the knowledge of the copyright owner. Additionally, the access and ownership scheme is different in the digital library environment. Where physical libraries loan out copyrighted materials that they lawfully own, digital libraries generally don't own the content they provide to patrons – they purchase licenses from copyright holders that allow patrons to access the digital materials (Chowdhury & Chowdhury, 2002; Mahesh & Mittal, 2009). Farber (2005) states that old copyright rules cannot just be translated into the digital world because the Internet is such a radically new technology. These new circumstances of the digital library environment necessitate the creation of access controls to prevent violations of applicable intellectual property laws and assurance of the authenticity of digital materials. The creation of new rules and guidelines is also necessary to protect the rights of owners and creators of digital materials (Chowdhury & Chowdhury, 2002; Mahesh & Mittal, 2009). Some scholars believe that the large-scale growth of digital libraries cannot occur until legislative action is taken to promote digital libraries and protect them from copyright infringement suits (Menell, 2007).

Google envisioned the largest online library by digitizing millions of books. However, to protect the intellectual property of the millions of authors and publishers involved, Google was charged with copyright infringement. Even after more than five years, Google is still in the process of trying to make its vision happen legally (Brew, 2010). Most copyright violations are not intentional; however, many people do not look at online material as someone's intangible property. Therefore, they do not seek permission to use the intellectual property of others. Many websites have had to take down a webpage or even the whole site due to copyright violations.

Digital Rights Management (DRM)

Digital rights management has been established to help protect intellectual property. It is used to control access to, track and limit uses of digital works (Digital Rights Management (DRM) & Libraries, 2010). This control is embedded in the materials, which prevents copyright infringement and enforces restrictions other than those stated in the copyright law. The problem with this is that it sometimes limits libraries and school in how they provide service to their communities. One of the restrictions is that of eliminating the "first sale" doctrine. The "first sale" doctrine allows libraries to purchase materials and lend them to encourage further purchases of the material. One of the other significant restrictions is the elimination of "fair use" (Digital Rights Management (DRM) & Libraries, 2010).

There are organizations that try to protect both the intellectual property rights and provide affordable public access, such as the World Intellectual Property Organization (WIPO) and the Digital Future Coalition (DFC). The WIPO is an agency of the United Nations dedicated to developing a balanced and accessible international intellectual property system (What is WIPO?, 2010). It was founded in 1967 at the WIPO Convention to promote the protection of Intellectual Property. The DFC was established in 1995 to promote collaboration between non-profit educational, scholarly, library and consumer groups together with major commercial trade associations to develop a balance between protecting Intellectual Property and affordable access. (Description of the Digital Future Coalition, 2010)

Digital libraries have created yet one more variable in the intellectual property realm. There is general agreement that the intellectual property holder is entitled to compensation (Lesk, 2005). However, there is much concern about how limiting the regulations of digital rights management are. Organizations such as WIPO and DFC try to ensure that both the intellectual property holder and public access are treated fairly.

The creator of a digital library of material that is not in the public domain must obtain written permission from the copyright owner and credit the creator rather than claiming the work as his own. An exception to copyright law would be if something would be considered "fair use," another legally murky area. Generally, fair use allows that portions of a material may be used, material may be used for educational purposes, material may be commented upon, or material may be used in distance learning. Fair use guidelines change frequently. For example, as of July of 2010, the non-commercial use of portions of video material is now considered fair use.

It is vital that digital librarians understand copyright law and set policies that both protect the intellectual property of contributors and give access to users. To aid libraries in developing such policies, Koulouris and Kapidakis (2012) have established a "policy route map." They surveyed several libraries across different nations and combined the results to create a "policy decision tree," which could guide libraries in developing their content-reproduction policies. This tree covers the content creation type (digitized or born digital), the acquisition method, copyright ownership, whether access is provided on-campus or off-campus, whether reproduction is for commercial or private use, and finally the conditions that apply to each use (i.e., fair use, permission and fee, forbidden, etc.) (p. 7-8).

11.2: Copyright and Copyright Laws

What is Copyright?

A copyright is intellectual property that protects original works of authorship for patents, trademarks, and any published or non-published original work of authorship in a tangible format.

Copyright is a bundle of rights that individuals receive for original works of authorship. These bundles of rights include: reproduction, preparation of derivative works, distribution, public performances (with certain exceptions), public displays (with certain exceptions), and performance of sound recordings (17 U.S.C. § 106).

There are two requirements for copyright: original work of authorship (the original work of authorship must involve a "modicum" of creative effort), and the work must be fixed in a tangible medium of expression.

There are two conditions with an unregistered copyright: with the fixation of an original work of authorship in a tangible medium of expression, the author has a copyright but it is an unregistered one; and a copyright holder cannot sue someone for infringement until the copyright is registered. To register a copyright one needs to complete the appropriate form, attach deposit copies, and pay certain fees at Copyright Office, 101 Independence Ave., S.E. Washington, D.C. 20559. The website is http://www.loc.gov/copyright/.

What can be copyrighted? The items that follow can be copyrighted: literary works; musical works (with words); dramatic works (with music); pantomimes, choreography; pictorial, graphic, sculptural; motion pictures, other AV materials; and sound recordings.

What CANNOT be copyrighted? Works that are not fixed cannot be copyrighted, these include ideas, facts, something already in the public domain, procedures/processes, systems, operation methods, concepts/principles, discoveries, etc.

What is infringement?

An infringement is a trespass on a piece of intellectual property. It could be a use of whole or part of an image without permission, use beyond the scope of a license, and/or adapting an image without permission.

Copyright Law

Copyright law is "a legal device that gives the creator of a work of art or literature, or a work that conveys information or ideas, the right to control how that work is used" (2008, Irving, p.144). The purpose of the copyright law is to "promote the progress of Science and the useful Arts. By securing for limited Times to Authors and Inventors the exclusive right to their respective Writings and Discoveries" (U.S. Constitution, Art. 1, Sec.8).

Copyright laws protect original, creative works such as poetry, movies, video games, videos, plays, paintings, sheet music, recorded music performances, novels, software code, sculptures, photographs, choreography, and architectural designs. Copyright grants the author exclusive rights to reproduce the work, prepare derivative works, distribute the work, and perform or display the work. Copyrighted works may not be used without permission from the copyright holder. (Shah, 2007; Stanford, 2007)

Up until the late 20th century, copyright applied to materials in the physical manifestations of created works. The rights and access to these types of materials was easier to control than works existing in the digital sphere. Copyright law covers these economic rights: reproduction, adaptations, derivative works, distribution, performance, and display (Besek, 2007, pp.331-332).

How should digital libraries handle materials they either own or have permission to use or those which fall under the public domain? Irving (2008) stated that it is "wise to operate under the assumption that all materials are protected by either copyright or trademark law unless conclusive information indicates otherwise" (p.150). A "better safe than sorry" mentality is a good approach to take with digital materials.

Copyright laws and digital libraries

Recognizing that the ubiquitous nature of digital libraries involves the legal systems of many countries. Since 1992, the World Intellectual Property Organization (WIPO) has focused on a digital agenda that addresses digital copyright issues, with the aim of amending the Berne Convention that was initially enacted more than a century ago. In December 1996, a WIPO conference produced drafts of three new treaties (Tang, 1999). One of the treaties, the WIPO Copyright Treaty of 1996 (WCT), contained model provisions that were designed to be incorporated into domestic laws to provide protections against copyright infringement in digital environments. The U.S. Digital Millenium Copyright Act (discussed below) was one of the first national laws to implement Articles 11 and 12 of the WCT, which provide recourse to copyright owners for the abuse of access/copy controls and rights management technology that protects digital information from unauthorized access. The Articles also make it unlawful to knowingly disable such protective devices, such as digital signatures, licenses, watermarks, etc. (Mahesh & Mittal, 2009).

11.3: Legal Issues and Copyright in the U. S.

As a digital librarian, you should know the basic concepts of United States copyright law and related policies. Two of the most frequently asked questions are: what is copyright about? and what are the United States laws regarding intellectual property? The Digital Millennium Copyright Act is the most comprehensive reform of copyright law that was formed and is one of the most significant pieces of Internet legislation. The CONTU "Fair Use" Guidelines contain very important provisions and information that digital librarians should learn. Lastly, all digital librarians should be familiar with some technologies used in cyberspace, the digital environment.

Here are some facts of the U.S. Copyright Laws. There are only federal laws and no state laws exist:

    1798-Books, maps, charts, with 14 years, 1 renewal
    1831-add music, and extend to 28 years
    1870-add printing, statues, fine arts, with 28years
    1909-Protection begins with publication, 28 years, 1 renewal
    1976-Copyright Act
    1998-Digital Millennium Copyright Act (DMCA)

Generally, works published after 1977 are protected under copyright for the life of the author plus 70 years. If the work was done for hire (created during the course of employment or was specifically commissioned) or was published anonymously or under a pseudonym, then copyright lasts between 95 and 120 years, depending on the date the work is published. Works published between 1923 and 1977 are protected under copyright for 95 years from the date of publication. (Stanford, 2007) For a chart maintained by Cornell University that sets forth time periods for copyright protection, see http://copyright.cornell.edu/resources/publicdomain.cfm.

All works published in the United States before 1923 are in the public domain, which means that the public owns these works, and not an author or artist. Works in the public domain are not protected by intellectual property laws and may be used by anyone without permission. Works can enter the public domain in 4 ways: (i) expiration of copyright; (ii) failure to renew copyright; (iii) the owner deliberately places it in the public domain; and (iv) no copyright protection is available for the particular type of work. (e.g. titles of books or movies, facts, ideas, or theories) (Stanford, 2007)

Today, copyright duration lasts for the life of the author plus 70 years, so no works copyrighted under the latest law are in the public domain. That is because the latest law went into effect on Jan. 1, 1978. Even if an author died on Jan. 2, 1978, only a day after his or her copyright became effective, the copyright would be in effect until 2048!

Early U.S. copyright law

All of the early copyright bills that existed in the United States were called "Acts to promote learning," which indicates that U.S. copyright law was meant to protect more than the rights of authors; copyright laws also exist for the greater cause of advancing knowledge and the public welfare of the nation. It was believed that education, access to knowledge, and encouragement of literature and science were cornerstones for a thriving democratic society (Menell, 2007; Shah, 2007). The first copyright law dates back to 1709 enacted under the new United States Constitution, and was designed to protect authors, creators, and publishers of print materials from those who sought to steal and illegally reproduce them (Lesk, 2005). Copyright is actually not just one right, but in reality, several rights including reproduction, adaptation, distribution, and performance or display (Kresh, 2007). Copyright laws protect the intellectual property of authors, creators, and publishers by dictating how and by whom a work may be used.

Major Copyright Legislation

The Copyright Act of 1976: Copyright Act: The definition of the works that are entitled to copyright protection is found in the Copyright Act of 1976 (Act of Oct. 19, 1976, Pub. L. 94-553, 90 Stat. 2541; 17 U.S.C. 101 et seq.).

The original copyright law has been revised numerous times. Current legislation holds that "there is no renewal requirement for works created before 1978: copyright is automatically given for a period of 95 years..." (Witten, Bainbridge& Nichols, 2010, p.31). Newer works are copyright protected for 70 years after an author's death (Witten et al., 2010). Copyright laws can be influenced by persons or entities. Therefore, it is important to keep aware of copyright laws to make sure that digital materials are processed correctly.

The Berne Convention Implementation Act of 1988: The Berne Convention, originally signed by international communities in 1886, holds that works do not need to be registered in order for the creator to have rights over their work/creation (Witten et al., 2010, p.30). According to the Berne Convention, "the minimum copyright duration is life plus 50 years [...] after the author dies" (Witten et al., 2010, p.31). Other important aspects of the Berne Convention include moral rights, "the right to the acknowledgment of their authorship, and to the integrity of their work" (Witten et al., 2010, p.30).

The Digital Millennium Copyright Act (DMCA) (1998): The Digital Millennium Copyright Act makes it illegal to create or write about any technology that circumvents technology created as a protection matter by copyright holders. Digital Millennium Copyright Act (DMCA) is to protect Intellectual Property Rights in Cyberspace. (1998, passed by the United States Congress, the Pub.L.No. 105-304, 112 Stat. 2860 (October 28, 1998). More in-depth information on DMCA and its effects on libraries can be found on the ALA's website under *Advocacy & Issues*.

What types of works are protected by the Digital Millennium Copyright Act?

Any original literary, artistic, musical, dramatic, pictorial or other type of original work which is fixed and is able to be communicated is protected under DMCA. For example, the article that you are currently reading is a work that is protected by the Copyright Act of 1976 -- this article is an original work, it is fixed (by written words), and it is able to be communicated (you are reading the article). In general, it is relatively easy to satisfy the definition of a copyrighted work.

The DMCA encourages copyright owners to use "technological measures;" that is, technology used to protect copyrighted works on their

Internet site. "Technological measures" fall into two categories: those which prevent access to your work and those which prevent copying of your work. An example of using the DMCA to prevent access to your work is prior to accessing the full text of the story, the individual is presented with a click wrap contract and has to obtain a password to view the story.

If an individual violates the DMCA, the government may request criminal penalties as follows: a fine of not more than $500,000 or imprisonment for not more than 5 years, or both, for the first offense; and a fine of not more than $1,000,000 or imprisonment for not more than 10 years, or both, for any subsequent offense.

Public domain material

If a work is in the public domain, it is not protected under copyright law. The author of the work may have declared it to be in the public domain, or perhaps the copyright has run out, because it went into effect under the 1909 law and has gone past the 56 year limit of that law. Or the material may be of the sort that cannot be copyrighted--federal documents cannot be copyrighted, for example. Facts cannot be copyrighted, nor can titles, tables of contents, most recipes, names, etc.

However, to avoid plagiarism charges, students and teachers do need to provide complete attribution for these works. For example, even though Shakespeare's works have never been protected under copyright law), it would be inappropriate for a student to claim that he or she authored the play "Romeo and Juliet." However, it is not generally a violation of copyright to provide a link to another site's home page. Providing a link is not seen as copying protected expression but merely providing an address to that expression.

11.4: Using Copyrighted Materials

What is Fair Use?

The National Commission on New Technological Uses of Copyrighted Works (CONTU) gives four rules for determining what is fair use. There are four factors for fair use as Stated in the US Law and Used by the Courts:
  1) Purpose & character of use
     Non-profit educational?
     Commercial?
     Mere copying?
     Transformative?
  2) Nature of Copyrighted work
     Fiction?
     Non-fiction?

Published?
Unpublished?

3) Amount & substantiality
How much was taken?
What was taken? If what was taken was the "heart" of the work, a very small amount could be too much.

4) Effect of use on value or market (The courts consider this the most important factor.)
Does the taking of the material:
Enhance the market? or diminish the market?
Enhance the value? or diminish the value?

Why is there a need for fair use:

Criticism & comment
Preparation for teaching
Scholarship or research
News reporting

Examples of fair use include class handouts of very short excerpts from a book, quoting for purposes of reporting the news or criticizing or commenting on a particular work of art, writing, speech or scholarship, making a collage for a school project; or manipulating an item such as an image to learn Photoshop or other software. You don't need to invoke fair use if you obtain permission to "use" a copyrighted work, but be sure that permission is in writing, and the person giving permission has the authority to do so.

Some schools' guidelines provide that a teacher may make one copy for herself of a chapter from a book, a periodical/newspaper article, a short story, essay or poem, a chart, graph, diagram, cartoon, or a picture from book.

For classroom copies, the following could be allowable under fair use: every copy must have notice, only one copy per student, only by the teacher or at teacher's request, immediate need (there is no time to get permission), no copying of consumables, no more than 9 instances for one class in one class term, limits on amounts and types of materials (Belfield).

For digital materials, the items in digital reserves, distance learning and electronic interlibrary loan (ILL) are fair use. However, there are some rules for fair use. For digital reserves, the print reserves factors should apply. In addition, copyright information should appear on the first screen, including a warning against further distribution by the user, and citations or attributions prominently on the items. For example, a statement on the digital reserve items can be this: "This material may be copyrighted by Title 17 of the U.S. Code and is intended solely for the use of students in Prof. Liu's ILS655-70 Course."

These materials should have limited access via passwords or other security measures. They must get permission from the copyright holder for subsequent use in new term, and they may retain material in electronic form while seeking permission.

Copyright Exceptions

An exception to copyright in the United States is the "fair use rule." Under fair use, researchers can cite sections of text from another work. Again as stated earlier, based on the United States Copyright Office, four factors that users need to know if a certain use constitutes fair use:

- The purpose and character of the use, including whether such use is of commercial nature or is for nonprofit educational purposes

- The nature of the copyrighted work

- The amount and substantiality of the portion used in relation to the copyrighted work as a whole

- The effect of the use upon the potential market for, or value of, the copyrighted work.

Libraries and archives are granted special permissions under section 108 of United States Copyright law. Section 108 specifies libraries and archives may make limited reproductions of published and unpublished works. Three copies of unpublished works are allowed for purposes of preservation, security, and deposit (Legal Information Institute, n.d., Section B). One copy of a published work may be reproduced (Legal Information Institute, n.d., Section A). There are many other aspects to this section of the law; however, the main idea behind the law is that under certain circumstances, libraries and archives may make additional copies of created works.

Permissions

It is important to understand that possession does not mean ownership: "When you buy a copy of a document, you can resell it, but you certainly do not buy the right to make further copies and redistribute them" (Written et al., 2010, p. 29). This is not to say that you cannot use copyrighted materials, but you must make sure your use is legal. If you determine that fair use is not in play, you have to get permission to use the material.

The first step is to determine who has ownership of the material. The creator is usually the initial owner. However, if it was created as work for hire, under an employer, then that employer owns the copyright. The creator can transfer or assign copyrights to others through a written contract: "What the creator does with the rights given is his own business. Rights are similar to property rights in that the owner may rent, lease, lend or sell outright any or all of the rights in the work" (Simpson, 2005, p.16). This can be permanent or temporary. Often authors sell these rights to publishing companies.

If you wish to use the material beyond the scope of fair use, you must get permission to do any of the following: reproduction, adaptations, derivative works, distribution, performance, and display. "The least expensive option is to get permission for the proposed use from the copyright holder or his agent. Failing permission, the only legal option is to pay for a license or royalty through a broker or directly to the copyright owner" (Simpson, 2005, p.155). These licenses may have very specific, restricted rights.

The copyright owner is often listed on the material, usually on the back page or a title page. Publishers' addresses can often be found in *Books in Print, The Literary Marketplace,* or other publishing industry directories. The Publisher may be able to broker permissions, or may direct you to the individual. Material may contain copyrighted works that are quoted with permission from that original copyright owner. You must also get separate permission to use that section (Simpson, 2005, p. 158). The United States Copyright office keeps records of all registered copyrights. If the material has been registered, you can obtain the name of the copyright owner. There are agencies that only broker permissions, such as the Motion Picture Licensing Corporation for films, or The American Society of Composers, Authors and Publishers (ASCAP) or Harry Fox Agency for music. The Copyright Clearance Center (CCC) was established to give several types of print permissions.

Once you identify the copyright owner, you must ask for *written* permission to use the material. You may be charged a fee for the permission. You may decline, but you then may not use the material. Remember also that no response does not mean that there is no objection. It is important that those involved in digitization projects understand copyright laws. Anything digitized and made available must comply with the laws or you will be left open to legal issues. Even donated materials must get permission. You must be sure that the donor is in fact the copyright holder.

Relinquishing Copyright &Creative Commons

Authors can relinquish their copyrights if they wish to, but they must take active steps. This can be somewhat difficult. Creative Commons is a nonprofit organization that has created licenses that people can attach to the content they create. It is expressed in three ways: a legal version, a human-readable everyday language, and a machine-readable tag. A CC on materials mean that copyright has not been waived, but there are more freedoms for others to use the material in ways beyond the scope of fair use. The freedoms may vary depending on the desire of the author for example, non-commercial use only (Witten et al., 2010, p, 32). Additional information on Creative Commons can be found athttp://creativecommons.org/.

The Creative Commons approach is a less restrictive, alternative method for controlling access to digital copyrighted works, which is a departure from the involved permission-gathering of DRM systems. Under the Creative Commons license, copyright holders inform users of the permissions they have been granted by the copyright holder by attaching machine searchable and readable licenses to the works. All Creative Commons licenses require proper attribution to the original author, and depending upon the copyright holder, may permit a narrow or broad range of uses. Over 16 million works of all kinds have been released under Creative Commons licenses, and despite the fundamental desire of the Creative Commons movement to remove copyright impediments to creativity, approximately one third of Creative Commons licenses do not allow the public to use the work or make adaptations or other derivatives without specific permission from the author (Zimmerman, 2007).

Copyright vs. Licensing[8]

The following information is derived from notes taken at the Plenary Address by Pamela Samuelson at the 2nd ACM International Conference on Digital Libraries, July 25, 1997, in Philadelphia.

The U.S. Supreme Court has held that private non-commercial copying of a document is presumed fair-use. Today, however, some feel the policy should be that every non-authorized copy is theft. Between these two views is a gap that needs to be defined. In the long term, this definition is essential to stabilize the legal environment in order to open up the development of digital libraries. In the short term, tollbooths are needed to manage access, else there will be total inoperability across digital libraries.

The hot issue in digital libraries and the Internet today is the question of whether it is lawful to link. The problems of linking are characterized by the total news coverage in the United States by CNN and the Washington Post on the Internet. These sites carry framing, advertising, and logos. It is possible to link to these sites in a way that bypasses the advertising, which is paying for the site and the logos, and mastheads that identify the source of the document. In contrast to this is "plain vanilla" linking--linking to the homepage only. Plain vanilla linking preserves the integrity of the linked-to site and seems to be legal.

---

[8]Acknowledgement: This lecture notes is updated from Dr. Mary Brown's lecture notes offered to the students of the course Digital Libraries at the Department of ILS, SCSU in 2000. It is originally derived from notes taken at the Plenary Address by Pamela Samuelson at the 2nd ACM International Conference on Digital Libraries, July 25, 1997, in Philadelphia.

Other issues include the lawfulness of using embedded links or annotating a text, and the indexing, archiving, caching, mirroring, and filtering of material. Publishers and some legal entities (e.g. current administration) hold that the copyright holder controls all RAM copying, where RAM is defined as a computer component in which data and computer programs can be temporarily recorded. In essence, this means any use of the Internet beyond personally created and owned documents, is illegal.

Current legal initiatives include: limiting liability of online service providers for infringement by users--with or without knowledge of the infringement; and giving databases protection against unauthorized use and extraction, including 25 years exclusive protection with no fair use.

A model standard law for intellectual property is needed. One candidate is the Uniform Commerce Code (UCC2B). Under UCC2B, books and other materials would be licensed rather than sold. Under the current UCC2B, however, there is no provision for fair use. Some want to build into the UCC2B a provision that licensing, for example of books, cannot override fair use. If this provision is included in the UCC2B, it is suggested that UCC2B could replace copyright law.

An interesting proposal for regulation and enforcement of copyright is the use of software agents in cyberspace to make contracts. That is, the software agent is activated when a user requests receipt of a document. The user's software-agent contacts the software-agent associated with the requested document and an automated negotiation for use and fee ensues, including billing of any fees to the user's account. Following successful negotiation, the document is transferred to the user. One question that arises is, can electronic agents exercise fair use? Fair use is a murky area in which all situations labeled (for example, classroom use) do not necessarily fall under fair use.

Another area of concern in digital libraries is the privacy of the user. For example, how do we maintain privacy, and the right to read anonymously, if the right (permission and access) to read a document is a matter of electronic record? There is also the issue of the deadbeat list, an automated compilation of users who have unpaid charges for Internet use. The deadbeat list could be used as a filtering device to exclude those who appear on it from gaining access to billable services. The deadbeat list is a problem in that if a user is disputing a charge with a vendor, his/her name could go on a deadbeat list before it is established that they in fact are in default of an actual owed amount.

General public license

The General Public License is another alternative copyright scheme that is used mostly by software developers to encourage the creation of derivative works. It is currently used to distribute approximately 60% to 70% of the open source software found on major sites, such as Linux and

Wordpress. (Zimmerman, 2007). The General Public License grants the four following freedoms:

    (i)   The freedom to run the program for any purpose;
    (ii)   The freedom to study how the program works and adapt it to your needs;
    (iii)   The freedom to redistribute copies so you can help your neighbor; and
    (iv)   The freedom to improve the program and release your improvements to the public, so that the whole community benefits (Creative Commons, n.d.).

Technologies Used for Copyright Protections

One of the technology tools, especially emerging tools that are used to protect intellectual property and copyright is *watermarking*, which allows an agent to locate the watermark at other sites, check the URL against legal copies, and execute some action against any non-legal copies found. Watermarking can also function as a search tool for locating information on potentially similar topics that center around an image.

Written regulations are one thing, enforcement is another. In the polymer industry there is a technique called doping that, using traces of elements as a fingerprint to identify the source of raw polymer, allows companies to trace unauthorized use of materials. Quite interesting research on a method analogous to doping is being conducted at the University of Geneva (Rauber, Ruanaidh & Pun, 1997). This research seeks to improve the security of online images. The work involves embedding hidden signatures in images using a digital watermarking tool. The watermark is capable of being searched and matched. Watermarking opens up interesting possibilities. Watermarking can also function as a search tool for locating information on potentially similar topics which center around an image.

For copyright protection of digital items, digital watermarking has become increasingly popular. Unlike traditional watermarks applied to visible media (like images or video), in digital watermarking the signal may be audio, pictures, video, texts or 3D models. A signal may carry several different watermarks at the same time. Digital watermarking is a passive protection tool, it marks data but does not degrade it or control access to the data ("Digital watermarking," 2020). Wikipedia also mentions that digital watermarking can be used for source tracking and has been used to detect the source of illegally copied movies.

11.5: Privacy and Security

Privacy and security measures are also important factors when creating digital libraries. If security measures are not in place, unauthorized users may view, download and even alter copyrighted material. You may be held legally liable for these actions. A second issue is the privacy of patron records. Traditionally, librarians have been very protective of patrons' records, such as the list of books they have read. Access to digital libraries leaves behind a clear record of patrons' actions. Data and web mining techniques can allow previously unprecedented access to personal information. Samuelson (1998) asks: "what responsibilities do or should digital library developers have to respect users' privacy or build in anonymity features to protect user privacy?" (p.1998). He further emphasized "this question is important because it is so easy to track what users are reading in digital library environments" (Samuelson, 1998, p. 16). Digital library creators can not only compile profiles of their users for their own purposes, but also sell or exchange the information.

Various image blurring and pixelization techniques can and have been employed in an attempt to protect privacy, however, recent development and applications of machine learning have rendered such obfuscation techniques ineffective for privacy preservation – one study has shown that Convolutional Neural Networks (CNN) are highly adaptable to standard obfuscation, and can re-identify up to 96% of pixelized faces (Liyue 2019). While libraries are probably not high on the target list of those unleashing such high-powered attacks, it does demonstrate the constant tension between opposing sides when it comes to how technology developments are used.

Authenticity

Authenticity, as note by Abby Smith, a former director of programs at the Council of Library and Information, "connotes precise, yet disparate things in different contexts and communities" (Introduction, 2000). For digital libraries, authenticity verifies that a document is authorized and legitimate. Digital copies of created works present a unique set of challenges. As noted by the United States Government Printing Office, "digital technology makes documents easy to alter or copy, leading to multiple non-identical versions that can be used in unauthorized or illegitimate ways" (Lazorchak, 2012, para.5). Security measures, therefore, are essential to maintaining the authenticity of digital materials.

Another type of authentication relates to user access of digital resources. Databases and digital libraries that are not open to the general public can restrict access to their content in three ways:
- logical: restricting access to an organization's network domain
- physical: restricting access to particular locations in the real world
- financial: restricting access to users who are prepared to pay (a "paywall")

(Witten et al., 2010, p.56)

Digital libraries may or may not require users to go through an authentication process. Public and academic libraries, for example, require that off-site users of their databases enter a library card number and pin. Other sites, such as the Perseus Digital Library and Project Gutenberg, do not require users to submit log-in information in order to use content. Reasons for limiting access to content can include licensing contracts, funding, and audience.

11.6: Examples of Legal Disputes

High profile efforts to digitize and provide access to works include the Google Books project and Project Gutenberg. Google has faced a myriad of legal challenges in its quest to digitize books. Project Gutenberg, on the other hand, deals with public domain literature, and handles another set of legal issues. Both examples help illustrate how the law applies to digital materials provided by commercial and non-profit organizations.

Google Books

One if the most famous copyright cases in the digital realm is the Google Books lawsuit, now in its seventh year. The Google Print Library project, commonly known as Google Books, was started in 2004. Google entered into an agreement with several libraries to scan their books into Google and have these books searchable via web searches. The book results offered short descriptions and "snippets" from the book. "While some books were already in the public domain and some publishers actually entered in to agreements with Google, most of the books were scanned without obtaining permission from the copyright owners" (Pike, 2012, p.1).

A number of groups sued Google for copyright infringement, including the Authors Guild, individual authors, the Association of American publishers, and other individual publishing companies. "For its part, Google defended its actions, claiming that the copying and showing of snippets was a fair use of copyright materials" (Pike, 2012, p. 32). A settlement with some of the groups in 2008 allowed for the development and marking of the books' database in return for payment of royalties. However, this settlement was rejected in federal court, "indicating that Google went too far in violating fundamental copyright laws and far beyond the original scope of the lawsuit which had been over the use of snippets and not full-text books" (Pike, 2012, p.32).

The newest strategy by Google has been a divide and conquer technique, saying that the groups did not have the right to sue for infringement because they are not the legal or beneficial owners of the copyrighted materials. Google claimed that the suit needed participation from all the individual members in order to be legitimate. However, the groups claim because they filed under a class action status, only a few individuals could represent the whole group. The publishers have been absent from these recent developments, which leads some to believe that they are closer to a settlement. "While changes in the copyright law were recommended by the courts as the best alternative to the rejected Google Books settlement, there does not seem to be any present action in Congress to suggest change" (Pike, 2012, p. 34). The Google Books lawsuit is still pending in court.

Project Gutenberg

Unlike the Google Books project, Project Gutenberg (PG) has focused only on public domain works. The legal process for acquiring materials and publishing them online for free public access is much simpler, as it does not require PG to acquire permissions. PG has made classic works accessible for users to read on their computers and/or portable e-reading devices. One major question that looms in the future for projects such as PG is whether or not copyright law will continue to change so as to prevent a growing number of books from becoming freely available in the public domain.

11.7: International copyright protections

Copyright law is national law, but due to the existence of several international copyright treaties, copyright protections are fairly similar worldwide. Under the principal international treaty on the subject, the Berne Convention of 1886, over 100 member countries have agreed to extend copyright protection to authors who are nationals of any member country. Member countries must provide protection that lasts at least for the life of the author plus 50 years, and the protection must be extended automatically, without requirements for the author to take any legal steps to preserve the copyright. (Mahesh & Mittal, 2009; Stanford, 2007)

There is no international copyright law, but there are some agreements playing important roles in intellectual property protections: International Copyright Treaties, Berne Convention, UCC, and GATT international agreement.

The General Agreement on Tariffs and Trade (GATT) treaty contains many provisions that affect copyright protection in signatory countries. Together, the Berne Convention and the GATT treaty provide copyright protections to U.S. authors in most industrialized countries, and reciprocally allow the nationals from member/signatory countries to enforce their copyrights in the U.S. (Stanford, 2007).

The International Copyright Treaties was promulgated on September 25, 1992 by Decree No. 105 of the State Council of the People's Republic of China, and became effective as of September 30, 1992. Its purpose is to protect the legitimate rights and interests of the owners of copyright in foreign works

The Berne Convention is shorthand for the Berne Convention for the Protection of Literary and Artistic Works. It was adopted at Berne in 1886, and first established the recognition of copyrights between sovereign nations. The Berne Convention provided that each contracting state would recognize as copyrighted works authored by nationals of other contracting states. Copyright under the Berne Convention is automatic: no registration is required, nor is the inclusion of a copyright notice.

The Uniform Commercial Code (UCC) regulates business transactions. It is a set of uniform laws governing commercial transactions. These laws help promote interstate commerce by making it simpler to pursue transactions in various jurisdictions. The Code covers the sales of goods, commercial paper, bank deposits and collections, letters of credit, bulk transfers, warehouse receipts, bills of lading, investment securities and secured transactions. (http://www.fact-index.com/u/un/uniform_commercial_code.html)

The General Agreement on Tariffs and Trade (GATT) is an international arrangement including a code of rules, an institution, and a forum for negotiations designed to achieve a more open trading system by reducing tariff and non-tariff barriers. The United States and 22 other countries adopted the GATT in1947, since then it has made major contributions to the rapid growth in international trade since World War II. A basic GATT principle, embodied in the most favored-nation clause, is that trade must be conducted on a nondiscriminatory basis.

Copyright law applies to everyone, and is therefore extremely important in the creation of digital libraries: "Collecting information and making it widely available to others has far-ranging social implication, and those who build digital libraries much act responsibly by making themselves aware of the legal and ethical issues that surround their particular application" (Witten et al., 2010, p, 29). It is not just a legal issue but also an ethical one. Whenever in doubt, seek the advice of legal counsel.

Study Questions for Chapter Eleven:

1. Lesk says that "many of the most important future issues of digital libraries involve legal questions" (Lesk, 1997, p.2). What are some of these legal issues and how do they relate to libraries? Use examples from your readings, personal knowledge, or examples from the most current literature to support your argument.

2. What new services or roles can you imagine that digital libraries will provide? Are there any privacy issues when a digital library can be mined for pictures or voices of people that might otherwise have always been thought of as insignificant or anonymous in the background of a picture or

audio file? Use those most recent studies/literature to support your arguments.

3. The Internet and Web have emerged from communities that believe in sharing information rather than restricting access to it. This has led to the perception, and perhaps even expectation that anything on the Web is freely available and may be redistributed at will (McCray &Gallagher, 2001). In light of this statement, what can digital libraries do to protect the rights of their contributors (publishers, artists, authors, etc.)? Find the most recent studies/literature to support your arguments.

4. In Holland's article "High Court Won't Hear Music Sharing Case" at http://www.siliconvalley.com/mld/siliconvalley/news/9899219.htm, she mentions the Digital Millennium Copyright Act and its possible implications on file-swapping in the present day. What are your thoughts on this issue? How do you feel about privacy in regards to piracy? How does this issue pertain to and affect digital libraries and their future creation? Use the most current studies that you can find to support your comments.

5. What legal issues did Google's digitization project face? What is the current status of these issues, and how do these legal issues affect our digital libraries? If you wanted to promote books on your digital library with images, excerpts, and a review, is this legal?

Chapter Twelve: Future Perspectives, Education and Research

Society calls for a new paradigm of information transfer. Digital libraries are responding to the new demand of society and their presence is going to grow. The future of digital libraries in society, their challenges, technological issues, research questions, and trends in growth are highly correlated with environmental conditions.

As information technologies continue to play a more prominent role in the education of library professionals, an emerging discipline, Digital Library Science, has emerged to respond to the need of preparing new digital librarians. Thus, another focus in this unit is education and research for digital libraries.

12.1: Future of digital libraries

Libraries will carve out a space for themselves if they remain adaptable and continue to provide excellent service in whichever format people prefer. The truth is that some people will always prefer to go to a library and borrow a book rather than downloading every book they wish to read. There will also be many people who will never have access to a fully virtual universal library due to a lack of technology at home (Mason, 2020).

Since the COVID-19 began, the practice has demonstrated how important digital libraries and digital resources are during times of national disaster. Digital libraries have been converting materials to be digital so that patrons can access them without having to physically visit the library. The future of brick-and-mortar libraries could be very similar to the future of digital libraries. This could imply additional outreach efforts and a focus on finding new ways to encourage people to use digital libraries. This could imply that digital and physical libraries collaborate to reach patrons and provide access in their homes.

What can we predict about future digital libraries?[9]

From reading the researchers' literature, we can confirm that various architectures are being suggested for digital libraries. Sanchez, Legett and Schnase (1997) observed a number of common characteristics among the various proposed architectures and predicted that 1) digital libraries would have highly distributed environments (that is, environments in which central collections store the information and queries go to the one repository to retrieve it as opposed to replication of repositories in multiple locations and

---

[9]This lecture notes is updated from Dr. Mary Brown's lecture notes offered to the students of the course Digital Libraries at the Department of ILS, SCSU in 2000.

queries going to one of the locations); 2) library objects would be served from digital libraries to clients (software residing on the user's computer) and these client services will request information and receive results through varied communication protocols; 3) the client services would make diverse interfaces available to the user; and 4) repositories on the server side would rely on advanced database management systems (DBMSs) for object storage, indexing and selective retrieval.

What can you expect as a user of digital libraries? You will be able to choose among screen display presentations and select one which best matches your needs. The screen presentation will include icons for agents, etc. which will take your queries. These agents will store information about you and histories of your information transactions. This stored information may be used in gaining information to satisfy your query. The agent may also recommend sources to which the query is most likely to retrieve a satisfactory response given your constraints, for example, of time or money or disciplinary interest. The agents will then translate your query into the form(s) specified by the sources to be queried, negotiate fair use and other contracts with source agents, receive the information requested, sort or arrange it in a sense-making scheme derived from your personal information use habits or specified information organization, and store aspects of this transaction in a personal profile of information needs and use. That is, digital libraries will be a service-oriented assortment of tools that will assist the patron in customizing a team of virtual specialists to broker the patrons' information needs.

Digital Library Models

Among the topics, models, and infrastructures used for developing national and/or international information resources, sharing consortia is a hot current topic. An influential founding program in this study area is International Digital Libraries Collaborative Research and Applications Testbeds, supported by the Division of Information and Intelligent Systems in the Directorate for Computer and Information Science and Engineering, National Science Foundation. The goal of this program is to "build on and extend prior Foundation efforts in international collaborative digital libraries research and applications."

What Models are used for developing national/international information resources sharing consortia?

As Lesk points out, many countries have digital library initiatives underway. Due to economies of scale and low entry costs, information technology is an appropriate national goal in many countries. Lesk contrasts the approaches used by these countries in supporting their digital library initiatives. Many nations decide to base digital library initiatives around either libraries or computer science research departments. At one extreme is the United States, where the digital library effort is run by the National Science Foundation (NSF). The focus is on computer science research, creating digital library tools, and new methods of access. The digital library collections are of less importance. It is felt that the tools developed in NSF supported projects can be applied by other institutions in building their collections. At the other extreme is Japan, where the major digital library initiative run by the National Diet Library is focused on collections. European nations are said to be following a mixed policy because they are focusing neither on tools nor collections exclusively.

In the United States, the government and the NSF have always been involved in information delivery research. Starting in the 1950s, the NSF and other government agencies provided the funding for research in information retrieval. This has led to the development of the U.S.'s world leadership in information services. As Lesk points out, government funding has led to the development of many private information services, such as DIALOG, which started as a venture between NASA and Lockheed. Other projects funded by the NSF have led to MOSAIC (an early browser capable of working with many different computing platforms), the Library of Congress' Thomas system, and Netscape, which grew out of the High Performance Computing and Communications program at the University of Illinois.

The NSF's major initiative in digital libraries (DLI-1) began in 1994. In cooperation with DARPA and NASA, six digital library projects were funded in the $30 million Phase 1 of the Digital Libraries Initiative. In 1999, the $55 million Phase 2 (DLI-2) included 36 projects supported by the NSF, DARPA, the National Library of Medicine, the Library of Congress, NASA, and the National Endowment for the Humanities, with the participation of the National Archives and the Smithsonian Institution. This funding was provided to develop innovative digital library technologies and applications. DLI-2 has also included a number of international digital library projects.

As stated previously, all of the NSF funded projects are intended to develop technological tools that will improve digital libraries' abilities to provide access to materials. The collections themselves are not the major focus of these projects.

As Lesk states (p. 252), other digital library projects have been more concerned with preservation and access to collections in digital format. In 1994, the same year as the NSF Digital Library Initiative, the Library of Congress created the National Digital Library. The National Digital Library Foundation is a joint effort with 15 large research libraries to provide a digital service that makes information on American heritage and history widely available. Different institutions are providing resources for the project. For example, Cornell and the University of Michigan are working together on the 'Making of America' project that will digitize important works and documents dealing with American history. The number of digital library projects has grown exponentially with the advent of the Internet. This growth makes it impossible to present even a cursory discussion of the varied projects and initiatives being undertaken.

Lesk mentions many of the initiatives being undertaken in the U.S. and internationally. The list is growing daily. Due to the relative ease of creating digital library projects and the trickle down of technologies developed by the larger DL projects, smaller local institutions and individuals are now undertaking their own projects. Since these projects are generally available on the WWW, they become part of a larger global information infrastructure. Items created locally and intended for a relatively small audience may be used by others and provide valuable information to information seekers elsewhere. Therefore, local digital library projects can serve a valuable function in supplementing the information provided by the larger institutions. The locally produced DL projects might provide expertise on subjects that may be overlooked by the larger institutions.

Due to the infrastructure provided by past research, especially that which is provided by government backed DLI initiatives, many institutions are now capable of making important collections available online. Digital libraries are not inexpensive propositions. An important challenge may be to come up with the appropriate funding to support digital libraries. Decisions to fund digital libraries must often come at the expense of traditional library services. This may be detrimental to the overall level of services provided by the institution. In order for digital libraries to meet their potential, proper funding mechanisms must be identified and developed.

We have seen that research into digital libraries has played an important role in their development. Although this process has been ongoing, it appears that 1994 was the watershed year when digital library research began in earnest with the NSF-funded creation of the 6 original DLI projects and the Library of Congress' NDL project.

User-centered Digital Libraries

When considering the future of digital libraries, "user friendly" becomes a key term, but "user-centered" is more appropriate. It is hard to envision a future for digital collections that does not further embrace the user and his/her input. In "Checking Out the Future Perspectives from the Library Community on Information Technology and 21st-Century Libraries," Jennifer C. Hendrix states "No collaborator will be more important or accessible than the library user. User participation and input will increasingly drive the adoption of technology, library services, and the design of physical and digital library spaces" (Hendrix, 2010). This is increasingly an individual-centered society. With a business-like librarianship, where the focus is serving the public, it makes sense that librarians, in developing their digital collections, will include participatory feedback from their patrons in the decisions that are made.

The now defunct Eye4YouAllianceIsland in Teen Second Life, a project based in Charlotte, North Carolina, was a prime example of the future focus on patron/library collaboration in a flexible online space where teens could exchange ideas, create content, and use linked sources like LSLWiki. This furthers the use of social networks in digital librarianship. Through using a way of communication and thinking the future of America is comfortable with, the NC Library and its collaborators (including the Alliance Library System, Trinity Episcopal School, National Public Radio, NASA, and the Technology Museum of Innovation) are pushing librarianship comfortably into the future (Hendrix, 2010).

Another user/library collaborative project cited by Hendrix is the Center for Digital Humanities and Culture at Indiana University of Pennsylvania found at http://wwww.digitalhumanities.net/. This project states in its mission: "The Center for Digital Humanities and Culture… support scholarship, proof-of-concept explorations and project applications of digital technologies in Humanities inquiry… today technology saturates the entire academic sphere, from classroom to library, to lab. The goal of the Center is to facilitate conversation, collaboration, and resource sharing amongst specialists within these disciplines." They offer non-residential fellowships, a student blog to "create a community of learners in dialogue," and collaborative projects like a "networked book," that will keep chapters "open for revision commentary and translation by online collaborators." This is a vision of the digital libraries of the future: fluid and open to contribution from users.

This user-centered sentiment is echoed by Peter Brantley in his article "Architectures for Collaboration: Roles and Expectations for Digital Libraries." In the article, Brantley (2008) gives his "musts" for the survival of libraries in the digital age. Libraries have to get better with use because "people—not library curators—enrich our collections." He also suggests that libraries must be portable. As he sees it, in an age where people rely on mobile phones and other portable devices, libraries have extensively offered a number of mobile access and services.

What challenges are digital libraries facing?

Many research issues remain to be studied. Many of the important research issues concerning digital libraries are discussed in two important documents: the report to the President, "Digital Libraries: Universal Access to Human Knowledge" (February 2001), which makes several recommendations for areas that need to be expanded for research, and a similar report entitled "Summary Report of the Series of Joint NSF-EU Working Groups on Future Directions for Digital Library Research" (February 1998), located at http://www.iei.pi.cnr.it/DELOS/NSF/Brussrep.htm, which gives similar recommendations.

The Information Infrastructure Technology and Applications (IITA) Working Group, the highest level of the country's National Information Infrastructure (NII) technical committee, held an invitational workshop in May 1995 to define a research agenda for digital libraries.

Objects of any type can be searched within and across different indexed collections in an entire net of distributed repositories (Schatz and H. Chen). In the short term, technologies must be developed to search across these repositories transparently, handling any variations in protocols and formats; for example, they may address structural interoperability (Paepcke). In the long term, technologies also must be developed to handle variations in content and meanings transparently. These requirements are steps along the way toward matching the concepts being explored by users with objects indexed in collections (Schatz).

The ultimate goal, as described in the IITA report, is the Grand Challenge of Digital Libraries, is

> deep semantic interoperability - the ability of a user to access, consistently and coherently, similar (though autonomously defined and managed) classes of digital objects and services, distributed across heterogeneous repositories, with federating or mediating software compensating for site-by-site variations...Achieving this will require breakthroughs in description as well as retrieval, object interchange and object retrieval protocols. Issues here include the definition and use of metadata and its capture or computation from objects, both textual and multimedia, the use of computed descriptions of objects, federation and integration of heterogeneous repositories with disparate semantics, clustering and automatic hierarchical organization of information, and algorithms for automatic rating, ranking, and evaluation of information quality, genre, and other properties.

Attention to semantic interoperability has prompted several NSF/DARPA/NASA funded large-scale digital library initiative (DLI) projects to explore various artificial intelligence, statistical, and pattern recognition techniques, e.g., concept spaces and category maps in the Illinois project (Schatz), textile and word sense disambiguation in the Berkeley project (Wactlar), voice recognition in the CMU project (Wactlar), and image segmentation and clustering in the UCSB project (Manjunath).

The ubiquity of online information has continued to push information and computer science researchers toward developing scalable artificial intelligence techniques for other emerging information systems applications.

In the Santa Fe Workshop on Distributed Knowledge Work Environments: Digital Libraries, held in March, 1997, a panel of digital library researchers and practitioners suggested three areas of research for the planned Digital Library Initiative-2 (DLI-2): system-centered issues, collection-centered issues, and user-centered issues. Scalability, interoperability, adaptability and durability, and support for collaboration are the four key research directions under system-centered issues. System interoperability, syntactic (structural) interoperability, linguistic interoperability, temporal interoperability, and semantic interoperability are recognized by leading researchers as some of the most challenging and rewarding research areas. (See http://www.si.umich.edu/SantaFe/)

Issues for Further Research

METADATA AND METADATA USE. Multimedia digital libraries present difficulties in describing information that cannot be described in simple text documents. Methods need to be developed to describe this media. For example, how should one describe a melody on a soundtrack, a video, or a musical score? Issues such as how to describe digital representations of images, paintings, sculptures, etc. must also be addressed. Methods for determining the provenance of content also require refinement. For example, a means needs to be developed to describe when, where, why, and how an object was created with details about its subsequent history. Metadata also needs to convey the reputation or trust one can place in a digital object. This might include a means to determine the accuracy of data sets or the authority of sources issuing digital documents. Research in creating metadata practices and standards along with a means for automating the creation of metadata is essential to the development of effective digital libraries.

SCALABILITY. Man produces terabytes of information daily. Fortunately, much of this material is now produced in digital form. However, only a small portion is in 'text' form. Research must solve the problem of moving from the manual collection management that was used in the past to using automated software-based methods. Software systems will need to understand and classify large amounts of multimedia materials and present them in a way that is understandable. Current research has yet to develop a scalable universal standard for a networked digital catalog of digital content that is able to interoperate with already established systems.

INTEROPERABILITY. Although progress has been made on this issue, ongoing research and the setting of standards can certainly lead to increased interoperability among digital libraries.

ARCHIVAL STORAGE AND PRESERVATION. Although many mistakenly believe that once an item is digitized it is preserved forever, this is not the case. Digitization is only the first step. Procedures for long-term storage and the capture of digital content that may be short-lived are issues that need to be resolved. Growing economic costs associated with the storage of digital materials is also problematic. For this reason, cost-effective long-term storage, efficient archiving, and preservation procedures are the focus of much research.

INTELLECTUAL PROPERTY ISSUES. The entire area of licensing, liability, and legislation dealing with intellectual property is in need of continuing research. Such research must come up with a means for digital libraries to manage and protect intellectual property rights while still providing users with meaningful access to materials.

PRIVACY AND SECURITY. Research to protect the privacy of users and to protect digital content from unauthorized use is key issues in the electronic environment. Research needs to continue in order to develop efficient means to protect the rights of all parties involved in digital transactions.

USABILITY. Research needs to be ongoing in order to ensure that digital libraries are able to provide access to users in the best manner possible. Usability covers a variety of issues. These issues may include the creation of effective interfaces, the provision of sufficiently wide bandwidth to effectively present multimedia materials, accessibility for those with handicaps, creation of improved means for searching, etc. Also, since the Internet makes digital libraries accessible globally, the issue of how to deal with diverse languages and cultures must be addressed. Research in all of these areas is essential to the future of digital libraries. As one can see, the issues that need continuing research are numerous and quite involved. Only a few of the major issues at the forefront of research have been touched upon here. Many other more complicated issues are being studied. The assistance of the government in funding research projects and large test-beds for the research and development of digital libraries has been beneficial in the past and it appears that it will continue to provide a major boost to advancements in this field.

Libraries must know where they are

An even grander technological advancement for digital libraries as seen by Brantley is "libraries must know where they are." Just as a mobile phone can pinpoint its user's geographical location, so should libraries. The portable digital libraries of the future, as seen by Brantley, will adjust to the user's geographical location, gathering information that is "relevant to location-based learning and geographic information services." (Brantley, 2008)

Brantley (2008) also wants to utilize more relevant media with his mantra: "Libraries must tell stories." In his opinion, digital libraries of the future should feature video and audio content, because that's more engaging than reading an article. Brantley (2008) says, "that TV engages us more easily than books do." So, videos of information will be more "direct."

In his mantra "Libraries must be tools of change," Brantley (2008) embraces what most see as a problem with information on the Internet: its fluidity. He states: "to publish today means publishing all the time—updating, commenting, changing. Publishing is fluid, punctuated, and diverse. And publishing is interactive, involving conversations in which libraries can play a key role." So, while some see it as a problem that information can no longer be contained in a published book, and is subject to constant change because it is now digital, Brantley views this fluidity as a good thing, and libraries can be instrumental in the process of altering information: "Libraries can lead the redefinition of new forms of scholarly communication" (Brantley, 2008).

Another Brantley mantra is "libraries must forge memory." Embracing the traditional library role of preservation. Brantley is realistic in his expectation that preservation will still be relevant in a digital format.

Brantley (2008) wants libraries to join with what is essentially their biggest threat to survival: the big search engines. "Google, Yahoo!, Amazon.com, and Microsoft are, obviously, important content holders, with massive scale and visibility." Their digital libraries are inevitable, so Brantley's (2008) 'can't beat them, join them' approach makes perfect sense. A digital library powered by Google, or Yahoo will be a really easy to use and efficient research tool.

What can we then expect of digital libraries of the future? All of these predictions are in some form being used now and will continue to be absorbed into digital libraries, but it is important to always remember that digital technology itself is fluid and there are things yet to be invented that will become part of digital libraries. For now, we can say that user-friendly websites that welcome user contribution, that are easily accessible from wherever the user is, and that are powered by the big web companies such as Google, are a good prediction of what we can expect in the future for digital libraries.

Pandamic

In the height of the pandemic, US libraries resorted to providing digital services during the pandemic's peak, but their physical locations remained closed. During the lockdown in March-May 2020, libraries were extremely vital because they supplied amusement, important COVID information, and learning tools for online schooling.

The COVID pandemic has brought attention to and emphasized the need for digital library services. To sustain their outreach services, digital library programs have extensively used Overdrive, Libby, and Hoopla, as well as synchronous and asynchronous reference services, online reference databases, and Zoom. The COVID pandemic has brought attention to and emphasized the need for digital library services.

During this time, vendors also offered libraries free extended trials of their databases to meet the needs of their library customers (Huffman, 2020). Libraries were able to take advantage of these promotions by providing more services to their customers and experimenting with new possible library resources. Libraries also provided "grab and go" services. A patron might use the library's online catalog to find the materials they wanted to borrow. After that, the books would be placed in a bag outside a table for them to take. Patrons were able to identify which resources were accurate for their information demands without physically viewing the item because to the extensive records kept by libraries.

As the pandemic draws to an end, libraries are faced with the decision of whether or not to keep the COVID-related services in place. When social distancing is no longer required, will the "grab and go" service be phased out? Should the library keep or cancel the extra digital subscriptions it purchased or acquired during the pandemic? "Would the novelty wear off after the crisis?" Huffman wonders. Would they just sit around and not be used, eventually costing money?" (2020).

Libraries need to make the difficult decision of what role they will play in the post-pandemic world. Will consumers regard digital libraries and digital services as a pandemic novelty? Are digital libraries and services becoming the new standard? Libraries must fully incorporate digital libraries within the academic community

12.2: Education for Digital Librarians

Due to the changing nature of librarianship resulting from the increasing amount of information available in digital format, educating digital librarians has become an important agenda within library and information science schools (Choi & Rasmussen, 2006).

An Emerging Discipline Based on the Web

Would "Digital Library Science" be an emerging discipline in higher education? A collaborative effort made from different disciplines, computer science, information science, library science, electronic engineering, management information systems, linguistics and others is forming an emerging discipline, Digital Library Science.

The state of education on digital libraries at this moment is unsettled; both Master and Doctoral degrees are being considered or beginning to be offered, responding to the need of preparing a new generation of information professions who can best serve for the future practice of digital libraries.

The Needs of Digital Librarians

In "How to Build a Digital Library," the authors, Witten & Bainbridge (2003) discuss the ever-present change in library development, especially in the digital realm. They quote one author as stating the attributes for digital librarians to be:

- Capacity to learn constantly and quickly
- Flexibility
- Innate skepticism
- Propensity to take risks
- Public-service perspective
- Aptitude for teamwork
- Facility for enabling and fostering change
- Ability to work independently (Witten & Bainbridge, 2003)

In a small study completed by Choi(Choi & Rasmussen, 2006), current practitioners who were in charge of digitization projects or digital library projects were surveyed. Among the group of questions asked were the skills and knowledge needed to perform from 23 sub-areas on a 5-point Likert scale. The five highest ranked choices were:

- Communication and interpersonal skills (4.60)
- Project management/leadership skills (4.56)
- Understanding of digital library architecture and software (4.52)
- Knowledge of the needs of users (4.42)
- Knowledge of technical and quality standards (4.33)

The survey also asked participants to indicate the most relevant courses they had taken in an LIS school for performing their current work. Twenty-one respondents replied. The most frequently mentioned courses were in the areas of cataloging, collection (electronic resources) development and management, systems analysis, and information technology. Digital libraries, as a course, was only mentioned once (Choi & Rasmussen, 2006). The survey respondents did not include the public library arena and out of the 146 surveys sent, less than half responded. Given this limitation, Choi and Rasmussen were still able to draw some conclusions: "It appears the LIS education needs to pay attention to additional education in interpersonal and communication skills and integration of practical skills and experience with digital collection management and digital technologies into curricula"(Choi & Rasmussen, 2006).

The Needs of Education

Challenges and issues surrounding the field are intensive. How can we acquire the resources needed to create balanced and complete collections? What software and construction will make them easily accessible and user-friendly? How can we organize and access this information? The problems, challenges, and issues of creating the resource and making it known and available to users are the current concern of digital library education. This is reasonable, because the technology and creation of these libraries is still so new that those involved are pioneers in a novel field. Other issues, such as preservation, and how to achieve access for all levels of society, while important, cannot be problems until the entity exists; until there is a library, we don't need to wonder how to access it. Thus, this trend in professional education is leading students to take a contributing and participatory role in the very newest technologies and discipline of our calling.

A recent survey by R. Varalakshmi found that professionals' expectations of library science programs are:

- To focus on producing knowledge managers instead of mere librarians;
- To focus on imparting knowledge on web-based services as the future belongs to the Web/Net;
- To organize more fields of study and interact with working librarians to gain knowledge on real time situations and enable them to blend the learning with working skills;
- To have a more practical component in curriculum as information technology is practice based.
- To offer specialization in the areas of Knowledge Management, Multimedia systems, Web design and development and Digital libraries.

Digital librarians should have what basic skills? Chowdhury & Chowdhury (year) recognize four major skills that digital librarians should strive to master in regards to digital library activities:

ICT (Information communications technologies) skills, which include:
- digitization and document management skills
- basic networking skills
- web design and development skills
- skills for design and evaluation digital library architecture, systems and software
- new digital library product and service design skills

Information skills, which include:
- collection management skills
- information organization skills
- information retrieval skills
- digital reference and information services skills
- skills related to various types of user studies, user educations, etc.
- skills for providing value-added information products and services.

Management skills, which include:
- general management skills such as vision, leadership qualities, strategic decision-making qualities, interpersonal communication skills, etc.

- personal and financial skills
- marketing skills
- customer relations and management skills

Research and project management skills, which include:
- research design and management skills
- fundraising skills
- project management skills
- learning skills
- publication and reporting skills

The primary emphasis in the field is on the nuts-and-bolts operations of digital libraries, which now is a cross-disciplinary field that resides in the intersection of several main study areas: computer science, information science, library science, electronic engineering, management information systems, linguistics and others.

Institutional Response

In 2004, Yan Liu, a professor at Southern Connecticut State University investigated the state of education for digital libraries. This study found the number of courses on the subject had more than doubled from 20 to 42. The educational emphasis was split into two camps: 1) "hands-off," which did not have a practical component (building an actual library), and 2) "hands-on," which did. Liu discovered the schools that combined library science with computer science emphasized metadata, databases and information retrieval. The schools of library or information science emphasized a balance of theory and technology. Most of the schools covered definitions, history and development, organization, storage, access, intellectual property, technology and maintenance (Yan Quan, 2004). Liu (2004) stated near the conclusion that although the digital courses offered suggested that quality and quantity had improved since 1999, there was need for improvement in the following areas: 1) Sharing access to digital libraries, as the "have-nots" did not receive much attention, 2) Courses should devote additional class time to the needs and information seeking behavior of the end-uses of digital libraries, and 3) Courses in digital libraries should provide students with both a theoretical study of, and practice in designing, constructing and evaluating digital libraries (Yan Quan, 2004).

In 2005, Barbara Blummer (2005) expanded the study of digital library course offerings and post-graduate offerings. She stated that traditional library skills are no longer adequate for maintaining a competitive edge in the field and post-graduate education in digital libraries offers information professionals an opportunity to broaden their knowledge (2005).

Blummer (2005) reviewed different modes of opportunity in achieving this knowledge. One was through continuing education. This included workshops, professional development sessions and continuing education courses. She cited Peter Jasco's 2003 article, "Training (beyond education) in Computer in Libraries" as providing an overview of sources of training. She further discusses several programs at the University of Wisconsin--Milwaukee, Texas A&M, University of Syracuse, University of Illinois at Urbana-Champaign, Wayne State University and others. All of these offered graduate, post-graduate study or certificates in digital library studies. Of note, two offered unique strategies worth mentioning.

Wayne State University's Library and Information Science Program utilized IMLS (Institute of Museum and Library Service) funds to provide a digital librarian master's degree program for underrepresented groups. This is a two-year degree that includes 15 hours interning at one of the WSU digital library programs. As of this current date (2010), this degree does not seem to be offered anymore but has been transformed to a graduate certificate in Arts and Museum Librarianship.(Graduate Certificate in Arts and Museum Librarianship - School of Library and Information Science - Wayne State University, 2010). It includes digital curation skills and museum library management.

Another IMLS funded program (2005) is a collaborative project with the University of Illinois Graduate School of Library and Information Science and the School of Library and Information Science at Indiana University. Indiana University offered "a research based master's degree level to educate librarians to work in digital library programs in libraries and archives"(Blummer, 2005). This did culminate in a degree offering of MLS with Digital Libraries Specialization starting in 2009 ("MLS Digital Libraries Specialization," 2010). These two examples alone show how much can change in five years.

12.3: Digital Library Science for Digital Librarianship

The new information technology era calls for new professionals. A number of academic programs in higher education have made the global community aware of the immense potential of the Internet for enhancing students' learning. Educating digital information professionals for the 21st century have been recognized by the following pioneering universities.

Johns Hopkins University has announced a new concentration, Digital Libraries, designed for librarians and information managers in their innovative master's degree that addresses the transformation of the information professions in the Digital Age. The program focuses mainly on emerging trends and sociological issues. Course of study include Communication law, Cultural differences, Digital objects, Digital rights, Electronic publishing, Emerging technologies, History of communications technology and Libraries in the digital age. The course "Libraries in the Digital Age" addresses issues concerning the "transformation of the traditional library and the changing impact libraries are having in academic, government, and community settings." Issues such as intellectual freedom and literacy, the centrality of information policies, and intellectual property and privacy are also examined.

The University of Pittsburgh now offers a Specialization in Digital Libraries with specific course electives that can be taken within the track, including: Introduction to Information Technologies, User Needs and Information Services, Information Architecture, Digital Image Collections, Automations of Library Systems and Services, Advanced Topics in Information Storage and Retrieval, Technologies for Information Management, Digital Libraries, Digital Preservation, Digitizing Library and Research Collections for Access, and Database Design and Applications (http://www.sis.pitt.edu/~dlis/academics/course_descriptions/course2600.html). These are all classes that support the digital library curricula and cover a variety of the issues mentioned above in a more in-depth manner than a generalized introduction course. The Specialization in Digital Library degree also offers objectives for its program: "The goals of the Digital Libraries specialization within the MLIS program is to provide a student with a course of study that affords a grounding in several key areas: information architecture, digital document design, and database design and implementation, as well as librarianship's core concerns" (http://www.sis.pitt.edu/~dlis/academics/course_descriptions/course2600.html).

Overall, every syllabus and curricula reviewed provide instruction about similar ideas, trends, and issues within the digital library field, and more importantly addresses each and every issue addressed in the current literature discussed above.

Syracuse University School of Information Studies' 2004 course descriptions list a Certificate of Advanced Studies in Digital Libraries, which requires 18 hours of completed coursework. There are three core classes: IST 676 Digital Libraries, IST 677 Creating, Managing, and Preserving Digital Assets, and IST 759 Planning and Designing Digital Libraries Services. The core classes, as their titles suggest, deal with the creation and management of digital libraries. The remaining courses, made up of electives, provide students with the opportunity to focus on a particular area of interest to them. These vary from the aforementioned information behavior (IST 641 Behavior of Information Users) to the detailed technological aspects (IST 731 Knowledge Organization Structures). This university provides a balanced course list, including both the library and the technical sides of the digital library concept. This is not particularly common, though it is generally more concentrated on one or the other. "If a course is offered through the computer science department, the emphasis tends to be on technology, metadata, databases and retrieval. If the course is included in the library or information science department offerings, the emphasis seems to be more on organizing, preserving, managing, and providing access to information" (Liu, 2004, p. 63-64).

Drexel University also now offers a Certificate in Digital Information. The Digital Information certificate prepares information professionals to manage digital information resources and processes, centering on the Internet and the World-Wide Web. Courses focus on mining Internet content, organizing digital resources for corporate use and developing local Web sites. Students with certificates who want to continue on to a master's degree will have the option of applying the certificate course credits toward a degree for up to 3 years after course completion. Submission of a full graduate application including official transcripts is required for admission to a master's program. Students cannot transfer more than 15 credits received as a non-matriculated student into a degree program. (http://www.drexel.com/Fields_of_Study/information_sciences/digital-info/index.shtml)

The University of North Carolina at Chapel Hill School of Information and Library Science is doing groundbreaking work in the field of digital libraries through its Center for Research and Development of Digital Libraries (CRADLE) program. The program identifies itself as a federation of interested parties devoted to the development of digital libraries and librarians, and they address all library service aspects of the field: creation, preservation, management and accessibility of resources, as well as transfer of information, research and testing involved in this developing area. CRADLE contains digital libraries of its own, and provides links to two dozen more. They also offer seminars every month discussing current topics in the field. The CRADLE program, with its concentration on the development and implementation of new methodologies, is a rich resource for graduate students in the university's Information and Library Science program, which is heavily geared to computer topics and proficiencies. Computer-based topics such as natural language processing, network management, data mining and information systems design are combined with computer/library topics such as introduction to databases and managing serials in an electronic age, and traditional library topics such as abstracting and indexing, preservation and archiving and school library media centers. The program offers a broad range of competencies from undergraduate minors and certificates of advanced study to Bachelors, Masters and Doctoral degrees.

The most recent exciting news is the newly established funding for "Recruiting and Educating Digital Librarians for the 21st Century" sponsored by the Institute of Museum and Library Services.

The Master's Program in Digital Libraries now is offered through a joint effort from the School of Library and Information Science at Indiana University--Bloomington, and the Graduate School of Library and Information Science at the University of Illinois--Urbana-Champaign. The new Master's program with emphasis on digital libraries is funded by the Institute of Museum and Library Services (http://www.imls.gov), which is "the creation of the first research-based, comprehensive master's-level and post-MLS degrees to educate librarians for work in digital library programs in libraries and archives." It has been developed as a collaboration between the iSchool at University of Illinois (http://alexia.lis.uiuc.edu/) and the Digital Library Program at Indiana University (http://www.dlib.indiana.edu/). They will award five fellowships to support a complete Master's degree with internship experience. (Digital Libraries Education Program, http://lair.indiana.edu/research/dlib/).

Similarly, the University of Texas in Austin offers Digital Library Master's and Doctoral Student Scholarships through the "Digitization in the Round Project," funded with $626,755 by the Institute of Museum and Library Services (IMLS) and begun in January 2005. The project "aims to recruit and educate library and information professionals in the art and science of creating and managing digital libraries. "Enormous challenges face libraries and special collections in their efforts to select, digitize, and manage digital libraries. A well-documented crisis faces the library and information profession to recruit and educate future librarians. This project acknowledges and addresses the need for librarians with specialized knowledge and skills in developing digital libraries."

Curricula for Digital Library Science

The concentration of courses for digital libraries differs from the schools. While some schools' courses center on social aspects of digital libraries, such as digital library user studies, user design, and human computer interaction, others focus on system aspects of digital libraries, such as metadata, information architecture, system interoperability, XML, and databases.

Courses for Master's Degree with Concentration in Digital Libraries from Indiana University include the following: Digital Libraries, Foundations of Information Architecture, User-Centered Database Design, Metadata, Computer Programming for Information Management, Network Technologies and Administration (Computer Science), Information Storage and Retrieval Theory, User Interface Design, Introduction to Human-computer Interaction, Information Usage and the Cognitive Artifact, Evaluation of Information Systems, Information Policies, Economics, and Law, Computerization in Society, Seminar in Intellectual Freedom, and Internship in Library and Information Science.

Courses required for the "Digitization in the Round" program in the School of Information the University of Texas are the following: Digitization Survey Class, Digitization for Preservation and Access; Research Seminar: Digitization for Digital Libraries and Archives; Introduction to Electronic and

Digital Records; Digital Libraries; Lifecycle Metadata for Digital Objects; and Problems in Retention of Electronic Records.

Only three courses for the "Certificate in Digital Information" at Drexel are required. They are: Internet Information Resource Design, Digital Libraries and Programming Internet Information Systems.

Based on the courses proposed by these universities, an ideal curriculum for the new discipline would be the following:

Core courses:
1. Digital Libraries, its theory and practice
2. XML and Digital Library Architectures
3. Digital Assets Creation and Management
4. Digital Libraries Services

Elective courses and Recommended tracks
1. Digital Image Collection
2. Digital Video and Multimedia Collection
3. Digital Media Design
4. Digital Preservation
5. Digital Heritage
6. Digital Library Evaluation
7. Digital Library Use Studies
8. Metadata for Digital Objects
9. Text Mining/Data Mining
10. Data Curation
11. Document Modeling
12. Artificial Intelligence & Virtual Libraries
13. Programming Internet Information Systems

Study on Master of Science in Digital Librarianship

A comprehensive review or meta-analysis is needed and long overdue to fully discover the educational avenues required for the current decade. Universities continue to expand and develop their curriculum, extending their specialization in digital libraries. To briefly see if the institutions have answered some of the shortcomings and needs expressed in the first section, a review of three university catalog offerings is explored. The shortcomings and needs listed above for digital library education and librarians were grouped together where they were best comparable and were measurable for outcome. The university catalogs reviewed were Drexel University (Philadelphia, PA), ("Online Degrees in Library Science provided by Drexel University Online," 2010),Indiana University (Bloomington, IN),("Comprehensive SLIS Course List," 2010) and San Jose State University,("SJSU SLIS | Course Descriptions," 2010). These three universities were randomly picked but represent different regional areas of the United States.

1). Communication and interpersonal skills and/or Project management/leadership skills

>Drexel offers Managing Information Organizations and Library Management. SJSU offers Information Organizations and Management and Interpersonal Communication Skills for Librarians and Systems Analysis. Indiana University offers Organizational Informatics, Library Management,

2). Sharing access to digital libraries with the "have-nots"/ The Digital Divide.

>Drexel offers Professional and Social Aspects of Information Services. SJSU offers course study in Information and Society and Library Services for Racially and Ethnically Diverse Communities. Though a course on social implications specifically wasn't found at Indiana University, they did offer a course for Resources and Services for People with Disabilities.

3). Courses should devote additional class time to the needs and information seeking behavior of the end-users of digital libraries.

>Drexel University offers Information and User Services and Human-Computer Interaction. SJSU offers Web Usability and Resources and Information Services in Professions and Disciplines. Though the course name may not directly cover digital libraries, this course covers digital humanities and cultural differences of users. Indiana University offers Human-Computer Interaction, and selective courses User-Interface Design, and Information Seeking and Use,

4). Courses in digital libraries should provide students with both a theoretical study of and practice in designing, constructing and evaluating digital libraries. This should also include knowledge of technical and quality standards. This also includes design architecture and software.

>Drexel offers a concentration in Digital Libraries. The student must take three courses: a) Internet Information Resource Design, b) Digital Libraries, and c) Digital Library Technology. An elective course in Information Architecture is also offered.

SJSU does not offer specific courses in Digital Libraries, but includes it in its course Seminar in Information Science. It does offer courses on Web Management and Design. SJSU states that "because of the depth and diversity of the faculty, students take part in a curriculum that can adjust quickly to changes in the LIS and the world"("SJSU SLIS | Program and Courses," 2010). Indiana University offers only one course on Digital Libraries. From the course description, there is no actual development of a digital library.

From these examples, there seems to still be some disparity on the development of curriculum for digital librarians. Universities such as Drexel, which is known for its high-tech computer education overall, have more in-depth technical courses. Universities such as San Jose, which is a culturally diverse city, have more course selections on social impact. Though SJSU has web development courses, it has not developed a digital course as a standard. Indiana has some of both, but does not seem to have a lab practical for its course in digital libraries. Like Drexel, Indiana does offer a MLS with a specialization in Digital Libraries. This combines standard library science courses with information technology courses and in-depth study of metadata and design("MLS Digital Libraries Specialization," 2010).

There are other universities which do have digital library courses and which may offer lab practices, such as Southern Connecticut State University, University of Michigan, University of Wisconsin-Milwaukee, and Virginia Tech. The student who wishes to develop digital libraries should further research the various institutions, for they are not standardized in their approaches to information science.

Continuing education

For the digital librarian and the self-starter, there are websites available such as Ebrary (Ebrary - Home). Using "digital librarian education, United States (limiter)" as search parameters, 15 chapters from several books were returned viewable at digital education for librarians. These were all available for viewing on the Internet. There are also websites such as the Digital Librarian at http://www.digitallibrarian.org. This is an informational/blog site designed by Jeremy Frumkin, Assistant Dean for the University of Arizona(Frumkin, 2010).

The American Library Association has webinars on different aspects of digital libraries ("ALA | Digital Libraries," 2010). This digital library includes the topics "Developing a Metadata Policy," "Digital Licensing Online eCourse," and "Perpetual Beta: Early Literature about Institutional Repositories and What Assessments Can Tell Us." These courses and continuing education should benefit digital librarians.

Certificate of Study

As reviewed by Blummer (2005), Certificates of Study have been available since 2005. At the University of Wisconsin, a graduate student may specialize in Digital Libraries. If the student is post-graduate, a Certificate of Study may be completed with 24 graduate credits selected by the student along with a faculty advisor ("Specialist Certificate," 2010). Syracuse University offers an 18-credit course resulting in a Certificate of Advance Study in Digital Libraries. It has 9 credits of core subjects and offers twenty courses ranging from architecture, managing projects to behavior of users and human-computer interaction ("CAS in Digital Libraries: Curriculum - iSchool - Syracuse University," 2010). Most of these Certificates of Study are available online.

Conclusion

Digital library education during the first decade of the new millennium has continued to expand. Not all schools of library science or information studies offer courses in digital libraries. Though the core graduate studies for a MLS are continually offered, specialization in studies such as digital libraries are also available. If the student already has a MLS or another professional degree, a certificate of study is obtainable in the area. Again, a published review of all schools and courses is indeed needed to thoroughly address the adequacy of education for digital librarians and some of the unmet needs.

What can we then expect of Digital Libraries of the futures? The predictions covered in this chapter are in some form being used now and will continue to be absorbed into digital libraries. It is important to always remember, digital technology itself is fluid and there are things yet to be invented that will become part of digital libraries.

Study Questions for Chapter Twelve:

1. It is particularly difficult to provide a survey of what is being done around the world in digital library projects. If you were to write a Fulbright to study digital libraries around the world, what qualities, issues or themes in digital libraries would you want to research?

2. With information so easy to access electronically, what do you think will become of the librarian as a professional? Vanevar Bush described the librarian as a "trailblazer" (pages 270-271 of Lesk). To quote, "librarians will not be those who provide the water but those who navigate the ship." Do you agree with this statement or disagree? Please support your answer.

3. What are the challenges and issues to Global Digital Library Collaborations, such as collection infrastructure issues, architecture issues, policy issues, technological challenges, and multilingual challenges? Provide examples from assigned readings, personal knowledge, or examples from the most current literature on the Web to support your arguments. Borgman suggests there are several challenges in developing a global digital library, one of them being "to transfer the technology and services to parts of the world with different traditions and practices than those of the Group of Seven major industrialized nations that laid the technical and political framework for a global information infrastructure." On page 240, he states, "availability...does not guarantee freedom of speech or access to information." Do you think there will ever be a global digital library? What do you feel is the future of the digital library?

4. What's next for digital libraries?

Bibliographical References

1. About.com. (2005). What is a portal, really? Retrieved from http://compnetworking.about.com/od/internetaccessbestuses/l/aa011900a.htm
2. Ackerman, M. S. and Fielding, R. T. (1995). Collection maintenance in the digital library. Retrieved from http://www.csdl.tamu.edu/DL95/papers/ackerman/ackerman.html#RTFToC15
3. ACM. (2003). Digital libraries across cultures: design and usability issues.
4. Adam, N. R., Bhargava, B. K., & Yesha, Y. (Eds.). (1995). Digital libraries: Current issues. Berlin: Springer-Verlag.
5. Allem. R.B. & Acheson, J. (2000). Browsing the structure of multimedia stories. Proceedings of the Fifth ACM Conference on Digital Libraries, 11-18.
6. Ambler, S. W. (2005). User interface prototyping tips and techniques. Retrieved from http://www.ambysoft.com/essays/userInterfacePrototyping.html
7. Anderson, J.D. &Carballo, J.P. (2005). Information Retrieval Design: Principles and options for information description, organization, display and access in information retrieval databases, digital libraries, catalogs, and indexes. St. Petersburg, FL: University Publishing Solutions.
8. Anyaoku, E. N., Echedom, A. U. N., & Baro, E. E. (2019). Digital preservation practices in university libraries: An investigation of institutional repositories in Africa. Digital Library Perspectives, 35(1), 41–64. https://doi.org/10.1108/DLP-10-2017-0041
9. Arms, W.Y. (1995, July). Key concepts in the architecture of the digital library. D-Lib Magazine. Retrieved from http://www.dlib.org/dlib/July95/07arms.html
10. Arms, W.Y. (2000). Chapter 1 - Background. In Digital libraries. Cambridge, MA: MIT Press.
11. Atkins,D.E., et al. (1996). Toward inquiry-based education through interacting software agents. IEEE Computer 29(5), 69-76.
12. Atlantic County Library System. (2018, April 12). What is the difference between Libby and the OverDrive app? Atlantic County Library System. https://www.atlanticlibrary.org/node/7368
13. Bajarin, T. (2016, July 18). 3 Things That Pokémon Go Says About the Future of Technology. Time. https://time.com/4410327/pokemon-go-technology/
14. Banerjee, K. & Reese, Jr., T. (2019). *Building digital libraries: a how-to-do-it manual for librarians* (2nd ed.). Chicago, IL: ALA Neal-Schuman.

15. Bansode, N. N., & Shinde, M. G. (2019). Impact of New Technologies in the Digital Libraries. Journal of Advancements in Library Sciences, 6(1), 279-283.
16. Bates, M. (1998). Indexing and Access for Digital Libraries and the Internet: Human, Database, and Domain Factors. Journal of the American Society for Information Science. 49 (13): 1185-1205
17. Baucom, E. (2019). Planning and Implementing a Sustainable Digital Preservation Program. Library Technology Reports, 55(6), 1–28. https://doi-org.scsu.idm.oclc.org/10.5860/ltr.55n6
18. Bielefield, A., **Liu, Y. Q.**, & Waimon, V. (2021). Private post-secondary library websites and the ADA: compliancy and COVID-19. *Universal Access in the Information Society*, 1-16.
19. Belkin, N. J. (1980). Anomalous states of knowledge as a basis for information retrieval. *Canadian journal of information science*. 133-143. Retrieved from https://faculty.washington.edu/harryb/courses/INFO310/Belkin1980_ASK.pdf
20. Belkin, N. J., Oddy, R. N., & Brooks, H. M. (1982). ASK for information retrieval: Part I. Background and theory. Journal of documentation.
21. Bell, L. & Peters, T. (2005). Digital Library Services for All. American Libraries, 36,8, 46-49
22. Benton Foundaton. (1996). Buildings, books, and bytes: Libraries and communities in the digital age. Washington, DC: Benton Foundation.
23. Biodiversity Heritage Library. (n.d.) Collection Development Policy. Retrieved from https://about.biodiversitylibrary.org/about/collection-management/collectiondevelopment-
24. Bishop, A, Peterson, A., Van House, N A., & Buttenfield, B. P. (2005). (Eds). Digital library use: Special practice in design and evaluation. Cambridge, MA: The MIT Press.
25. Bishop, A. P., Van House, N. A. (2003). Digital library use: social practice in design and evaluation. Cambridge, Mass.: MIT Press.
26. Board of Trustees of the Leland Stanford Junior University. (2004). Copyright and fair use overview. Retrieved from http://fairuse.stanford.edu/Copyright_and_Fair_Use_Overview/index.html
27. Boateng, F., & **Liu, Y. Q.** (2014). Web 2.0 applications' usage and trends in top US academic libraries. *Library Hi Tech*.
28. Borgman, C. L. (1999). What are digital libraries? Competing visions. Information Processing & Management. 35, 227-243.

29. Borgman, C. L. (2000). From Gutenberg to the global information infrastructure: Access to information in the networked world. Cambridge, MA: MIT Press.
30. Borgman, C. L. (2002). Challenges in building digital libraries for the 21st century. In Digital Libraries: People, Knowledge, and Technology: 5th International Conference on Asian Digital Libraries (pp. 1-13). London: Springer-Verlag.
31. Borgman, C.L. (1997). From Acting Locally to Thinking Globally: A Brief History of Literary Automation. The Library Quarterly: Information, Community, Policy, Vol. 67, (No. 3) pp. 215-249. https://www-jstor-org.scsu.idm.oclc.org/stable/pdf/40039721.pdf?refreqid=excelsior%3Affee5cf74bf027be8159579bd9fac79d
32. Börner, K. & Chen, C. (Eds.). (2002). Visual interfaces to digital libraries, LNCS 2539. New York: Springer Verlag.
33. Boynton, R. S. (2005). Book forum: Righting copyright, fair use and "digital environmentalism". Retrieved from http://www.bookforum.com/archive/feb_05/boynton.html
34. British Educational Communications and Technology Agency. Retrieved from http://www.becta.org.uk/technology/infosheets/html/metadata.html
35. Broughton, V. (2006). The need for a faceted classification. *Aslib Proceedings: New Information Perspectives*, *58*(1/2) , 49-72.Library of Congress Subject Headings and Name Authority List available at
36. Brown, A. (2006). Archiving Websites, a Guide for Information Management Professionals. Neal-Schuman Publishers.
37. Brown, M.S. & Seales, B. (2000). Beyond 2D images: Effective 3D imaging for library material. Proceedings of the Fifth ACM Conference on Digital Libraries, 27-36. New York: ACM Press.
38. Bush, Vannevar. (1945, July). As We may Think. Atlantic Monthly. Retrieved from http://www.theatlantic.com/unbound/flashbks/computer/bushf.htm
39. Calado, P.P., et al. (2003). The Web-DL environment for building digital libraries from the Web. In Proceedings of the 3rd ACM/IEEE-CS Joint Conference on Digital Libraries (pp. 346-357). Washington, DC: IEEE.
40. Campbell, J. D. (2006). Changing a cultural icon: The academic library as a virtual destination. *Educause* 41 (1). 16-30.
41. Cardenas, S. & Zelkowitz, M.V. (1990). Evaluation criteria for functional specifications. In Proceedings of the 12th International Conference on Software Engineering. Washington, D. C: IEEE Computer Society Press.

42. Chambers, S., & Myall, C. (2010). Cataloging and classification. Library Resources &Technical Services,54(2), 90-114.
43. Chapman, S. (2001). Digital Library Federation: Report of imaging practitioners meeting on 30 March 2001 to consider how the quality of digital imaging systems and digital images may be fairly evaluated. Retrieved from http://www.diglib.org/standards/imqualrep.htm
44. Choi, Y. and Rasmussen, E. (September 2006). What is Needed to Educate Future Digital Librarians: A study of current practice and staffing patterns in academic and research libraries. *D-Lib Magazine*, 12 (9). (
45. Choudhury, S.; et al. (2002). A framework for evaluating digital library services. D-Lib, 8(78). Retrieved from http://www.dlib.org/dlib/july02/choudhury/07choudhury.html
46. Chowdhury, Gobinda G., &Chowdhury, S. (2003). Introduction to Digital Libraries. London: Facet Publishing.
47. Cleveland, G. (1998). UDT occasional paper #8: Digital libraries: Definitions, issues and challenges. Retrieved from http://www.ifla.org/VI/5/op/udtop8/udtop8.htm
48. Cleveland, Gary, (1998), Digital Libraries Definitions, Issues and Challenges. International Federation of Library Associations and Institutions. Occasional Paper 8, 1-8.
49. Cohen, S., et al. (2000). MyLibrary: Personalized electronic services in the Cornell University Library. *D-Lib*, 6(4).
50. Cohen, S., et al. (2000). Personalized electronic services in the Cornell University Library. *D-Lib*, 6(4).
51. Committee on Intellectual Property Rights and the Emerging Information Infrastructure, et al. (2000). The digital dilemma: Intellectual property in the information age. Washington, D.C.: National Academy Press.
52. Cornell University Library. (2000). Moving theory into practice: Digital imaging tutorial. Retrieved from Cornell University Library, Research Department Website: http://www.library.cornell.edu/preservation/tutorial/contents.html
53. Cousins, S. B., et al. (1997). The digital library integrated task environment (DLITE). Retrieved from http://dbpubs.stanford.edu:8090/pub/1997-69
54. Cuneiform Digital Library Initiative. (2005). CDLI. Retrieved from http://cdli.ucla.edu/
55. Cuvillier, J. (2007). Indexing grey resources: considering usual behavior of library users and the use of Dublin core metadata via a database of specialized vocabulary. Publishing Research Quarterly, 23(1).

56. Dahl, m.; Banerjee, K. & Spalti, M. (2006). Digital Libraries: Integrating Content and Systems. Chandos Publishing (Oxford).
57. Davis, J. R. &Lagoze, C.. (2000). NCSTRL: Design and deployment of a globally distributed digital library. Journal of the American Society for Information Science, 51(3), 273-280.
58. Del Galdo, E. M. & Nielsen, J.> (Eds.). (1996). International user interfaces. New York: Wiley.
59. Digital Library Copyright Project, (n.a., 2020). Berkeley Law, University of California. Retrieved 02/29/20 from https://www.law.berkeley.edu/experiential/clinics/samuelson-law-technology-public-policy-clinic/digital-library-copyright-project/
60. Digital Library Federation. (2004). Digital library standards and practices. Retrieved from http://www.diglib.org/standards.htm
61. Digital Library of Georgia. (2001). Digital library of Georgia digitization guide. Retrieved from http://dlg.galileo.usg.edu/guide.html
62. Digital Library Perspectives, 34 (1), 60–69. https://doi.org/10.1108/DLP-09-2017-0035
63. Digital watermarking, (2020). In Wikipedia. Retrieved from https://en.wikipedia.org/wiki/Digital_watermarking
64. Digitizing Hidden Collections: Success Stories from Small and Medium-sized Digitization Projects. http://www.districtdispatch.org/2011/10/digitizing-hidden-collections-success-stories-from-small-and-medium-sized-digitization-projects-webinar-announcement/
65. Dillon, A. (1999). TIME - A multi-level framework for the design and evaluation of digital libraries. International Journal of Digital Libraries, 2(2/3), 170-177.
66. Disney. (n.d.). MagicBands & Cards – Frequently Asked Questions. Walt Disney World. https://disneyworld.disney.go.com/faq/bands-cards/how-to-use-magic-band/
67. DiStaso, M.W. and Khan, A. (2015, January 12). *What You Should Know About Location-Based Services.* Institute for Public Relations. https://instituteforpr.org/know-location-based-services/
68. Dublin Core Metadata Initiative. (2005). DCMI metadata terms. Retrieved from http://dublincore.org/documents/dcmi-terms/
69. Edelberg, E. (2019). Accessibility Laws for Private Colleges. Retrieved from https://www.3playmedia.com/2017/10/13/accessibility-laws-private-colleges/
70. Eden, B. (2004). MARC and metadata: METS, MODS, and MARCXML: current and future implications. Part 1. *Library High Tech,22*(1).

71. Eden, B. (2004). MARC and metadata: METS, MODS, and MARCXML: current and future implications. Part 2. *Library High Tech,* 22 (2).
72. EGNOS and Galileo LBS Brochure. (2014). In Pereira (2018). Location-Based Services. Navipedia. https://gssc.esa.int/navipedia/index.php/Location_Based_Services
73. Fondren, E., & Menard McCune, M. (2018). Archiving and Preserving Social Media at the Library of Congress: Institutional and Cultural Challenges to Build a Twitter Archive. Preservation, Digital Technology & Culture, 47(2), 33–44. https://doi-org.scsu.idm.oclc.org/10.1515/pdtc-2018-0011
74. Fox, E., et al. (2002, October). Toward a global digital library: Generalizing US-Korea collaboration on digital libraries. *D-Lib Magazine*, 8(10).
75. Fox, E.A. (1998). DL self-study: definitions. Retrieved from: http://ei.cs.vt.edu/~dlib/def.htm
76. Fox, E.A., Pomerantz, J., Sanghee O., Seungwon Y., Wildemuth, B.M. (2006). Digital Library Education in Library and Information Science Programs http://www.dlib.org/dlib/november06/pomerantz/11pomerantz.html
77. Fox, Edward A. (2001). Overview of digital library components and developments. Retrieved from http://www.unm.edu/~jreenen/dlbook/chapter4.html
78. FRANAR. (2007). Functional Requirements for Authority Data: A Conceptual Model (The Hague: International Federation of Library Associations) www.ifla.org/VII/d4/FRANAR-ConceptualModel-2ndReview.
79. Franklin, R. (2003). Re-inventing subject access for the semantic Web. Online Information Review,27(2), 94-101.
80. Gibbons, G. (2011). Catching Glimpses of the Future of Libraries through Library User Studies. Speech at Glimpsing the Future through User Studies. http://www.loc.gov/today/cyberlc/feature_wdesc.php?rec=4937
81. Global Digital Library Development. (1999). Proceedings of the 10th and 11th International Conference on New Information Technology.
82. Global Information Locator Service (GILS) – making it easier to find all the information. (2000). Retrieved from http://www.gils.net/
83. Goodrich, R. (2018, January 22). Location-Based Services: Definition & Examples. Retrieved February 8, 2020, from https://www.businessnewsdaily.com/5386-location-based-services.html

84. Gould, E. M., & Goslen, A. (2019). Digital Preservation in Libraries: Preparing for a Sustainable Future (An ALCTS Monograph). *Library Resources & Technical Services, 63*(3), 217–218.
85. Green, D. (1997, July/August). Beyond word and image: Networking moving images: More than just the "movies": A two-part examination of networking cultural heritage materials. D-Lib Magazine. Retrieved from http://www.dlib.org/dlib/july97/07green.html
86. Greene, S., Marchionini, G., et al. (2000). Previews and overviews in digital libraries: Designing surrogates to support visual information seeking. *Journal of the American Society for Information Science, 51*(4), 380-393.
87. Greenstein, D. (2000, Fall). Digital libraries and their challenges. Library Trends. Retrieved from http://www.findarticles.com/p/articles/mi_m1387/is_2_49/ai_72274397
88. Guilford Free Library [GFL]. (N.D.) Shoutbomb: a new text messaging service. Retrieved from http://www.guilfordfreelibrary.org/my-account/shoutbomb/
89. Gul, S., & Bano, S. (2019). Smart libraries: An emerging and innovative technological habitat of 21st century. *The Electronic Library, 37*(5), 764–783. https://doi.org/10.1108/EL-02-2019-0052
90. Guo, Y. J., **Liu, Y. Q.**, & Bielefield, A. (2018). The provision of mobile services in US urban libraries. *Information Technology and Libraries, 37*(2), 78-93.
91. Guo, Y., Yang, Z., Yang, Z., **Liu, Y. Q.**, Bielefield, A., & Tharp, G. (2020). The provision of patron services in Chinese academic libraries responding to the COVID-19 pandemic. *Library Hi Tech*.
92. Hahn, J. (2017). The Internet of Things: Mobile Technology and Location Services in Libraries. United States: American Library Association.
93. Han, Z., Huang, S., Li, H., & Ren, N. (2016). Risk assessment of digital library information security: A case study. The Electronic Library, 34(3), 471–487. https://doi.org/10.1108/EL-09-2014-0158
94. Hanani, U & Frank, A. J. (2000). "The parallel evolution of search engines and digital libraries: their convergence to the Mega-Portal," Proceedings 2000 Kyoto International Conference on Digital Libraries: Research and Practice, Kyoto, Japan, 2000, pp. 211-218. Retrieved from https://u.cs.biu.ac.il/~ariel/download/ird665/kyoto.pdf
95. Harris-Pierce, R. L., & **Liu, Y. Q.** (2012). Is data curation education at library and information science schools in North America adequate?. *New Library World*.

96. Harter, S. (1997). Scholarly communication and the digital library: Problems and issues. Journal of Digital Information, 1(1). Retrieved from http://journals.tdl.org/jodi/article/view/jodi-3/4
97. Hitchcock, S., et al. (1997). Citation linking: Improving access to online journals. Proceedings of the 2nd ACM International Conference on Digital Libraries, 115-122.
98. Hughes, L. (2004). Digitizing Collections, Strategic Issues for the Information Manage. Neal-Schuman Publishers.
99. Hutnik, A. Z. (2012, March 12). Location-Based Services: Why Privacy "Dos and Don'ts" Matter. IAPP. https://iapp.org/news/a/2012-03-08-location-based-services-why-privacy-dos-and-donts-matter/
100. Iannella, R. and Campbell, D. (1999). The A-Core: metadata about content metadata. Retrieved from http://metadata.net/admin/draft-iannella-admin-01.txt
101. IFLA Working Group on Functional Requirements and Numbering of Authority Records
102. IFLA. (1999, September 29). Digital libraries: Metadata resources. Retrieved from http://www.ifla.org/II/metadata.htm
103. IFLA. (2010, October 7). IFLA Manifesto for Digital Libraries. Retrieved from http://www.ifla.org/publications/ifla-manifesto-for-digital-libraries
104. ISDL. (1997). Proceedings of international symposium on research, development and practice in digital libraries, ISDL'97. Retrieved from http://www.dl.slis.tsukuba.ac.jp/ISDL97/proceedings/
105. Jantz, R. C. (2017). A Vision for the Future: New Roles for Academic Librarians. Academic Librarianship Today, 223–235. https://doi.org/10.7282/T30867SB
106. Jones, D. (1999). Collection development in the digital library. In D. Stern (Ed.) Digital libraries: Philosophies, technical design considerations, and example scenarios. (pp. 27-37). New York: The Haworth Press, Inc.
107. Jones, E. (2017). The Public Library Movement, the Digital Library Movement, and the Large-Scale Digitization Initiative: Assumptions, Intentions, and the Role of the Public. Information & Culture, 50, (2), 229-258.
108. Jones, Elisabeth. (2017). The Public Library Movement, the Digital Library Movement, and the Large-ScaleDigitization Initiative: Assumptions, Intentions, and the Role of the Public. Information & Culture, 52(2), 229-263.
109. Jung-ran, P., & Tosaka, Y. (2010). Metadata creation practices in digital repositories and collections: schemata, selection criteria, and interoperability. *Information Technology & Libraries,29*(3), 104-116.

110. Jung-ran, P., & Tosaka, Y. (2010). Metadata creation practices in digital repositories and collections: schemata, selection criteria, and interoperability. Information Technology & Libraries,29(3), 104-116.
111. Kalbach, J. (2000). Designing for information foragers: A behavioral model for information seeking on the World Wide Web. Internet Technical Group (ITG) Publication, 3.3. Retrieved from http://www.internettg.org/newsletter/dec00/article_information_foragers.html
112. Kamel, S. (Ed.). (2003). Managing globally with information technology. Hershey, PA: IRM Press.
113. Khalil, M. A. (1998). Are end-users satisfied by using digital libraries? In J. Corbina& T. Baker (Eds.), Research and Advanced Technology for Digital Libraries: 4th European Conference, ECDL 2000, Lisbon, Portugal, September 2000. Proceedings. New York: Springer-Verlag.
114. Kirriemuir, J. (2001). Establishing a digital library center. Ariadne Issue 29. Retrieved from http://www.ariadne.ac.uk/issue29/kirriemuir/
115. Kling, R. & Elliott, M. (1994). Digital library design for usability. Retrieved from http://www.csdl.tamu.edu/DL94/paper/kling.html
116. Leiner, B.M. (1998). The scope of the digital library: Draft prepared by Barry M. Leiner for the Dlib working group on digital library metrics. Retrieved from http://www.dlib.org/metrics/public/papers/dig-lib-scope.html
117. Lesk, M. (2005). Digital Searching to Digital Reading; presentation at LITA session at ALA conference, Chicago 2005. Retrieved from http://lesk.com/mlesk/diglib.html
118. Lesk, M. (2009). Understanding Digital Libraries. San Francisco: Morgan Kaufmann Publishers.
119. Lesk, M. (n.d.). Why digital libraries? Retrieved from http://www.lesk.com/mlesk/follett/follett.html
120. Levy, D. (2000). Digital libraries and the problem of purpose. D-Lib, 6(1). Retrieved from http://www.dlib.org/dlib/january00/01levy.html
121. Levy, D. M. & Marshall, C. C. (1995.) Going digital: A look at assumptions underlying digital libraries. Communications of the ACM, 38(4), 77-84.
122. Li, S., Jiao, F., Zhang, Y., & Xu, X. (2019). Problems and Changes in Digital Libraries in the Age of Big Data From the Perspective of User Services. The Journal of Academic Librarianship, 45(1), 22–30. https://doi.org/10.1016/j.acalib.2018.11.012
123. Li, X., & Wu, B. (2009, June). An Ontology Based Knowledge Sharing Approach in E-learning. In *2009 Second Pacific-Asia Conference on Web Mining and Web-based Application* (pp. 205-208). IEEE.

124. Libraries Get Creative With E-Books And Other Online Offerings. (2020, Mar 27). NPR. Retrieved from https://www.npr.org/2020/03/27/822728334/libraries-get-creative-with-e-books-and-other-online-offerings
125. Library of Congress. (2003). Understanding MARC: Bibliographic machine-readable cataloging. Retrieved from http://www.loc.gov/marc/umb/umbhome.html
126. Library of Congress. (2005). Encoded archival description (EAD). Retrieved from http://www.loc.gov/ead/
127. Liddy, E. D., et al (1994). Research agenda for the intelligent digital library. Retrieved on from http://www.csdl.tamu.edu/DL94/paper/liddy.html
128. Limani, F., Latif, A., & Tochtermann, K. (2016, September). Scientific social publications for digital libraries. In International Conference on Theory and Practice of Digital Libraries (pp. 373-378). Springer, Cham.
129. **Liu, Y. Q.** (2003). Digital library infrastructure: Rethinking its models. In Symposium on the libraries' sustainable development innovation. Symposium conducted in Beijing, China.
130. **Liu, Y. Q.** (2004). Best practices, standards and techniques for digitizing library materials: A snapshot of library digitization practices in the USA. Online Information Review, 28(5), 338–345. https://doi.org/10.1108/14684520410564262
131. **Liu, Y. Q.** (2004). Best practices, standards and techniques for digitizing library materials: A snapshot of library digitalization practices in the USA. Online Information Review, 28(5), 338–345. https://doi.org/10.1108/14684520410564262
132. **Liu, Y. Q.**, & Wnuk, A. (2009). The Impact of Digital Resource and Service Use on Urban Residents in New England Public Libraries—A Survey Report. *Public Library Quarterly*, *28*(1), 4-23.
133. **Liu, Y. Q.** (2014). *Surfing the World of Knowledge -- Analytical Case Studies of Digital Liberties in the United States*. Beijing: Ocean Press. http://www.amazon.com/Twenty-first-Century-Library-knowledge-Overview/dp/7502788301/ref=sr_1_4?ie=UTF8&qid=1411522497&sr=8-4&keywords=yan+quan+liu
134. Liu, Y. Q., Bielefield, A., & McKay, P. (2019). Are urban public libraries websites accessible to Americans with Disabilities? *Universal Access in the Information Society*, 18(1), 191–206. https://doi.org/10.1007/s10209-017-0571-7
135. **Liu, Y. Q.**, Martin, C., Roehl, E., Yi, Z., & Ward, S. (2006). Digital information access in urban/suburban communities: A survey report of public digital library use by the residents in Connecticut. *OCLC Systems & Services: International digital library perspectives.*

136. Liyue, Fan (2019). Differential privacy for image publication. University of North Carolina. Retrieved from https://webpages.uncc.edu/lfan4/pdf/TPDP2019.pdf
137. Lougee, W. P. (2002). Diffuse libraries: Emergent roles for the research library in the digital age. Washington, DC: CLIR.
138. Maggio, L., Bresnahan, M., Flynn, D., Harzbecker, J., Blanchard, M., & Ginn, D. (2009). A case study: using social tagging to engage students in learning Medical Subject Headings. *Journal of the Medical Library Association, 97*(2), 77-83.
139. Mahesh, G., & Mittal, R. (2009). Digital content creation and copyright issues. The Electronic Library.
140. Manduca, C. A., Iverson, E. R., Fox, S., &McMartin, F. (2005, May.) Influencing user behavior through digital library design: An example from the geosciences. D-Lib Magazine. Retrieved from http://www.dlib.org/dlib/may05/fox/05fox.html
141. Mann, T. (2008). On the Record' but off the track: A review of the report of the Library of Congress Working Group on the Future of Bibliographic Control, with a further examination of Library of Congress cataloging tendencies.www.guild2910.org/WorkingGrpResponse2008.pdf
142. Marchionini, Gary. & Fox, Edward A. (1999). Progress toward digital libraries: Augmentation through integration. Information Processing & Management, 35(3), 219-225.
143. Marcum, D. (2003). Research questions for the digital era library. Library Trends v. 51, no. 4, pp. 636-651.
144. Marshall, C. (1997) Annotation: From paper books to the digital library. Proceedings of the 2nd ACM International Conference on Digital Libraries, 131-140.
145. Mason, M.K. (2020). Future of libraries. Retrieved from http://www.moyak.com/papers/digital-future-libraries.html
146. McGinty, John. (2009). Digital Libraries Need Digital Organization: Identifying, Defining, and Creating New Academic Library Management Structures. ACRL Fourteenth Conference, March 12-15, 2009. Seattle: WA. Retrieved from http://www.ala.org/acrl/sites/ala.org.acrl/files/content/conferences/confsandpreconfs/national/seattle/papers/298.pdf
147. Menial, C. & Klotz, V. (2006, January). The first 10 years of the ECCC digital library. Communications of the ACM. 49(1), 131-134.
148. MIC metadata strategies: Thinking beyond asset management, by Jane D Johnson. Journal of Digital Asset Management. Houndmills: Jan 2006. Vol. 2, Iss. 1; pg. 59, 10 pgs.
149. Michalek, G. V. (2002, June). The universal library and the million-book project. D-Lib Magazine. 8(6). Retrieved from http://www.dlib.org/dlib/june02/06inbrief.html#MICHALEK

150. Minow, M. (2005). Infopeople webcasts: "Borrowing" graphics or text for library web pages: Fair play, and fair use. Retrieved from http://infopeople.org/training/webcasts/03-03-05/
151. Mitchell, E. & Gilbertson, K. (2008, March/April). Using Open Source Social Software as Digital Library Interface. D-Lib. Retrieved from http://www.dlib.org/dlib/march08/mitchell/03mitchell.html
152. Mitchell, S. (1999). Interface Design Considerations in Libraries. Digital Libraries Philosophies, Technical Design Considerations and Example Scenarios. New York, NY: Haworth Press.
153. Morales-del-Castillo, J., Pedraza-Jiménez, R., Ruíz, A., Peis, E., & Herrera-Viedma, E. (2009). A semantic model of selective dissemination of information for digital libraries. Information Technology & Libraries,28(1), 21-30.
154. Morgan, E. L. (2005). M Library. Retrieved from http://dewey.library.nd.edu/mylibrary/
155. Morgan, E. L. (2005). Making information easier to find with MyLibrary. Retrieved from http://infomotions.com/musings/mylibrary-access/
156. Nabil R., Adam; Bhargava, Bharat K. and Yesha, Yelena. (Eds, 1995). Digital Libraries: Research and Technology Advances. ISBN 3540614109
157. National Information Standards Organization. (2007). A framework of guidance for building good digital collections. Retrieved from http://www.niso.org/framework/
158. Network Development MARC Standards Office, Library of Congress. (2000, May 3). Encoded archival description (EAD). Retrieved from http://www.loc.gov/ead/
159. Neuby, B. L. (2016). Organizational Technology. Retrieved from https://link.springer.com/referenceworkentry/10.1007/978-3-319-31816-5_30-1
160. Nicholson, S. (2004). A conceptual framework for the holistic measurement and cumulative evaluation of library services. *Journal of Documentation*, 60(2).
161. NIUDL. (2017, June 8). Collection development policy. NIUDL. https://digital.lib.niu.edu/policy/collection-development-policy_back
162. NOLO. (2003). Proposed guidelines for students or instructors preparing multimedia works. Retrieved from http://fairuse.stanford.edu/Copyright_and_Fair_Use_Overview/chapter7/7-c.html#3
163. Pace, A. K. (2001). Should MyLibrary be in your library? Computers in Libraries, 21(2), 49-51.
164. Parabhoi, L., Bhattacharjya, N., & Dhar, R. (2017). Use of QR code in library. Retrieved from

https://www.researchgate.net/publication/318259063_Use_of_QR_Code_in_Library
165. Pereira, R. B. (2011). *Location-Based Services*. Navipedia. https://gssc.esa.int/navipedia/index.php/Location_Based_Services
166. Perell, B.C., Williams, M. E. (Eds.). (1998). Copyright law and its effects on the dissemination and accessibility of electronic journals. In Proceedings of the 19th National Online Meeting --1998. (pp. 257-263). Williams, NJ: Information Today.
167. Peterson Bishop, A. (1998). Logins and bailouts: Measuring access, use, and success in digital libraries. Journal of electronic publishing, 4(2).
168. Pisaniello, H. L., & Dixon, W. G. (2020). What does digitalization hold for the creation of real-world evidence? Rheumatology, 59(1), 39–45. https://doi.org/10.1093/rheumatology/kez068
169. Prasad, A, and Guha, N. (2008) Concept naming vs. concept categorization: a faceted approach to semantic annotation. *Online Information Review,32*(4), 500-510.
170. Rajashekar, T.B. (2002). Digital library and information services in enterprises: Their development and management.
171. Reeves, T., Apedoe, X., & Hee Woo, Y, (2003). Evaluating digital libraries: A user-friendly guide. Retrieved from http://dlist.sir.arizona.edu/archive/00000398/
172. Regents. (2005). Copyright, Intellectual Property Rights, and Licensing Issues. Retrieved from http://sunsite.berkeley.edu/Copyright/
173. Reimer, Jim. (1997, July). Keynote address. 2nd ACM International Conference on Digital Libraries.
174. Rhyno, Art. (2004). Using open source systems for digital libraries. Porthsmouth, NH: Libraries Unlimited.
175. Robertson, S., Jitan, S., & Reese, K. (1997). Web-based collaborative library research. Proceedings of the 2nd ACM International Conference on Digital Libraries, 152-160.
176. Roeder, R. (2010). A year of cataloging research. Library Resources & Technical Services,54(1), 2-3.
177. Saffady, W. (1995, May-June). Digital library concepts and technologies for the management of library collections: An analysis of methods and costs. Library Technology Reports, 221-380.
178. Sateli et al. (2017), ScholarLens: Extracting Competences from Research Publications for the Automatic Generation of Semantic User Profiles. PeerJ Comput. Sci. 3:e121; DOI 10.7717/peerj-cs.121
179. Schatz, B., et al (1994). Digital library infrastructure for a university engineering community. Retrieved from http://www.csdl.tamu.edu/DL94/paper/schatz.html

180. Schatz, G. (2021, January 12). Active Vs. Passive RFID For Location Tracking [2021 UPDATE]. AirFinder. https://www.airfinder.com/blog/active-vs-passive-rfid
181. Schiller, J., and Voisard, A. (2004). In *Wikipedia*. https://en.wikipedia.org/wiki/Location-based_service#cite_note-15
182. Schwartz, C. (2000). Digital libraries: an overview. The Journal of Academic Librarianship, 26(6), 385-393.
183. Schwartz, C. (2008). Thesauri and facets and tags, oh my! A look at three decades in subject analysis. Library Trends,56(4), 830-842.
184. Schwartz, C. (2008). Thesauri and facets and tags, oh my! A look at three decades in subject analysis. *Library Trends,56*(4), 830-842.
185. Sharma, C., & Nakamura, Y. (2003). *Wireless Data Services: Technologies, Business Models and Global Markets*. Retrieved from https://archive.org/details/wirelessdataserv0000shar_s7b4
186. Shen, Y. (2019). Emerging scenarios of data infrastructure and novel concepts of digital libraries in intelligent infrastructure for human-centered communities: A qualitative research. Journal of Information Science, 45(5),691-704
187. Shiri, A. (2005). Knowledge Organization Systems in Canadian Digital Library Collections. Online Information Review, Vol. 29(6). https://pdfs.semanticscholar.org/2b39/f7f1e74259bcba05a31b76aa613911cd065b.pdf
188. Sicilia, M. (2006). Metadata and semantics research. Online Information Review,30(3), 213-216.
189. Simic, J., & Wick, R. (2019). Sharing Oregon's Cultural Heritage: Harvesting Oregon Digital's Collections into the Digital Public Library of America. OLA Quarterly, 24 (4). https://doi.org/10.7710/1093-7374.1962
190. Sloane, A. (1995). The digital library and the home-based user. In N. R. Adam, B. K. Bhargava, & Y. Yesha (Eds.). Digital libraries: Current issues (pp. 203-208).
191. Smith, M. K., et al. (2002). Web ontology language (OWL.) Retrieved from http://www.w3.org/TR/2002/WD-owl-guide-20021104/
192. Smith, M., et al. (2003). DSpace: An open source dynamic digital repository. D-Lib Magazine, 9(1).
193. Sorge, A. (1991). Strategic fit and the societal effect: Interpreting cross-national comparisons of technology, organization and human resources. Organization Studies, 12(2), 161-190.
194. Stoker, D. and Cooke, A. Evaluation of networked information sources. Proceedings of the 17th International Essen Symposium, 287-312.
195. Sun Microsystems, Inc. (2002). Digital library technology trends. Retrieved from http://www.sun.com/products-n-solutions/edu/whitepapers/pdf/digital_library_trends.pdf

196. Svenonius, E. (2000). The intellectual foundation of information organization. Cambridge, Mass.: MIT Press.
197. Tadic, L. (2002). Copyright in a digital world: A practical workshop: The permissions process. Retrieved from http://digitalcooperative.oclc.org/copyright/CopyrightDocs/TAdic/NINCH_toolkit_permissions.doc
198. Taylor, A. &Joudrey. (2010). The Organization of Information. Westport, Conn: Libraries Unlimited.
199. Tennant, R. (2004). A Bibliographic metadata infrastructure for the twenty-first century. *Library High Tech,22*(2), 175-181.
200. Tennant, R. (1999, October). User interface design: Some guiding principles. Library Journal, 124(17), 28-29.
201. Thaller, M. (2001, February). From the digitized to the digital library. D-Lib Magazine, 7(2). Retrieved from http://www.dlib.org/dlib/february01/thaller/02thaller.html
202. The Digital Library Curriculum Project at Virginia Tech. (2006). Retrieved from http://fox.cs.vt.edu/DLcurric/
203. The Dublin Core web site. Retrieved from: http://dublincore.org/.
204. The Open University. (2002, October). Personalization and digital libraries. Seminar presentations, The Open University. Retrieved from http://www.dlib.org/dlib/december02/12clips.html#OPEN
205. Theng, Y. L., Duncker, E., MohdNasir, N., Buchanan, G. &Thimbleby, H. (1999). Design guidelines and user-centered digital libraries. In S. Abiteboul & Vercoustre. A. (Eds.). Lecture notes in computer science: Research and advanced technology for digital libraries, Third European Conference ECDL'99 (pp. 167 - 183). Heidelberg: Springer.
206. Thong, J. (2002?). Understanding user acceptance of digital libraries: What are the roles of interface characteristics, organizational context, and individual differences? International Journal of Human-Computer Studies, 57(3), 215-242.
207. Tillman, H. N. (2000). Evaluating quality on the net. Retrieved from http://www.hopetillman.com/findqual.html
208. Todd, C. R. (2018). Librarian as data migrator: A functional pathway from Millennium to Koha.
209. TULIP - The University Licensing Program. Retrieved from https://www.google.com/search?client=safari&rls=en&q=TULIP+-+The+University+Licensing+Program.&ie=UTF-8&oe=UTF-8#
210. Van House, N A., Butler, M. H., Ogle, V., & Schiff, L. (1996, February). User-centered iterative design for digital libraries the cypress experience. D-Lib Magazine.
211. Vise, D. (2005, November 22). World digital library planned. Washington Post, p. A27.
212. W3C. (2019). About W3C. Retrieved from https://www.w3.org/

213. What is Libby? (2020, January 3). Libby Help. https://help.libbyapp.com/6144.htm
214. Wiederhold, G. (1995.) Digital libraries, value, and productivity. Communications of the ACM, 38(4), 85-96.
215. Wikipedia. (2021). *Recommender system*. Retrieved from
216. Wilson, C. (1997). User interface design bibliography. Retrieved from http://www.uie.com/biblio.htm
217. Witten, I. H. (2002, December). Examples of practical digital libraries: Collections built internationally using greenstone. Paper presented at the 5th International Conference on Asian Digital Libraries, Singapore. DLib Magazine, 9(3). Retrieved from http://www.dlib.org/dlib/march03/witten/03witten.html
218. Witten, I. H., & Bainbridge, D. (2003). How to build a digital library. San Francisco: Morgan Kaufmann Publishers.
219. Witten, I. H., Brainbridge, D. & Nichols, D.M. (2010). (2nd). How to Build a Digital Library.
220. Witten, Ian H. (2002). Examples of practical digital libraries: Collections built internationally using Greenstone. 5th International Conference on Asian Digital Libraries, ICADL 2002, Singapore, December 11-14, 2002. Proceedings. Lecture Notes in Computer Science
221. Wolf, G. (2002). Exploring the unmaterial world. *Wired Magazine*, 8(6).
222. Wolverton, Jr., R. (2006). Becoming an authority on authority control: An annotated bibliography of resources. *Library Resources & Technical Services,50*(1), 31-41.
223. Xie, I., Babu, R., Lee, T. H., Castillo, M. D., You, S., & Hanlon, A. M. (2020). Enhancing usability of digital libraries: Designing help features to support blind and visually impaired users. Information Processing & Management, 57(3), 102–110. https://doi.org/10.1016/j.ipm.2019.102110
224. Yang, W., Zhao, B., **Liu, Y. Q**., & Bielefield, A. (2020). Are Ivy League Library Website Homepages Accessible?. *Information Technology and Libraries (Online)*, *39*(2), 1-18.
225. Yale Law School. (2001, October 5). YLS Avalon Project Provides Link to History.
226. Zeng, M. & Qin, J. (2008). *Metadata*. New York: Neal-Schuman.

Appendix 01

The List of the US Digital Libraries

National Science Digital Library--Serving science, technology, engineering, and mathematics education.
https://nsdl.oercommons.org/oer/providers/sets?startswith=A

Typical Digital Libraries:

1. A Science Odyssey http://www.pbs.org/wgbh/aso/
2. Alberta Folklore and Local History Collection http://folklore.library.ualberta.ca/
3. Alexandria Digital Library http://www.alexandria.ucsb.edu/
4. Alsos: Digital Library for Nuclear Issues http://alsos.wlu.edu/default.asp
5. American Overseas Digital Library [changed to] DLIR http://dlirwww.aiys.org/aodl/index.php
6. Avalon Project at Yale http://avalon.law.yale.edu/subject_menus/15th.asp
7. Ames Imaging Library System http://ails.arc.nasa.gov/ails/?st=1&so=cdate&v=thumbs&o=0&h=1&page=1
8. Astronomy Digital Image Library http://imagelib.ncsa.uiuc.edu/imagelib.html
9. Awesome Library http://www.awesomelibrary.org/
10. BookHive http://www.bookhive.org
11. British Columbia International Digital Library http://bcdlib.tc.ca/
12. Bureau of Economic Analysis Digital Library http://library.bea.gov/
13. California Digital Library http://www.cdlib.org/
14. CalPhotos http://elib.cs.berkeley.edu/photos/
15. Cary Collection http://wally.rit.edu/cary/index.html
16. Centennial Exhibition Digital Collection http://libwww.library.phila.gov/CenCol/index.htm
17. Center for Retrospective Digitization http://gdz.sub.uni-goettingen.de/search-entry.shtml
18. Charles H. Templeton Ragtime Sheet Music Collection http://library.msstate.edu/ragtime/
19. Children's Digital Library http://www.storyplace.org/
20. Computational Science Education Reference Desk http://www.shodor.org/cserd/
21. Computer Vision Education Digital (CVED£© http://www.cved.org/
22. Cuneiform Digital Library Initiative http://cdli.ucla.edu/
23. Digital Archive Network for Anthropology (DANA-WH) http://www.dana-wh.net/
24. Digital Asia Library / PAIR http://digitalasia.library.wisc.edu/
25. Digital Learning Sciences http://dlsciences.org/index.html

26. Digital Library Federation http://www.diglib.org/Washington, DC
27. Digital Library for Earth System Education http://www.dlese.org/
28. Digital Library Collection for Computer Vision Education http://www.cved.org/
29. Digital Library for the Humanities http://www.perseus.tufts.edu/
30. Digital Library Network for Engineering and Technology http://www.dlnet.vt.edu or http://www.ceage.vt.edu/node/243
31. Digital Library of Appalachia http://www.aca-dla.org/
32. Digital Library of the Commons http://dlc.dlib.indiana.edu/
33. Digital Library of Georgia http://dlg.galileo.usg.edu/?Welcome
34. Digital Library of Wielkopolska http://www.wbc.poznan.pl/dlibra
35. Digital Library Service Integration (DLSI) http://is.njit.edu/dlsi/
36. Digital Morphology Library http://www.digimorph.org/
37. Digital Multimedia Library for Health Sciences Education http://www.healcentral.org/
38. Digital Public Library of America http://dp.la/
39. Digital South Asia Library http://dsal.uchicago.edu/
40. Distributed Information Filtering System for Digital Libraries http://sifter.indiana.edu/
41. DSpace at MIT: an Institutional Repository http://dspace.mit.edu/
42. Earth and Space Science Brower (ESSB) http://www.si.umich.edu/Space/index.html [project in question?]
43. Earth Exploration Toolbook http://serc.carleton.edu/eet/index.html
44. eCUIP Digital Libraryhttp://www.lib.uchicago.edu/ecuip/diglib/index.htm
45. Electronic Text Center http://etext.lib.virginia.edu/index.html
46. Electronic Encyclopedia of Earthquakes, A digital library of http://sceccore.usc.edu/e3/index.php
47. Enhancing Searching of Mathematics http://www.dessci.com/en/reference/searching/
48. eSkeletons Project Digital Library http://www.eskeletons.org/
49. Federation of American Scientists http://www.fas.org/index.html
50. Franklin D. Roosevelt Library http://www.fdrlibrary.marist.edu/
51. Gateway to Educational Materials (Gateway to 21st Century Skills?) http://www.thegateway.org/
52. Harvard-Smithsonian, Digital Video Library http://www.hsdvl.org/
53. Health Education Assets Library http://www.healcentral.org/index.jsp
54. HyHistory Online http://www.hyperhistory.com/online_n2/History_n2/a.html
55. iConn http://www.iconn.org/AboutIconn.aspx
56. Informedia Digital Video Library http://www.informedia.cs.cmu.edu/
57. International Children's Digital Library http://www.icdlbooks.org/
58. Internet Archive: Moving Image Archive http://www.archive.org/details/movies
59. Internet Library of Early Journals http://www.bodley.ox.ac.uk/ilej/

60. Internet Public Library http://www.ipl.org
61. Internet Scout Project http://scout.wisc.edu/
62. JSTOR or Journal Storage http://www.jstor.org
63. Kentuckiana Digital Library http://kdl.kyvl.org/
64. Kinematic Models for Design Digital Library (K-MODDL) http://kmoddl.library.cornell.edu/
65. Learning Page http://memory.loc.gov/ammem/ndlpedu/index.html
66. Making of America http://quod.lib.umich.edu/m/moagrp/
67. MathDL Mathematical Sciences Digital Library http://mathdl.maa.org/
68. Meeting of Frontiers http://international.loc.gov/intldl/mtfhtml/mfhome.html
69. Medicinal Spices Exhibit - UCLA Biomedical Library- History & Special Collections http://unitproj1.library.ucla.edu/biomed/spice/index.cfm
70. Missouri Botanical Garden Library http://www.mobot.org/MOBOT/molib
71. National Digital Library of Korea http://www.dlibrary.go.kr/NEL_ENG/Index.jsp
72. National Gallery of the Spoken Word (NGSW) http://www.historicalvoices.org
73. National Library of Scotland Digital Library http://www.nls.uk/digitallibrary/index.html
74. National Science Foundation Online Document System http://www.nsf.gov/home/menus/publications.ht
75. Network of Excellence on Digital Libraries (DELOS)
76. New York Public Library' Digital Collections http://www.nypl.org/digital/
77. New Zealand Digital Library http://nzdl.sadl.uleth.ca/cgi-bin/library
78. Newton Project / Newton Manuscript Project http://www.newtonproject.ic.ac.uk/index.html
79. NICI Virtual Library http://www.vlibrary.org
80. NOAA Photo Library http://www.photolib.noaa.gov/
81. Nuclear Pathways http://www.nuclearpathways.org/
82. Operational Social Science Digital Data Library http://thedata.org/
83. OriginalSources http://www.originalsources.com
84. Pedagogic Services for Digital Libraries http://serc.carleton.edu/sp/index.html
85. Perseus Digital Library http://www.perseus.tufts.edu/
86. Picture Australia http://www.pictureaustralia.org/
87. Project Gutenberg, the oldest digital library, http://www.gutenberg.org/
88. Public Library of Science http://www.plos.org/
89. Sciencedirect http://www.info.sciencedirect.com/
90. SIMPLE Science: Image-based learning tools for K-12 education http://www.simplescience.org/
91. SIOExplorer http://siox.sdsc.edu/
92. Spices - Exotic Flavors & Medicines http://unitproj1.library.ucla.edu/biomed/spice/index.cfm

93. StoryPlace http://www.storyplace.org
94. Texas A&M Digital Library http://digital.library.tamu.edu/
95. Tufts Digital Library http://dl.tufts.edu/
96. U. S. Army Corps of Engineers Digital Visual Library http://www.spa.usace.army.mil
97. U.S. Fish and Wildlife Service Digital Library System http://images.fws.gov/
98. United States Digital Map Library http://www.rootsweb.com/~usgenweb/maps/table2.html
99. University of Michigan Digital Library http://www.lib.umich.edu/digital-library-production-service-dlps
100. University of Pittsburg Digital Library http://www.library.pitt.edu/libraries/drl/
101. Utah State University Digital Library Collections http://digital.lib.usu.edu/
102. Villanova Digital Library http://digital.library.villanova.edu/
103. Virginia Tech Digital Library http://scholar.lib.vt.edu/
104. Virtual Telescopes in Education (TIE) http://vtie.gsfc.nasa.gov/
105. Visible Earth http://visibleearth.nasa.gov
106. Wirtz Labor Digital Library (U.S. Dept. of Labor) http://library.dol.gov/ Main Page: http://www.dol.gov/oasam/library/digital/main.htm
107. World Digital Library http://www.worlddigitallibrary.org/project/english/index.html
108. World Digital Mathematics Library (WDML) http://www.wdml.org/

Appendix 02 Rubric Evaluation Criteria of "Digital Library Review"

CRITERIA	UNACCEPTABLE (1)	ACCEPTABLE (2)	TARGET (3)
Paper is presented with 5 required component parts	Paper has poor or no formation of 5 components.	Paper is formatted with 5 components.	Paper has clearly organized with 5 components and appropriated subheadings.
Project background	Background info is not clearly stated or with vague terms	Background info is basically covered.	Background info is addressed fruitfully.
Resource Organization	Poor or no description on its resource organization.	Resource organization is described specifically.	Organization information is described sufficiently
Service Features	Poor or no presentation on its service features.	Main service features are presented.	Service feature is presented t adequately.
Technologies	Poor or discussion on its technology used.	Technology used is somewhat discussed.	Technology used is discussed in detail.
Comments	Poor or no comments on the strengths and weaknesses of a chosen digital library.	The strengths and weaknesses of a chosen digital library are superficially provided.	The strengths and weaknesses of a chosen digital library with suggestions for future development are well provided.
Bibliographic references	No references or poorly presented reference list.	Reference list is presented in APA or a preferred citation style.	Consistent citation and reference list in APA or a preferred citation style are neatly

			presented with error free.

* This assignment measures the following student learning outcomes.

What you would review to a chosen digital library, examples of features/elements for each of evaluation criteria are below:

- **Background,** including title, URL, responsible parties, mission/goal/objectives, target users, community, funding, collaboration, creation, historical development, snapshots of main page ....

- **Organization,** including collection policy, selection criteria, databases, collections, resource types, file formats, catalog, headings/categorizations, classifications, metadata scheme/treatment or resources description, subject heading scheme, tag styles, digitization policies/methods/regulations, file/record management, file open plug-ins, copyright or legal issues on collection

- **Service Features**, including search engines, browsing capability, navigation mechanisms, access & use policies, indexes, site map, catalogs, circulation, remote services, mobile services, upload/download, full-text, reference services, contact info, help tools, discussion forum, web/lib 2.0 tools/software, blog, podcast, enhancement and/or evaluation, maintenance plan ...

- **Technologies**, including interface design, colors/fonts/graphics/icons, multimedia, layout, sidebars, menu (drop-down, mouse over), software structures, digitization techniques, markup languages (HTML, SGML, XML), database architecture, hardware components, server, system or database interoperability ....

- **Comments**, including your input on the strengths/weaknesses, effectiveness of service/organization/interface, and suggestions for further improvements of the chosen digital library.

- **Bibliographic references**, including publication and related URLs, etc:

Provided by Dr. Yan Quan Liu, ILS SCSU.

Appendix 03 Rubric Evaluation Criteria for the Digital Library Project

#	Criteria/ Levels	UNACCEPTABLE (1)	ACCEPTABLE (2)	TARGET (3)
1	Mission statement	No written mission with target users and/or no 'About' or like section.	The mission or goals are stated and focused on target audiences or users in an 'About' or like section.	The mission or goals are clearly stated and focused on target audiences or users in an 'About' or like section.
2	Collection policy	No or usefulness selection criteria for the chosen collection.	Selection criteria are fairly presented and collection is suitable to the mission.	Selection criteria are specifically detailed and collection is appropriate & sustainable to the mission.
3	Organization of collection	Collection is either not or poorly organized with meaningful labels.	Collection is fairly organized with meaningful labels.	Collection is well-organized with meaningful subject/index terms or category headings.
4	Resource descriptions	No metadata schema is provided or inconsistent metadata are employed.	Resource descriptions are fairly provided with a metadata schema.	Resource descriptions are standardized and consistent throughout collection items with a well-adopted metadata schema.
5	Access and use	Access and use are poorly provided.	Access and use are supported with basic browsing mechanism &	Access and use are easy, quick and friendly throughout with well designed

			navigation strategies.	browsing mechanism & navigation strategies, such as search engine, site map and/or smooth linkages and transitions.
6	Services features	There are no recommended service features and/or poor services are provided.	One or more recommended service features are provided effectively.	Three or more recommended service features are provided effectively.
7	Interface design	Interface is poorly designed with distractive fonts, color, graphic, layout and orders.	Interface is intuitive with proper use of textural and graphic elements and neatly layout of web pages.	Interface is intuitive with excellent use of textural and graphic elements that make the site attractive and have a professional appearance & high level of usability.
8	Enhancement, Evaluation &/or Maintenance plan	No or poor enhancement and evaluation plan.	Maintenance and evaluation are partially planed & structured.	Maintenance and evaluation are deliberately planed & structured.
9	Acknowledgment or copyright-like statement	No acknowledgement of site responsibility.	Acknowledgement is partially presented.	Acknowledgement for the course project is prominently presented.

| 10 | Project overall | The project does not stay on task. | The project stays on task. | The project stays on task very well. |

Key concepts and elements suggested for each criterion:

1. Mission statement - What are the goals and objectives of the DL? Have you identified a clear user group? Who is your target audience?

2. Collection policy - What rules or criteria do you want to use to collect? What are your resources or collections, including media format, language, and scope? Do you provide a comprehensive but manageable collection policy? What information resources do you provide? Of note, the collections may include, but are not limited to hyperlinks, images, electronic publications, digitized items such as texts, sounds, pictures and many others.

3. Organization of collection - How do you want to sort, classify, categorize, and/or index the resources you collect? Of note, the collection can be arranged by media type, place of publication, data of publication, content of resources, process of data presented, among many others.

4. Resource descriptions - What standard or metadata method, such as Dublin Core, simplified Dublin Core, MARC, or others, do you want to use to describe each item or resource you collect?

5. Access and use - What access methods, such as browsing mechanism, navigation strategies (such as Go back button), search engine (such as FreeFind), site map, etc., would you provide to achieve high accessibility?

6. Services features - What services would you provide for your users beyond your resource collection? For example, catalog/indexing systems, discussion forum, blog, RSS feed, news/announcement bulletins, podcast, email feedback, chat, Q&A, help documents, object/document uploading and downloading, book renew, circulation record checking, interlibrary loan request, full text or document delivery, digital reference services, and others?

7. Interface design - What does your digital library look like? How do you want to display your digital resources or collections with use of color icon, line, graphic, different size/type of fonts, and background images or texture presentation to make the site more attractive and eye appealing? Is everything neat, orderly and easy to use and navigate? Is each page well laid out? Is the site well organized? Does the site have an attractive and professional appearance?

8. Enhancement, Evaluation &/or Maintenance plan - What is your plan to further develop the DL? What is your method to receive and monitor feedback? What is your plan to preserve your collection? How will you keep your web site updated? Who will be the contact?

9. Acknowledgment – Have you presented a copyright-like statement containing the course info, the instructor and site creator(s)'s names?

10.Project overall – How would you rate this project overall?

Provided by Dr. Yan Quan Liu, ILS SCSU.

Acknowledgement

This book was compiled in inspiration from the VT modules to serve for students in the course, Digital Libraries, offered at Southern Connecticut State University.

The contributors to this text include both professors and graduate students within the Master in Library Science program at Southern Connecticut State University (SCSU) in New Haven, Connecticut, as well as researchers and helpers from other universities.

The author wants to thank Dr. Mary Brown whose encouragement, inspiration and contributions to the book. The appreciations also go to students who successfully conducted their "Digital Aspects" assignment for ILS655 with Dr. Mary Brown and I at SCSU. Aspects concerning digital libraries are discussed. Thanks for Dale E. Roydauphina is and Mariana Psenicnik who took this and contributed to the compilation of this product respectfully; as well as Alison Weber who worked as a TA partially for this book and made great contribution to the book's compilation. Ms. Kim Jones made a great contribution on this book since its initiation. Ms. Tian Sue reformatted some contents of this book that also made the text easy to read.

Names of students who also made contributions are as follows (please see Appendix Z for a list of contributing papers):

Morissa Antosh, Eva N. K. Betjemann, Jeffrey Bourns, Rachel Bray, Dante Buccieri, Eileen Bujalski, InuwaBukar, Sarah Campany, Caitlin Carbonell, David Cirella, Ruth Cowles, Chris Cudworth, Kurtis Darby, Amanda dos Santo, Patricia Dunn, Rolando Garcia Millian, Timothy Guay, Hilary Gindi, Guillermo Gomez,Marisa Gorman, Anne Gresham, Gene Hayes, Michael Hermann,
Jessica HinksonDesmarais, Hanem Ibrahim, Kari LaPoint, Jose Lopez, Kelly Loveday, Kyle Lynes, Sean Marsh Glover, Diane Marques, Laura Matthews, Kristie McGarry,Katherine Meyrick, Brook Minner, Phillip Modeen, Robert F. Musco, Janet Nelson, Bernadette Niedermeier, Jamie Oltmans, ConorPerreault, Rachel Priest Baelz,Julie T. Rio, Joaquin Rodriguez, Nicole Rodriguez, Dale E. Roydauphinais,Marjorie Ruschau, Becky Schneider, Rita Scrivener, Kate Slavinski, Heather L. Tebbs, Kerri Vautour, Catherine F. Wong, Krista Woodbridge, Norma Wright, and Christopher Zollo.